The Yoke of Christ:
Martin Bucer and Christian Discipline

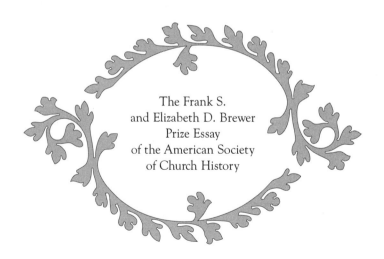

The Frank S.
and Elizabeth D. Brewer
Prize Essay
of the American Society
of Church History

Habent sua fata libelli

Volume XXVI
of
Sixteenth Century Essays & Studies
Charles G. Nauert, Jr., General Editor

ISBN 0-940474-28-X

Composed by NMSU typographer Gwen Blotevogel,
Kirksville, Missouri
Cover design by Teresa Wheeler, NMSU Designer
Printed by Edwards Brothers, Ann Arbor, Michigan
Text is set in Goudy Old Style 10/12

The Yoke of Christ:
Martin Bucer and Christian Discipline

Amy Nelson Burnett
Volume XXVI
Sixteenth Century Essays & Studies

This book has been brought to publication with the
generous support of
Northeast Missouri State University

Library of Congress Cataloging-in-Publication Data

The yoke of Christ: Martin Bucer and Christian discipline / Amy Nelson Burnett.
    p.   cm. — (Sixteenth century essays & studies ; v. 26)
    "The Frank S. and Elizabeth D. Brewer prize essay of the American Society of Church History"
    Includes bibliographical references and index.
    ISBN 0-940474-28-X (alk. paper)
    1. Bucer, Martin, 1491-1551. 2. Church discipline—History—16th century. 3. Strasbourg (France)—Church history—16th century.
    I. Title. II. Series.
    BV740.B87 1994   93-47542
    262.9'84'092—dc20   CIP

Contents

Abbreviations

ARC   *Acta Reformationis Catholicae ecclesiam Germaniae concernentia Saeculi XVI. Die Reformverhandlungen des deutschen Episkopats von 1520 bis 1570.* Ed. Georg Pfeilschifter. 6 vols. Regensburg: Friedrich Pustet, 1959–1974.

ARG   *Archiv für Reformationsgeschichte.*

AST   Archives du Chapitre de Saint-Thomas, in the Archives Municipales of Strasbourg.

BCor   *Correspondance de Martin Bucer.* Martini Buceri Opera Omnia, Series III. Studies in Medieval and Reformation Thought. Leiden: E.J. Brill, 1979–.

BDS   *Martin Bucers Deutsche Schriften.* Martini Buceri Opera Omnia, Series I. Ed. Robert Stupperich. Gütersloh: Gerd Mohn, 1960–.

BOL   *Martini Buceri Opera Latina.* Martini Buceri Opera Omnia, Series II. Paris/Gütersloh, Leiden: E.J. Brill, 1955–.

BSLK   *Die Bekenntnisschriften der evangelisch-lutherischen Kirchen.* 9th ed. Göttingen: Vandenhoek & Ruprecht, 1982.

CO   *Iohannis Calvini opera quae supersunt omnia.* Ed. W. Baum, E. Cunitz and R. Reuss. Corpus Reformatorum 29–87. Braunschweig: Schwetschke, 1863–1900.

CR   *Philippi Melanchthonis opera quae supersunt omnia.* Ed. Karl Bretschneider and H. Bindseil. Corpus Reformatorum 1–28. Halle/Braunschweig: 1834–1860.

DTC   *Dictionnaire de théologie catholique.* Ed. A. Vacant, E. Mangenot and E. Amann. 15 vols. in 30. Paris: Letouzey et Ané, 1915–1950.

Friedberg   Friedberg, Emil, ed. *Corpus Iuris Canonici.* 2 vols. 2d ed. Leipzig: Tauschnitz, 1879–1881.

Herminjard   Herminjard, Aimé-Louis, ed. *Correspondance des réformateurs dans les pays de langue française recueillie et publiée avec d'autres lettres relatives à la Réforme et des notes historiques et biographiques.* Geneva: H. Georg, 1865–1897; repr. Nieuwkoop: B. De Graaf, 1965.

LB   *Desiderii Erasmi Roterodami Opera Omnia.* 10 vols. Ed. Joannes Clericus, Leiden, 1703; repr. London: Gregg, 1962.

Lenz	Lenz, Max, ed. *Briefwechsel Landgraf Philipp's des Grossmüthigen von Hessen mit Bucer*. 3 vols. Publikationen aus den königlichen preussischen Staatsarchiven, 5, 28, 47. Leipzig: G. Hirzel, 1880–1891.
MGEGDE	*Fragments des anciennes chroniques d'Alsace*. Mittheilungen der Gesellschaft für Erhaltung der geschichtlichen Denkmäler im Elsass, II. Reihe 13-15, 17-19, 22-23. Strasbourg: R. Schultz, 1888–1911.
MPG	Migne, J. P., ed. *Patrologiae Cursus Completus. Series Graeca*. Paris, 1857–1936.
MPL	Migne, J. P., ed. *Patrologiae Cursus Completus. Series Latina*. Paris, 1844–1864.
PC	*Politische Correspondenz der Stadt Straßburg im Zeitalter der Reformation*. 5 vols. in 6. Urkunden und Akten der Stadt Straßburg, Abth. 2. Strasbourg/Heidelberg: Trübner/Carl Winter, 1882-1933.
Psalms	Bucer, Martin. *Sacrorvm Psalmorvm libri qvinqve*. . . . Strasbourg: Georgius Vlricherus Andlanus, 1532. Stupperich #25b.
QGTS 2	*Quellen zur Geschichte der Täufer in der Schweiz*. Vol. 2: *Ostschweiz*. Ed. Heinold Fast. Zürich: Theologischer Verlag, 1973.
RP	*Ratsprotokolle*. Minutes of the *Rat und XXI* in the Archives Municipales of Strasbourg.
SA	Bucer, Martin. *Scripta Anglicana fere omnia . . . collecta*. . . . Basel: Petrus Perna, 1577. Stupperich #115.
Schieß	Schieß, Traugott, ed. *Briefwechsel der Brüder Ambrosius und Thomas Blaurer 1509-1567*. 3 vols. Freiburg i. Br.: Fehsenfeld, 1908–1912.
Sentences	Petrus Lombardus. *Sententiae in IV Libris Distinctae*. 2 vols. 3d ed. Spicilegium Bonaventurianum 4-5. Grottaferrata (Rome): Collegium S. Bonaventurae ad Claras Aguas, 1971-1981.
Stupperich	Stupperich, Robert, ed. *Bibliographia Bucerana*. Schriften des Vereins für Reformationsgeschichte 169 (58/2). Gütersloh: C. Bertelsmann, 1952.
Sum. Theol.	Thomas Aquinas. *Summa Theologiae*. Cura et studio Instituti studiorum medievalium Ottaviensis, ad textum S. Pii pp. V iussu confectum recognita. Ottawa: Studium generalis O.P., 1941.
TAE	Krebs, Manfred, Hans Georg Rott, et al., ed. *Quellen zur Geschichte der Täufer. Elsass I.–IV. Teil. Stadt Straßburg*. 4 vols. Quellen und Forschungen zur Reformationsgeschichte 26-27, 53-54. Gütersloh: Gerd Mohn, 1959-1988.
TB	*Thesaurus Epistolicus Reformatorum Alsaticorum*. Copied by Johann Wilhelm Baum, et al. Manuscripts in the Bibliothèque nationale et universitaire de Strasbourg.
TRE	*Theologische Realenzyklopädie*. Ed. Gerhard Krause and Gerhard Müller. Berlin/New York: de Gruyter, 1977-.

WA	*D. Martin Luthers Werke. Kritische Gesamtausgabe.* Weimar: Hermann Böhlau, 1883–1983.
WABr	*D. Martin Luthers Werke. Briefwechsel.* Weimar: Herman Böhlau, 1930–1983.
Z	*Huldrich Zwinglis sämtliche Werke.* Ed. E. Egli et al. Corpus Reformatorum 88–. Berlin/Leipzig/Zürich, 1905–.
1527 Gospels	Bucer, Martin. *Enarrationvm in evangelia Mattaei, Marci, & Lucae, libri duo.* . . . 2 vols. Strasbourg: Johannes Herwagen, 1527. Stupperich #14.
1530 Gospels	——. *Enarrationes perpetvae in sacra qvatvor evangelia, recognitae nuper & locis compluribus auctae.* . . . Strasbourg: Georgivs Vlrichervs Andlanvs, 1530. Stupperich #28.
1536 Gospels	——. *In sacra qvatvor evangelia, Enarrationes perpetvae, secvndvm recognitae, in qvibus praeterea habes syncerioris Theologiae locos communes.* . . . Basel: Ioannes Hervagivs, 1536. Stupperich #28a.

Acknowledgments

This book could not have been written without the support of both individuals and institutions. It began as a dissertation under the guidance of Robert Kingdon at the University of Wisconsin; both as his student and since, I have benefited greatly from his sage counsel. A year spent at the Bucer-Forschungsstelle in Münster not only increased my familiarity with Bucer's works but also enabled me to profit from the expertise of Marijn de Kroon and Hartmut Rudolph. Dr. de Kroon's careful reading of an earlier draft of the manuscript helped enormously in the process of revision. In Strasbourg, Jean Rott graciously helped me decipher the nearly illegible minutes of the Strasbourg City Council sessions and pointed out other documents in the Archives municipales of Strasbourg which were pertinent to my research. The staffs of the Archives municipales and the Bibliothèque nationale et universitaire in Strasbourg, as well as those of the Staatsarchiv Zürich, the Zentralbibliothek Zürich, and the Basel Universitätsbibliothek were always extremely helpful and very efficient in making the resources of their institutions available to me. In this country, Terrance Dinovo, curator of the Lutheran Brotherhood Foundation Reformation Research Library, has worked with the interlibrary loan staff of Love Library at the University of Nebraska-Lincoln to provide me with microforms of Bucer's works.

The original research for this book was supported in part by a Fulbright-Hays fellowship and a Charlotte W. Newcombe Dissertation Fellowship. I would also like to thank both the Oecolampad-Stiftung of Basel, Switzerland, which helped underwrite the original dissertation, and the Brewer Prize Committee of the American Society of Church History, whose award of the Brewer Prize in 1991 has helped make publication of this book possible.

Last but certainly not least, my husband, Stephen, has been an invaluable critic, willing sounding board, and patient proofreader since I first began work on Bucer. Without his support this book would not have been written. Katy and Daniel have helped in their own way as well, by reminding me that there is more to life than Reformation scholarship. To the three of them I dedicate this book.

Matthew 18:15-20

¹⁵Moreouer, if thy brother shall trespasse against thee, goe and tell him his fault betweene thee and him alone: if he shall heare thee, thou hast gained thy brother.

¹⁶But if he will not heare thee, then take with thee one or two or more, that in the mouth of two or three witnesses, euery word may be established.

¹⁷And if hee shall neglect to heare them, tell it vnto the Church: But if he neglect to heare the Church, let him be vnto thee as a heathen man, and a Publicane.

¹⁸Verily I say vnto you, Whatsoeuer ye shall bind on earth, shall bee bound in heauen: and whatsoeuer yee shall loose on earth, shall bee loosed in heauen.

¹⁹Againe I say vnto you, that if two of you shall agree on earth as touching any thing that they shall aske, it shall bee done for them of my father which is in heauen.

²⁰For where two or three are gathered together in my Name, there am I in the midst of them.

–Holy Bible–1611 Edition, King James Version

Introduction

Near the end of his life, the exiled reformer Martin Bucer expressed his fervent prayer that the Strasbourg church "would willingly accept [the Lord's] most easy yoke, i.e. his discipline, without which the church will certainly not be able to last." The "discipline of Christ," he continued, consisted in this,

> that all the members of Christ recognize and embrace each other most intimately and lovingly, and that they build one another up in the knowledge of and obedience to the son of God most zealously and efficaciously, and that the ministers of the churches know, care for and tend the individual sheep of Christ, as the chief pastor Christ set the example. . . . In countless places in Scripture, the Lord described and set forth for us this [discipline] which we also have proclaimed so clearly for so many years in life and writings and sermons.[1]

Bucer had indeed devoted much of his life, writings, and sermons to establishing a system of discipline in Strasbourg and elsewhere which he believed would conform to the teaching of Scripture. The system of Christian discipline which he advocated was much broader than simply the punishment of sinners.[2] As his words imply, discipline was the means by which the entire life of each and every Christian was shaped and guided. It included not only excommunication but contained other elements, such as catechetical instruction and confirmation, which together formed an integrated system for religious instruction, moral oversight, and pastoral care. The goal of this system was the internalization of religious values and moral norms which would ultimately lead to a new, Christian society whose members lived in accordance with evangelical teachings.

Bucer's understanding of Christian discipline, like other aspects of his theology, evolved over the course of his career. It grew out of certain fundamental theological convictions expressed in his earliest writings, but it was also shaped by his long experience as pastor, teacher, and church organizer. From childhood he was exposed to two powerful intellectual currents, humanism and the teachings of Thomas

---

[1]CO 13:237–238 (no. 1177, April 26, 1549).

[2]For this reason I use the phrase "Christian discipline" to describe Bucer's system and limit "church discipline" to the measures applied by the church specifically for the correction of sinners.

Aquinas, which would shape his later thought.[3] Born in 1491, Bucer probably attended the famous Latin school in his home city of Schlettstadt (Sélestat) in Alsace before entering the Dominican order at the age of fifteen.[4] As a Dominican friar he was thoroughly grounded in Thomist theology, but he retained his early humanist interests and was an avid admirer of Erasmus. A list of books in his possession in 1518 includes most of the works of the Dutch humanist along with Thomas' *Summa Theologiae*, his commentary on the *Sentences*, and several of his commentaries on Aristotle.[5]

Bucer's encounter with Martin Luther started the young Dominican down a new path. In April 1518, Bucer attended Luther's disputation at the University of Heidelberg; he enthusiastically described both the disputation and his subsequent meeting with Luther in a letter to Beatus Rhenanus written a few days later.[6] Bucer's staunch support for Luther made his position within the Dominican order untenable, and in the spring of 1521 he obtained papal dispensation from his religious vows. He served briefly as chaplain to the Count-Palatine Friedrich, then became a parish pastor in territory under the jurisdiction of Franz von Sickingen. During this time he testified to his evangelical convictions by marrying Elisabeth Silbereisen, a former nun. In early 1523 Bucer took the post of evangelical preacher in the small city of Wissembourg and remained there until May, when he was forced to flee after von Sickingen's defeat and death. He took refuge in Strasbourg, where his father was a citizen.

In the months following his arrival in Strasbourg, Bucer published his first works—a summary of what he had preached at Wissembourg, a self-defense in response to charges brought against him by the bishop of Strasbourg, and a pamphlet entitled, *That No One Should Live for Himself but for Others, and How We May Attain This*. The pamphlet reflected not only Bucer's commitment to the evangelical message of justification by faith alone, but also his deep concern for the responsibility of each

---

[3]Martin Greschat, "Der Ansatz der Theologie Martin Bucers," *Theologische Literaturzeitung* 103 (1978):82–96; Friedhelm Krüger, *Bucer und Erasmus. Eine Untersuchung zum Einfluss des Erasmus auf die Theologie Martin Bucers (bis zum Evangelien-Kommentar von 1530)*, Veröffentlichungen des Instituts für europäische Geschichte Mainz 57 (Wiesbaden: Franz Steiner, 1970), 38–51; Lambert Leijssen, "Martin Bucer und Thomas von Aquin," *Ephemerides Theologicae Lovanienses* 55 (1979):266–296.

[4]Martin Greschat, *Martin Bucer, Ein Reformator und seine Zeit* (Munich: C.H. Beck, 1990), discusses Bucer's background and his early years, 13–32; this biography is the most detailed presentation of Bucer's life. Hastings Eells, *Martin Bucer* (New Haven: Yale, 1931), the only biography of Bucer in English, contains many errors of detail.

[5]BCor 1:42–58 (April 30, 1518; no. 2); cf. Martin Greschat, "Martin Bucers Bücherverzeichnis von 1518," *Archiv für Kulturgeschichte* 57 (1975):178–185; idem, "Martin Bucer als Dominikanermönch," in *Bucer und seine Zeit: Forschungsbeiträge und Bibliographie*, ed. Marijn de Kroon and Friedhelm Krüger, Veröffentlichungen des Instituts für europäische Geschichte Mainz 80 (Wiesbaden: Franz Steiner, 1976), 30–53.

[6]BCor 1:58–72 (May 1, 1518; no. 3); cf. Martin Greschat, "Die Anfänge der reformatorischen Theologie Martin Bucers," in *Reformation und Humanismus, Robert Stupperich zum 65. Geburtstag*, ed. Martin Greschat and J. F. G. Goeters (Witten: Luther-Verlag, 1969), 124–140; Ernst-Wilhelm Kohls, "Martin Bucer als Anhänger Luthers," *Theologische Zeitschrift* 33 (1977):210–218.

Christian for others. "God has created all things according to his will," the treatise began, and "because he has created us and all creatures so that his goodness becomes known, . . . we, his creatures, should be of service to him in the administration of his goodness. That is, each created being is to serve all others for good with all that God has made and given it."[7] The original harmony of the created order was broken by sin, but through faith in Christ it could be restored. As a consequence of this restoration, "we serve and accede to God gladly in all acts of love towards our neighbors, which he has demanded above all from his people. Because we are ourselves saved as children and heirs of God, it is certain that we will suffer no lack here and in the future life; we also have this requirement to serve our brothers in all true and unadulterated love from faith."[8] Bucer's emphasis on love for one's neighbor and the responsibility of each Christian to serve others remained a hallmark of his theology, and it played a central role in his understanding of Christian discipline.[9]

Bucer quickly became involved in the turmoil of events which led to Strasbourg's acceptance of the Reformation. In the spring of 1524, the parishioners of St. Aurelien chose him as their pastor in a landmark case which resulted in the city council's assuming control of pastoral appointments in the city. Over the next several years Bucer became the unofficial leader of the Strasbourg church. During the early years of the Reformation, he directed his energies against the remnants of Catholic worship in Strasbourg. Although the city was essentially Protestant by 1525, the mass continued to be read in the collegiate churches until, after years of petitioning by the pastors, the magistrate finally abolished it in 1529. In the meantime a new threat had arisen in the form of various Anabaptist and sectarian groups which had spread to the city. Bucer attacked the positions held by these radicals both in popular pamphlets and in the biblical commentaries he published during the later 1520s. Gradually he became convinced that the city's church needed an officially recognized creed and a fixed institutional structure in order to withstand the challenges posed by the radicals. Accordingly, he helped direct the Strasbourg synod of 1533, which resulted in the city's first ecclesiastical ordinance.

Bucer's importance for the Strasbourg church was reflected by the positions he held within it. In 1531 he was appointed pastor of St. Thomas, a large and important parish church in the center of Strasbourg, whose college of canons was the only one in the city to accept the Reformation. Ten years later he was elected to the chapter of St. Thomas, and in 1544 he was chosen as its dean. That same year his place as leader of the Strasbourg church was officially recognized when he was named president of the *Kirchenkonvent*, the body of pastors and assistants which met biweekly to discuss the needs of the church.

[7]BDS 1:45.13, 29-46.4; cf. Greschat's description of the work, *Martin Bucer*, 68-70.
[8]BDS 1:63.1-10.
[9]Marijn de Kroon has described *pietas*, defined as faith in Christ and love for neighbor, as a "key concept" for Bucer's theology, *Martin Bucer und Johannes Calvin, Reformatorische Perspektiven, Einleitung und Texte* (Göttingen: Vandenhoeck & Ruprecht, 1991), 125-141; cf. Karl Koch, *Studium Pietatis: Martin Bucer als Ethiker*, Beiträge zur Geschichte und Lehre der Reformierten Kirche 14 (Neukirchen: Neukirchener Verlag, 1962), 43-50; 99-106.

Outside of Strasbourg Bucer became known for his role in the eucharistic controversy which dominated the 1520s. Although his earliest works reveal his debt to Luther, the outbreak of the controversy made Bucer aware of his affinities with Ulrich Zwingli through the common bond of Erasmian humanism. In works published during the 1520s Bucer upheld the Swiss interpretation of the sacrament against the Lutherans. Nevertheless he was convinced that agreement on the issue of the Lord's Supper was possible. In 1529 he attended the meeting at Marburg between Luther and Zwingli, and after obtaining Luther's grudging consent at the time of the Diet of Augsburg, he devoted himself to bringing about a reconciliation of the two parties. His efforts finally achieved partial success in the signing of the Wittenberg Concord in 1536.

Bucer's theology was thus elaborated in response to Catholic, Anabaptist, and Lutheran positions, and his interaction with these different groups led to a significant evolution of his own views. This evolution is best demonstrated by his changing conception of the relationship between internal and external.[10] In his earliest writings Bucer stressed the internal working of the Holy Spirit on the individual believer and criticized external rituals and practices as useless or even harmful because they promoted reliance on one's works. He also emphasized the spiritual and invisible nature of the church as opposed to the institutional and visible structure defended by Catholic theologians. The dichotomy of internal/spiritual and external/institutional affected other areas of Bucer's theology as well, including his understanding of the sacraments. However, the extreme spiritualism of many of the Anabaptists he encountered during the later 1520s caused Bucer to rethink his position and to place more emphasis on the link between external sign and internal significance. His growing rapprochement with the Lutherans on the issue of the Lord's Supper during the early 1530s both made possible and was a result of his increased appreciation of the concept of sacramentality. The greater importance which Bucer was willing to grant to external actions had implications for his system of Christian discipline.

By the mid-1530s Bucer was one of the most prominent Protestant churchmen in Germany. The Strasbourg magistrate relied on his theological expertise at meetings of the Schmalkaldic League and at several imperial diets, while Landgraf Philip of Hesse came to regard him as one of his most trusted advisors. During the 1540s Bucer worked actively to reunite the German church, representing the Protestant side at the religious colloquies held between 1539 and 1541. His support for concord led to an invitation from the Archbishop of Cologne, Hermann von Wied, to participate in the reformation of the territories under his secular jurisdiction. Despite the eventual failure of the Cologne reformation, Bucer continued to advocate the reform and

---

[10]The importance to Bucer of his pairing of internal and external, especially in his early years, is discussed in most studies of his theology; see especially Johannes Müller, *Martin Bucers Hermeneutik*, Quellen und Forschungen zur Reformationsgeschichte 32 (Gütersloh: Gerd Mohn, 1965), 169-178; René Bornert, *La réforme protestante du culte à Strasbourg au XVIe siècle (1523-1598): Approche sociologique et interprétation théologique*, Studies in Medieval and Reformation Thought 28 (Leiden: Brill, 1981), 306-322.

reconciliation of the entire German church, publishing pamphlets and participating in colloquies until the outbreak of the Schmalkaldic War in 1546. With the defeat of the Protestants and the imposition of the Augsburg Interim, Bucer was forced to leave Strasbourg. He went to England at the invitation of Archbishop Thomas Cranmer and was appointed Regius Professor of theology at Cambridge. The constant theme of his preaching and teaching there was the need for discipline.

A topic so central to Bucer's theology as discipline has frequently been discussed in more general studies of the reformer's life and thought. At the turn of this century August Lang drew attention to the evolution of Bucer's theology, including his understanding of the church's ministry and the power of the keys as reflected in the three editions of his commentary on the Gospels.[11] Some three decades later Jaques Courvoisier published his study on the development of Bucer's ecclesiology which highlighted the important place Bucer gave to church discipline in his mature theology.[12] Most recently, Willem van't Spijker has discussed the power of the keys and church discipline as important elements in Bucer's understanding of church office.[13] Because these works have examined Bucer's views on discipline in the context of a larger topic, whether his theology as a whole, his ecclesiology, or his view of the ministry, they have not been able to give the reformer's understanding of discipline as much attention as it clearly deserves.

Erich Roth, in *Die Privatbeichte und die Schlüsselgewalt in der Theologie der Reformatoren*,[14] has considered one element of Bucer's system of Christian discipline more directly. Roth's book focuses primarily on Luther and includes shorter sections on the Swiss reformers Zwingli, Oecolampadius, and Bullinger, and on Bucer and Calvin. His analysis of Bucer's understanding of confession and the power of the keys, based on two works from the later 1530s,[15] presents only a partial picture of the Strasbourg reformer's views. Roth does not discuss how Bucer's ideas developed before 1536, nor does he show how they continued to evolve during the 1540s. This is a significant shortcoming, given the extent to which Bucer's views on Christian discipline changed over time. Moreover, Roth's analysis of Bucer is severely hampered by his use of Luther's theology as the standard against which all else is measured. Bucer and Calvin are depicted as taking the "middle ground" between Saxony and Switzerland, but Bucer receives a fair amount of criticism for not having attained the enlightenment of Luther with regard to the power of the keys and private absolution.

---

[11]August Lang, *Der Evangelienkommentar Martin Butzers und die Grundzüge seiner Theologie*, Studien zur Geschichte der Theologie und der Kirche II/2 (Leipzig, 1900; repr. Aalen: Scientia, 1972), 181–187; 298–316.

[12]Jaques Courvoisier, *La Notion d'Église chez Bucer dans son développement historique*, Études d'histoire et de philosophie religieuses publiées par la faculté de théologie protestante de l'université de Strasbourg 28 (Paris: Félix Alcan, 1933), 22–40.

[13]*De Ambten bij Martin Bucer*, 2d ed. (Kampen: Kok, 1987), passim.

[14]Eric Roth, *Die Privatbeichte und die Schlüsselgewalt. . .*(Gütersloh: Bertelsmann, 1952.)

[15]Roth uses extracts from the third edition of Bucer's Gospels commentary published in 1536 and from the 1538 treatise *Von der waren Seelsorge* contained in a nineteenth-century collection of *loci communi* drawn from the writings of the reformers.

Roth's focus on Luther, and to a lesser extent on the scholastic interpretation of the sacrament of penance and the power of the keys, also blinds him to other influences, most notably the position held by Erasmus which is reflected in the thought of the Swiss and South German reformers.

In contrast to the methodological and conceptual flaws of Roth's work, two other recent studies stand out in their careful analyses of relevant aspects of Bucer's thought. René Bornert, in his *La réforme protestante du culte à Strasbourg au XVIe siècle*, analyzes the role played by Bucer and his Strasbourg colleagues in establishing a new theological consensus for the city and in devising forms of public worship to reflect that consensus. As a part of his study, he examines how the Catholic sacrament of penance was replaced in the Strasbourg church by other liturgical and disciplinary forms.[16] Bornert's book provides a wealth of information about the actual liturgical changes in Strasbourg which resulted from the Reformation, but again, because it is so broad in scope, it gives only a tantalizing glimpse of how Bucer hoped to establish a system of Christian discipline in Strasbourg.

The most important recent work to discuss Bucer's views on discipline is *Entre la Secte et la Cité*, Gottfried Hammann's masterful study of the reformer's ecclesiology. Hammann describes Bucer's view of the church as "the Christian community, at the same time open to all, identical with the social body of the city, and the body of Christ, community of the elect called to sanctification."[17] According to Hammann, this "dualist conception of the church" had important consequences for Bucer's view of discipline. The form of discipline applied to individuals within "the church of the multitude" was intended "to guide their evolution towards a comportment testifying to their membership in the true church of Christ." It consisted of gathering them together to hear the word of God, surveillance to ensure regular participation in the Lord's Supper for the faithful and to prevent unworthy reception by sinners, and coercive authority "to control the faith and morals of all members of the *corpus mixtum*." For "the professing community," the elect within the larger church, there was an additional need for a "discipline of edification," which went beyond simple religious instruction to include shaping of character, and a "discipline of accompaniment," which consisted of admonition and penitential discipline. At both the levels of the multitude and the professing church, discipline retained its "double aspect of pastoral preoccupation and coercive practice," although the pastoral concern always predominated.[18] Excommunication, although a part of discipline, was to be used only rarely. Bucer saw excommunication as "a limited solution," used only as a last resort. It could not be exercised where there was only a "church of the multitude" but was instead an element of discipline used within the professing church for the edification and sanctification of its members.[19]

---

[16]Bornert, *Réforme protestante*, 389–417.

[17]Gottfried Hammann, *Entre la Secte et la Cité. Le Projet d'Église du Réformateur Martin Bucer (1491-1551)*, Histoire et Société 3 (Geneva: Labor et Fides, 1984), 56; cf. 162–166.

[18]Ibid., 234–239.

[19]Ibid., 245–248.

Hammann's perceptive analysis of Bucer's dualist ecclesiology and its implications for church discipline provides a useful framework for understanding the reformer's thought. Starting from Hammann's recognition of the complexity of Bucer's ideas on discipline, this study will trace the evolution of Bucer's understanding of Christian discipline—"the yoke of Christ"—and examine his attempts to impose this yoke both inside and outside of Strasbourg. The first chapter will sketch the background for Bucer's ideas by describing the penitential and disciplinary structures which existed in the medieval church and surveying the criticisms aimed at them by humanists and reformers during the early years of the Reformation. The next three chapters will follow the development of Bucer's ideas during the first two decades of his career, concentrating on the key theological issues underpinning his understanding of Christian discipline: the power of the keys, private confession and absolution, and the goals and methods of disciplining sinners. By the end of the 1530s Bucer's system of Christian discipline was essentially complete. The remaining chapters will examine several different situations during the 1540s in which that system of discipline became a subject of discussion or controversy: with Catholics, as Bucer became involved in attempts to reunite the German church and to reform the territories of the Archbishop of Cologne; in Strasbourg itself; and finally in England, where Bucer spent his last years in exile.

Bucer held that the ministry of Christian discipline, "the yoke of Christ," properly belonged within the church. Therefore this study will discuss only indirectly the responsibility of the state in the exercise of discipline. Bucer certainly granted the Christian magistrate an important place in promoting the spiritual welfare of its subjects, but in the exercise of Christian discipline its tasks were limited and largely punitive. Through its use of civil discipline, it was to prevent, deter, or punish that which hindered true doctrine and piety. By taking action against those who deviated in faith or morals, it kept the church from harm. The magistrate also had more positive, although indirect, supervisory responsibilities. It was to see that the clergy performed their duties faithfully and that their doctrine and conduct were above reproach; it was to create and maintain structures which allowed the clergy better to carry out their ministry; it was to ensure that its citizens gathered to hear the word and receive the sacraments. But Bucer emphasized that these responsibilities and the motives underlying civil discipline were quite different from the more pastoral duties and goals of the ministers in exercising Christian discipline.[20]

Martin Bucer certainly was not unique in his desire to see that the reformation of the church brought about a reformation both of the individual and of society as a whole, but he stands out as one who thought long and hard about how to achieve that reformation. Although he held firm to his evangelical convictions, Bucer was

---

[20]On the magistrate's role in the church, cf. Hammann, *Entre la Secte*, 309-322; cf. Bucer's own discussions of the responsibilities of the magistrate for pastoral care, *Von der waren Seelsorge*, BDS 7:147.6-151.38; 188.31-191.34; and the distinction he makes between the civil and ecclesiastical regiments in a letter to Ambrosius Blarer, Schieß 2:225-228 (Dec. 22, 1543, no. 1055); *Von der kirchen mengel vnnd fähl*, BDS 17:159.31-164.20.

ready to modify his concrete proposals for discipline to fit different circumstances and situations. The creative tension between theological principle and practical experience resulted in the formation of a system whose components continued to evolve even after the basic institutional foundations had been laid. Bucer's approach to discipline is distorted by focusing on only one aspect of the entire system. This study aims to redress the imbalance by examining the development and elaboration of the varied components of Christian discipline. The end result will be not only a deeper appreciation of a crucial aspect of Bucer's theology, but also a better understanding of how one of the most creative and practically minded of the reformers hoped to create a self-disciplined, God-fearing evangelical society.

1

Penance, Discipline, and the Reformation

Bucer's system of Christian discipline was meant to replace the penitential and disciplinary system of the late medieval church. Bucer himself occasionally contrasted "the yoke of Christ" with "the papal yoke" or "the yoke of the anti-Christ."[1] Although his references to the Catholic system were hostile, he also drew more positive lessons, particularly with regard to praxis, from the history of the church. Despite his rejection of Catholic theology, Bucer was schooled in scholastic thought and familiar with contemporary Catholic practice. Thus it was only natural that his evangelical system of discipline would bear traces of his Catholic background. Moreover, during the early years of the Reformation, the terms of the debate between Catholics and Protestants were determined by the teaching and practice of the late medieval church. Thus Bucer made some of his earliest statements on important elements of Christian discipline in the course of criticizing the Catholic sacrament of penance and the Catholic use of excommunication. Even during the 1540s, however, Bucer continued to interact with the Catholic system as a result of his involvement in the religious colloquies and the attempted reformation of the archiepiscopal territories of Cologne.

Bucer's rejection of the sacrament of penance had significant ramifications for his system of Christian discipline. In addition to its theological function of transmitting forgiveness, the various elements of the sacrament met other religious and social needs. Bucer had to incorporate into his system of discipline measures which would meet those needs but would be more in accordance with his own evangelical principles. He drew many of those elements from the church's past, as he attempted to purge a system perceived as full of abuses and to restore the penitential and disciplinary system which had existed in the early church.

Another factor influencing the development of Bucer's views on discipline was the controversy within the evangelical camp regarding the validity of certain elements of the medieval penitential system. Although the reformers were united in their criticism of Catholic theology and practice, they disagreed among themselves on issues such as the value of private confession and absolution. To place Bucer's ideas in prop-

---

[1]Cf. for example his letter to an unknown prince, CR 10:152 (March 9, 1540), no. 7122; *De vi et usu sacri ministerii*, SA 600.

er perspective, this chapter will briefly summarize the development of the Catholic penitential and disciplinary system and describe the controversy regarding the elements of the sacrament of penance during the early years of the Reformation.

By the fourth century, the early church had developed a penitential system whose chief characteristic was its rigor.[2] Christians who had committed grave sins were excluded from the church. As excommunicates, they were forbidden to enter the church, prohibited from receiving the Eucharist, eliminated from the prayers and suffrages of the church, unable to give oblations, and denied a church burial. Excommunicates who refused to be reconciled with the church were also to be shunned by the faithful in both religious and secular affairs.[3] These remained the basic consequences of excommunication throughout the Middle Ages.

Repentant sinners could be reconciled with the church by undergoing public penance: after being formally admitted to the order of penitents, they were required to perform acts of penance for a period before being absolved through the imposition of hands by the bishop. In the western church, penitents were to stand with the catechumens in a special section of the church and required to leave the church with them before the communion liturgy began. The bishop determined the length of the period of penance. For serious sins such as murder or apostasy, that period could be several years, although it was not as long for lesser offenses; by late antiquity, it was common for penitents to be enrolled on Ash Wednesday and reconciled with the church on Maundy Thursday.

The penances imposed on repentant sinners were demanding and included fasts, vigils, sexual continence, and almsgiving. Many of the prohibitions imposed on penitents continued in force after their reconciliation with the church; thus they could not marry or were required to abstain from sexual relations if already married, and were not allowed to hold public office, engage in commerce, serve in the military, or attend public functions such as baths, games, or feasts. Public penance could be performed only once, and sinners who relapsed after they had been absolved could not again be reconciled with the church; there was even some question about the spiritual status of reconciled penitents who did not again commit grave sin but who did not observe the lifelong injunctions imposed by the penitential state.[4] Individuals guilty of lesser sins could voluntarily enroll as penitents, but as the system gradually placed

[2]On penance in the early church, see, "Pénitence," DTC 12/I:748-931; Bernhard Poschmann, Penance and the Anointing of the Sick, trans. & rev. F. Courtney, S.J., Herder History of Dogma (New York: Herder & Herder, 1964),19-121, which draws on Poschmann's earlier, more detailed works on the history of penance, some of them cited below; Herbert Vorgrimler, Busse und Krankensalbung, Handbuch der Dogmengeschichte IV/3 (Freiburg: Herder, 1978), 28-92. The classic older work by H. C. Lea, A History of Auricular Confession and Indulgences in the Latin Church, 3 vols. (Philadelphia: Lea Brothers, 1896), is still informative despite its obvious hostility to Catholic practice.

[3]Paul Hinschius, System des katholischen Kirchenrechts mit besonderer Rücksicht auf Deutschland, 6 vols. (Berlin: Guldentag, 1869-1897; repr.: Graz, 1959), 4:698-705.

[4]Bernhard Poschmann, Die abendländische Kirchenbusse im Ausgang des christlichen Altertums, Münchener Studien zur historischen Theologie 7 (Munich: Pustet, 1928), 58-61.

more weight on the lifelong consequences of penance, fewer people were willing to accept its rigors. As a consequence, public penance was virtually limited to cases of serious sin, and it became the custom to postpone acceptance of penance until late in life or on one's deathbed. By the sixth century it had fallen into disuse, and during the Middle Ages it was imposed only for the most grave and notorious sins.[5]

Another reason for the gradual disappearance of public penance during the early Middle Ages was the spread of a system of private penance associated especially with Irish monasticism. This system differed from public penance in that it was repeatable and could be administered by a priest rather than by the bishop. It combined two factors: private confession for spiritual direction, an important feature of early monasticism, and tariff penance, a system of fixed penalties for specific sins.[6] This form of private penance was brought to the continent during the sixth and seventh centuries by Celtic missionaries. By the Carolingian period it was largely accepted by the church, although the adage that private penance should be imposed for secret sins and public penance for notorious sins influenced the type of satisfaction imposed by the priest.[7] In a significant development, it was becoming common for the priest to absolve the penitent before the penance had been completed.[8]

Private penance itself underwent important changes with the rise of scholastic theology.[9] By the mid-twelfth century, penance had been included among the seven sacraments of the church. Although monastic practice had allowed confession to a layman, it was gradually accepted that serious sins had to be confessed to a priest, who had the authority to forgive them on the basis of the power of the keys given by Christ to St. Peter (Matt. 16:19). The developing emphasis on the priest's authority to forgive or retain sin raised other problems, however, for it seemed to negate the obviously important role of repentance or contrition in obtaining forgiveness. During the twelfth century, theologians speculated on the relative value of the sinner's contrition and the priest's absolution in an attempt to reconcile the subjective and objective elements of the sacrament. Peter Lombard held that in absolution the priest did not forgive sins but merely declared or pronounced them forgiven. Most of his contemporaries shared this view.

A new understanding developed in the thirteenth century, however, as theologians distinguished between attrition and contrition. Although attrition was sufficient to bring a sinner to confession, it had to be transformed into contrition for the sinner to receive pardon for sin, a transformation brought about by absolution. John Duns Scotus was eventually to take the distinction between attrition and contrition to its

---

[5]Poschmann, *Ausgang*, 300–303; Lea, *History*, 2:78–81.

[6]On monastic confession, see Poschmann, *Ausgang*, 230–239; on tariff penance, idem, *Die abendländische Kirchenbuße im frühen Mittelalter*, Breslauer Studien zur historischen Theologie 16 (Breslau: Müller & Seiffert, 1930), 8–24.

[7]Poschmann, *Mittelalter*, 92–101.

[8]Ibid., 111–114.

[9]On penance in scholastic theology, see "Pénitence," DTC 12/I:931–1050; Poschmann, *Penance*, 155–193; Vorgrimler, *Busse*, 114–153.

logical conclusion. He taught that perfect contrition resulting in forgiveness was possible, although very difficult, for most sinners to achieve. For this reason God had established a second means of forgiveness through the sacrament of penance by which grace was infused through priestly absolution, changing attrition into contrition. In Scotus' view, the absolution granted by the priest was the sacrament of penance; contrition, confession, and satisfaction were necessary in preparing one for reception of the sacrament but were not part of the sacrament itself.[10] Thomas Aquinas, on the other hand, had taught that the acts of the one confessing—contrition, confession, and satisfaction—were the matter of the sacrament, while absolution was its form. All four elements worked together to bestow forgiveness of sin. This position was endorsed by the Council of Ferrara-Florence in 1439.

The elaboration of scholastic doctrine concerning the sacrament of penance had implications for the practice of excommunication.[11] Influenced by the Augustinian teaching that baptism conferred an indelible character, theologians moved away from the original understanding of excommunication as exclusion from the church to interpret it as a loss of the privileges of church membership. From the thirteenth century it was the church's official teaching that excommunication did not affect one's salvation unless it was ignored or condemned.[12] Although the priest's authority to impose both excommunication and satisfaction was derived from the power of the keys, the two actions were gradually separated as theologians distinguished between the *forum judiciale*, in which the ecclesiastical courts exercised their jurisdictional authority, and the *forum poenitentiale*, in which priests forgave sins through the sacrament of penance. As a consequence of this distinction, excommunication increasingly became a disciplinary penalty used by ecclesiastical courts.[13]

During the early Middle Ages neither the terminology concerning excommunication nor the specific consequences resulting from it were very precise, but this had changed by the thirteenth century. Major excommunication or the ban was the penalty which had evolved from the practice of the early church, which entailed loss of the rights of church membership. In theory, it could be imposed only for contumacy, which canon lawyers interpreted as the failure to appear before a court when cited or refusal to obey a judgment of the court.[14] In addition to its religious and social consequences, it now included a host of legal disabilities which restricted the excommunicate's rights in both ecclesiastical and secular courts. As early as the fifth century civil penalties were associated with excommunication, and from the thirteenth cen-

---

[10]Poschmann, *Penance*, 184–190.

[11]On the development of excommunication and its forms, see Elisabeth Vodola, *Excommunication in the Middle Ages* (Berkeley: University of California, 1986), 1–43; Hinschius, *Kirchenrecht*, 5:1–51.

[12]Vodola, *Excommunication*, 42–43.

[13]François Russo, S.J., "Pénitence et Excommunication. Etude historique sur les rapports entre la théologie et le droit canon dans le domaine pénitentiel du IXe au XIIIe siècle," *Recherches de science religieuse* 33 (1946):257–279; 431–461.

[14]Vodola, *Excommunication*, 36–37.

tury the imperial ban was automatically incurred by excommunicated persons who were not absolved within a year.[15] Excommunicates who did not seek reconciliation with the church could also be anathematized, or formally excommunicated in a solemn ceremony. Anathema was occasionally described as complete exclusion from the church and as eternal damnation, but the term was also often used as a synonym for excommunication itself.[16]

Ostracism was an important part of the penalty of excommunication.[17] From at least the third century both clergy and laity who associated with an excommunicate could themselves be excommunicated. Over the centuries, this provision was softened. A ninth-century canon limited the penalty for association with excommunicates to exclusion from the sacraments, and by the end of the twelfth century this was the accepted consequence for such contact; in the early thirteenth century sacramental exclusion was given the name of minor excommunication. From the eleventh century, an excommunicate's spouse, children, servants, and other dependents, as well as those ignorant of the excommunicate's status, were exempted entirely from incurring any form of excommunication.[18] The requirement to avoid excommunicates was complicated by the development, in the twelfth century, of the sentence of *excommunicatio latae sententiae*. This form of excommunication was incurred immediately and automatically when an individual committed a forbidden act, in contrast to the traditional form *(excommunicatio ferendae sententiae)* which was publicly imposed by those with the proper jurisdictional authority in the church. Canonists debated whether individuals should avoid an acquaintance whose excommunication was not public, and the church itself required that secret excommunicates be publicly denounced once they had been identified, so that they would be subject to the full consequences of the sentence.[19]

From about the eighth century, church canons began to require individuals to confess once, twice, or even three times a year. This confession was often regarded as a preparation for receiving communion, and by the tenth century it was widely held that such confession was a necessary prerequisite for participation in the sacrament.[20] The Fourth Lateran Council of 1215 made the linkage between confession and communion permanent. Its decree *Omnis utriusque sexus* required every Christian to confess all mortal sins to his or her parish priest and then receive communion at least once a year. The decree thus recognized a practice which had become standard and provided a new legal basis which made that practice universal and its neglect punishable.

---

[15]"Bann IV," TRE 5:172–173, 176–178.

[16]Hinschius, *Kirchenrecht*, 5:7–10, 513–514; Vodola, *Excommunication*, 45–46.

[17]On the social consequences of excommunication, Vodola, *Excommunication*, 44–69.

[18]Vodola, *Excommunication*, 17–18, 24–27.

[19]Ibid., 28–32, 48–50.

[20]Peter Browe, "Die Kommunionvorbereitung im Mittelalter," *Zeitschrift für katholische Theologie* 56 (1932):375–415; Poschmann, *Mittelalter*, 172–180.

Omnis utriusque sexus led to further developments in theology, canon law, and popular piety during the later Middle Ages. One consequence of the decree was a debate concerning the obligatory nature of auricular confession.[21] Writing before the Fourth Lateran Council, Gratian and Peter Lombard recognized that there was disagreement concerning the necessity of confession to a priest. Gratian left the final decision regarding the necessity of confession to his readers, stating that "both sides had supporters who were wise and religious men."[22] Peter Lombard, while acknowledging the disagreement, was more willing to take a stand, citing James 5:16 and various patristic authorities to demonstrate the necessity of confessing first to God and then to a priest.[23] Canon lawyers after the Fourth Lateran Council acknowledged the obligation to confess but based the obligation on the tradition of the church, arguing that Scripture passages adduced to support the necessity of confession were inconclusive and that the Greek church did not require it. This position was repeated as late as the fifteenth century by the Sicilian conciliarist Niccolo de Tedeschi, called Panormitanus.

Theologians, on the other hand, soon began to interpret *Omnis utriusque sexus* as at least implying the divine (rather than human) institution of auricular confession. Bonaventure absolved Gratian and Peter Lombard from any accusation of heresy since they had written before the decrees of the Fourth Lateran Council, but he stated that after the decrees had been issued, those who denied the necessity of confession were heretics because they thus implicitly denied the power of the keys. Thomas Aquinas went further to assert that confession was mandated by divine law. Later theologians tried to base this divine command on several different passages of Scripture but were unable to agree on which text could serve as the definitive basis for the obligation. John Duns Scotus thought Christ's words to his disciples after the Resurrection (John 20:22-23) seemed the most likely basis for obligatory confession, but he was willing to accept Christ's oral teaching to the disciples, not contained in Scripture, as the basis for the church's requirement of auricular confession.[24]

The requirement that every Christian confess at least once a year contributed to the development of literature intended to aid priests in hearing confession. Penitential manuals listing certain penances to be imposed for specific sins had been in existence for several centuries. By the time of the Fourth Lateran Council, however, a new emphasis had emerged which focused not so much on the sin and the penance to be imposed for it as on the individual sinner and the way in which the priest could

[21]When discussing confession after 1215, I use the term "auricular confession" (sometimes called "secret confession" by the Protestant reformers) for the confession of all mortal sins to a priest required by *Omnis utriusque sexus*, which was part of the sacrament of penance, and "private confession" for the voluntary confession of sin advocated by some of the reformers.

[22]Friedberg 1:1189.

[23]*Sentences* IV, dist. XVII, 2-3.

[24]Pierre-Marie Gy, "Le précepte de la confession annuelle et la nécessité de la confession," *Revue des sciences philosophiques et théologiques* 63 (1979): 529-547.

best help him recognize his sin.[25] The *Corrector sive Medicus*, part of a longer canonical collection by Burchard of Worms at the beginning of the eleventh century, was the first work to include questions which the confessor could use in examining the penitent along with the usual list of penitential canons. Such manuals became more numerous from the end of the twelfth century, and two of the most influential, written by the Dominicans Raymond de Peñaforte and Johannes von Freiburg, were composed in the thirteenth century.[26] As P. Michaud-Quantin has stated, the confessor's manuals were the means by which the theological debates on ethical action and Aristotelian moral philosophy were able to trickle down from the closed environment of the universities to the masses of the faithful.[27]

The questions used by priests in examining individuals during confession often followed a pattern—the seven deadly sins, sins of the five senses, the seven cardinal virtues, the six works of mercy, or the eight beatitudes. At the end of the fourteenth century the Ten Commandments assumed a prominent place in the confessional literature and became firmly established there over the course of the next century.[28] Popular devotional books intended to help the laity prepare for confession also often contained other elements considered necessary for each Christian to know, especially the Apostles' Creed, the Lord's Prayer, the Ave Maria, and a list of the sacraments.[29] Children received no special instruction from the church before making their first confession or receiving the Eucharist for the first time. Parents and godparents were responsible for their religious instruction, and statutes from the Carolingian period

---

[25]On the development of the *summae confessorum* and other types of literature related to the confessional, see Pierre Michaud-Quantin, "A propos des premières *Summae confessorum*. Théologie et droit canonique," *Recherches de théologie ancienne et médiévale* 26 (1959):264-306; idem, *Sommes de casuistique et manuels de confession au moyen âge, XIIe – XVIe siècles*, Analecta Mediaevalia Namurcensia 13 (Louvain: E. Nauwelaerts, 1962); Thomas Tentler, *Sin and Confession on the Eve of the Reformation* (Princeton: Princeton University Press, 1977), 28-53. Johannes Geffken, *Der Bildercatechismus des fünfzehnten Jahrhunderts und die catechetischen Hauptstücke in dieser Zeit bis auf Luther. I. Die zehn Gebote, mit 12 Bildtafeln nach Cod. Heidelb. 438* (Leipzig: T.O. Weigel, 1855), 28-49, gives an overview of works intended for learned confessors, aids for unlearned priests, and vernacular works for the laity from the end of the Middle Ages.

[26]Michaud-Quantin, *Sommes de casuistique*, describes the most important confessors' *summae* of the later Middle Ages; he discusses the works of Raymond de Peñaforte and Johannes von Freiburg, 34-50. While Raymund's *Summa* apparently declined in popularity at the end of the Middle Ages, it and its gloss were cited by later authors of popular confessors' *summae* and manuals such as Astesanus of Asti and Guido de Monte Rocherii, Tentler, *Sin and Confession*, 31-32, 37.

[27]Michaud-Quantin, *Sommes de casuistique*, 109-110.

[28]John Bossy describes the gradual acceptance of the Ten Commandments in the fourteenth and fifteenth centuries, especially in Germany, and some of the consequences of this acceptance in the early modern period in "Moral Arithmetic: Seven Sins into Ten Commandments," in *Conscience and Casuistry in Early Modern Europe*, ed. Edmund Leites, Ideas in Context (Cambridge: Cambridge University Press, 1988), 214-234.

[29]Geffken, *Bildercatechismus*, 20-22; Rudolf Padberg, *Erasmus als Katechet. Der literarische Beitrag des Erasmus von Rotterdam zur katholischen Katechese des 16. Jahrhunderts. Eine Untersuchung zur Geschichte der Katechese*, Untersuchung zur Theologie der Seelsorge 9 (Freiburg: Herder, 1956), 22-44.

decreed that all godparents must be able to repeat the Creed and the Lord's Prayer to the priest to demonstrate their ability to carry out their responsibility to teach their godchildren. Likewise in confession priests were encouraged to examine penitents to see if they knew the Creed and Lord's Prayer.[30]

Confession thus came to be one of the few means available for religious instruction, clerical oversight, and the internalization of moral values. In this capacity the sacrament served as an influential method of social control.[31] Roberto Rusconi has observed that in shifting the emphasis from external repentance or satisfaction to internal repentance or contrition, the penitential literature of the later Middle Ages emphasized the *erubescentia* of the penitent as a reflection of genuine penitence.[32] Thomas Tentler goes further to assert that the confessors' *summae* popular at the end of the Middle Ages "are intended to bring guilt down on people who deviate. That is not to deny that they try to strengthen the pusillanimous, or to offer reconciliation to the sinner, or console the anxious. But their system of social control is predicated on an ecclesiastical authority's theology of law, guilt, and absolution."[33]

Whether or not the consolation of absolution was sufficient to allay the sense of guilt aroused by the priest's detailed probing of conscience is a question much debated since Steven Ozment proposed that it was "the burden of late medieval religion," with its emphasis on perfect penance and ascetic clerical values, which made the early reformers' message of Christian liberty so attractive to the urban laity.[34] Certainly in the well-known case of Luther, auricular confession could not alleviate the guilt. On the other hand, Lawrence Duggan argues that the degree of clerical control and hence the oppressiveness of the penitential system was weakened by poor enforcement of the requirement to confess to the parish priest, by rivalry between secular

[30]Peter Browe, "Der Beichtunterricht im Mittelalter," *Theologie und Glaube* 26 (1934):437–442; see also H. Holzmann, "Die Katechese des Mittelalters," *Zeitschrift für praktische Theologie* 20 (1898):1–18, 117–130, esp. 4–18.

[31]Thomas N. Tentler, "The Summa for Confessors as an Instrument of Social Control," in *The Pursuit of Holiness in Late Medieval and Renaissance Religion*, ed. Charles Trinkaus and Heiko A. Oberman, Studies in Medieval and Reformation Thought 10 (Leiden: E.J. Brill, 1974), 103–126; cf. the critique by Leonard E. Boyle, "The Summa for Confessors as a Genre, and its Religious Intent," in ibid., 126–130, and Tentler's "Response and Retractio," 131–137.

[32]Roberto Rusconi, "De la prédication à la confession: transmission et contrôle de modèles de comportement au XIIIe siècle," in *Faire Croire. Modalités de la diffusion et de la réception des messages religieux du XIIe au XVe siècle*, Collection de l'école française de Rome 51 (Rome: École Française, 1981), 81.

[33]Tentler, "The Summa for Confessors," 124; cf. Hervé Martin, "Confession et contrôle social à la fin du Moyen Age," in Groupe de la Bussière, *Pratiques de la Confession des Pères du désert à Vatican II. Quinze études d'histoire* (Paris: Cerf, 1983), 127–132. John Mahoney recognizes the influence which the sacrament of penance and the practice of auricular confession have had on Catholic moral theology, particularly with regard to its preoccupation with sin, its concentration on the individual, and its obsession with law in *The Making of Moral Theology. A Study of the Roman Catholic Tradition* (Oxford: Clarendon, 1987), 27–36.

[34]Steven Ozment, *The Reformation in the Cities: The Appeal of Protestantism to Sixteenth-Century Germany and Switzerland* (New Haven: Yale University, 1975); Ozment uses the phrase as the heading for his discussion of confession, 22–32.

and regular clergy over hearing confession, and by the category of reserved sins which could only be absolved by the bishop's penitentiary.[35] Tentler concludes from his examination of confessors' *summae* that one can argue both for and against confession as being Pelagian, magical, purely legalistic, excessively lax, creating scrupulosity, subjecting laity to the clergy: "the meaning of every judgment of sacramental confession—favorable or unfavorable—depends on what evidence you choose, what part of the institution you pay attention to."[36]

Of course no matter how closely a confessor examined the penitent in order to uncover sin and promote contrition, such a detailed scrutiny would have less effect if done only infrequently. The requirement of yearly confession gave the church the leverage it needed to bring the consciences of all the faithful under its moral scrutiny. Synodal statutes of the thirteenth century required priests to submit the names of those who had not made their annual confession.[37] Less official but perhaps more effective was the social pressure to confess in an urban parish or rural village where failure to receive the Eucharist during the Easter season was public evidence that an individual had not confessed and been absolved. Preachers of the later Middle Ages exhorted their hearers to make confession and would hear confessions themselves after their sermons. This emphasis on more frequent confession is manifested in the statutes of religious confraternities which often required their members to confess two, three, or four times a year.[38]

On the eve of the Reformation, then, the sacrament of penance and the church's related disciplinary practices performed major religious and social functions in addition to their primarily theological function of transmitting forgiveness of sin and restoring the penitent to a state of grace. The popular *Beichtbüchlein* used by the laity to prepare for confession and the private meeting with the priest served as the chief

---

[35]Lawrence Duggan, "Fear and Confession on the Eve of the Reformation," ARG 75 (1984):165–173.

[36]Tentler, *Sin and Confession*, 363–364. Ozment points out, however, that "the further one moves from the balanced scholastic tract, and the closer one gets to the short vernacular *Beichtspiegel* for ordinary people, the more legalistic, fiscalized, and psychologically burdensome penitential practice appears," *Reformation*, 176 n. 50.

[37]Peter Browe, "Die Pflichtbeichte im Mittelalter," *Zeitschrift für katholische Theologie* 57 (1933):372–375.

[38]Lester K. Little, "Les techniques de la confession et la confession comme technique," in *Faire Croire*, 87–99. Little cites Italian examples; on the more frequent practice of confession and communion in Alsace, see Medard Barth, "Beicht und Kommunionen im mittelalterlichen Elsass; Ein Durchblick," *Freiburger Diözesanarchiv* 74 (1954):88–99. Rusconi, "de la prédication," and Nicole Bériou, "Autour de Latran IV (1215): la naissance de la confession moderne et sa diffusion," in *Pratiques de la Confession*, 73–92, also discuss the link between preaching and confession. Lawrence Duggan believes that despite occasional complaints in synodal statutes of the fourteenth and fifteenth centuries about those who did not confess, the documents give the impression that confession was the general practice, and he cites the popularity of indulgences which required contrition and confession from the penitent as further indirect evidence of the general acceptance of confession at the close of the Middle Ages, "Fear and Confession," 159–161.

means of religious instruction for the faithful. Confession was used to instill in the masses a deeper appreciation of right and wrong, relying on guilt or shame to produce genuine contrition and on the power of sacramental absolution to console guilty consciences and assure them of forgiveness. Moreover the shame of confessing all one's sins to a priest and the desire to avoid the duty of performing any form of penance or satisfaction served as a deterrent to socially unacceptable behavior. The requirement to confess before receiving the Eucharist enabled priests to examine their parishioners and ensured that those receiving the sacrament were worthy to do so. The imposition of excommunication also functioned as a punishment for disobedience to the church and, by making an example of the sinner, had a deterrent effect on others as well.

In the years immediately following Luther's posting of his Ninety-five Theses the sacrament of penance and the church's related penitential practices were attacked from many different quarters. Luther and other reformers were loud and vigorous in their criticism of auricular confession, if not always united on the question of whether it should be reformed or rejected altogether. The practices associated with confession were also assailed by Erasmus. A comment by the Dutch humanist in his *Annotations on the New Testament* sparked a heated exchange on the origin and significance of penance which stretched over several years.[39] The note on Acts 19:18 ("many of those who believed now came and openly confessed their evil deeds") in the first edition of the *Annotations,* published in 1516, stated that "there was of old some form of confessing a life of evil-doing, but it was a public confession, in my opinion, and a general one, and we do not read that it was compulsory." In the second edition three years later Erasmus added that secret confession began as a private consultation with bishops made by those with troubled souls.[40]

Edward Lee, an English theologian teaching at Louvain, listed this note as one of Erasmus' three hundred errors in a book published in February 1520.[41] In reply, Erasmus published three treatises defending his views; the last included a lengthy discussion of secret confession. In this *Response* to Lee, he argued that auricular confession had been established indirectly by the Spirit of Christ working through the church rather than directly by Christ himself.[42] He rejected Scripture passages adduced by Lee to prove the divine institution of auricular confession, saying that they

---

[39]John B. Payne, *Erasmus: His Theology of the Sacraments* (Richmond, VA: John Knox Press, 1970), 183–184; Erika Rummel, *Erasmus' "Annotations on the New Testament": From Philologist to Theologian,* Erasmus Studies 8 (Toronto: University of Toronto, 1986), 152–156. J. P. Massaut, "La position 'oecuménique' d'Érasme sur la pénitence," in *Réforme et Humanisme, Actes du IVe Colloque, Montpellier, Octobre 1975,* ed. Jean Boisset, Centre d'Histoire de la Réforme et du Protestantisme (Montpellier: Université Paul Valéry, 1977), 241–281, gives a good summary of Erasmus' understanding of the sacrament based on several of the humanist's works.

[40]LB 6:507F–508E; translation from Rummel, *Erasmus' "Annotations,"* 154.

[41]BCor 1:107 n. 20 (no. 12).

[42]LB 9:255C.

relied too heavily on allegory, which had no weight in determining doctrine.[43] On the other hand, Erasmus quoted Chrysostom, Origen, Cassian, Ambrose, and Basil as evidence that the church fathers did not give secret confession a more important role in obtaining forgiveness of sins than other methods of expressing repentance and humility. He mentioned Gratian's unwillingness to state whether confession was obligatory or not and cited both Durandus of St. Pourçain and Panormitanus as two more recent authorities who believed that the obligation to confess was based on human rather than divine law.[44]

The human institution of auricular confession was an important issue, because it implied that what the church had instituted, it could also eliminate "for the well-being of the people."[45] Erasmus believed that a practice instituted to relieve troubled souls and to promote piety had been twisted by the clergy to increase their own control over their spiritual charges.[46] In stating this opinion, however, Erasmus tried to avoid any possible charges of heresy: he declared that he was not criticizing confession per se, but only the method of confession, which had been so perverted. It did not seem to him that this type of confession could have been instituted by Christ, but he would freely submit to the judgment of the church.[47]

As might be expected, Luther was much more vehement in his criticism of mandatory auricular confession.[48] In *De captivitate Babylonica*, published in October 1520, Luther accused the papists of totally destroying the sacrament of penance, "so that not a trace of it remained."[49] While Luther held that confession of sins was both necessary and commanded by God, mandatory auricular confession had no basis in Scripture. He praised private confession as being useful, even necessary, and stated that he was glad that the church had such confession, since it was a "unique remedy" for troubled and afflicted consciences. But this beneficial form of confession had been warped by the tyrannous requirements of the pope that all secret sins be revealed to a specified person. Luther also criticized the requirement to confess the circumstances connected with the sin committed. "For Christians," he said, "there is only one circumstance, which is that a brother has sinned."[50]

---

[43]Ibid., 257B–258B.

[44]Ibid., 259D–261E.

[45]Ibid., 259C.

[46]Ibid., 258C–D.

[47]Ibid., 259A–B, 262E.

[48]Emil F. Fischer, *Zur Geschichte der evangelischen Beichte*, 2 vols., Studien zur Geschichte der Theologie und der Kirche, 8/2 and 9/4 (Leipzig: Dieterich, 1902–1903), is the most detailed study of the development of Luther's views on confession and absolution and of the changes made in the practice of confession at Wittenberg in the early years of the Reformation. Jos E. Vercruysse, "Schlüsselgewalt und Beichte bei Luther," in *Leben und Werk Martin Luthers von 1526 bis 1546. Festgabe zu seinem 500. Geburtstag*, ed. Helmar Junghans, 2 vols. (Göttingen: Vandenhoeck & Ruprecht, 1983), 1:153–169; 2:775–781, is a more recent summary citing most of the relevant secondary works.

[49]WA 6:543.12–13.

[50]Ibid., 547.17–548.17; citation at 548.10.

The growing controversy over auricular confession was fueled by a work published in April 1521, written by the humanist and later reformer of Basel, Johannes Oecolampadius, and entitled *Quod non sit onerosa christianis confessio, Paradoxon.*[51] Oecolampadius sharply condemned the *psychotyranni* who had made confession burdensome by demanding confession of all sins, an impossible task that would take more than one lifetime.[52] He described three types of confession: the first type made to God, the second type made to a priest in the name of the church, and the third type made to a brother for the sake of mutual prayer. Like Erasmus, he argued that auricular confession did not exist in the early church. The penitential practices of the early church were intended to maintain the purity of the congregation and dealt only with grave, manifest sin. In accordance with the decree of the Fourth Lateran Council, individuals should confess sins of a more public nature to their priest, but the confession of secret sins or sins of thought was unnecessary.[53] Oecolampadius' treatise on confession proved so popular that it was reprinted twice as well as translated into German.[54] In his edition of Tertullian which was published in July 1521, Beatus Rhenanus referred his readers to Oecolampadius' book, which he said was a help to all who had been caught by superstitious traditions about confession.[55]

Luther also spoke highly of Oecolampadius' book but judged that there was still room for another work on the topic written in the vernacular.[56] His book *Von der Beicht, ob die der Bapst macht habe zu gepieten,* was published in September 1521. In it Luther repeated and intensified all the criticisms he had earlier made of auricular confession, but he also restated his fundamental belief that although there was no scriptural basis for secret confession it was still a beneficial and salutary institution when purged of abuses. Luther argued that no one could be compelled to confess; nevertheless the absolution which one obtained in private confession was a great gift of God. He attacked the view that the priest was to judge whether to absolve the sinner on the basis of his confession; rather, if a person confessed, the priest was obligated to absolve him: "confession is my decision, not yours, and absolution is my right, not your right."[57] Luther asserted that the power to bind and loose sins which the papists claimed was exercised in auricular confession actually applied only to public binding or loosing, that is, in excommunicating unrepentant sinners, as Matthew,

[51]The first edition was printed in Augsburg by Sigismund Grimm. Ernst Staehelin summarizes this work in *Das theologische Lebenswerk Johannes Oekolampads,* Quellen und Forschungen zur Reformationsgeschichte 21 (Leipzig: M. Heinsius, 1939), 121–134.

[52]*Quod non sit onerosa,* fol. B1b–C1b.

[53]Ibid., fol. L1b–M3a.

[54]Staehelin, *Lebenswerk,* 134. A pamphlet entitled *De penitentia evangelica et confessione secundum veteres theologiae doctores,* which contains Luther's 1520 *Confitendi ratio* and excerpts from Erasmus' *Response* to Lee as well as quotations from Origen, Chrysostom, Ambrose, and other church fathers, has also been attributed to Oecolampadius, although there is no proof that he was actually responsible for the publication, ibid., 122 n. 1.

[55]Ernst Staehelin, ed., *Briefe und Akten* 1:367 n. 4.

[56]WABr 2:347.24–29; cf. introduction to *Von der Beicht,* WA 8:131.

[57]WA 8:157.4–9.

chapter 18, taught. This power to bind a sinner belonged to the congregation or to the pastor as its representative, and it should be used only against manifest sin.[58]

Other critics of auricular confession were more radical in their attitudes toward the institution of confession. Ulrich Zwingli went beyond Luther in his discussion of confession in the *Schlußreden*, published in 1523. In Article 52 he stated that confession made to a priest or to a neighbor was made not to receive forgiveness of sins but rather to obtain advice. Here Zwingli criticized "certain learned men who teach that although the priest does not forgive sins, a person should still go to him to be reassured, because the going and receiving absolution is a sign by which the sinner is assured that his sins are forgiven." This view, Zwingli stated, had no basis in Scripture. Rather, "as soon as we believe that God forgives us our sins through his son and we are confident in this belief, then our sins are forgiven."[59] If a person did not have this confident faith, his sins would not be forgiven "even though he were to confess to a priest a thousand times." Those weak in faith could go to the priest for counsel; the priest's duty was to teach the penitent to trust in God through Christ. This, Zwingli asserted, was binding or loosing a person from his sin: if the penitent believed the word of the gospel which was taught, he was loosed; if he did not believe, he had come to the priest in vain and remained bound.[60] Obviously Zwingli did not hold confession in the same high esteem that Luther did. For the Swiss reformer, the focus shifted from the penitent's confession of sin to his instruction by the priest—or by a layman—in the word of God. Moreover, Zwingli denied that the words of absolution to which Luther attached such importance had any power to console or reassure the sinner.[61]

Zwingli recognized these differences with Luther in the understanding of absolution and the power of the keys, and in his *Amica Exegesis*, written in 1527, he used them to support his claim that he had discovered the gospel independently of Luther. If he had learned the gospel from Luther, why did they not hold the same understanding of the power of the keys? Zwingli accused Luther of not understanding properly what the keys were. Our absolution, Zwingli wrote, comes when we believe in Christ Jesus, the Son of God, but Luther still held to the view that "the conscience had to be reassured by someone chanting an absolution."[62] He was even more critical of Luther's understanding of absolution in his response to Luther, *Daß diese Wort: Das ist mein Leib usw., ewiglich den alten Sinn haben werden*, published in 1527. The Swiss reformer asserted that Luther had never recognized "the broad and glorious appearance of the gospel," or if he had, that he had lost it again.[63] He accused Luther of

---

[58]Ibid., 159.36–160.15.

[59]Z 2:393.8–394.5.

[60]Ibid., 396.13–397.16.

[61]Roth, *Privatbeichte*, discusses the views of Zwingli, Bullinger, and Oecolampadius on confession and absolution and compares them to Luther's views, 71–132.

[62]Z 5:715.14–716.3.

[63]Ibid., 819.15–17; cf. 820.15–18.

emphasizing that absolution had to be pronounced for anyone who wanted to be sure that his sins were forgiven, and that this absolution was the power of the keys. But, Zwingli argued, assurance of faith came from the gospel; if faith in the gospel existed, there was absolution and release from sins. He repeated what he had expressed four years earlier in the *Schlußreden*: if a man says a thousand times, "your sins are forgiven you," still no one will be sure of this forgiveness unless he has been assured in his heart by God. For Zwingli it was only logical that assurance and faith in the gospel were identical. When someone says, "your sins are forgiven through the death of Jesus Christ and you have also been made into a son of God through him," he is stating the gospel.

> But no one accepts Christ Jesus unless the Father has drawn him. From this it follows: as soon as he is drawn he believes. If he believes he is already assured [of forgiveness], for wherever there is no assurance, there is no perfect faith; but if there is faith, there is assurance. Why then is there a need for the assurance of men or absolution?[64]

Given the reformers' criticism of auricular confession, it is not at all surprising that changes in practice were soon introduced in the cities and territories where evangelical beliefs were adopted. The differences among evangelical pastors and preachers over the value of confession and the theological interpretation of absolution led to differences in practice as well. In Wittenberg, mandatory auricular confession was effectively abolished during Luther's stay at the Wartburg, when Andreas Carlstadt distributed communion in both kinds to the entire congregation on Christmas Day, 1521, without requiring that confession be made beforehand.[65] Confession remained voluntary in Wittenberg for almost two years, but in his Maundy Thursday sermon of 1523 Luther warned his hearers that this situation would soon be changed:

> I'll let it go once more for this year, that each person receive the sacrament according to his conscience, but next time we will have to order things so that no one is allowed to the sacrament unless he has first been questioned and it is clear how his heart stands, and if he knows what the sacrament is and why he receives it.[66]

The following December, in the *Formula Missae*, Luther wrote that all those wishing to receive communion were to go to the pastor beforehand to be examined concerning their understanding of the sacrament and their worthiness to partake of

---

[64]Ibid., 819.21–820.9.

[65]Fischer, *Geschichte* 2:141–185; Kurt Aland, "Die Privatbeichte im Luthertum von ihren Anfängen bis zu ihrer Auflösung," in idem, *Kirchengeschichtliche Entwürfe. Alte Kirche, Reformation und Luthertum, Pietismus und Erweckungsbewegung* (Gütersloh: G. Mohn, 1960), 461–472; Bjarne Hareide, *Die Konfirmation in der Reformationszeit. Eine Untersuchung der lutherischen Konfirmation in Deutschland, 1520–1585*, Arbeiten zur Pastoraltheologie 8 (Göttingen: Vandenhoeck & Ruprecht, 1971), 87–100.

[66]WA 12:477.20–478.4.

it. This examination was not intended as a binding law required of everyone before receiving communion. Luther stated that a yearly examination was sufficient for those who wished to commune, while some individuals might be examined only once in their lifetime or not at all. In accordance with Luther's views, Johannes Bugenhagen, the pastor of Wittenberg's parish church, introduced the precommunion examination of faith and morals during Lent of 1524. Four years later the *Unterricht der Visitatoren* made the precommunion examination standard for all of electoral Saxony. The *Unterricht's* importance as a model meant that the requirement of a pre-communion examination was incorporated into church ordinances for other Lutheran territories.

Although Luther differentiated between this examination and the private confession of sin, it is obvious that the distinction could easily be missed by the laity and the examination seen as a new form of confession. Melanchthon made the link between the precommunion examination and confession explicit in Article XXV of the *Augsburg Confession*, which stated that "confession has not been abolished by the preachers of our confession, for we have retained this custom that the sacrament is not given to those who have not previously been examined and absolved. In addition, the people are diligently taught how consoling the word of absolution is and how high and dear they should consider absolution."[67]

In Zürich on the other hand no attempt was made to replace auricular confession. Although the followers of Zwingli who had eaten meat during Lent in 1522 were required by the Zürich city council to confess and perform the penance imposed on them, the Lenten fast and pre-Easter confession were rejected two years later by most citizens. In this they were encouraged by the pastors and preachers who taught that confession before receiving the sacrament was unnecessary and that it sufficed to confess to God alone.[68]

Notorious sinners were to be kept from receiving the Lord's Supper through the use of excommunication. In his recommendations concerning the Lord's Supper written in April 1525—when the Catholic mass was abolished and a new reformed communion service introduced in Zürich—Zwingli wrote that those guilty of grave public sin such as adultery, blasphemy, drunkenness, murder, theft, or usury were to be excluded from the sacrament.[69] If the magistrate did not expel such sinners from the city, the faithful would be instructed to avoid them in their daily activities. The city council rejected Zwingli's proposal to excommunicate usurers, but it incorporated the excommunication of those guilty of sexual sins in the *Ehegerichtsordnung* issued a

---

[67]Translation of the German version, BSLK:97–98.

[68]Gottfried Locher, *Die Zwinglische Reformation im Rahmen der europäischen Kirchengeschichte* (Göttingen: Vandenhoeck & Ruprecht, 1979), 142; Emil Egli, ed., *Aktensammlung zur Geschichte der Zürcher Reformation in den Jahren 1519–1533* (Zürich: J. Schabelitz, 1879; repr: Nieuwkoop: B. de Graaf, 1973), 76–77 (no. 236) and 216–217 (no. 498).

[69]See his *Ratschlag betreffend Ausschließung vom Abendmahl für Ehebrecher, Hurer, Wucherer, etc.,* Z 4:31–34; on the connection between the recommendations and the communion ordinance, Roger Ley, *Kirchenzucht bei Zwingli,* Quellen und Abhandlungen zur Geschichte des schweizerischen Protestantismus 2 (Zürich: Zwingli-Verlag, 1948), 38–39 n. 1.

month later. The ordinance authorized the pastors to exclude adulterers and fornica-
tors from the Lord's Supper, while the magistrate retained the right to impose fines
or other civil penalties.[70] A year and a half later the council issued a new ordinance
which automatically excluded adulterers from the Lord's Supper, barred them from
guild membership, and prohibited their election to public office. Imprisonment and
fines were also imposed, increasing in severity with repeated offenses. The authority
to lift the penalties and reconcile the adulterer with the church after he had reformed
was reserved to the city council acting as representative of the church.[71]

Known sinners, or at least those guilty of sexual sins, were thus kept from scan-
dalizing the church by their participation in the Lord's Supper. All others, Zwingli
wrote a short time later, were left to their own consciences concerning reception of
the sacrament. Every individual had committed secret sins which may have already
been washed away by his repentance; these people could not be kept from the sacrament, both because God and not man is the judge of secret sins, and because any
attempt to punish such sins only resulted in hypocrisy.[72] According to Zwingli, the
church had only two options in dealing with its members. Notorious sinners were
excommunicated, which entailed not only exclusion from the sacrament but also
avoidance by the faithful and civil punishment imposed by the magistrate. Everyone
else was granted full acceptance in the church with the right to receive communion.
There was no middle way of simple exclusion from the Lord's Supper.[73]

Another approach was taken to the problem of screening communion participants in Basel. Here the *Reformationsordnung* of April 1, 1529, required that the pastors of each parish summon all children between the ages of seven and fourteen four
times a year for catechetical instruction. Those children about to receive the Lord's
Supper for the first time were to be especially instructed regarding the sacrament by
the pastor or the deacon.[74] In addition the pastors and deacons were charged with
oversight of their parishioners and given the authority to ban notorious sinners if they

[70]Z 4:186.26-187.2.

[71]Egli, *Aktensammlung*, 521-523 (no. 1087); cf. Ley, *Kirchenzucht*, 48-59.

[72]*Amica Exegesis*, published in February of 1527, Z 5:727.3-15.

[73]Ley points out in a general way the link between Zwingli's ideas on exclusion from
the Lord's Supper and the conflict with Luther, *Kirchenzucht*, 70-71. More specifically the di-
vergence between Zwingli and Luther on the use of minor excommunication was related to
the differing positions of the two reformers regarding reception of the sacrament by the unworthy, a topic which became especially significant during the negotiations which led to the
signing of the Wittenberg Concord. To go further into this issue is clearly beyond the scope
of this study; both Walther Köhler, *Zwingli und Luther. Ihr Streit über das Abendmahl nach
seinen politischen und religiösen Beziehungen*, 2 vols., Quellen und Forschungen zur Reformationsgeschichte 6-7 (Leipzig/Gütersloh: C. Bertelsmann, 1924-1953), and Ernst Bizer, *Studien zur Geschichte des Abendmahlsstreits im 16. Jahrhundert*, Beiträge zur Förderung
christlicher Theologie, 2. Reihe, Sammlung wissenschaftlichen Monographien 46 (Gütersloh: C. Bertelsmann, 1940), cover the topic in great detail.

[74]Paul Roth, ed., *Aktensammlung zur Geschichte der Basler Reformation in den Jahren
1519 bis Anfang 1534* (Basel: Verlag der historischen und antiquarischen Gesellschaft, 1937),
3:389-390 (no. 473).

did not heed admonitions to reform.[75] Semiannual catechism instruction had been held in Zürich possibly as early as the spring of 1522,[76] but the examination of children before their first communion was an innovation specific to Basel. The examination allowed the pastors to see that all future communicants rightly understood the significance of the sacrament.[77]

By the end of the 1520s there was thus not only a range of opinion among Protestants regarding the value of confession and absolution, but a variety of measures to replace some of the elements of the Catholic penitential and disciplinary system as well. These methods were based on the theological presuppositions of those who proposed them. During the first half of his career the Strasbourg reformer Martin Bucer moved across this range of opinion, both absorbing and reacting to the positions of the other reformers as he began to formulate a new system of Christian discipline.

[75]Ibid., 394.

[76]In the *Schlußreden* Zwingli states that such instruction had been instituted a year earlier, Z 2:123.24-32.

[77]Staehelin, *Lebenswerk*, 586-592. Wilhelm Maurer discusses these examples of catechization as predecessors of evangelical confirmation, *Gemeindezucht, Gemeindeamt, Konfirmation. Eine hessische Säkularerinnerung*, Schriftenreihe des Pfarrervereins Kurhessen-Waldeck 2 (Kassel: Stauda, 1940), 57-60.

2

The Theological Foundations: Penance,
Church Discipline, and the Power of the Keys,
1523-1530

During the decade of the 1520s, Bucer's discussions of church discipline, the power of the keys, and the elements of penance—confession, absolution, and satisfaction—were largely theoretical. His treatment of these issues was not static, however. Rather, it evolved over the decade, reflecting his own concerns and priorities as a reformer and theologian. In the first years after his arrival in Strasbourg, all Bucer's energies were directed towards defending evangelical reforms and eliminating Catholic opposition in that city. Consequently much of what he wrote during this period was either apologetic or polemical in nature. In particular his discussions of penance and church discipline were critical of Catholic doctrine and practice. Nevertheless, these issues received relatively little attention in comparison to other more controversial topics. Bucer discussed such questions as the power of the keys or the value of private confession only briefly and did not give a thorough or complete presentation of his ideas.

In contrast to the incidental character of Bucer's statements on these issues before 1525, his discussions over the next few years were much more detailed and systematic. From the time of his arrival in Strasbourg Bucer had given public lectures on various books of the Bible, and in the second half of the decade he published a series of commentaries which were based on those lectures. His commentary on the Synoptic Gospels appeared in 1527, and a commentary on the Gospel of John followed in 1528. In these commentaries Bucer wrote at length for the first time on the power of the keys, the proper forms of confession and absolution, the purpose of satisfaction, and the methods and goals of church discipline, basing his ideas on the exegesis of key biblical texts. Although somewhat milder in tone than his earliest works, the Gospels commentaries continued to criticize Catholic doctrine and practice; they also revealed his new disagreements both with the Lutherans and with the Anabaptists who were becoming established in Strasbourg.

Bucer took a different, less polemical approach to the issues of penance, discipline, and the power of the keys beginning with his commentary on the Psalms in

1529. In an effort to win readers to his point of view, he began to emphasize positions held in common, minimizing or glossing over differences. Bucer first employed this method of presentation to appeal to Catholics, but he used it especially in dealing with the Lutherans as he became increasingly involved in efforts to establish an evangelical political and religious alliance at the time of the Diet of Augsburg in 1530. The many memoranda which he wrote both before and after the Diet reveal this tendency to emphasize commonalities with the Lutherans on the issues of private confession and absolution. This chapter will trace the evolution of Bucer's ideas through the phases of anti-Catholic polemic, evangelical exegesis, and growing irenicism.

There are indications from his correspondence that Bucer followed with interest the controversy over the sacrament of penance which broke out during the early years of the Reformation. In August of 1521, he wrote to Wolfgang Capito expressing his enthusiasm for Erasmus' *Response* to Edward Lee, in which the Dutch humanist argued that the requirement to confess was based on human rather than divine law. The work was circulating both in Latin and in German translation, Bucer reported. In his opinion, "it had done more to destroy the power of secret confession than any book of Luther"; indeed, it made the author look even more like a supporter of Luther.[1] Less than a month later, Luther published *Von der Beicht*, which went far beyond Erasmus in its criticism of mandatory auricular confession. In the book's dedicatory epistle, written to Franz von Sickingen, Luther asked the knight to convey his greetings to Bucer, who had stayed at von Sickingen's castle of Ebernburg that spring. The Strasbourg humanist Nicholas Gerbel wrote to Bucer at the end of September, asking him to send a copy of Luther's latest book on confession along with two other works.[2] The discussions in these letters imply that Bucer agreed with the criticisms expressed by humanists and reformers against mandatory auricular confession.

References to the sacrament of penance or its components in Bucer's earliest published works allow another glimpse of his views during the first years of his career as a reformer. In the *Summary seiner Predig*, the defense he wrote of his preaching at Wissembourg during the first half of 1523, Bucer mentioned that the Franciscans in Wissembourg had refused to hear confessions during Lent and had done "many other anti-Christian things" as well.[3] He explained the incident more clearly a few pages later, stating that certain friars had refused to hear the confessions of those who had eaten eggs or dairy products during the Lenten fast. Bucer expressed his anger and echoed Luther's sentiment in *Von der Beicht* when he wrote that the monks were obliged by divine law not to deny absolution, let alone confession, to anyone who desired it.[4]

---

[1]BCor 1:171.21–28, no. 37 (August 27, 1521).

[2]Ibid., 178.25–26, no. 39 (September 30, 1521). Gerbel had not yet received a copy of *Von der Beicht* a month later, when he repeated his request, ibid., 179.4–12, no. 40 (November 5, 1521).

[3]BDS 1:126.30–127.2.

[4]Ibid., 140.15–22. Luther faced a similar situation in 1520, when certain priests were requiring their parishioners to surrender any copies of Luther's books in their possession before granting them absolution. Luther wrote his *Unterricht der Beichtkinder über die verboten*

In another work, the *Handel mit Cunrat Treger* published in 1524, Bucer presented his evangelical understanding of the power of the keys. He began on a polemical note, denying the Catholic claim that the pope "gives the keys as he wishes to others who are anointed and tonsured so that they can loose souls from sin if people diligently confess to them, or bind souls and give them to the devil if they speak or act against the Roman See."[5] On the contrary, he asserted, the keys given to St. Peter are the power by which people are either brought into the church or excluded from it through the proclamation of God's word: "to open heaven is to preach forgiveness of sins in the name of Jesus our Savior, to preach, 'whoever believes and is baptized shall be saved.' To close heaven is to preach, 'he who does not believe is condemned,' and 'no immoral or impure or greedy person has an inheritance in the kingdom of Christ.'"[6]

Bucer repeated his definition of the power of the keys in the context of Matt. 18:15-17, which prescribes the procedure followed in disciplining a sinner: "If your brother sins against you, reprove him first without hesitation through the word of God. For this is the keys which open or close heaven." Bucer outlined the next stages of discipline—private admonition in the presence of two or three witnesses, then denunciation before the church—and described the purpose of excommunication: "if he will not listen to [the church] and no rebuke helps, let him be as a Gentile and give him to the devil. But this is only so that the flesh of the external man may suffer shame and hardship, because Christians will not accept him, so that he may sooner come to knowledge of himself."[7] Implicit in this discussion are several important ideas. First, the power of the keys was equated with the proclamation of the word of God, not only through public preaching but also through individual admonition. Second, this authority was not restricted to ordained priests. Every layman had the right to exercise the power of the keys through private admonition. Finally, the chief goal of the disciplinary process was the repentance of the sinner. All of these are themes which Bucer developed further over the following years.

Bucer addressed another aspect of church discipline, exclusion from the Lord's Supper, in another work published at the end of 1524. His *Grund und Ursach auß gotlicher schrifft* was a justification of the innovations in doctrine and ceremonies in the Strasbourg church. Although much of it was intended for Catholic opponents, Bucer also defended the Strasbourg church against charges that it had not gone far enough in its introduction of reforms. According to Bucer, these more radical evangelical critics held that the Lord's Supper should be received by the entire congregation. This practice would enable the reintroduction of a Christian ban, so that those

---

Bücher early in 1521 in response to this situation, and it underlay the vehemence of his argument in *Von der Beicht* that a priest had no right to deny absolution. WA 7:290.7-12; WA 8:157.1-13; cf. also the introductions to each of these works.

[5]BDS 2:59.10-19.
[6]Ibid., 59.24-37.
[7]Ibid., 127.20-29.

who had shown by their deeds that they were not Christians could be kept from the Supper and thus more obviously excluded from Christian fellowship.[8]

Bucer acknowledged that this view was based on Scripture and that it accorded with the practice of the early church, but he opposed compulsory reception of the sacrament. The Lord's Supper was only "an external thing, that is not necessary in itself," he argued, and therefore the Strasbourg pastors could not compel its reception, "so that the old superstitions are strengthened or new ones planted, as if the Lord's Supper itself saved a person or made him pious."[9] Citing the example of the early church, which accepted and gradually instructed those who had not yet been baptized, Bucer could not in good conscience expel from the church those who did not receive the sacrament, but instead he was glad that so many wished to hear God's word preached.[10]

Bucer then gave three reasons why the Strasbourg church could not follow the example of the early church in celebrating the Lord's Supper with the entire congregation. First, in the early church only those who had "given themselves entirely to the word of Christ" were baptized and accepted into fellowship, while in Strasbourg there were many who heard the sermons but were not yet wholly committed to Christ. Second, the early church had the ban and could exclude from the church all who offended it by their lives or teaching, whereas the Strasbourg pastors had no such power of exclusion but had to allow everyone, good and bad, to take communion. Third, the early church had not been led astray by false teaching about the Lord's Supper, but the evangelical preachers had to wait patiently until their hearers "learned the right use [of the sacrament] through the word."[11] Bucer accepted the present situation but clearly sympathized with more radical critics: "Whoever desires more, that is, that we should hold the Lord's Supper only with the whole congregation and in doing so exercise the Christian ban against those whose lives offend, let him ask God that in this and in other things he help us and make us perfect."[12]

Like his earlier statements on the power of the keys, Bucer's discussion of compulsory reception of the sacrament expressed an idea which assumed greater prominence in later years. In citing the early church as a model for Strasbourg practice, Bucer distinguished between those who had "given themselves completely to Christ's word"—the full members of the church—and those who were not yet baptized but were being instructed in the faith—the catechumens. Although this distinction did not exist in Strasbourg, Bucer saw a parallel between those who desired to receive the sacrament and those who listened to the sermons but abstained from the sacrament.

Both *Grund und Ursach* and *Handel mit Cunrat Treger* contained hints of Bucer's understanding of penance and church discipline; his Gospels commentaries of 1527

---

[8]BDS 1:243.23–244.14.
[9]Ibid., 244.20–30.
[10]Ibid., 244.37–245.1.
[11]Ibid., 245.5–18.
[12]Ibid., 245.20–24.

and 1528 gave a much more complete picture. The positions which Bucer set forth
in the commentaries were based on the Scripture texts, but they were also formulated
in response to the arguments of Bucer's theological opponents, whether Catholic,
Lutheran, or Anabaptist, and they reflected his sympathies with the Swiss reformers
Zwingli and Oecolampadius. Bucer's discussion of the power of the keys, based on
Matt. 16:18-19, was the foundation for his other views. He defined the keys to the
kingdom of heaven as the word of God preached in the power of the Holy Spirit. The
two worked together, for the Holy Spirit empowered the preacher who used the word
to touch his hearers.[13] Bucer attacked the Catholic teaching that the keys were given
to Peter alone and to the pope as his successor,[14] and he rejected the use of the passage to establish the practice of auricular confession. In his view the power of the keys
was exercised more when adults were received into the church through baptism as
repentant believers than when someone confessed to a priest.[15]

Bucer emphasized equally the power to bind and the power to loose. Binding
and loosing were both the work of the Spirit and the word; it was the hearers' faith
or lack of faith which determined whether they were loosed or bound:

> The disciples, endowed with the spirit of the Lord, opened the kingdom
> of heaven to all believers, that is they promised remission of sins and eter-
> nal life, allowing entrance into the church of Christ. In this way they
> loosed and forgave sins. On the other hand they closed the kingdom of
> heaven to those who did not believe by the same spirit and through the
> same word, that is, they refused remission of sins and preached eternal
> death, by refusing the communion of the church. In this way they bound
> and retained sins, but all of this in the power of the spirit of God and
> through the word of God.[16]

---

[13] 1527 Gospels 1:181r: "Neque enim aliud claves istae sunt, quam spiritus sanctus, et
verbum Dei. Spiritus Sanctus in praedicatore haec potestas est, sed per verbum exeritur erga
auditores."

[14] Ibid., 181v-183r.

[15] Ibid., 183r: "Non minus abutuntur hoc loco, qui ex eo confessionem secretariam volunt stabilire. . . . Etenim nequaquam hic de absolutione illa, qua illusum confitentibus fuit,
sed de praedicatione cum veniae poenitentibus et Christo credentibus fienda, tum iudicij et
condemnationis comminatione, qua impoenitentes et Christum reijcientes, ab Ecclesia
Christi repelli debent, hic agitur. Eoque collatione baptismi adultis quo in Ecclesiam Christi,
tanquam credentes ac poenitentes recipiuntur, magis haec potestas exeritur, quam erga con-
fitentes, licet et hi dum eis Evangelion Christi et inde consolatio praedicatur, recte solvi
dicantur, ut ligari, quibuscunque iudicium et condemnatio ex verbo Dei praedicitur."

[16] Ibid., 180v-181r: "Spiritu itaque Domini praediti discipuli, credentibus omnibus regnum caelorum aperuerunt, hoc est, remissionem peccatorum et vitam aeternam promis-
erunt, aditu in Ecclesiam Christi concesso. Sic solverunt, et peccata remiserunt. Rursus non
credentibus ex eodem spiritu, et per idem verbum, caelorum regnum clauserunt, hoc est,
peccatorum remissionem negarunt, et aeternam mortem praedixerunt, communione Ecclesiae negata. Sic ligarunt, et peccata retinuerunt, omnia autem vi spiritus Dei et per verbum
Dei."

Because the power of the keys had become so closely linked with priestly absolution, the debate over the power of the keys tended to focus on the priest's authority to forgive sins. For Bucer, however, the power to bind or retain sins was as important as the power to loose or forgive them.

Not surprisingly, Bucer's discussion of the power of the keys echoed the position held by other reformers. Both Zwingli and Oecolampadius identified the keys with the preaching of the word of God.[17] Luther also linked the power of the keys, as the proclamation of the forgiveness of sins, to the preaching of the gospel, but he saw this power exercised especially in the words of absolution. In this sense absolution was a means of preaching the gospel, whether to the individual in private confession or to the congregation after a general confession of sins.[18] The Swiss reformers, however, saw no need for the assurance offered by private absolution, and Bucer followed their interpretation when he limited the keys to the word of God impressed in the hearts of its hearers by the Holy Spirit. In his understanding of the power of the keys, as in his sacramental theology in general, Bucer inclined towards a Zwinglian position.

At the end of his discussion of the power of the keys Bucer referred his readers to Matthew 3:6, where he gave his own understanding of confession and criticized both the Catholic and Lutheran positions. His entire discussion of confession was strongly influenced by Melanchthon's treatment of repentance in the first edition of his *Loci Communes*, published in 1521. Bucer followed Melanchthon's pattern of describing three scriptural types of confession, subdividing the third type into two categories, and then condemning Catholic auricular confession.[19] The first type of confession, and the source of the other two, was the acknowledgment before God that one was a sinner. This confession to God compelled the individual to make the second type, the public confession of sin to others.[20] The third type was private confes-

---

[17]Z 2:374.4–11; 380.16–20; 385.19–386.13; Z 3: 723.22–24; 738.8–11, 31–33. Johannes Oecolampadius, *Elleboron pro Iacobo Latomo* (Basel: Cratander, 1525), F7r–F8v; cf. Staehelin, *Lebenswerk*, 261.

[18]Laurentius Klein, *Evangelisch-Lutherische Beichte. Lehre und Praxis*, Konfessionskundliche und Kontroverstheologische Studien 5 (Paderborn: Bonifacius, 1961), 38; cf. Vercruysse, "Schlüsselgewalt," 153, 168–169.

[19]CR 21:217–219. Both Oecolampadius, in his 1521 pamphlet *Quod non sit Onerosa Christianis Confessio Paradoxon*, and Luther, in his *Sermon von der Beichte und dem Sakrament* of 1524, describe three types of confession. Luther held that only two types, confession to God and confession made to a neighbor against whom one has sinned, were commanded by God. The third type, private confession made to a priest, was required by the pope but had no scriptural mandate. No one was to be forced to make such a confession, but the confession itself was beneficial and advisable, WA 15:482.21–485.22. Oecolampadius' three categories were closer to those of Melanchthon: confession to God, confession of grave sins to a priest made either publicly or privately, and private confession to a brother for counsel and consolation. However, he included auricular confession in the second category.

[20]1527 Gospels 1:63v–64r: "Prima et fons reliquarum est, qua ex animo coram Deo, nos peccatores agnoscimus, qua utique ita humiliamur, ut coram universo mundo, si id vel in gloriam Dei, vel commodum proximorum cessurum constaret, omnem nostram iniquitatem detegere, nihil gravaremur . . . Haec peccatorum coram deo agnitio et confessio, ubi vera ac viva

sion, whether made for the sinner's own sake or for the sake of others. In the former case, a sinner needing consolation or counsel sought out a wise brother who could assure him of forgiveness or provide guidance in living piously and avoiding sin.[21] In the latter case, the sinner asked those he had offended for forgiveness.[22]

Catholic auricular confession was not included among the three legitimate types of confession: "Scripture recognizes this many forms of confession; whatever is brought in beyond them is a human invention and therefore it cannot not be harmful. Of this kind is the secret confession which the pope has required." Bucer condemned auricular confession because it taught people to trust in their own works rather than in Christ and led to overscrupulosity and despair.[23] He asserted that the scriptural passages used by Catholics to defend auricular confession pertained not to it but to one of the three genuine types of confession already described.[24]

Bucer likewise dismissed the argument that a priest could not loose specific sins if he did not know that the sinner had been bound by them. He equated the loosing and forgiveness of sins with public admission into the church:

> This is normally done by the church of Christ first through baptism, and after that as often as anyone who has been ejected from the communion of the church because of his sins merits readmittance by his genuine repentance. For this there is scarcely any need to list individual sins to a priest, just as God forgives sins not one by one but all simultaneously. . . .

---

fuerit, impellit mox, ut facto et verbis peccatorem se coram hominibus quoque, quando cunque eis occasio est, ingenue fatearis. . . . Atque haec altera confessio est, cum interna illa peccatorum coram Deo agnitio, compellit, illa et hominibus fateri. Ea autem, a nonnullis fit, citra spem veniae, ex importabili duntaxat conscientiae tormento. . . . Porro eorum, qui certi de remissione peccatorum, magis ex ardenti, divine bonitatis praedicandae affectu, quam aestu male sibi conscij cordis, ea confitentur."

[21]Ibid., 65v–66r: "Tertia confessio privata est, qua vel tui vel proximi caussa commissum aliquod tuum, aut affectum, fratri cuipiam privatim confiteris. Tui caussa, si quando haereas aut animo sis consternatior, quod vel consilio habes opus, vel consolatione. . . . Haec sane affectuum et consiliorum privata apud fidelem animum, detectio et confessio, ad modum frequens ijs est, quos vera pie vivendi solicitudo, et peccandi tenet formido. Suspecta enim habent semper sua pij, eoque cum fratribus de ijs libentissime consultant."

[22]Ibid., 67r: "Verum privata confessio, quae alterius fit gratia, est, eum quem offendisti, confitens tuum in illum peccatum, oras veniam, atque ita tibi curas cum placare."

[23]Ibid., 67r–v: "Tot novit genera confessionum scriptura, quicquid praeterea invectum est, humanum est commentum, eoque non potest, non esse noxium. Qualis est illa secretaria confessio, quam praecepit pontifex, sacerdoti quot annis, ad minimum semel, de omnibus peccatis fieri, ita ut qui non etiam cogitata omnia, quibus peccato vel consensit vel fuerit eo, non nihil in animo titillantus, enunciaverit, nullam possit spem habere salutis. O inventum noxium, quo non tam tortae, quam perditae fuere innumerae animarum myriades. Hac enim confessione crediderunt, peccata prorsus deponi, ita pernitiosissime doctae fuerunt, suo opere fidere, misso Christo."

[24]Ibid., 68r: "Nam quas scripturas pro ea stabilienda afferunt, nequaquam huic, sed vel confessioni quae Deo fit, vel quae in genere Ecclesiae, a suscipientibus, in adulta aetate baptismum, aut reconciliandis post excommunicationem, aut alias a volentibus impensam sibi Dei misericordiam depraedicare, vel quae privatim fratri fit, pro consolatione aut consilio, aut denique quod ipsum offenderis, pro venia, competere, quicunque eas excusserit, manifesto videbit."

Surely since the loosing of the church is public reception into the church, so also publicly known sin ought to be confessed before the church by those who are loosed. . . . But if you wish to confess your sins in private with some profit, you should not look to someone who has been chosen for this duty by a bishop but to someone whom the Lord has made suitable for consoling, admonishing and counseling by his word and Spirit.[25]

Bucer did not limit his criticism to Catholic auricular confession. He also disagreed with those "who seem to attribute too much value to absolution and who teach that it has singular power when someone hears the gospel privately and is pronounced absolved," thus reassuring the individual sinner that the absolution pertained to him. This criticism was aimed directly at Melanchthon, who had stated that absolution was as necessary as baptism and that private absolution assured an individual that he had been forgiven.[26] Bucer saw no scriptural basis for this view:

Certainly a private discussion in the Lord and friendly consolation through the word of God has wonderful power to console and encourage souls on the basis of what the Lord himself says, "where two or three are gathered in my name, there I am in their midst"; but it is human reasoning, arisen without the word of God, to think that being individually absolved by man, that is, to hear in private the promise of grace, has any effect of itself for strengthening consciences, and that you may be made more certain that the gospel pertains to you individually when you are privately and individually absolved. For whether the word of grace is preached publicly or privately, it belongs to the Lord alone to give the increase, that is, to believe that this also applies to me.[27]

---

[25]Ibid., 68r-v: "Istam solutionam a peccatis, et remissionem peccatorum . . . esse publicam in Ecclesiam admissionem, in numerum scilicet eorum, quos a peccatis salvat Christus, id quod primum baptismo, postea quoties quis ob sua scelera e communione Ecclesiae eiectus, vera poenitentia recipi meruerit, solet a Christi Ecclesia fieri. Ad quod haud quaquam opus est sacerdoti singula peccata enarrare, sicut neque singula ordine, sed simul omnia Dominus condonat . . . . Certe ut Ecclesiae solutio non est, nisi publica in Ecclesiam receptio, ita palam coram Ecclesia etiam peccata sunt, a solvendis confitenda. . . . Secreto sane si volueris cum fructu tua commissa confiteri, non sane spectandum qui ab Episcopo, ad id muneris sit delegatus, sed quem Dominus verbo et Spiritu suo fecerit, ad consolandum, monendum, et consulendum te idoneum."

[26]CR 21:220.

[27]Ibid., 68v-69r: "Ex nostris sunt, qui plus satis secretariae confessioni videntur tribuere, affirmantes singularem energiam habere, si privatim quis Evangelion audiat, et sese pronunciari absolutum. Tum demum, inquiunt, certus es id ad te proprie pertinere, cum tu privatim ac proprie absolveris. Haec quoniam nulla scriptura confirmant, mittenda sunt. Habet certe privatum in Domino colloquium, et amica per verbum Dei consolatio, miram vim ad consolandum, et erigendos animos, ex eo, quo Dominus ipse ait: Ubi duo vel tres congregati sunt in nomine meo, ibi sum in medio coram, at quod privatim absolvi ab homine, hoc est, seorsim audire gratiae promissionem, per se momentum aliquod ad confirmandam conscientiam habeat, et tum demum certus reddaris, Evangelion ad te proprie pertinere, quum tu privatim, ac proprie absolueris, cogitatio humana est, sine verbo Dei nata. Sive namque publicitus, sive privatim verbum gratiae praedicetur, Domini solius est, dare incrementum, hoc est, ut credam illud ad me quoque pertinere."

Bucer explained the efficacy of private admonition and consolation in psychological terms. People often attended public worship out of habit rather than out of a genuine desire to hear God's word, but they did not seek private consolation unless afflicted in spirit. Moreover, in private confession the word of God could be presented in such a way as to meet the individual needs of a "famished soul." The resulting psychological relief was what others had recognized, Bucer stated, but they had then unwisely attributed some kind of power to private confession and absolution, as if individual absolution were more effective than the general proclamation of forgiveness. "We must always beware lest we speak as though we attribute anything to our own works or to those of others and not to Christ," he warned.[28] Although Bucer acknowledged that private confession and individual instruction had consolatory power, he was closer to the Zwinglian position that the individual was consoled through private instruction in God's word rather than by a divine promise of forgiveness mediated through the spoken absolution of an ordained minister.

Bucer discussed the sacrament of penance at other points in his commentaries as well. He specifically rejected the allegorical interpretation of passages such as Christ's healing of the ten lepers (Matt. 8:4) or the raising of Lazarus (John 11:44), both favorite scholastic arguments for the power of priestly absolution.[29] Proofs based on such allegories were nonsense which should have no place in Christ's church, he stated. He claimed that the fifth petition of the Lord's Prayer ("and forgive us our debts . . .") should not be understood as stating a condition for forgiveness. It was fraudulent to teach that through confession and works of satisfaction, whether done by us or by others, our sins could be expiated. Sinners were forgiven through the satisfaction accomplished by Christ, since it was impossible for anyone to offer satisfaction for even the least sin.[30] This was standard evangelical criticism of scholastic teaching on satisfaction.

[28]Ibid., 69r–v: "Quod enim generali et publica, privata plerunque verbi admonitio, atque consolatio efficacior sentitur, ex eo potius est, quo animo famelico haec magis, quam illa fere queritur, cum publicas et solennes conciones plus ex more saepenumero, quam vera verbi fame adeamus, privatas autem consolationes non nisi afflictis animis, verbique Dei serio sitientibus, petamus, tum quod in privatis illis colloquijs atque consolationibus, expositis animi morbis, ex ijs potissimum scripturae locis medicina profertur, qui sic laborantem animum proprie respiciunt, qui denique pro laborantis captu quoque tractantur, cum in generali concione, generalia tractari soleant, et non semper, nec quae ad meos morbos proprie faciunt, neque eo modo, quo me potissimum levarent. Haud vero facile crediderim, notatae sententiae authores, aliter sua quoque intellexisse, quanquam imprudentiores quidam, ut privatae et confessioni, et absolutioni, per se aliquam virtutem ab illis putant attributam, ita fortuer ipsum praedicant, ignari quid dicant aut affirment. Quasi si frater mihi dicat: Confide, ego absolvo te a peccatis tuis, plus haberet momenti, quam si in genere dicatur: Fiditote domino, per Christum condonavit vobis peccata omnibus. Postquam videmus proclives adeo nos, ad hoc, ut nostra opera, alicuius habeamus, debemus certe sumopere cavere, ne ita loquamur etiam, quasi nostris vel aliorum operibus aliquid tribueremus, et non Christo omnia."
[29]1527 Gospels 2:8v: "Explosi pridem sunt, qui hoc Christi dicto, confessionem illam secretariam fundare conati sunt, quasi vero ijdem essent nostri Presbyteri, qui legis sacerdotes, et ostendere, confiteri singula peccata, et lepra peccatum significaret"; cf. BOL 2:363.
[30]1527 Gospels 1:199v–200r: "Non enim conditio, sed similitudo hic significatur . . . quilibet videt, quanta impostura fuerit, docere per confessionem et nostra quaedam ac aliorum

Nevertheless, Bucer was willing to recognize the linkage of contrition, confession, and satisfaction when the three terms were rightly defined. He gave his definitions of contrition and satisfaction in the discussion of "legal and evangelical repentance" which was associated with Matt. 4:17. Legal repentance occurred when the soul was tormented by the sight of its own impiety; evangelical repentance was a "coming to one's senses" done in the hope of salvation and accompanied by the amendment of life. While these two types were once called by the common name of repentance, they had more recently been divided and the first called contrition, the latter satisfaction. Between these two was placed confession which, if done piously, was a work and fruit of true contrition. Satisfaction was rightly understood to be a continual practice of piety and reformation of life.[31] Bucer bluntly rejected scholastic teaching on repentance: "What the sophists have written about repentance is nonsense, corresponding neither to Scripture nor to the thing itself. For since they do not know Christ, it is impossible that they would rightly know anything which pertains to true Christianity." Finally, Bucer mentioned the penance which was once imposed on sinners by bishops, comprised of fasts and other physical disciplines, and referred his readers to the discussion of church discipline in Matthew 18.[32]

While Bucer's discussions of the power of the keys and confession were shaped by his disagreements with Catholics and Lutherans, the locus on church discipline clearly reflected his debates with the Anabaptists who had come to Strasbourg over the latter half of 1526.[33] Given Bucer's conviction that the Anabaptists were leading people astray with their emphasis on adult baptism, it is significant that he began his discussion of the disciplinary process outlined in Matt. 18:15-20 with reference to the preceding verses in which Christ warned his disciples:

---

hominum opera satisfactoria, ut vocarunt, et pontificias denique condonationes, peccata posse expiari Deus est, cui soli peccando debitores constituimur, unus igitur ipse quoque est, qui bonitate sua debita haec nostra remittat; quanquam non absque satisfactione, sed Christi, non nostra, quandoquidem nobis, nunquam pensum nostrum persolventibus, ut iam dixi, impossibile est, vel pro minimo peccato satisfacere, unum itaque ipsum etiam debitorum remissionem debemus orare, eamque ab ipso solo expectare."

[31]Ibid., 109v: "Prior illa legalis erat, et animum conspecta iam impietatis abominatione excarnificabat, altera vero Evangelica, nimirum spe salutis suscepta resipiscentia, vitam cum hilaritate emendabat. . . . Haec duo et veteres poenitentiae nomine intellexerunt, recentiores prius contritionem, posterius satisfactionem vocarunt, mediam inserentes peccatorum confessionem, quae si pie fiat, verae contritionis opus et fructus est. . . . Quod aut isti satisfactionem, qui recte sentiunt, perpetuam pietatis meditationem, vitaeque innovationem recte intelligunt, et vocant carnis ac peccatorum mortificationem, vitae conversionem, studiorum correctionem, sive, ut dixi, poenitentiam Evangelicam, satisfactionem, Christo uni, qui scilicet pro omnibus in se credentibus satisfecit, tribuentes."

[32]Ibid., 110r: "Quae sophistae de poenitentia scripserunt, fere nihil nisi nugae sunt, neque scripturis, neque rei ipsi respondentia. Ut enim Christum ipsum ignorant, ita impossibile fuit, eos quicquam eorum, quae ad verum Christianismum attinent, recte nosse. De poenitentia illa, quam vulgo vocarunt, quam Episcopi olim iniunxerunt ijs qui peccaverant, certa scilicet ieiunia, et alias corporis castigationes, dicam infra in caput 18."

[33]On the importance of this period for the growth of Anabaptism in Strasbourg, see Hans-Werner Müsing, "The Anabaptist Movement in Strasbourg from early 1526 to July 1527," *Mennonite Quarterly Review* 51 (1977):91-126.

to beware lest you offend anyone, and especially these little ones, for you ought to be concerned about working together for the salvation of everyone with me, who came to seek and to save the lost. Apply your most diligent efforts not so that you do offend anyone, but so that you are able to lead every one all together to salvation. And therefore, when a person sins in the presence of another, [Christ] wishes to admonish him for that sin.[34]

Following Christ's prescription, sinners were to be admonished first privately, then in the presence of one or two witnesses; if they refused to repent they were to be made known to the church. Throughout this process, Bucer added, "we should not easily give up hope for sinners before we have tried everything." Those who refused to heed the admonition before the church were to be "regarded as Gentiles and publicans by all those to whom this is known."[35] The power to bind and loose sins and the promise of answered prayer guaranteed divine confirmation of the disciplinary process.

Bucer then raised several points concerning the exercise of church discipline, all of them intended to refute Anabaptist separatism.[36] He first defined those who were subject to the disciplinary process. The Anabaptists claimed that the ban could be imposed only on those who had been baptized as adults,[37] but Bucer argued that discipline should be applied more broadly. He granted that Christians were not to judge those who were outside the church, although they were to make every effort to bring them into the church. But, he continued, "woe to us if we do not admonish those who wish to be considered brothers!"[38] Moreover, the essence of discipline was not the imposition of the ban but rather the frequent use of mutual admonition:

[34]1527 Gospels 2:212v: "Monui quantopere necesse sit cavere, ne quem, praecipue autem pusillos, offendatis, debetis enim solicite, ad salutem quorumlibet mihi cooperari, qui veni, ut quod perijt, quaeram et servem. Ne quem igitur offendatis, sed ut ad salutem quot quot omnino licuerit, perducatis, diligentissimam curam impendite. Eoque cum quis coram aliquo peccarit, is admonere illum peccati uelit. . . ."

[35]Ibid., 213r: "Adeo non facile, de peccatoribus, desperandum est, sed ante tentanda omnia. At si ne Ecclesiam quidem, admonitus iam a pluribus audierit, habeatur, ab omnibus, quibus ita cognitus fuerit, tanquam Ethnicus et publicanus."

[36]Bucer's arguments seem directed in particular at the positions expressed in the Schleitheim Articles, drawn up by Michael Sattler and published at the end of February 1527, one month before the Gospels commentary appeared. Sattler had been in Strasbourg at the end of 1526 and had discussed with Bucer and Capito "several articles which I have agreed on together with my brothers and sisters on the basis of Scripture . . . [concerning] baptism, the Lord's Supper, [secular] power and the sword, oaths, the ban, and all the commandments of God"; TAE 1:68.9–18, no. 70 (Sattler's farewell letter to Bucer and Capito, written in late 1526 or early 1527). Sattler may have been referring to a draft of his *Brüderliche Vereynigung etzlicher kinder gottes*, i.e. the Schleitheim Articles.

[37]Cf. the first two of the Schleitheim Articles, QGTS 2:28–29 (no. 26, Feb. 24, 1527).

[38]1527 Gospels 2:213v: "Notandum praeterea, quod ait frater tuus. Nam iudicare de ijs, quae foris sunt, nihil ad nos. Quanquam ut et ipsi in Ecclesiam veniant, et fratres nostri evadant, omnem operam impendere oporteat. At qui fratres haberi volunt, vae nobis, si peccantes non admonuerimus."

The argument is very certain that those who neglect such a serious precept of Christ and a thing so useful and so very fruitful have too little faith and love. For who sees himself sufficiently clearly that he does not need continual reminder? . . . Since we are members one of another, and that ought to be our greatest desire by which we are all furthered in piety and the true worship of God, if we cease to admonish one another, what other way is left, I ask, by which we may demonstrate the love of Christ among ourselves when we have ceased in this chief duty? And if there is no true love between us, how may we boast of being Christians, when this is the unique mark of a Christian?[39]

Bucer then considered the circumstances in which the ban should be used. Christ's phrase "tell it to the church" did not mean the public excommunication during the worship service of those who had ignored two previous admonitions, since during Christ's ministry there were no such public gatherings of Christians. The power of the keys belonged to the entire gathering of the faithful, but this gathering could consist of as few as two or three people. Moreover, public excommunication was not feasible given the current situation of the church:

there are now too many who are impure in our gatherings, and the number of those who have completely dedicated themselves to Christ is small, and for the sake of public tranquillity the unfit may not be excluded from gatherings of the church, and so, as things now stand, excommunication cannot be exercised publicly in the public gatherings of the church unless where God graciously causes the greater part of all the people, together with the magistrate, to be converted to Christ with their whole heart.[40]

In view of these concerns, Bucer proposed the private exercise of church discipline: those "who had more fully received Christ" should reestablish the practice of mutual admonition in their households and with their friends and neighbors. Anyone who disregarded such admonition was to be excluded from the fellowship of this more dedicated group of family and friends. In the meantime, "not only the ministers

[39]1527 Gospels 2:213v-214r: "Nimis certum est argumentum, ijs perparum fidei et dilectionis esse, qui tam serium Christi praeceptum acrem adeo utilem et frugiferam tantopere neglexerint. Quis enim sibi ipsi satis oculatus sit, qui non continuo monitore egeat? . . . Ad haec cum membra invicem sumus, et summum studium nostrum esse debeat, quo in pietate veroque cultu Dei omnes promoveamus, si monere nos mutuo cessamus, quid quaeso reliquum est, quo Christi inter nos esse dilectionem demonstremus, cum ea in praecipuo officio cesset? Atqui si nulla inter nos vera dilectio fuerit, quid quaeso Christianos nos gloriabimur, quando haec proprium Christianismi insigne sit?"

[40]Ibid., 214v: "Iam nostri conventus impuri adhuc nimis sunt, et sane parvus numerus eorum, qui sese penitus Christo dediderint, neque licet per pacem publicam, arcere a conventibus Ecclesiae non probatos, quare in publicis Ecclesiae conventibus, ut hodie res fere habent, excommunicatio publicitus exerceri non potest, nisi ubi Dominus eam gratiam faceret, ut maior totius populi pars, cum magistratu, ad Christum pleno corde converterentur."

of the word but also everyone else" were to see that "those who disgraced the name of Christ by their flagrant sins" were kept from the Lord's Supper. The ultimate goal of these Christians was to see that "this most salutary institution of the Lord would be embraced and observed by all those who wish to be considered part of Christ's church."[41]

Bucer thus saw the private practice of mutual admonition and shunning as a means of eventually reforming the entire church. He vigorously condemned the Anabaptist view that because the church had not yet reached a point where excommunication could be publicly imposed, it had "no gospel, no Christ."[42] Although Bucer conceded that the communion of the Lord's Supper should be kept pure, it was wrong to insist that only the pure be allowed to public assemblies where the word of the Lord was preached. During his earthly ministry Christ had not held "that only the upright were included in the church and the rest were excluded from it." The line separating the pure from the impure was to be drawn not by adult baptism but rather by participation in the Lord's Supper.[43]

In his exposition of Christ's prayer for the unity of the church (John 17), Bucer explained more fully why he opposed the exclusivity taught by the Anabaptists. It was a trick of Satan, he wrote, that some thought it more pious to separate from those considered sinners than to exhort them to repent. Their excuse was that because such people had not been baptized as believers, they were not brothers and therefore should not be admonished. But, Bucer argued, avoidance was the last remedy to be used on fallen brothers. Our first duty was to admonish in private those whom we had heard confess Christ, and they should be warned to repent, not to undergo bap-

[41]1527 Gospels 2:214r–215r: "Ubi id non datur, necesse est, ut qui plenius Christum receperunt, sanctissimum hoc et saluberrimum Christi institutum inter sese reducant, ut quoscunque familiares, vel vicinos habent, qui Christo nomen dederunt, diligenter et libere moneant, cumque monitiones aliqui contemnere pergunt Ecclesiae, quam ipsi inter se habent, vel ex vicinitatis, vel alias familiaritatis consortio, aut denique ratione cognationis, atque familiae, contemptores monitionis deferant, quae illos si pergant contemnere, postea e sua communione eijciat, donec a pluribus, sancta haec Christi lex recipiatur. Utcunque autem res interim habeant, Christianorum profecto fuerit, tam ministrorum verbi quam aliorum, ut Domini panem cum nemine palam Christi nomen flagitijs suis infamante frangant , et eo continuo enitantur, quo quae Christi Ecclesiae haberi volunt, institutum hoc Domini saluberrimum amplectantur, sanctumque servent."

[42]Ibid., 215r: "Quod autem dum huc venire non datur, propterea nullum habeatur Evangelion, nullus Christus, ut Anabaptistae blasphemant, commentum est Satanae, Christum conantis ita rursus nobis eripere." Cf. the fourth Schleitheim article, on separation from evil, QGTS 2:29–30. The Anabaptists in Strasbourg complained that after four years of evangelical preaching there had been little improvement in the city's church; TAE 1:64.26–31 (no. 67, late 1526).

[43]1527 Gospels 2:215r: "Christus siquidem ipse, et vere adfuit electis, quibus cum carne vixit, et non sine fructu ipsis praedicavit, neque tamen Ecclesiam habuit, in quam probati tantum admissi, et reliqui ab ea exclusi fuissent. . . . Attamen utcunque feratur impuritas conventuum, ubi verbum praedicatur, quam Christus et Apostoli quoque tulerunt, caenae tamen communio, ut dixi, pura esse debet. Nam publica est, de redemptione gratiarum actio, atque circa hanc, ut communio, ita et excommunicatio potissimum exercenda est, et non circa baptismum."

tism or renew vows or something similar. Both Christ and Paul taught that those who were more spiritual were to admonish, exhort, and entreat others to live in a manner worthy of their calling, and only when everything else had been done were they to exclude a person from their fellowship. Even then such people were not to be held as enemies, for they were still to be admonished when occasion arose.[44]

Underlying Bucer's entire discussion of church discipline is his disagreement with the Anabaptists concerning the composition of the church. He emphasized that only those within the church were to give or receive fraternal admonition, but his definition of membership in the church was much broader than that of the Anabaptists, who limited their definition of the church to those who had been baptized as adults. For Bucer, the chief criterion of church membership, and thus the obligation to mutual admonition, was a person's desire to be considered as a Christian. Bucer also made it clear that discipline consisted primarily of brotherly admonition, with the goal of progress in true piety and the worship of God. Such admonition was the responsibility of every Christian, not just of the minister, and it was to be a constant, ongoing activity, not restricted to a formal procedure of three stages. One should not give up on a sinner before having tried everything to bring him to repentance, and so excommunication was to be used only as a last resort.

Excommunication itself, which Bucer defined as exclusion from the fellowship of "those dedicated to Christ," was limited in scope. As in his *Grund und Ursach* published three years earlier, Bucer stated that public excommunication was the eventual goal of the church, but he implied that the conditions under which it could be established—the "full conversion" of magistrate and the majority of citizens—did not yet exist. He could not endorse the strict separatism of the Anabaptists or their stringent use of public excommunication and ostracism, but he did acknowledge the validity of the principles of church discipline which they advocated. For this reason he proposed a modified version of the disciplinary process which included the private practice of mutual admonition and the limited ostracism of the unrepentant by those aware of his sin.

Bucer's proposal for the private exercise of discipline was a logical outgrowth of his view that the power of the keys belonged to any group of believers, no matter how small. In its prescriptions that secret sins should not be made public and that a contumacious sinner should be shunned only by those who knew of his sin and his refusal to repent, it echoed the treatment recommended by canon law and penitential manuals for sinners whose excommunication was not publicly known.[45] Bucer was concerned about the purity of the eucharistic fellowship, stating that known sinners should be kept from receiving the sacrament, but he did not specify how this should be done. Public worship, on the other hand, should be open to all, as was clear from his rejection of Anabaptist separatism. This also followed logically from his interpre-

---

[44]BOL 2:483-484; cf. the pastors' statement to the Strasbourg Council, "if, God willing, private admonition were really to be put into practice, we would then have the real ban," TAE 1:210.2-3 (no. 171, Jan. 23, 1529).

[45]Vodola, *Excommunication*, 48-50.

tation of the power of the keys and his view of the importance of admonition. Denying sinners the opportunity to hear the gospel preached would eliminate a powerful
means of bringing them to repentance.

In 1529 Bucer published his third major exegetical work, a commentary on the
book of Psalms. In this commentary, published under the pseudonym Aretius Feli-
nus, Bucer moved away from the polemical stance of his earlier works. The more detached manner in which Bucer discussed topics at issue between Protestants and
Catholics and his use of a pseudonym were connected: as he wrote in a letter to
Zwingli, he thought that he would have a better opportunity to demonstrate his pro-
ficiency in interpreting Scripture if the commentary was not known to be written by
him and so rejected out-of-hand by both Catholics and Lutherans. Moreover, the use
of a pseudonym, a translation of his own name into Greek, would make it easier for
the persecuted brethren in France to obtain the commentary, since it was illegal to
bring books by Protestants into France.[46]

Bucer's more detached manner is evident in his discussion of confession and the
sacrament of penance associated with Psalm 32. He did not directly attack mandatory
auricular confession but instead cited the church fathers, canon law, and even
Thomas Aquinas to present an evangelical view of confession. He defined confession
as a recognition before God of those sins by which we have offended him and therefore deserve eternal punishment. Such a confession left a person humble and contrite
but also resulted in an increased desire to do God's will and to confess his sins to
someone who could teach him about God. The confessor could be a priest who was
especially learned in the law of God and a true doctor of souls, but he could also be
any Christian who was able to advise.[47]

Bucer dismissed the debate as to whether confession of sins to another was required by divine law or human law; it was a divine law, he argued, that we use any
and every means possible by which we might move away from sin and towards righteousness. He then cited several authorities who upheld the value of private confession:

[46]Z 10:198.1-15, no. 871; similar comments to Ambrosius Blarer, Schieß 1:204, no.
158. R. Gerald Hobbs, "An Introduction to the Psalms Commentary of Martin Bucer," 2
vols., Th.D. diss., Strasbourg, 1971, 1:77-90, discusses the mildness of Bucer's tone with regard to both Catholics and Lutherans.

[47]Psalms, 131C-D: "Hoc autem pacto peccata confiteri, est vere, solideque et tanquam
coram Deo ipso, peccata agnoscere et ea, eiusmodi tamque gravia, ut quibus, sicut condi-
torem nostrum Deum Opt. Max. offendimus, ita extrema, eaque sempiterna mala merueri-
mus. Hoc pacto, qui peccata sua agnoverit, fassusque Deo fuerit, is vere demum se exuerit,
plane humiliarit, penitus cor contritum, adflictumque spiritum habuerit, peccata vere detes-
tabitur, Deo sese prorsus consecrabit, et omni studio, totisque viribus voluntati eius studebit,
eoque facile veniam omnium scelerum, totiusque pravitatis suae abolitionem a Deo exorabit.
Utque nullius rei sitientior fuerit, quam vivendi ex sententia Dei, quicunque de ea ipsum
docere poterit, quam lubens illi, quam prompte non commissa solum, sed quaevis etiam, ac
quamlibet occulta animi vitia confitebitur. Non iam soli sacerdoti, Legis Dei singulariter doc-
to, et vero mentium medico, sed cuivis etiam Christiano, qui vel mediocriter monere potis
sit." The 1532 edition of the commentary cited here is a reprint of the 1529 edition. The section on confession has only a few minor stylistic changes.

It should not be believed that either Panormitanus, a man of much erudition, or the author of the gloss, who had an outstanding reputation among experts in canon law, or other experts in the law or theologians (for there are many who affirm that secret confession is a human tradition) were so foolish as to teach that this confession, by which an efficacious remedy for sin, that is, salutary admonition and instruction, is sought and which the fathers of the western church taught, is only a human institution. Much less should it be supposed that St. John Chrysostom allowed such confession to be neglected. . . . And least of all should it be thought that the Greek church ever slighted this kind of confession or slights it now.[48]

The patriarchs of the Greek church did not believe that confession, "such as I have described and the fathers of the western church taught it," was to be neglected or that it was only human tradition. It was certain, Bucer asserted, that "since we are commanded to love God with all our heart, all our soul and all our strength, whatever is conducive to this love is also required, in other words, whatever results in a life more purified from sin and more instructed in holiness."[49]

Bucer's careful qualification of what he meant by confession was important, for he had defined it in such a way that it was no longer the auricular confession required as a part of the sacrament of penance. The confession "taught by the fathers of the western church" was for him an opportunity to seek advice and instruction, not an enumeration of all mortal sins in order to receive absolution from a priest. Bucer's emphasis was not so much on the penitent's confession as on the admonition and instruction he received after making his confession.

The importance Bucer placed on the counsel received in confession led him to consider the character of the person to whom confession was made and the problem of the unworthy confessor. Surely it was not the desire of the church fathers, he wrote, that sins be confessed to a man unable to train one in piety, to say nothing of a priest

---

[48]Ibid., 131D-132A: "Nihil enim morabitur, quod confessionem peccatorum, quae homini fiat, alij iuris divini, alij humani faciunt. Iuris divini agnoscet esse, uti omnibus rebus, quibus promoveri huc possit, ut a peccatis recedat longius, accedat propius iustitiae. . . . Nec sane credendum, aut Panormitanum tantae eruditionis virum, aut Glossae authorem, inter iuris canonici consultos praecipui nominis, vel alios sive iurisconsultos sive Theologos, plurimi enim sunt, qui secretam illam confessionem, traditionem hominum tantum esse affirmant, sic desipuisse, ut talem confessiorem [sic], qua efficax adeo peccatis remedium, salutaris scilicet monitio et instructio petatur, qualem utique sancti patres Occidentalium Ecclesiarum docuerunt, institutionis humanae fecissent. Multo minus putandum, talem permissam negligi a Divo Chrysostomo. . . . Minime omnium vero existimandum, Graecorum Ecclesiam, talem confessionem posthabuisse unquam, aut posthabere hodie, quae quidem vere Christi Ecclesia fuerit."

[49]Psalms, 132A-132B: ". . . propterea haud quaquam censuerunt, talem qualem paulo ante descripsi, et sancti Occidentalis Ecclesiae patres tradiderunt confessionem negligendam, ut quae traditionis humanae tantum esset. Certe cum praeceptum est, Deum ex toto corde, tota anima, totisque viribus deligere, praeceptum simul est, quicquid dilectio tanta Dei requirit, quae utique requirit, quicquid quovis modo ad id conducit, quo vita evadat peccati purior, et sanctimonia instructior."

from whom one expected what was offensive rather than a remedy for sin. Again Bucer cited medieval authorities to support his position:

> The sacred canons not only wish that you fear such priests, but that you shun those who are so blind and do not know the ways of God, and for this reason they even decree that it would be better to confess to your neighbor, a layman (as they call him) than to a priest who you justly fear will either be made worse himself by such a confession or who will make you worse, and St. Thomas also supports this view.

Bucer referred specifically to the passage in canon law which described the qualifications of a good confessor: someone who was blameless in character and able to aid the one confessing through prayer, instruction, and admonition.[50] Bucer implied that a confession made to an unworthy confessor was useless or even harmful. He recommended that his readers choose as a confessor someone who would help them rather than hinder or even contaminate them with serious sins. To support his position, he once more cited Thomas, who taught that the precepts of positive law, that is, "whatever is established beyond the manifest and express precept of God," did not extend beyond the intention of the lawgiver. Bucer stated that the intention of those who ordered secret confession was clear from the canons he had cited. And so,

> when you avoid a priest who cannot make you better, you do not transgress against a precept of the church, as St. Thomas says, since the precept requires you to confess to one who will free you from sin and who will train and promote you in piety, nor are you doing any injury to the priest, since as St. Thomas writes, whoever abuses the power given to him deserves to lose the privilege.[51]

---

[50]Psalms, 132B: "Certe neque Occidentalis Ecclesiae patres unquam voluerunt, ijs peccata fateri, a quibus non queas ad pietatem eruditi, expectes autem tibi vel illi offendiculum potius, quam peccati remedium. . . . At sacri Canones, non solum a quibus tanta timeas, sed et eos vitari volunt, qui tantum caeci sunt, viae Dei ignari, et adeo quidem, ut proximo et Laico (ut vocant) confitendum potius statuerint, quam ei sacerdoti, quem vel ipsum ex confessione deteriorem fore, vel te deteriorem redditurum, iure metuas; Id quod et Divus Thomas probat in articulo quarto, Quest. septima de partibus poenitentiae. Proinde in Canone: Qui vult, de poenitentia dist. 6. Praecipitur ut quaeras, a quo non negligaris, et ideo melior, qui haberi possit, qui non sit ab unitate Ecclesiae divisus, in nullo eorum iudicandus, quae in alio iudicare debeat. Deinde ita munere scientiae instructus, ut cognoscere queat, quae iudicare debeat, qui valeat morbum, quamlibet latentem agnoscere, didicerit, confitenti esse benevolus, onus eius portare, charitatem ardentem in omnibus exhibeat, iuvet confitentem, orando, docendo, monendo, consolando." Cf. De penitencia, dist. VI (Friedberg 1:1242–1244); Thomas Aquinas, Sum. Theol. Suppl., q. 8, a. 2, and a. 4, esp. ad 5.

[51]Psalms, 132C: "Quare cum in Ecclesia Christi veris agendum est, et confessione peccatorum praecipue spectandum, ut peccatis liberetis, certe non levi diligentia circumspiciendum, ut talem confessionis tuae arbitrum tibi deligas, qui ad hoc ipsum momentum aliquod conferat, non qui remoretur, aut etiam peccatis gravioribus te inquinet. . . . At quando admodum pie Divus Thomas, loco iam citato scribat praecepta iuris positivi, ut loquitur, hoc est, praeter manifestum et expressum Dei praeceptum constituti, non extendere

Throughout his entire discussion Bucer neatly sidestepped the issue of the necessity of confession by focusing instead on the question of its divine institution. Despite his argument that whatever promotes holiness is required by divine law, it is evident from the authorities he cited that he did not believe private confession was divinely instituted. Indeed, by emphasizing the high regard in which the Greek church and the canonists held confession even though they did not believe it was divinely instituted, Bucer subtly reminded his readers that there were authorities who held that confession was not *de iure divino*.

In fact, Bucer was guilty of misleading his readers through his selective citation of authority. It is true that both Panormitanus and the *glossa ordinaria* on the Decretum taught that confession was established by the tradition of the western church and not instituted by divine law, whether derived from the Old or New Testament. This does not mean that they regarded auricular confession to be voluntary, however. While both recognized that the Greek church did not require confession, they concluded that the tradition of the western church obligated Latin Christians to confess all mortal sins.[52]

Bucer's use of Thomas to support his contention that it was better to confess to a layman than to an unworthy priest is also misleading. Thomas held that confession could indeed be made to a layman in case of necessity, but this confession, although sacramental in nature, was not a perfect sacrament because of the absence of a priest. And although Thomas did make the concession Bucer cites, he was careful to specify that permission to confess to another must first be sought from the priest himself or from a higher authority. Only if one failed to obtain permission could he act as in a case of necessity where there was no priest and confess to a layman.

The influence of Erasmus is especially clear in Bucer's discussion. All of the authorities which Bucer cited, with the exception of Thomas Aquinas, were used by Erasmus in his *Response* to Lee which Bucer had greeted with enthusiasm when published eight years earlier. Erasmus used Panormitanus, Chrysostom, the *Historia Tripartita*, and the gloss on the Decretum as clear support for his contention that confession was instituted by human law and could thus be modified by human law. Bucer's use of these texts was more indirect, for he quoted them to emphasize the importance and value of private confession. It is only upon further reflection that the

---

se ultra intentionem praecipientis, quae sit finis praecepti, nempe charitatem, ut Divus Paulus inquit, ad utilitatem, et verae pietatis instaurationem omnia instituentem. . . . Quare cum praeteritur sacerdos, qui meliorem reddere te nequeat, nec praeceptum Ecclesiae, ut Divus Thomas inquit, transgreditur, quia illa ei confiteri praecipit, a quo peccatis libereris, et in pietate erudiaris, ac promovearis, nec fit ulla sacerdoti eiusmodi iniuria, nam ut ibidem Divus Thomas scribit, privilegium meretur amittere, qui concessa sibi abutitur potestate."

[52]Gloss on *de poenitentia*, V, 1, in *Decretum divi Gratiani, totius propemodum ivris canonici compendium, summorumque pontificum decreta atque praeiudicia, vna cum variis scribentium glossis et expositionibus* . . . , Lugduni (Lyon), 1555, col. 1765; *Abbatis Panormitani Commentaria in Primum-Quintum Decretalium Libros. Quamplurium Iurisconsultorum, qui probe hucusque aliquid ijs addidisse apparuerunt, et nunc demum Alexandri de Neuo Adnotationibus illustrata.* vol. 7, Venice, 1591, fol. 228v; cf. Gy, "Le précepte," 532–534.

reader becomes aware that Bucer's view of the divine institution and necessity of private confession is something quite different from the understanding of divine institution taught by Catholic theologians. For Bucer, private confession was in general commanded by God as a salutary aid to instruction in piety and amendment of life, but it was nowhere commanded that individual sins be confessed. By avoiding any mention of the yearly confession of all mortal sins, he obscured the radical difference between his position and that held by Catholic theologians.

Bucer also followed Erasmus in his emphasis on the importance of confession for training in piety and in his criticism of the immorality which made priests unfit to be good confessors. From the discussion one would judge that the central issue was the character of the person to whom confession was to be made. Bucer's position cannot be called Donatistic because he denied the sacramental nature of priestly absolution entirely; but he did make the value of private confession largely dependent on the moral and spiritual qualifications of the confessor. This position separated Bucer not only from the Catholics but from Lutherans as well, since for the latter the power of absolution was independent of the character of the one pronouncing it. In addition, Bucer ignored the Catholic church's claim that the power of the keys was given to St. Peter and through him to the priesthood. Bucer acknowledged that a priest might be preferable to a layman as a confessor, but only if he had a better understanding of God's word. By emphasizing the pedagogical value of confession and avoiding discussion of the significance of priestly absolution and its role in obtaining forgiveness, Bucer diverted attention from the underlying conflict of his position with the Catholic—and the Lutheran—understanding of the power of the keys.

Despite its deceptively conciliatory tone, the Psalms commentary does not set forth a position on confession fundamentally different from the one presented in the Gospels commentary. Bucer stressed the positive aspects of confession and condemned the harm caused by unworthy confessors, scrupulously avoiding any polemic which would immediately label the commentary as a Protestant work. Instead he emphasized even more the pedagogical value of confession, without elaborating a definition of it which would make obvious his rejection of the auricular confession required by the Catholic church.

Bucer may have first used a more irenic approach to theological issues in an effort to appeal to Catholic readers, but the technique of emphasizing commonalities and ignoring differences would be particularly useful to him over the next few years as he worked to heal the division within the evangelical movement. Only a few weeks after the Psalms commentary was published, Bucer accompanied Zwingli to his meeting with Luther at Marburg in an unsuccessful attempt to reconcile their differences. Although he may not have been aware of it at the time, the Marburg Colloquy proved to be an important turning point for Bucer. The participants could not agree on the interpretation of the sacrament, but they did sign a mutual statement of faith covering other issues, including the value of private confession. Article 11 stated that "confession or the seeking of counsel from a pastor or neighbor should be voluntary and not compulsory, but it is a very useful thing to a conscience that is distressed and assailed by temptation, burdened with sin or fallen into error, particularly for the sake of absolution or consolation from the gospel, which is the genuine absolution."[53] Zwingli later stated that he had accepted this article after it had been modified so that "confession" was equated with "the seeking of counsel" and "absolution" identified with "consolation" and "preaching of the gospel."[54] These changes shifted the emphasis of the article away from the confession of sins and the minister's words of absolution to the broader use of the gospel to teach and console the sinner.

Bucer's concerted efforts to reconcile Luther and Zwingli began in earnest after the Marburg Colloquy. Luther's willingness to accept this broadening of the term "absolution" in the Marburg Articles provided the basis for Bucer's attempts to minimize the differences and to draft a position on absolution that would be acceptable to both sides. Despite his assertions of doctrinal agreement, however, Bucer shared Zwingli's distrust of the emphasis placed by the Lutherans on the words of absolution. This distrust was reflected in Bucer's critique of the statement on confession in the Schwabacher Articles formulated by the Wittenberg theologians in the summer of 1529. The article endorsed the practice of private confession "because in it, absolution, which is God's word and judgment, is spoken so that the conscience is loosed and set at rest from its cares."[55] Bucer objected to the wording of the article, stating that "the terms 'absolution' and 'loosed by judgment' were suspect; it would be sufficient to say that such instruction and seeking of counsel and consolation was salutary for all burdened consciences because of the private instruction and consolation which were given to them from God's word, when they sought them from a brother who was rightly instructed in God's word."[56] Like Zwingli, Bucer stressed the pedagogical value of confession and was wary of anything which would seem to give absolution some objective power to forgive or loose sins.

In March of 1530 Bucer published the second edition of his Gospels commentary. This volume contained both the 1527 Synoptic Gospels and the 1528 John commentary and was marked by numerous changes and improvements.[57] The new edition reflected Bucer's growing tendency towards irenicism and conciliation, now especially directed towards the Lutherans. In the preface Bucer stated that he had softened passages which were too harshly expressed in the first edition of the commentary.[58] The bulk of the preface was a lengthy plea for the unity of the church and a defense of the articles agreed upon at Marburg the previous October. With regard to confession Bucer reminded his readers that both sides had agreed that the gospel was the true absolution. To the Zwinglians, he stated that the words "absolution" or "con-

---

[53]BDS 4:352.25-29.

[54]Z 6/II:550.19-22.

[55]BDS 3:469.1-9.

[56]Ibid., 468.10-15.

[57]Lang, *Evangelienkommentar*, 70-80. Lang notes in passing that Bucer has moderated his criticism of Catholic practices such as auricular confession (p. 76), but he does not discuss the specific changes or the similarity of the revised passages with Bucer's Psalms commentary.

[58]The entire preface is reprinted in ibid., 386-410; citation at 387.

fession" should offend no one, while he reminded the Lutherans that Zwingli and his followers would never ridicule such confession, although such charges had been made against them. On the contrary, they had always held that it was a salutary thing to seek counsel from experienced Christian brothers when someone had a troubled spirit or did not sufficiently recognize his own sin.[59]

In the body of the commentary, Bucer's views on church discipline and the power of the keys were essentially unchanged. Nor, at first glance, does the section on confession seem much different from that of the first edition. The discussion of the three types of confession taught in Scripture—privately to God, publicly to man, and privately to a brother for consolation, counsel, or reconciliation—has only minor stylistic changes. These modifications clarify and sharpen Bucer's statements. If anything, the more sober and exhortative tone gives the impression that in his practical experience as pastor at Strasbourg, Bucer was learning that people were not as eager to confess their sins, either publicly or privately, as he had rather optimistically assumed three years earlier. For example, instead of simply stating that it is a pleasure to be able to confess to one another, Bucer now urged his readers to make this kind of confession.[60]

There is a significant change of focus in Bucer's discussion of auricular confession, however. While he was still critical of it, he was now much more careful to specify what he opposed in the Catholic practice and why he opposed it. Auricular confession was no longer rejected because it was a human invention per se but rather because it went beyond the word of God. Bucer still blamed auricular confession for the ruin of many souls, but his argumentation had moved from simple name-calling to a more reasoned attempt to prove that the present practice was not based on Scripture. In listing the most objectionable characteristics Bucer focused not on confession as a whole but rather on what was required in confession: the yearly confession of all sins, along with the individual circumstances, and thoughts which either approved of sin or were themselves sinful.[61]

This description is similar to the passage of 1527, but Bucer omitted one important element which he had earlier criticized, that confession be made to a priest. Indeed, on this point Bucer made a remarkable about-face. While in 1527 he had stated that men should diligently be taught that it is useless to worship God with human precepts, including secret confession, he now wrote that "men should be taught that it is indeed Christian sometimes to confess their sins to men, but to confess to a cer-

[59]Ibid., 406–407.

[60]1530 Gospels, 22C: "Hortari tamen ad eam convenit, quod et Divus Iacobus fecit Iaco. 5., Cum ait: Confitemini invicem peccata vestra, etc. Nam de eo confessionis genere locutum non dubito." Cf. 1527 Gospels 1:66v–67r: "Quos vero ardens iustitiae studium habet, ij mirifice delectantur, invicem alius alij delicta confiteri, et orare pro se invicem ut salventur, de quo confessionis genere, Iacobus 5, videtur scripsisse." The reference is to James 5:16.

[61]1530 Gospels, 22C: "Quale illud est quod eos gehennae addicunt, qui non quottannis, vel semel peccata sua singula, cum singulis circumstantijs, ac etiam cogitationes quibus peccato vel consenserunt, vel fuerunt eo, non nihil in animo titillati enunciaverint."

tain man at a certain time each individual sin, even sins of thought, is a human tradition."[62] Bucer supported his argument by appealing to the authorities he had cited in the Psalms commentary: "Panormitanus, the author of the gloss and many other legal experts and theologians." Thomas Aquinas was again quoted to the effect that a Christian could not be bound by what did not lead to an increase in piety, and Bucer brought in a new authority, Jean Gerson, who taught that it was not possible to require the confession of forgotten sins. Bucer now blamed the "more recent theologians and writers of *summae*" for trying to establish secret confession on the basis of scriptural passages which actually referred to the three genuine types of confession.[63]

Bucer continued to argue as he did in 1527 that if one chose to confess privately, he should go not to some priest delegated by a bishop to hear confessions but to someone made suitable for consoling, admonishing, and counseling by the word and Spirit of God. He now added, in defense of his position, that the church fathers had recommended confession to a priest because in those days priests were better able to console, admonish, and give counsel. But today, he lamented, no truly pious person would seek out a priest before all others if he suffered from a troubled conscience, because "no one leads a more vice-filled life" than the priests of today.[64] Bucer's criticism echoed what he had written in his Psalms commentary.

Bucer's greater willingness to see some value in private confession carried over into his critique of the Lutheran position. He no longer stated that their view was unscriptural; instead he gave a sort of apology: "I scarcely think that they feel that what they call private absolution has any ability of itself to soothe consciences, but rather that when brothers meet together and console one another, the Spirit of Christ, who renders efficacious the gospel so heard in private, is not absent."[65]

The 1530 Gospels commentary was a great deal more explicit in its approval of private confession than was the 1527 edition. It reflected Bucer's respect for the role

---

[62]Ibid., 23A: "Docendi igitur sunt homines , christiani quidem esse, et homini nonnunquam sua peccata confiteri, sed confiteri homini certo, certo tempore, et peccata singula, etiam cogitationum, id humanam esse traditionem." The passage replaced from the first edition, 1527 Gospels 1:68r: "Diligentissime igitur doceantur homines, frustra Deum timeri mandato hominum . . . quale omnino est hoc, de secretaria ista confessione."

[63]1530 Gospels, 23A: ". . . quod et Panormitanus, author glossae, multique alij, et Iureconsulti, et Theologi agnoverunt, eoque Christianos illa non amplius teneri, quam ea, ad pietatis incrementum conduxerit, quod et Thomas Aquinas censet, nec posse obmissam peccato obstringere, ut Gerson pie docuit. Etenim quas scripturas pro stabilienda hac sua secretaria confessione recentiores Theologi quidam et Summatij afferunt, nequaquam illi [confessione]."

[64]Ibid., 23B: "Quod autem Sacerdotibus praecipue confitendum veteres censuerunt, caussa fuit, quod horum sit, alijs ad docendum, monendum, et consolandum, esse instructiores. Quales si et hodie haberentur, nemo vere pius, non illos prae alijs consulet, si quando conscientiae aestibus laboraverit. At ut vulgo sunt, quid quaeso consilij, quid doctrinae ab eis tibi petas, quibus nemo fere in orbe vivit sceleratius."

[65]Ibid.: "Verum haud puto istos sentire, privatam illam, quam vocant absolutionem, per se momentum aliquod, ad tranquillandam conscientiam habere, sed quo ita convenientibus fratribus, et se invicem consolantibus, non desit spiritus Christi, qui Evangelion sic secreto auditu, reddat efficax. Hoc sane experiuntur pij, privatim in Domino colloquium. . ." cf. 1527 Gospels, cited in n. 27 above.

and function of private confession apparent in the 1529 Psalms commentary. Although Bucer continued to condemn what he saw as the perversions of auricular confession by the Catholic church, all of which grew out of *Omnis utriusque sexus*, he was much more careful to emphasize the positive effects of private confession. While Bucer had not adopted the high view of absolution which the Lutherans held, he made an extra effort to extol the value of private confession and to encourage its practice. In this he had moved beyond the position of Zwingli, who spoke highly of the importance of personal counsel and private instruction but did not place any particular importance on the confession of sin to another individual.

The situation in Strasbourg and his experiences with the practical problems of establishing the new church there may have had some influence on Bucer's views on the importance of confession.[66] Although there is little record of the practice of private confession in Strasbourg,[67] there are some indications of the changes that occurred during the 1520s. Not surprisingly, all references to confession in contemporary chronicles[68] appear in the week or two before Easter when every Catholic was required to make his or her yearly confession to a priest. Although evangelical practices had become fairly well established by the spring of 1525, the city council was still unsure how to deal with inhabitants who sought out and made their confessions to monks still in the city or to the priest at the church of St. Andreas who remained faithful to the Catholic church. When the matter was brought to their attention during Holy Week, the council ordered the priests to stop hearing confessions but also decided to write to Nürnberg to find out what was being done about this problem in that city.[69] In 1526, it took more decisive action: informed that the priest of St. Andreas and his assistant were hearing confessions and saying masses behind locked doors against the council's command, the council had the offending priests arrested and jailed. Two weeks later the council, without much debate, resolved to forbid the hearing of confessions and other practices in the cathedral and in the chapters which had remained Catholic.[70] The following year it issued a decree on Good Friday forbidding the city's inhabitants to make confessions or to light candles before the statues and pictures in the choir of the cathedral; all monstrances were also

---

[66]René Bornert has shown that the period from 1524 to 1530 was a time of development and establishment of new liturgical forms and that gradually the Strasbourg reformers began to appreciate more the traditions and practices of the early church, *Réforme protestante*, 84-153.

[67]Ibid., 403-404.

[68]Or rather, the fragments of contemporary chronicles, since most of the chronicles themselves perished in the fire which destroyed Strasbourg's library during the Franco-Prussian War. Excerpts from some of the chronicles were published between 1888 and 1911 in the series *Mittheilungen der Gesellschaft für Erhaltung der geschichtlichen Denkmäler im Elsaß* (MGEGDE). Miriam Chrisman describes the chronicle fragments published in the series, *Strasbourg and the Reform: A Study in the Process of Change*, Yale Historical Publications, Miscellany 87 (New Haven: Yale University Press, 1967), 320-322.

[69]*Annales de Sébastien Brant*, vol. 2, MGEGDE 19:117-118 (no. 4601).

[70]Ibid., 135-136 (no. 4668).

to be emptied.[71] Although most Strasburghers accepted the reformers' innovations, there was still a minority which clung to the Catholic church and sought to fulfill their yearly obligation to confess.

To the outside world, however, the reformers confidently asserted that they had managed to eliminate auricular confession and other Catholic practices from the city. In a description of the changes in the Strasbourg church dating from late August or September, 1529, written at the request of Ulm's city council, Bucer depicted what had happened to the practice of auricular confession in Strasbourg:

> Because [the practice of] confession gave rise not only to false confidence but also to great offense, we abolished it long ago. But we want to instruct our charges both publicly and in private through friendly meetings. We also summon individuals to give account and answer for their affairs; we do this every day and we meet with many people but without the methods and the procedures of auricular confession.[72]

The abolition of auricular confession did not enhance the reputation of Strasbourg or its pastors in certain circles. When Erasmus wrote his *Epistola contra pseudoevangelicos* in 1529, he charged that since the Protestants no longer required confession, many people no longer confessed even to God; Christian liberty was only a pretense for Epicurean license.[73] Bucer refused to accept the blame for this, however. As he argued in his response to Erasmus, the *Epistola Apologetica*, the Protestant pastors had not eliminated the type of confession which encouraged men to trust in God's pardon, but rather constantly recommended it to the people in their sermons and worship services. Nevertheless, no Christian could be compelled to confess, and it was useless to require those who did not confess to God to confess to man, since this only created hypocrites and mocked God.[74]

Opposition to the mandatory confession of all sins and the beneficial aspects of voluntary confession are two themes which were incorporated into the document which Strasbourg drew up in 1530 to justify the religious innovations which it had adopted. Intended to be given to the emperor at the Diet of Augsburg, the justification was the joint work of Bucer, Wolfgang Capito, and the patrician councillor Jakob Sturm, one of Strasbourg's delegates to the Diet.[75] Concerning auricular confession, the first draft of the justification repeated the assertion that no one was forbidden to confess, but there was no requirement concerning when and to whom confession was

---

[71]*Chronique de Jacques Wencker*, MGEGDE 15:156 (no. 3039).

[72]BDS 4:368.16-22. For a description of the circumstances surrounding Ulm's request for this description, Walther Köhler, *Zürcher Ehegericht und Genfer Konsistorium*, Quellen und Abhandlungen zur Schweizerischen Reformationsgeschichte 6–7 (Leipzig/Gütersloh: Bertelsmann, 1924-1953), 2:12.

[73]LB 10:1578E.

[74]BOL 1:156.8-18.

[75]The existing drafts of this apology reveal corrections by all three men; BDS 3:339-341.

to be made, since there was no command from God's word concerning these things.[76] This emphasis on the voluntary nature of confession was even more strongly emphasized in the final version of the apology. Here confession was discussed together with fasting as something which should be practiced "from the free spirit of truth and only to please God," and not because it was compelled. Requiring such practices by law only led to hypocrisy and was opposed to the teaching of St. Paul that no one should coerce consciences.[77]

Strasbourg never presented its justification to the emperor, but Bucer used the document, as well as a copy of the *Confessio Augustana*, when he and Capito composed the *Confessio Tetrapolitana*, a statement of faith submitted by Strasbourg and three other cities unable to accept the article on the Lord's Supper in the Lutheran confession.[78] The *Tetrapolitana* combined themes which Bucer had emphasized in his earlier works, but it also showed a further development in Bucer's theology. For example, he wrote in Article 13 that the clergy had the keys to the kingdom of heaven and the power of remitting and retaining sin, but only to the extent that they were ministers of Christ, who alone possessed the right and power to open heaven and forgive sins. No one was suitable for this ministry in and of himself, Bucer stated; rather, God made those whom he willed to be ministers and used them to bring people into the new covenant of grace. The ministers opened heaven to and forgave the sins of those to whom they preached the doctrine of faith mediated by grace and the Spirit of God.[79] The similarity with Bucer's exegesis of Matthew 16 in the Gospels commentary is clear: the word of God (doctrine) and the Spirit work together to open heaven. With his instrumental view of the ministry, however, Bucer was beginning to place more emphasis on the visible, institutional church.[80] Bucer applied the instrumentality of the minister to the preaching of the gospel rather than to the specific words of absolution, reflecting his definition of the keys as the word of God. This view of the minister as instrument would become increasingly important as Bucer's understanding of the power of the keys continued to evolve over the next few years.

Article 20, on confession, summarized the position taught in both the Gospels and Psalms commentaries. Bucer rejected the divine institution of auricular confession and stressed that the human requirement to confess only led to abuse. He also referred to

[76]Ibid., 347.12–19.
[77]Ibid., 386.8–23.
[78]On the background and contents of the *Tetrapolitan Confession*, see Marc Lienhard,"Evangelische Alternativen zur Augustana? Tetrapolitana und Fidei Ratio," in *Bekenntnis und Geschichte: Die Confessio Augustana im historischen Zusammenhang*, ed. Wolfgang Reinhard (Munich: Vogel, 1981), 81–100.
[79]BDS 3:99.21–101.20.
[80]Bucer's view of the instrumentality of the minister also distanced him from Zwingli. Referring to priestly absolution, the Zürich reformer disagreed with those "who grant all power to the word of God, but its administration to the priest as little more than an instrument or tool"; Z 3:724.6–11.

the schoolmen who write that one should confess to a layman rather than to a priest from whom one cannot hope for amendment. In summary, where confession does not arise from true contrition and sorrow for sin, it causes more offense than amendment, and since God grants contrition and sorrow, in such things nothing fruitful can be accomplished by human commandments. Unfortunately, experience has made this only too clear.[81]

In this article Bucer largely held to the position he had stated in earlier works. It reflected the issues he saw as most important: rejection of compulsory confession and emphasis on the moral character of the confessor. As in his Psalms commentary, Bucer focused on confession itself and said little about the value or significance of absolution. He was vehement in arguing for the voluntary nature of confession, and he stressed the pedagogical benefits of confession—consolation, counsel, instruction, and exhortation—rather than the assurance of forgiveness obtained through the words of absolution. His concern with the moral character of the confessor reflected a similar interest in the pedagogical and ethical value of confession. This contrasts with the *Augsburg Confession*, in which Melanchthon deliberately linked Lutheran and Catholic practice in stating that no one was allowed to receive the Lord's Supper without prior confession and absolution. Confession was acknowledged to be valuable for instruction, especially for the young and unlearned, but absolution was as essential as confession because through it sinners were assured of pardon. For Melanchthon the moral character of the confessor was in this respect irrelevant; his emphasis was on the voice of God which spoke in absolution.[82]

Nevertheless, despite the different interpretations of absolution, there was an underlying common understanding of confession, and the Strasburghers' offer to sign the *Augsburg Confession* without agreeing to the article on the Lord's Supper[83] shows that Bucer was not averse to Melanchthon's formulation and was willing under the circumstances at Augsburg to accept the Lutheran view of absolution as expressed in the confession. Another document sheds greater light on Bucer's understanding of and willingness to accept the *Augsburg Confession*. In May 1532, in preparation for negotiations with imperial representatives concerning the possibility of a truce until a general council could be called, Bucer wrote a memorandum to clarify Strasbourg's position if negotiations were to be based on adherence to the *Augsburg Confession* rather than the *Tetrapolitana*. In the memo he glossed over any conflict between the Lutheran position on private confession and absolution and his own view, stating that there was nothing in the *Augustana* and its *Apology* that "could be difficult for a Christian to confess" and that in all things the *Augustana* agreed with Strasbourg's

---

[81]BDS 3:143.20-145.35. The unnamed "schoolmen" is a reference to the position held by Thomas Aquinas, whom Bucer cited by name in his commentaries.

[82]BSLK, 66, 97-100; cf. the *Unterricht der Visitatoren*, WA 26:220.7-19, which established the precommunion examination in electoral Saxony.

[83]BDS 3:19; cf. Justus Jonas' letter to Luther, WABr 5:427.27-29.

Tetrapolitana.[84] Bucer also saw no essential difficulties with the second half of the *Augustana*, concerned with church practices and ceremonies. Citing Article 7 of the *Confession* and its explanation in the *Apology*, he wrote that uniformity of the ceremonies instituted by man was not necessary.[85] Bucer pointed out that the signatories of the *Augustana* did not have uniform practices among themselves. For instance, the *Confession* stated that no one was allowed to the Lord's Supper unless he had confessed, been examined and absolved, but in Nürnberg neither confession nor examination was required before reception of the Lord's Supper.[86]

Bucer continued to pursue his policy of stressing commonalities and avoiding discussion of differences in his response to the open letter Luther wrote in early 1533 to the Frankfurt clergy criticizing their teaching on the Lord's Supper and on private confession. In a draft pamphlet which he wrote as a response for the Frankfurt ministers, Bucer praised Luther for freeing consciences from human traditions and laws. In this context, he mentioned Luther's position that confession should be highly regarded because it was the consolation of the gospel and a medicine when used rightly, but that it could not be compelled, nor was it necessary that all sins be confessed—the two facets of Christian freedom in confession which Bucer had emphasized in the *Tetrapolitan Confession*.[87] Similarly, Bucer did not mention absolution, but he did discuss the power of the keys, administered by the church's ministers at God's command. The power to open heaven to repentant believers and to close it to unrepentant unbelievers was given by the Lord to his church, and those who exercised it were only servants of Christ and dispensers of the mysteries of God who were to be faithful in their ministry of tending Christ's flock.[88] Again, there are clear echoes of Bucer's discussion of the keys in the *Tetrapolitan Confession*, especially in the Scripture passages used to justify the arguments.

A more intriguing section of the draft is a paragraph on the number of sacraments which Bucer wrote and then crossed out. In it he rejected the view that penance or absolution was a sacrament, since Christ's promise regarding the power to bind and loose was not accompanied by a visible sign equivalent to water in baptism or bread and wine in the Lord's Supper. Nevertheless, he asserted, the practice of re-

---

[84]BDS 4:419.11-14. In a letter to Bonifacius Wolfhart and the other pastors of Augsburg written the end of May 1532, Bucer defended Strasbourg's acceptance of the *Augsburg Confession*, stating again that there was nothing in the first section of the *Confession*, on doctrine, to which a Christian could object, with the exception of two clauses from the articles on baptism and the Lord's Supper. Moreover, Strasbourg had not abandoned the *Tetrapolitan Confession* but retained it along with the *Augsburg Confession*; J. V. Pollet, *Martin Bucer, Etudes sur la Correspondance avec de nombreux textes inédits*, 2 vols. (Paris: Presses Universitaires, 1958-1962), 1:92-93, doc. 11.

[85]BDS 4:420.14-421.11.

[86]Ibid., 419.16-420.1. This was changed the next year, when the Brandenburg-Nürnberg church ordinance made a precommunion examination mandatory; Emil Sehling, ed., *Die evangelischen Kirchenordnungen des XVI. Jahrhunderts*, vol. 11/I (Tübingen: Mohr, 1961), 185-187.

[87]BDS 4:484.30-485.4.

[88]Ibid., 488.8-16.

pentance, confession, and absolution should be highly regarded.[89] This was the only time Bucer used this argumentation to deny the sacramentality of penance, or, more precisely, of absolution. It is all the more noteworthy because a year later he would argue that the imposition of hands was a quasi-sacramental sign which could be used to symbolize the granting of forgiveness in absolution.

Bucer's *Bericht* to the Frankfurt clergy was never published. Instead, after consulting with the other Strasbourg pastors, Bucer wrote to the Frankfurt preachers with advice on how to defend themselves against Luther's charges, urging them to use the *Tetrapolitan Confession* in their own reply to Luther.[90] The *Bericht* serves, however, as yet another example of the approach to private confession and the power of the keys which Bucer took at the Diet of Augsburg and after, in his attempts to achieve concord with the Lutherans. Its statements reflect Bucer's basic understanding of the power of the keys and the related issues of confession, absolution, and church discipline. The power of the keys was the word of God given by Christ to his church. It was exercised in the public preaching of the gospel. Confession was a useful means of instruction and assurance for troubled consciences, but its value depended on the abilities of the confessor to teach the penitent from the word of God. The absolution given in confession was nothing more than this private instruction and reassurance based on the gospel. Although useful and salutary for those who desired it, confession could never be compelled. Church discipline also involved the exercise of the keys, by the congregation rather than by a priest claiming to be the successor of St. Peter. All Christians were to admonish those who fell into sin, and excommunication was to be imposed only as a last resort. In these extreme cases family, friends, and neighbors were to use social pressure and some degree of ostracism to bring the sinner to repentance and the pastors were not to allow such sinners to receive the Lord's Supper, but excommunication could not be publicly pronounced, given the present circumstances of the church.

[89]Ibid., 490 n. d. This position directly opposed Melanchthon's statement in the *Apology* to the *Augsburg Confession* that absolution could properly be called a sacrament, *Apol.* XII, 41; BSLK, 259. This lack of an external sign is, however, the reason why Luther did not include penance among the sacraments properly so-called at the end of *De captivitate Babylonica*, WA 6:572.12-17. On the Lutheran view of absolution as a sacrament, see Holsten Fagerberg, *Die Theologie der Lutherischen Bekenntnisschriften von 1529 bis 1537* (Göttingen: Vandenhoeck & Ruprecht, 1965), 227-231.

[90]Bucer's advice was obviously followed, for when the Frankfurt pastors published their official response in March, they took part of the section on confession directly from the *Tetrapolitana*; cf. BDS 4:316.14-17 (*Entschuldigung*) and BDS 3:142.4-6 (*Tetrapolitana*). It has long been assumed that Bucer wrote the *Entschuldigung der Diener . . . zu Franckfurt*, and the work is included in the critical edition of Bucer's works, but the editor of Bucer's *Bericht* casts doubts on Bucer's authorship of the *Entschuldigung*: in part because of its detailed portrayal of the use of confession in Frankfurt which implies an intimate knowledge of the city's church; in part because of its frequent literal citation of the article on the Lord's Supper in the *Tetrapolitan Confession* rather than on the ideas emphasized in the *Bericht* and the letter to the Frankfurt preachers. This latter argument is strengthened by the literal citation of part of the *Tetrapolitana* on confession as well; cf. the editor's introduction to the *Bericht* in BDS 4:465-468.

Bucer formulated these positions in his earliest polemical exchanges with Catholics, in his commentaries, and in various memoranda written over the course of the 1520s. At the same time, however, he remained open to new ideas. As he became more involved in attempts to reach concord with the Lutherans, he demonstrated his willingness to change the language in which he expressed his positions. Gradually he began to modify those positions as well, reflecting his growing concern for the bond between visible and invisible, the internal working of the Spirit and the external signs of that working. In 1530 he had only begun this process, but his increased respect for private confession and the instrumental role of the minister were indicators of the direction which his thought would take over the next decade. Moreover, as he was confronted with the task of church organization both inside and outside of Strasbourg, Bucer was forced to become more specific and practical in his definition of the power of the keys and how it was exercised in the church in accordance with the ideas and principles he had expressed earlier. The first half of the 1530s proved to be an important time of development for Bucer's understanding of penance and especially for the practice of church discipline.

3

The Effect of Experience: Church Discipline and Church Order, 1531-1534

If Bucer's discussions of penance and church discipline during the 1520s were chiefly theoretical and theological, his treatments of these topics in the early 1530s were primarily practical. During these years Bucer directed his energies towards two tasks: promoting concord between Lutherans and Zwinglians and establishing an institutional structure for the evangelical church in Strasbourg. Both of these activities forced Bucer to think through the implications of his ideas on penance and church discipline. In his efforts to reach agreement with the Lutherans Bucer reexamined his positions on private confession and absolution. His experiences in church organization gave him the opportunity to translate his theoretical statements on church discipline into concrete procedures. As a consequence, his writings from 1531 to 1534 focused on issues such as the need for regular religious instruction, the value of a pre-communion examination, the steps to be taken in disciplining an unrepentant sinner, and the use of excommunication. Significantly, for the most part Bucer wrote about these questions in German—either in church ordinances or in popular works intended to reach a broad audience.

Bucer's earliest statements concerning the establishment of church discipline in Strasbourg occur in a description of that city's church sent to Ulm in 1529.[1] The pastors, he wrote, hoped soon to establish a Christian ban, with the magistrate's consent. The ban was to be closely linked to the punishment of those who had offended against the city's moral code, the *Constitution*, which had just been issued by the Strasbourg city council.[2] The primary purpose of the Christian ban, Bucer stated, was to ensure that these sinners would not be able to participate in the Lord's Supper. It would also allow "pious Christians" to point out such sinners so that they could be excluded.[3]

---

[1]BDS 4:365-373; above, 49.
[2]On the *Constitution*, see Köhler, *Ehegericht* 2:388-394.
[3]BDS 4:368.23-369.3.

Bucer implied that the ban consisted not only of exclusion from the sacrament but also entailed some degree of social ostracism or shunning. Such ostracism, however, was limited in scope: "the obstinate sinner is excluded by those who know him, such as his neighbors, before whom he is ashamed and whom he has offended and injured, unless, as I said, he is a public offense to everyone."[4] Bucer's description of the practice of exclusion by the sinner's neighbors accorded with his position in the Gospels commentary that excommunication was not to be publicly proclaimed.

Characteristically, Bucer emphasized the need for brotherly admonition "for as long as there is hope of amendment." He cautioned that exclusion of an obstinate sinner had to be done with great circumspection and thorough examination, "since diligent teaching and admonition are better able to improve, maintain and satisfy the Strasbourg church than is exclusion."[5] Public ostracism was a drastic measure, and Bucer repeated the caution that it was not to be used lightly. The motives of improving, preserving, and keeping peace within the congregation were always uppermost in Bucer's mind, and for these goals brotherly admonition was much more effective than exclusion from the church community.

Bucer did not go into specific details concerning the use of excommunication, such as how it was to be imposed and by whom. Over the next two years, however, developments outside of Strasbourg caused him to think more deeply about the use of excommunication and church discipline in general. In June of 1530, Johannes Oecolampadius gave a lengthy speech to the city council of Basel defending the necessity of church discipline and describing how it could be established in the city's church. He recommended that the responsibility for church discipline be entrusted to a college of twelve censors or *Bannherren* , composed of four ministers, four council members, and one layman from each of the city's four parishes. Following the pattern of Matthew 18, these men would admonish a known sinner first individually, then with two or three others, and finally as a body. They would pronounce contumacious sinners excommunicated and absolve the excommunicated sinner after the appropriate penance had been performed.[6]

Oecolampadius hoped that his system would be adopted not only in Basel but in other churches in south Germany and Switzerland as well, and to this end he tried to win the support of his fellow reformers for it. Bucer and Zwingli apparently discussed the proposal in mid-October 1530, while Bucer was on a trip through Switzerland.[7] According to Zwingli's later account of their discussion, Bucer "wanted nothing to do with" Oecolampadius' plan.[8] The two men had agreed that it was the

[4]Ibid., 369.5–8.
[5]Ibid., 369.3–11.
[6]Staehelin, *Briefe und Akten* 2:448–461 (no. 750); cf. Staehelin, *Lebenswerk*, 507–514; Köhler, *Ehegericht* 1:142–144; on Oecolampadius' views of church discipline more generally, see Akira Demura, "Church Discipline according to Johannes Oecolampadius in the Setting of his Life and Thought" (Th.D. diss., Princeton Theological Seminary; Ann Arbor: University Microfilms, 1964).
[7]Bucer was in Zürich on October 12; Schieß 1:226.
[8]"doch wolt Bucer gar nit drinn sin," Staehelin, *Briefe und Akten* 2:547.

duty of the Christian magistrate to punish sin, although where the magistrate was negligent in this responsibility, the church had the right to take action "so that the congregation may be preserved clean and pure."[9] Bucer himself expressed another concern in a letter to Zwingli written on October 19, soon after the Strasbourg reformer had returned home. He had stopped in Basel and discussed the issue of church discipline with Oecolampadius, but he still had reservations about Oecolampadius' model. He restated his fear that no system of church discipline could be established "which would not hamper a Christian magistrate." Moreover, he questioned the fitness of the clergy to exercise church discipline, "for there are many who are too querulous"; in his opinion even Oecolampadius was likely to be too severe in the use of church discipline.[10]

Despite his best efforts, Oecolampadius was unable to persuade any of the other cities to adopt his proposal. At a meeting in November, delegates from the evangelical cities rejected the adoption of a uniform means of exercising church discipline, stating that it was up to each city to decide "how to punish evil."[11] One month later, the Basel city council issued a mandate establishing the exercise of church discipline in the city and surrounding territory. The council modified Oecolampadius' original proposal to match its own priorities. Instead of giving oversight of the entire city to a group of twelve *Bannherren*, the mandate specified that the three *Bannherren* from each parish were to be responsible for their fellow parishioners. The mandate also made the *Bannherren* an entirely lay body more closely tied to the city council: two of the three *Bannherren* from each parish were to be council members, while the third was a layman. Although the parish pastor and his helpers were to have general oversight of their parishioners, they were not brought into the disciplinary process until the third admonition. If the sinner rejected this third warning and was guilty of manifest sin, he was banned and the sentence of excommunication was publicly pronounced by the pastor. Likewise, excommunicates wishing reconciliation with the church were to appear before the three *Bannherren* and the parish pastor to ask forgiveness. They would then be absolved and their reconciliation publicly proclaimed by the pastor; there was no requirement that penance be either imposed or performed before absolution. If an excommunicated sinner did not seek reconciliation within a month, he or she would be subject to discipline by the magistrate and guilds as well.[12]

Although he had earlier expressed misgivings about Oecolampadius' proposal, Bucer now began to view the Basel ordinance as a model to be followed elsewhere.[13]

---

[9]Ibid., 548.

[10]Z 11:199.5–14, no. 1118.

[11]Staehelin, *Briefe und Akten* 2:528 (no. 800).

[12]Ibid., 536–538 (no. 810). A copy of this mandate was sent to Strasbourg soon after it was published on December 14.

[13]W. van't Spijker discusses Bucer's apparent change of mind and suggests that it was due to the growing criticisms of the Strasbourg church by Anabaptists in the city, *Ambten*, 208–209; Bucer's mention of the Anabaptists in his letter to Blarer and the other pastors at Memmingen supports this view.

Other pastors in the south German cities looked to the Basel ordinance as a model as well, particularly as they began to debate whether their churches should adopt a uniform church ordinance which would, among other provisions, establish a common form of church discipline.[14] In late February 1531, pastors and city representatives met in Memmingen to discuss the issues and then draft a model disciplinary ordinance, known as the Memmingen Articles.[15] Bucer was unable to attend this meeting, but he stated his position on the issues to be discussed in a letter to Ambrosius Blarer and the other pastors gathered there. Concerning church discipline, he was disturbed that the evangelical church did not practice "the public penance of those who have publicly offended the church" and tentatively recommended the Basel ordinance: "It scarcely seems that the practice of excommunication . . . which has been established in Basel will be without fruit." The Anabaptists, he stated, were able to lead "simpler souls" astray in part because the magisterial church did not follow the disciplinary practices of the early church. This was the first time that Bucer explicitly endorsed the use of public penance. He also suggested that the pastors consider "whether it would be beneficial to establish a public profession of Christianity in the church after formal instruction in the catechism, a practice which has been usurped by papistic confirmation." This suggestion was also aimed at the Anabaptists, who complained that the practice of infant baptism did not allow for a public confession of Christian faith.[16]

Bucer drew heavily on the Basel ordinance and, to a lesser degree, the Memmingen Articles when he was given his first opportunity to design a system of church discipline. In May of 1531 he joined Oecolampadius and Blarer in Ulm to assist in the reorganization of that city's church in the wake of its official adoption of the Reformation. Among his many other responsibilities, Bucer undertook the task of writing a new church ordinance for the city.[17] His draft ordinance was divided into three sections devoted to doctrine, church ceremonies and practices, and the Christian life. The final section, on Christian life, was further subdivided into sections on civil and ecclesiastical discipline. In the section concerned with civil discipline, Bucer urged that Zuchtherren be appointed and given the authority to summon and punish those who spoke or acted against God and the magistrate. Bucer left the determination of

[14]Cf. Conrad Sam's proposals contained in a memo drawn up for the Memmingen meeting, Julius Endriß, Das Ulmer Reformationsjahr 1531 in seinen entscheidenden Vorgängen (Ulm: Höhn, 1931), 97–100; Köhler, Ehegericht 2:20–21.

[15]On the Memmingen meeting and the resulting Articles, see Köhler, Ehegericht 2:14–41.

[16]Schieß 1:245, no. 187 (Feb. 20, 1531).

[17]On the Ulm church ordinance and the events surrounding its adoption, see Gustav Anrich, "Die Ulmer Kirchenordnung von 1531," Blätter für württembergische Kirchengeschichte 35 (1931):95–107; Endriß, Reformationsjahr, 88–100; Carl Theodor Keim, Die Reformation der Reichstadt Ulm. Ein Beitrag zur schwäbischen und deutschen Reformationsgeschichte (Stuttgart: Belser, 1851), 221–263; Ernst-Wilhelm Kohls, "Ein Abschnitt aus Martin Bucers Entwurf für die Ulmer Kirchenordnung vom Jahr 1531," Blätter für Württembergische Kirchengeschichte 60/61 (1960/1961):177–213; idem, "Martin Bucers Anteil und Anliegen bei der Abfassung der Ulmer Kirchenordnung im Jahre 1531," Zeitschrift für evangelisches Kirchenrecht 15 (1970):333–360.

misdeeds and their specific punishment to the city council, but he commended the Memmingen Articles as a model for them to follow.[18]

Bucer began the section "On the Christian Ban" with a justification for church discipline based on the example of the early church. From the very beginning, the Holy Spirit had established that, along with public preaching and private admonition, the properly ordered church would have a system whereby those who lived in ways unbefitting a Christian could be warned and admonished to reform. Sinners who ignored this warning were excluded from Christian fellowship until they had recognized their sin and humbly asked to be reaccepted by the church. Those guilty of grave, manifest sin were not immediately reconciled, even though they repented, but were kept from the Lord's table for a period and placed among the penitents in order to demonstrate their contrition and repentance.[19]

This system of discipline, ordained by Christ, instituted by the apostles, and practiced in the early church, was to be restored in the church of Ulm. To this end, eight pious and God-fearing men—three from the city council, three from the community, and two pastors—were to serve as "ministers of Christian discipline." Bucer recommended that they be elected by a special committee composed of four city council members plus a representative from each of the guilds. The ministers of discipline would oversee the entire church, but to make this task easier Bucer suggested that each minister be responsible for a different section of the city.[20] The ministers of discipline would have the authority to admonish or warn only those who had publicly sinned against the Ten Commandments.[21] Where such sin became apparent, one of the ministers of discipline was to admonish the sinner to reform; this private admonition was to continue "for as long as there is hope that it will be fruitful." If individual admonition was not heeded, two or three of the ministers were to approach the sinner and again admonish him repeatedly, until it became clear that he would not repent. At this point he was summoned before all eight ministers for final warning, and if this failed, he was recognized as banned. The ministers of discipline were then to authorize the pastor to proclaim from the pulpit that this person had "denied the power of the Christian life and had fallen from Christ back to the devil"; he was proclaimed to be "expelled from the congregation and excluded with such earnestness and zeal that fear would come upon the whole congregation."[22]

If and when the banned sinner was moved to repent and asked to be readmitted to the congregation, the ministers of discipline were to console him but also to impose a period during which he was to demonstrate his repentance. If during this time he kept his promise and testified to his change of heart by his deeds, he was brought before the church, which was told to regard him once more as a Christian, and was

---

[18]BDS 4:397.7–22.
[19]Ibid., 392.15–36.
[20]Ibid., 393.1–24; 395.24–30.
[21]Ibid., 393.29–394.12, with a list of specific sins against the Ten Commandments.
[22]Ibid., 394.13–37.

then readmitted "to all the fellowship of the sacraments." If the sinner continued his offensive life despite the excommunication, so that he gave injury to the entire city, he was to be turned over to the guilds or to the magistrate for further punishment.[23] Although the draft did not specify the full consequences of excommunication, the provisions concerning the public proclamation of excommunication and reconciliation imply that the congregation was expected to shun or avoid the sinner.[24]

The draft did not explicitly grant the pastors the authority to refuse the Lord's Supper to anyone who had not been publicly banned, but it did suggest measures to protect the sacrament from profanation by unworthy recipients. Before celebration of the sacrament, for example, the pastors "were to point out who should refrain from the fellowship of the Lord's Table," thus allowing for self-imposed abstention from the sacrament.[25] Bucer also suggested that those who wished to receive the sacrament should attend the Saturday Vespers service and meet with the deacon afterwards. This meeting was not a precommunion examination but rather had a practical purpose, "so that if it looked like there would be too many [to receive communion the next day], the group could be divided and some asked to wait until the following Sunday." At the same time, however, Bucer added that "where the deacon saw that there were some young and uneducated people, while they were all gathered together he could explain the service of the Lord's Supper and admonish to its proper use."[26] Bucer also recommended regular catechetical instruction: each parish church was to provide instruction on the Lord's Prayer, the Creed, and the Ten Commandments every Sunday afternoon for children and servants. In addition, a special catechism service which all children and servants were required to attend was to be held four times a year.[27] The weekly catechism services were modeled on a similar practice in Strasbourg which had been established in three of the seven parish churches in 1526 and had quickly spread to all the churches.[28]

[23]Ibid., 394.38-395.19.

[24]Further indirect evidence that the ban entailed more than just exclusion from the Lord's Supper comes from Basel. The Basel *Bannordnung* of December 1530, which Bucer used as a model for the Ulm ordinance, required unrepentant sinners to be publicly banned and barred from receiving communion in their own church or any of the other churches in Basel. The actual proclamation of excommunication was more explicit. Here the congregation was ordered to shun the sinner, who was not to be allowed to participate in the Lord's Supper or in other Christian ceremonies so that "we do not damage our consciences, stain our churches and deny the commandment of our Lord." Under pain of fine, the congregation members were told not to have any fellowship with the banned sinner; Roth, *Aktensammlung* 5:61, no. 76. Given Bucer's earlier statements about the consequences of excommunication, he no doubt understood the consequences of public excommunication to include shunning by the entire congregation. This would also explain the negative reaction of the Ulm city council to the use of the word "ban" in the ordinance.

[25]BDS 4:388.17-21; the final ordinance was more precise in listing specific sins, 243.24-244.4.

[26]Ibid., 387.30-388.8.

[27]Ibid., 385.16-25. These recommendations were incorporated into the final ordinance as well; 229.11-198.

[28]August Ernst and Johann Adam, *Katechetische Geschichte des Elsasses bis zur Revolution* (Strasbourg: F. Bull, 1897), 115-116; François Wendel, *L'Eglise de Strasbourg, sa constitution et son organisation (1532-1535)*, Etudes d'histoire et de philosophie religieuses 38 (Paris: Presses universitaires, 1942), 47.

The provisions concerning catechetical instruction were adopted by the city council, but the section on discipline proved to be much more controversial, as is clear from the number of changes made to it before the final publication of the ordinance. Even the use of the word "ban" appeared suspicious to the Ulm city council, so that in the published ordinance it was replaced with "Christian exclusion." The published ordinance no longer contained Bucer's justification for the reestablishment of church discipline according to the model of the early church. Instead, a new section devoted to Christian doctrine at the beginning of the ordinance contained a paragraph explaining the power of the keys and laying the theological basis for the exercise of church discipline. It emphasized the use of the keys not just in preaching but also in admonishing and disciplining sinners. The keys to the kingdom of heaven were "the power to forgive sins and to preserve the congregation in true unity and edification through daily teaching, admonition, reproof and discipline"; they were God's word and the gospel which truly opened heaven to those who believed and truly closed it to those who scorned the gospel, and this "both at the beginning of conversion and afterwards, so we are admonished to continue in Christian deeds. For this reason Christian admonition and exclusion as well as pardon and forgiveness of sin should be in constant use in the church."[29] The section on church discipline also cited the power of the keys given by Christ to the apostles as justification for the "fraternal admonition and rebuke" which would be restored in the Ulm church.[30]

More significantly, the city council modified Bucer's draft so that it had a greater role in exercising discipline and was the final authority in imposing or lifting the sentence of excommunication. Like their counterparts in Basel, the Ulm council would not grant its pastors any authority to act independently of the magistrate. Therefore the final version of the ordinance specified that the eight ministers of discipline were to be chosen by the city council rather than by an independent committee. Four of the ministers of discipline were to be from the city council itself, which in essence gave it control over any decisions made by the body.[31] Moreover, the ministers of discipline no longer had the authority to excommunicate a person directly. Instead, they were to refer the case to the city council, which would make the decision whether to apply temporal punishment, banish the person from the city, or have him publicly proclaimed as banned. Excommunication thus became only one of the options open to the city council in disciplining contumacious sinners. The ordinance emphasized that the final authority and decision belonged in every case to the city council. Repentant sinners were pardoned by the city council, although they were also to seek readmission to the congregation from the ministers of discipline.[32] The final ordinance encouraged the pastors to great diligence "in genuine fraternal, friendly admonition and reproof," and told them to report anyone "who would not repent and was an offense to the whole church" to the ministers of discipline.[33] The ordinance implicitly

[29]BDS 4:218.26-219.13.
[30]Ibid., 251.14-24.
[31]Ibid., 251.23-27.
[32]Ibid., 253.11-254.1.
[33]Ibid., 254.20-25.

acknowledged the pastors' right to prevent sinners from receiving the sacrament by differentiating these individuals from those who had been publicly excommunicated.[34]

The Ulm church ordinance provided Bucer with his first opportunity to design a system of church discipline, but its importance should not be overrated. Bucer wrote the entire draft ordinance in the space of a few days, and he had very little time to work out all the practical implications of his own ideas.[35] In describing how discipline was to be administered, he closely followed the provisions of the Basel *Bannordnung*. He was surely encouraged to do this by Oecolampadius, who worked with him in Ulm. For this reason it is difficult to determine the extent to which the Ulm draft accurately reflects Bucer's own ideas. Bucer did incorporate some of his chief concerns into the section on discipline, such as the repeated assertion that admonition should be continued at each stage for as long as there was hope for reform. However, the ordinance's provisions for the public excommunication of contumacious sinners seem to conflict with Bucer's preference, stated in his Gospels commentaries, that the sentence of excommunication not be publicly pronounced. Free from the constraints of time and friendly pressure, Bucer proposed a different method of church discipline in the Strasbourg church ordinance of 1533. Although he retained some elements from his proposal for Ulm, the Strasbourg ordinance demonstrates that his ideas about church discipline would take him in another direction.

There is one other important source of information concerning Bucer's views on church discipline which dates from the period between the Ulm church ordinance and the Strasbourg church ordinance: a letter which Bucer wrote in March of 1532 to Simon Grynaeus and his fellow pastors in Basel. The letter was occasioned by a divisive quarrel among the Basel clergy concerning the public excommunication of those who refused to receive the Lord's Supper, as the city council had specified in a mandate issued the previous April.[36] Grynaeus had written to Bucer in hopes that his authority would resolve the conflict,[37] and the Strasbourg reformer promptly responded with a letter giving his position on "the use of the keys, that is, the administration of ecclesiastical censure, and especially towards whom it is to be exercised and to what extent."[38]

---

[34]Ibid., 254.4-6.

[35]Writing a church ordinance was not Bucer's only task in Ulm; he also preached, helped examine both the rural and urban clergy, became involved in a disputation with Dr. Georg Oßwald, a staunch defender of the Catholic church, and wrote a lengthy defense of the Ulm reformation for the rulers of the surrounding territories; see Endriß, *Reformationsjahr*, 18-43.

[36]Roth, *Aktensammlung* 5:194-195 (no. 217). There is a brief description of the controversy in Friedrich Rudolf, "Oswald Myconius, der Nachfolger Oekolampads," *Basler Jahrbuch* (1945):14-30.

[37]TB 5:31r-32v (Feb. 27, 1532).

[38]Staatsarchiv Zürich, E-II 338:1359r: "De usu clavium, hoc est administratione censurae Ecclesiasticae nos rogatis, maxime vero in quos exercere hanc debeatis et quatenus." There is a copy of this letter in the Simler'sche Sammlung of the Zentralbibliothek Zürich, Msc. S 31, fol. 63vff. I wish to thank Dr. Marijn de Kroon for bringing this letter to my attention.

Bucer listed four principles governing the exercise of church discipline. First, the magistrate should be encouraged to check false doctrine and blasphemy against the word of God and the sacraments, just as it acted against other crimes. Second, the pastors should consider all those who wished to be regarded as Christians as being under their care. It was the duty of the pastors to admonish not only publicly but also privately; the presbyters of the Basel church were to assist in such admonition.[39] Third, those who openly rejected the word of God were to be held as "Gentiles and publicans" if they would not accept admonition and refused to give up that which they acknowledged to be wrong. Bucer added that "if the magistrate is pious and wishes to perform its duty, it will see that the church uses this power without stirring up the city." The church imposed the sentence of excommunication, but the magistrate was to see that excommunication did not disrupt public peace. To those who protested that they had been wrongfully excommunicated, Bucer advised a sharp response: "You wish to be considered as a Christian, but your life is unworthy of this name. These men are pastors of the Christian flock. God has commanded them to cast out such yeast, so that the rest are not infected. Act and live out what you say and they will recognize you to be that which you desire to be called."[40] Fourth, Bucer emphasized again the importance of admonition. Every Christian ought to be subject to admonition concerning every part of the Christian life. Those who did not partake of the Lord's Supper were to be admonished to do so, though they were not to be pressured.[41]

Referring specifically to the controversy in Basel, Bucer urged greater toleration of individuals who abstained from the Lord's Supper. Those who could not in good conscience receive the sacrament but whose lives were blameless in other areas were not to be excommunicated but rather considered as catechumens. They could not be excluded from the kingdom of Christ as long as they called on Christ, honored his teaching, and submitted to admonition.[42] This was the practice of the early church,

[39]Ibid., 1359v-1360r:"Primum debetis magistratum huc hortari, ut sicut alia crassiora flagitia, ita et blasphemiam in verbum Dei atque sacramenta, falsam item doctrinam coerceat. Deinde quia omnes volunt Christi esse, omnem debitis vobis curam impositam credere, eoque non solum publicitus, sed etiam privatim monere, quoscumque potestis. . . . Praespyteris tamen Ecclesiae simul utendum est, quos habetis."

[40]Ibid., 1360r: "Tertio, si quis huc prorumpat, quisquis sit, ut palam verbum Dei contemnat, non sustineat se verbo Christi moneri et ab alijs revocari, quae satis novit mala esse, de quibus omnibus boni viri iudicio conscientiam praetexere non potest, hunc certe ut Ethnicum et publicanum vos habendum iudicare debetis. . . . Hic, si magistratus pius est et suo munere volet fungi, curabit ut Ecclesia hic sua potestate utatur sine turbatione Reipublicae. . . . Dicent eiusmodi excommunicationem indigne ferenti: Tu vis Christianus haberi, iam haec tua vita hoc nomine indigna est. Hi sunt Christiani gregis pastores. His Deus praecepit, ut tale fermentum expurgent, ne reliqua inficiantur. Age, vive quod diceris, et agnoscent te hi, quem dici te cupis."

[41]Ibid.: "Quarto, admonitio sicut erga omnes, ita de omni et toto Christianismo fueri debet, ac ideo volumus moneri etiam hos qui nondum sacram adeunt caenam, sed non urgeri, hoc quod vobis adhuc controvertitur."

[42]Ibid., 1360r-v: "Si qui autem nihilominus perstent in sententia, conscientiam semper excusantes, et caetera tamen viverent, quod posset conscienta videri, non heretica pervicacia, temperentque sibi a blasphemanda Ecclesia eiusque salutari doctrina, numerandi nobis videntur quasi inter Cathechumenos, Christi enim regno excludi non possunt dum illum serio nobiscum invocant, dum doctrinam eius colunt, dum moneri se sustinent."

"which always had a class of those who were neither regarded as Gentiles, clearly banished from the kingdom of Christ, nor were they worthy of full communion. You should place such people in this category."[43] Bucer acknowledged that refusal to receive the sacrament might be a mark of "heretical obstinacy," but he was willing to give such individuals the benefit of the doubt: "we prefer to err on the side of allowing as errors of conscience that which could actually be stubbornness and hypocrisy, than to condemn in the name of obstinacy that which is nothing more than error of conscience."[44] If, however, those who refused to receive the sacrament also committed grave sin and refused to heed admonition to repent, then they were to be excommunicated.[45] Moreover, in the exercise of discipline Bucer warned the Basel pastors not to use doctrinal disagreement as the chief criterion for excommunication, "for we are such that we are often too lenient towards those who agree with us and accept our teaching and too severe towards those who dissent and do not yet accept our teaching. . . . It is the greatest calamity to recognize as ours only those who accept all our doctrine, thereby neglecting many who truly belong to Christ."[46]

Throughout the letter Bucer stressed two points. First, all those who professed to be Christians and did not contradict this profession by their deeds were to be regarded as part of the church and hence subject to discipline. The definition of church membership could not be limited only to those who were considered orthodox doctrinally, especially on the question of the Lord's Supper. The only essential doctrine was faith that "Christ is the unique savior of mankind, true God, true man, from whom we await all things."[47] Bucer was ready to admit that this broad definition included Catholics: "there are many who belong much more to Christ among those who are considered papists than among those who seem to be evangelical."[48] Like-

[43]Ibid., 1360v: "Ergo ut res apud vos habere credimus, nolimus quemquam excommunicari ob id, quod non adijt sacram mensam, si conscientiam aliqua verisimilitudine excuset. Vetus Ecclesia semper habuit eorum quoque ordinem quos nec habebat sicut Ethnicos a regno Christi plane extorres, nec dignabatur communione plena. In hunc vos tales redigite."

[44]Ibid.: "Hic quoque mallemus nos in hanc partem peccare, quod ut conscientiae errorem ferremus quae esset vera pervicacia et hypocrisis, quam ut pervicaciae nomine damnaremus quod nihil quam error esset conscientiae."

[45]Ibid.: "si quis Eucharistiae disputationem excuset, qui alijs flagitijs madeat a quibus etiam quamlibet monitus non resipiscat, hunc iam licebit excommunicare ob ea, quae non admittunt conscientiae emendationem."

[46]Ibid., 1360v-1361r: "probe attendite vobis hic ut nullam personam respiciatis et semper quae praecipue cum Christo pugnant, in ea praecipue quoque severi sitis. Sic omnes sumus ut in consentientes nobis nostraque adprobantes admodum lenes nos exhibeamus, plus autem quam severos in dissentientes et nostra nondum recipientes. . . . Summa pernitiosum putamus eos tantum nostros agnoscere qui omnia nostra dogmata recipiunt, plurimos enim qui vere Christi sunt negligeremus."

[47]Ibid., 1359r: "putamus eos amplectendos nobis interque Christianos numerandos esse, quicumque Evangelio Christi, hoc est, huic praedicationi: Christus unus est humani generis servator, verus Deus, verus homo, a quo sunt expectanda omnia, se fidem habere fatentur, nec ijs factis negant, quae cum hac fide nullatenus consistunt."

[48]Ibid., 1360r: "Saepe longe plus Christi est apud eos qui habentur adhuc Papistae, quam apud multos quibus nihil videtur magis Evangelicum."

wise, neither Lutherans nor Anabaptists, both of whom would disagree with the Basel clergy over the interpretation of the Lord's Supper, were to be considered outside of the church because of their doctrinal disagreement. "You should not think that ecclesiastical censure should only be exercised on those who accept all of your doctrines and testify to this by receiving the sacraments, for you would exclude a great multitude from the fellowship of Christ whom he does not wish excluded, and you would deny this healing work of yours to those who especially need it and would neglect those whom you should especially watch over."[49] The pastors' mandate to exercise discipline was very broadly defined, extending over the entire population of a Christian city.

Bucer's second emphasis was the centrality of admonition in the process of discipline: "church discipline does not consist in excommunication alone; the more important part of discipline is friendly admonition, and this you owe to all who profess the name of Christ and do not openly reject it." Moreover, admonition was to be repeated as long as the individual would listen. Bucer interpreted the disciplinary procedure of Matthew 18 not as some kind of magical formula but as a figure of speech, "for the Lord used a specific number to mean an indeterminate one, which he expressed as three-fold. He wished to signify completeness, so that we would not cease to admonish before we have satisfied Christian love."[50] Excommunication was imposed only when the sinner refused to heed admonition.[51] It was better to allow hypocrisy within the church, Bucer reasoned, than mistakenly to expel from the church those whose consciences were misled but who truly were Christians. The weeds would not be eliminated from the church during this age, he stated, referring to the parable of the wheat and the tares.[52] The emphasis on admonition and the corresponding de-emphasis on excommunication reveals yet again Bucer's pastoral concern.

Bucer's letter becomes even more instructive when it is compared to the procedure for church discipline instituted at Ulm. Bucer's reference to the "presbyters"—

---

[49]Ibid., 1359v: "Hortamur itaque vos in Domino et per regni Christi amplitudinem obtestamur, ne huc adduci vos patiamini, ut censuram ecclesiasticam erga eos tantum exercendam vobis putetis qui dogmata vestra recipiunt omnia, et simul id usu Sacramentorum testati sunt. Quantam enim multitudinem exclusuri essetis societate Christi quos ille non vult exclusos, et quibus maxime opus, hic operam vestram medicam essetis negaturi, et eos piussissimum neglecturi, quibus unice oportet invigilare."

[50]Ibid.: "Disciplina Ecclesiastica non sola excommunicatione constat, potior eius pars est amica admonitio; hanc debetis omnibus qui Christi nomen profitentur nec dum aperte illud reiecerunt, nec magica superstitione ternarius hic numerus observandus, certum enim pro incerto posuit Dominus, quod enim ternarium expressit. Significare voluit perfectum, ut non ante monere desinamus, quam plene satisfactum sit charitate Christianae, quae lucrandis fratribus nihil non tentat, nihil non impendit."

[51]Ibid., 1359v: "Etenim cum eos consideramus, quos Ecclesia proscribi Christus et Apostoli iusserunt, vidimus, primam huius causam fuisse, noluisse admittere admonitionem."

[52]Ibid., 1360v: "Evellere quoque zizanias omnes non est huius temporis." For the function of this parable (Matt. 13:24–30) in Bucer's ecclesiology, see Hammann, *Entre la Secte*, 90–92.

presumably the *Bannherren*—indicates that he had accepted this element of Oecolam-padius' plan for church discipline. Moreover, by identifying this group of laymen with the elders of the New Testament, Bucer gave their office scriptural justification. On the other hand, Bucer opposed the public excommunication of those who volun-tarily abstained from the Lord's Supper. He repeated the argument against compul-sory reception of the sacrament which he had first used in *Grund und Ursach* almost eight years earlier. As long as an individual would accept admonition, Bucer was re-luctant to have him or her publicly cut off from the church; therefore he proposed the category of "catechumens" as a middle ground between full membership and complete exclusion from the church. The Ulm ordinance—and the Basel *Bannord-nung* which was its model—did not officially recognize this middle category of church membership.

Although Bucer continued to play an active role as organizer and advisor outside of Strasbourg, his own church provided him with the greatest opportunity to develop an institutional structure to replace the Catholic system of penance, instruction, and discipline. The last official traces of Catholicism disappeared from Strasbourg with the abolition of the mass in 1529, but it was several years before the new evangelical church could institutionalize its own practices. Beginning in the 1520s the pastors and their assistants had met informally each week in what was called the *Kirchenkon-vent* to discuss the concerns of the church. In early 1531 the *Kirchenkonvent* submit-ted a lengthy memorandum to the city council with concrete suggestions for strengthening the church. Among other proposals, it pointed out to the council that, in addition to public preaching, the church needed some form of private religious in-struction, such as catechization for children and private confession for the repentant. To meet this need, it recommended that the council require all householders to bring their children and servants to catechism instruction. The ministers noted that other churches required a precommunion examination, a practice which not only provided an opportunity for individuals to be consoled or instructed but also strengthened the ties between the pastor and his parishioners. The Strasbourg clergy acknowledged that they could not require such an examination, but they proposed as a substitute that each pastor, with his assistants, periodically visit the householders of his parish to instruct them and their families in the faith.[53]

The city council ignored these and most of the other proposals made by the clergy, but they did adopt one of the recommendations—the establishment of a commission to supervise the city's pastoral corps. In a mandate published at the end of October 1531, the council ordered the appointment of twenty-one *Kirchenpfleger*: each of the city's seven parishes was to have as its representatives one council member, one mem-ber of the *Schöffen*, the large advisory council of elected guildsmen, and one lay resi-dent. These twenty-one men, appointed for life, were responsible for overseeing the

---

[53]AST 84, no. 27; printed in abridged form with a summary of this point, TAE 1:327–330 (no. 244), where the document is dated on or after February 25, 1531; cf. Köhler, *Ehegericht* 2:404–407.

doctrine and conduct of the pastors and their assistants. In addition, a standing committee was chosen from among the *Kirchenpfleger* to deal with matters pertaining to the church on a daily basis. If necessary this committee would refer more difficult problems to the entire group of *Kirchenpfleger*. At least once every three months the entire committee was to attend the *Kirchenkonvent*, and one *Kirchenpfleger* was required to attend every meeting. If anyone had any complaints about the clergy, they were to report them to the *Kirchenpfleger*.[54] Although patterned after the Basel *Bannherren* and the Ulm ministers of discipline in composition, the Strasbourg *Kirchenpfleger* differed from these two groups in function. The official body envisioned by the Strasbourg pastors and established by the magistrate had no responsibility or authority to supervise the morals of the laity but was concerned only with the doctrine taught and the moral example set by the clergy. They were also to play a more active role in the day-to-day functioning of the church than did their counterparts in Basel and Ulm.

The *Kirchenpfleger* and the pastors directed the Strasbourg church as well as they could, but their informal authority was not enough to handle effectively the many pressures that the church faced, especially those caused by the large number of sectarians in the city. Strasbourg's reputation for clemency towards religious dissenters led to an influx of Anabaptists who had been expelled from other cities. The presence in Strasbourg of prominent religious dissidents such as Melchior Hoffmann and Caspar Schwenckfeld made the situation even more difficult for the church.[55] The magistrate's mandate against harboring Anabaptists, first issued in 1527 and renewed in 1530, did little to weaken the movement.

It was as a response to Anabaptist pressure and to the failings of the church that the first Strasbourg synod was held in June of 1533. The synod began the lengthy process of officially establishing the Strasbourg church, a process which culminated in the publication of the Strasbourg church ordinance a year and a half later.[56] One of its most important acts was to adopt the *Tetrapolitan Confession* and the 16 Articles

[54]This mandate is printed in Timotheus W. Röhrich, *Mittheilungen aus der Geschichte der evangelische Kirche des Elsaß* (Strasbourg: Treuttel & Würz, 1855), 1:257-260; cf. Köhler, *Ehegericht* 2:408-410. Köhler's analysis of this mandate and of the preachers' memorandum should be used with caution, since his misinterpretation of Bucer's motives concerning magisterial oversight of church discipline distorts his analysis of the role of the *Kirchenpfleger*; cf. Hammann, *Entre la Secte*, 234-238, on Bucer's view of the magistrate's role in church discipline.

[55]For a description of the various radicals in Strasbourg, see Klaus Deppermann, *Melchior Hoffman. Soziale Unruhen und apokalyptische Visionen im Zeitalter der Reformation* (Göttingen: Vandenhoek & Ruprecht, 1979), 149-193. George H. Williams summarizes much of the recent research on the Anabaptist movement in Strasbourg, *The Radical Reformation*, third ed., Sixteenth Century Essays and Studies 15 (Kirksville, MO: Sixteenth Century Journal, 1992), 363-431. The best of the older works on the Strasbourg Anabaptists is A. Hulshof, *Geschiedenis van de Doopsgezinden te Straatsburg van 1525-1557* (Amsterdam: Clausen, 1905).

[56]Wendel, *L'Eglise*, describes the synod, 69-96; excerpts from the synod protocol in TAE 2:35-55, 70-90, nos. 373 and 384; Williams, *Radical Reformation*, 410-431, describes the disputations with several Anabaptist leaders held as a part of the synod.

drawn up by Bucer as the city's official teaching. While the *Tetrapolitan Confession* defended Protestant doctrine against Catholic opponents, Bucer wrote the 16 Articles to counter Anabaptist views which were gaining adherents within Strasbourg. The four Articles relating to church discipline reflected this goal. They asserted that participation in the Lord's Supper was open to all who recognized Christ as their savior and did not testify to the contrary by leading a life of obvious impenitence. Those who taught that one should first demonstrate genuine improvement of life or be baptized, "thus scaring people away from the Lord's Supper," only created schisms in the church.[57] Moreover, those who were "one body and bread in Christ . . . should show Christian concern for each other through mutual instruction, admonition, reproof, and encouragement in all mildness and humility." This held true even if one Christian had no greater ties or connection with another than the bond of faith.[58] No one was to be excluded from the congregation unless he had committed any of the grave sins listed in the Pauline epistles and would not heed admonitions to repent. Those who used the ban in any other way achieved only destruction.[59] The power of the keys was exercised by the church "according to God's word and from God's Spirit"; no other power is given to any man, "be he pope or bishop," and especially not by means of laws which were not based on the word of God. Christians were free from all laws, commands, and vows which did not serve to produce true piety.[60] The rejection of eucharistic rigorism, the importance of admonition, the use of excommunication only as a last resort, and the definition of the power of the keys are all familiar elements of Bucer's thought.

At the end of the synod a committee of four pastors and four *Kirchenpfleger* was appointed to draft a church ordinance for the city. This draft, composed by Bucer and with corrections and additions in his hand, was presented to a second session of the synod held in October 1533.[61] As in the Ulm ordinance, Bucer made no provision for a precommunion examination but emphasized instead the need for regular religious instruction. Parents who wished their children to receive communion for the first time were to bring them to the pastor during the Sunday catechism for examination. The weekly catechism services were to be continued, during which the Creed, Lord's Prayer, and Ten Commandments were to be explained to the children "in the most brief and clear way." All parents were earnestly to be exhorted—but not required—to send their children and servants to special catechism services to be held every three months.[62] These provisions concerning religious instruction formalized the existing practices in Strasbourg.

[57]BDS 5:391.5-12 (Article 10).

[58]Ibid., 391.13-18 (Article 11).

[59]Ibid., 391.19-23 (Article 12).

[60]Ibid., 391.24-35 (Article 13).

[61]See the introduction to the church ordinance, BDS 5:19-21; Wendel, *L'Eglise*, 97-107.

[62]BDS 5:412.15-34, "Der Juget halb." These provisions were adopted without change in the final version of the ordinance, ibid., 34.13-33. The quarterly catechisms were catechetical sermons, to be distinguished from the weekly *Kinderberichten*, Ernst and Adam, *Katechetische Geschichte*, 115-117. On the custom of catechetical services, see Bruno Jordahn, "Katechismus-Gottesdienst im Reformationsjahrhundert," *Luther. Mitteilungen der Luthergesellschaft* 30 (1959):64-77.

The draft ordinance also expanded greatly the role and responsibilities of the *Kirchenpfleger*. They were to see that no one taught against or criticized the city's officially recognized doctrine, either publicly or privately. The draft recommended that a new commission, comprised of city council members, *Kirchenpfleger*, and pastors, be established to examine anyone who wished to preach or teach in the city.[63] The *Kirchenpfleger* were also to participate in the process of appointing new pastors to vacant positions.[64] In addition, two *Kirchenpfleger* were to attend the meetings of the *Kirchenkonvent*, which was to meet biweekly instead of weekly so that the attendance requirement would not be too burdensome.[65] The most significant change for the *Kirchenpfleger*, however, was the extension of their responsibilities of oversight to include the laity. Together with the pastors, the *Kirchenpfleger* were to watch over the inhabitants of their parishes to see that they proved themselves true members of the church. To fulfill this responsibility, the draft recommended that the pastors and *Kirchenpfleger* meet every Sunday and that they be given the authority to summon parishioners to appear before them if necessary. Bucer added on the margin of the draft that as an alternative to summoning, the *Kirchenpfleger* and pastors could appoint someone to approach in private those needing admonition, "where they recognize this to be more profitable"—a practical outworking of his constant stress on the importance of private admonition to bring about amendment.[66]

Those who had separated themselves completely from the church, neither attending sermons nor receiving communion, were to be asked "with all gentleness . . . why they rejected what the magistrate and the whole city recognized as and held to be Christian." If their only reason for avoiding worship services was "little fear of God," they were to be admonished "to heed God more and hold him before their eyes."[67] If they agreed to attend the sermons but would not receive the sacrament, they were to be left alone after being encouraged "to pray that God grant that they give themselves to him completely." This group of people were like the catechumens of the early church who had accepted Christian doctrine but had not yet joined the full fellowship of the church through the sacraments. The draft stressed that "no one who does not desire it from his heart should be allowed to the Lord's Supper . . . not to mention compelled to receive it."[68]

The distinction between those who were willing to attend public worship and those who steadfastly refused was an important one for Bucer, since the draft went on to state that those who continued to scorn God's word "should be let alone and handed over to divine judgment." In his own hand Bucer emphasized that this contempt had to be obvious and public, thus further differentiating such individuals from

---

[63]BDS 5: 402.6–403.22.
[64]Ibid., 406.10–407.35.
[65]Ibid., 408.10–26.
[66]Ibid., 415.24–416.5.
[67]Ibid., 416.6–13.
[68]Ibid., 416.13–23.

the "catechumens." In a phrase which was crossed out, the draft identified those "handed over to divine judgment," as "those who have been banned by Christ himself." With such people the pastors and *Kirchenpfleger* could do nothing, since they had already separated themselves from the church and showed no desire to be reconciled with it. The draft did state, however, that "one should still offer them every civil friendship and help with all gentleness and good will. . . . For Christians, like their heavenly father, should do good to everyone and live without offense with all men, even Jews and heathens." The same treatment was prescribed for those who attended the sermons and received the Lord's Supper and thus "showed that they were some kind of Christians," but whose lives gave public offense and were a disgrace and a shame to Christ and his church. Again, Bucer added in his own hand the qualification that those individuals must have refused to reform when admonished.[69] The draft underlined the responsibility to care for the salvation of everyone "who is baptized and bears the name of Christ, since the Lord has commanded this . . . the Lord desires so greatly that doctrine, admonition and fellowship are accepted in the church that he has said, whomever the church on earth binds or looses shall be bound or loosed in heaven, and whosesoever sins it retains or forgives will be retained or forgiven."[70]

The procedures for congregational oversight and church discipline described in the draft ordinance for Strasbourg are much different from those outlined in the draft ordinance which Bucer wrote for Ulm. The two draft ordinances describe different procedures applied to different groups and with different goals. The Ulm draft was concerned with how to discipline, and if necessary excommunicate, sinners: it included a list of sins for which a person could be disciplined, a procedure to be followed when disciplining that person, and provisions concerning how to reconcile an excommunicated sinner to the church. The Strasbourg draft, on the other hand, was concerned primarily with separatists, those who did not participate in public worship by attending sermons or receiving the sacrament. Its goal was not so much to discipline or excommunicate as it was to reintegrate individuals into the life of the church; it referred only in passing to contumacious sinners who were regular churchgoers. In comparison to the Ulm ordinance, it is striking in its vagueness. Instead of an elaborate three-stage process with multiple admonition, the Strasbourg draft mentioned only the authority either to summon an individual for questioning or to approach that person privately. It said nothing concerning exclusion from the sacrament, other than the self-imposed exclusion of those who refused to receive it, and there was no clear or explicit mention of excommunication, although the phrase "hand over to divine judgment" implies that individuals were considered to be excommunicated.[71]

[69]Ibid., 416.23–417.2.

[70]Ibid., 417.2–15.

[71]Because of the vagueness of these provisions scholars disagree whether the final church ordinance allowed for the imposition of excommunication. Werner Bellardi interprets the ambiguous phrase "hand over to divine judgment" to mean "exclusion from the sacrament and thus from the ecclesiastical congregation," and he regards the qualification concerning main-

The absence of any specific procedures governing the imposition of public excommunication in the Strasbourg church ordinance has generally been attributed to the magistrate's opposition to Bucer's intentions. There is, however, no indication that Bucer proposed or even desired to establish a procedure for public excommunication in Strasbourg. Like other sections of the ordinance, the provisions regarding pastoral oversight were specifically intended to eliminate the sectarian threat to the Strasbourg church. Since many of the city's Anabaptists had already excluded themselves from the official church, there was little purpose in outlining a formal procedure whereby they would be publicly excommunicated. Instead, the draft ordinance attempted to differentiate between the convinced separatists who would have nothing to do with the church and those who the pastors hoped could be won back into the full fellowship of the church. To the extent that the pastors and Kirchenpfleger decided when further admonition was useless, they had the authority to determine when an individual was considered to be banned. Because the sentence of excommunication was not to be publicly pronounced, however, its social effects were limited. Moreover, the draft ordinance specifically limited the civil consequences of even this restricted form of the ban. In this respect its provisions reflected the aversion to public excommunication and complete ostracism which Bucer had shown in his Gospels commentary and in his letter to the Basel pastors.

It was another year before the final version of the church ordinance was approved and published.[72] While large sections of the ordinance were identical with Bucer's draft, a few significant changes were made which limited the authority which the draft ordinance had given to the pastors. As in Ulm, the Strasbourg city council had little understanding of or appreciation for Bucer's distinction between the responsibilities of the church and those of the magistrate, and consequently it regarded the Kirchenpfleger as its own representatives in regulating church affairs. The ordinance specified that three Kirchenpfleger attend the biweekly Kirchenkonvent, and it gave them the authority to refer difficult or controversial matters to the whole body of Kirchenpfleger or to the city council itself. The Kirchenkonvent was forbidden to make important decisions or to undertake any innovations without the prior knowledge and, it is assumed, approval of the council.[73] The ordinance followed the draft

---

tenance of civil fellowship as "a special form of the lesser ban," *Die Geschichte der "christlichen Gemeinschaft" in Straßburg. Der Versuch einer "zweiter Reformation,"* Quellen und Forschungen zur Reformationsgeschichte 18 (Leipzig: Heinsius, 1934), 17-18. Wendel, relying on the 16 Articles and on Bucer's 1534 Catechism to interpret the church ordinance, also concludes that the authority of the Kirchenpfleger included the power of excommunication, *L'Eglise,* 118-120, 222-227. Köhler disagrees, arguing that although the section may legitimize the principle of excommunication, it does not bestow the legal authority to excommunicate, *Ehegericht* 2:423-424. It should be noted that during the 1540s the Strasbourg pastors regarded some of the city's inhabitants to be excommunicated; see p. 175 below.

[72]Wendel, *L'Eglise,* 108-125, and Köhler, *Ehegericht* 2:416-418, describe the pastors' attempts to hasten the redaction of the church ordinance and the city council's discussion of the proposed ordinance.

[73]BDS 5:31.1-10.

in describing the various categories of people to be admonished, with the exception that Bucer's condemnation of compulsory participation in the Lord's Supper was omitted. However, it placed the authority to admonish solely in the hands of the *Kirchenpfleger*. The three *Kirchenpfleger* in each parish were to meet once a week to fulfill this responsibility, and where necessary they could seek the advice of the pastors, but the pastors themselves had no part in the disciplinary process.[74]

The changes made to the ordinance destroyed the balance between magistrate and clergy which Bucer had tried to establish in the Strasbourg church. Whereas Bucer had intended the pastors and *Kirchenpfleger* of each parish to work together in the oversight of the laity, the city council gave this responsibility entirely to its representatives, the *Kirchenpfleger*. What Bucer proposed as a harmonious means of cooperation between clergy and lay representatives of the magistrate was altered to become another opportunity for the city council to strengthen its control over the church. In essence the *Kirchenpfleger* were responsible for admonition, and the pastors had only an advisory role. This would become a source of conflict between clergy and magistrate in the years to come.

At the same time that the Strasbourg church ordinance was being finalized, Bucer was still formulating his ideas on church discipline and pastoral oversight. During the course of 1533 and 1534 he published several works in which he discussed the power of the keys and added an important new element to his understanding of discipline. Two of the books were aimed specifically at a Catholic audience: *Furbereytung zum Concilio*, published in the late summer of 1533, was a dialogue between a Protestant and a Catholic intending to show how concord could be established between the two churches, while *Defensio adversus axioma catholicum*, published a year later, was a response to criticism directed against Bucer by Robert Cénan, the bishop of Avranches. These works discussed issues relating to the sacrament of penance that were disputed between Protestant and Catholic: the power of the keys, the authority of the minister and the imposition of public penance or satisfaction. Bucer wrote two other pamphlets meant for the Anabaptists of Münster. The first of these, *Quid de baptismate infantium iuxta scripturas Dei sentiendum*, was published in December 1533, and the second, *Bericht auß der heyligen geschrift*, appeared in March 1534. In them, Bucer considered problems associated with attempts to preserve the purity of eucharistic fellowship. Finally, Bucer wrote a catechism for the Strasbourg church which was published in the spring of 1534. This catechism summarized arguments made in the earlier works. Significantly, one of its purposes was to teach the inhabitants of Strasbourg the proper use and goals of church discipline. Although written for different reasons and intended for different audiences, these works all testified to Bucer's growing concern about the need for religious instruction, moral oversight, and church discipline.

In *Furbereytung* and *Defensio*, Bucer combined his understanding of the power of the keys with his ideas on church discipline to develop a model of penitential dis-

[74]Ibid., 37.15–38.19.

cipline which he hoped would be acceptable to both Protestants and Catholics. As he had done in his Psalms commentary, Bucer made frequent use of scholastic theologians to support his arguments where it suited his purposes. This is evident in the lengthy section of *Furbereytung* devoted to the church's power to bind and loose sins. Bucer explained that the ministers of the church exercised the power of the keys in three ways. The first type of binding and loosing was the proclamation of the gospel, accompanied by the baptism and reception into the church of those who accepted it, and the binding to condemnation of those who rejected it.[75] The second type of binding and loosing concerned the use of excommunication and public reconciliation: those already in the church who sinned and would not repent despite repeated admonition were excluded from the church, or bound; they were loosed when they submitted to penance, whether publicly or privately, were consoled through the gospel, and were reaccepted into the church.[76] The third type of binding and loosing was the imposition of penance and exclusion from the Lord's Supper for those who had fallen into grave, manifest sin and the lifting of these measures after the sinner had demonstrated his repentance.[77]

Bucer's three types of binding and loosing parallel the description of the power of the keys contained in the *Sentences* of Peter Lombard.[78] Bucer did not mention the *Sentences* when describing the second and third types of binding and loosing, but he did cite it when discussing the power of the keys in general:

> [Peter Lombard] teaches, and supports this with quotations from the fathers as is his custom, that God alone and of himself forgives sins and looses people from them. He has not granted this to the priests but has given them the authority to show which people are bound before God and which are loosed. . . . And so the binding and loosing which is given to the priests is nothing other than through God's word to proclaim and to reveal those who are bound or loosed before God.[79]

Bucer's citation of the *Sentences*, like his earlier use of scholastic authority in his Psalms commentary, was somewhat disingenuous. The Lombard clearly tied the first use of the keys to the absolution of the priest in the sacrament of penance. Bucer, on the other hand, linked it to the sacrament of baptism. Although he continued to em-

---

[75]BDS 5:306.3-10.

[76]Ibid., 306.36-307.3.

[77]Ibid., 308.12-25.

[78]*Sentences*, Dist. XVIII, c. 6-7. The first type of binding and loosing, according to Peter Lombard, occurred when priests "judge and display the sins which have been remitted or retained by God." The second occurred when they imposed satisfaction on those who made their confession or admitted those who had performed such satisfaction to the sacrament, while the third type was the imposition of excommunication and the reconciliation of the penitent to the church. Bucer differed from the *Sentences* by replacing the first type of binding and loosing with his own definition, transposing the second and third type, and by defining his third type as the imposition of penance rather than of satisfaction.

[79]BDS 5:304.1-5, 18-20; cf. *Sentences*, Dist. XVIII, c. 5-6.

phasize the preaching of the gospel, as in his earlier discussions of the power of the keys, he now stated that forgiveness of sins occurred when those who had heard the gospel responded to it by confessing their faith and seeking baptism for themselves and for their children. The actual use of the keys occurred not simply when the minister preached the word but when he baptized those who had accepted the word in faith and repentance. This was much different from the Lombard's first use.

Bucer did not devote much space to scholastic argumentation, however. He brought up the disagreement between Thomists and Scotists concerning the role of the keys in mediating forgiveness in the sacrament of penance, but then peremptorily dismissed their theories:

> I see clearly that we hold the keys and the power to retain and forgive sins much higher than you do . . . for we simply stick to the word of the Lord and say whom the church binds on earth must be bound in heaven and whom it looses on earth must be loosed in heaven, not that it is only revealed who should be bound or loosed or who is instrumentally prepared. The words of the Lord are clear and unambiguous.[80]

This clear rejection of scholastic teaching was a corollary of Bucer's identification of the power of the keys with the proclamation of the gospel. Individuals could be assured that their sins had been loosed by the very fact that they had heard and responded to its message, whether through baptism or through reconciliation with the church.

Bucer maintained that "there is only one forgiveness by God and by the church; God forgives through the church."[81] In so doing, he made use of the ministers of the church. Earlier in the book, Bucer had referred to the analogy of the clergy as God's instruments or tools: "all authority, office and ministry of the clergy is from God, and God not only bestows such authority and office as a king installs a governor but must also bring about the use of this authority and ministry and do everything in and through the ministers."[82] Now he applied this analogy to the power of the keys:

> The minister is God's tool, who in this his work cannot move himself; the Lord must work through him. If I say, 'the plane has made the board smooth,' I do not exclude the carpenter through this manner of speaking but rather include him. Our dear God has willed that we remain together

---

[80]BDS 5: 304.29–305.6.

[81]Ibid., 305.8–9. This statement is a direct refutation of the Lombard's position that through absolution the priest displays the divine forgiveness already granted to the repentant sinner, *Sentences*, Dist. XVIII, c. 5–6: "Hoc sane dicere ac sentire possumus, quod solus Deus dimittit peccata et retinet; et tamen Ecclesiae contulit potestatem ligandi et solvendi, sed aliter ipse solvit vel ligat, aliter Ecclesia. Ipse enim per se tantum dimittit peccatum, qui et animam mundat ab interiori macula, et a debito aeternae mortis solvit. . . . Non autem hoc sacerdotibus concessit, quibus tamen tribuit potestatem solvendi et ligandi, id est, ostendendi homines ligatos vel solutos."

[82]BDS 5: 302.15–36.

on earth in such a way and in doing so has highly honored us, that he uses us with each other even to the accomplishment of our salvation.[83]

If the minister actually had the power to forgive or retain sin, the question then arose whether he could abuse this power by loosing the unrepentant or binding the innocent. Bucer stated that in exercising the first type of binding and loosing, such abuse was not possible, since it was the hearers' rejection or acceptance of the gospel preached by the ministers that determined whether they were bound or loosed. The minister was merely the tool that God used to proclaim the gospel.[84] To prevent the misuse of the keys in the second type of binding and loosing, the imposition of excommunication, Bucer stressed that ministers were to ban only those who had knowingly committed those sins explicitly condemned in the Pauline epistles, and then only after the sinner had scorned the admonition of the church. He cited Thomas Aquinas in support of this position.[85]

Discussion of the third type of binding and loosing, the imposition of penance, led to criticism of the Catholic sacrament of penance. Bucer admitted that the Protestants were at fault in not imposing such penance as that practiced in the early church, which itself accorded with the teaching and example of the New Testament. On the other hand, he was just as critical of Catholic practice: "Unfortunately we are lacking much in true discipline and obedience to the church, but we cannot establish anything good with such imposition of penance as you use, and you [accomplish] just as little when you impose a few 'our Fathers,' fasts and other things that accord little with Christian faith, and then lift [these same penances] for money."[86] Bucer had nothing but scorn for such penances:

> We can never justify that for each and every sin that one is forced to confess, even the secret sins, a certain penance is imposed such as fasting, praying, entering a monastery and so on, as one still finds in the Penitentials—that some should spend their entire lives, some seven years, others more or fewer years in special fasts and other [practices]. . . . Through these practices many people are scared away from genuine repentance, others are taught to rely on their own works, and since only rarely can one live according to such severity, the practice gradually developed that

---

[83]Ibid., 305.8-15. The analogy was used by Thomas Aquinas, who himself took it from Pseudo-Dionysius; *Sum. Theol. Supp.*, q. 18 a. 4, Resp.; cf. Bucer's *Defensio*, C6r: "Thomas sane inter Scholasticos facile princeps, scribit Ecclesiae ministrum usu clavium agere ut instrumentum, quod efficaciter nihil praestare potest, nisi quatenus motum est a principali agente. Ad quod comprobandum adducit D. Dionysium in fine Ecclesiasticae Hierarchiae confirmantem, sacerdotes uti oportere virtutibus hierarchicis, quomodo eos divinitas moverit."

[84]BDS 5:305.33-306.33.

[85]BDS 307.5-15, 17-22; *Sum. Theol. Supp.*, q. 21 a. 3 Resp.

[86]BDS 5: 308.32-309.2.

people were allowed to use money to replace the penance imposed, which is the origin of indulgences.[87]

Bucer also condemned mandatory auricular confession. The church fathers had required confession only as part of public penance, and private confession had remained voluntary until the time of Innocent III. Confession itself was useful when it sprang from genuine repentance and when it was made to a confessor able to give consolation and counsel, but it could not be compelled.[88] Likewise, he rejected the scholastic position that God accepted human works as sufficient and that the *opera supererogationis* could be used as satisfaction for sin. The doctrines of a papal treasury of merit, indulgences, the "states of perfection," and of purgatory had all developed from scholastic teaching and led to many abominable practices in the church.[89]

On the other hand, Bucer endorsed the term "satisfaction" when it was interpreted according to patristic rather than scholastic usage: it was "the penance imposed through which one satisfies the church, not at all with the idea that through it one can repay or compensate God for what good we have omitted and what evil we have committed through sin, but rather so that the people will be kept from future sin."[90] Satisfaction also helped the church in that through it, sinners proved their genuine contrition for sin. In upholding the value of works of satisfaction, Bucer drew a line at the point where the works themselves were seen as meritorious. God allowed us to do penance for our sins and accepted the penance as satisfaction, but we could never

---

[87]BDS 310.3-14; cf. *Defensio*, C7v: "Sed ubi vigilantia et studium Episcoporum refrixit, caeperunt condi leges: et praescribi quantum cuique pro quolibet peccato indici ieiuniorum, vigiliarum, precum et eleemosynarum deberet. . . . Ubi vero iam ista se veritas puniendi delinquentes in ecclesia, in literis potius quam in hominum observatione locum haberet, inventa statim ratio est, eleemosynis et recitatione psalmorum ieiunia redimendi. Hinc ortae indulgentiae sunt, condonationes illae Pontificiae. . . . Hoc inventum tam recens est, ut Magister Sententiarum nihil de eo meminerit. . . . Huic manifestae poenitentiae eversioni, et totius disciplinae ecclesiasticae abolitioni, certe non assentimur."

[88]BDS 5:347.16-23; 348.7-10.

[89]BDS 345.7-20.

[90]BDS 346.8-13; cf. *Defensio*, C77r-C77v: "Habet et Ecclesia suam vindictam scelerum, suas quoque de peccantibus sumit poenas, non quidem ut ijs quod peccatum est, aboleant, id enim solo sanguine Christi confit: sed ut eorum seria poenitentia emendent et instaurent, quos peccantium flagitia corruperant et offenderant, tum eos ipsos sic humiliatos, cautiores reddant in posterum. . . . Eiusmodi vero vindictam in eos veri olim Episcopi exercebant, qui vel flagitijs suis Ecclesiam palam contaminassent; vel acti vera eorum, quae clam admisissent poenitudine, ipsi se castigationi Ecclesiasticae ultronea confessione obtulissent. Ea vero castigatio constabat ieiunijs, vigilijs, accubationibus in terra, eleemosynis, precibus, et caeteris cum carnis castigationibus, tum pietatis exercitijs. His dicebantur homines satisfacere pro peccatis, non quod eo pacto compensare possent, id quod peccassent: sed quod eiusmodi solidae poenitentiae attestatione, Ecclesiam rursus aedificarent, quam suis improbe admissis, laeserant: tum etiam petulantiam carnis suae ea ratione retundebant. Inde ea satisfactio a D. Augustino definiebatur, esse peccatorum causas excindere, et eorum suggestionibus aditum non indulgere." Bucer also cited this definition of satisfaction in the *Furbereytung*, where he was more cautious about attributing it to Augustine. The definition is taken from *De dogmatis ecclesiasticis*, attributed to Augustine but actually written by Gennadius of Marseilles; MSL 42:1218, cap. XXIV.

do more good than we were obligated to do. Sinners were to pray for forgiveness and strength to avoid the sin in the future; they were also to fast, humble themselves, and do all that was a part of true repentance. But in all this, every consolation of forgiveness had to be based on God's grace and Christ's merit.[91]

Many of Bucer's statements are familiar from his earlier works. There is the same stress on the voluntary nature of confession and the identification of the keys to heaven with the word of God. In *Furbereytung zum Concilio*, however, his discussion of these issues was much more detailed. In particular he had expanded the power of the keys from the simple preaching of the gospel into the authority to regulate membership in the visible, institutional church through preaching and baptism, excommunication and reconciliation, church discipline and the imposition of penance. He had moved away from his earlier, more spiritualized view of the power of the keys and had enlarged on the role and authority of the minister in exercising that power. In the *Tetrapolitan Confession* he had upheld the minister's responsibility in exercising the keys, but he was now much more explicit in linking the power of the keys with the ministry, while at the same time emphasizing that the ministers had this authority only as instruments which God used to accomplish his will. By expanding the definition of the power of the keys to include public penance, excommunication, and reconciliation with the church, Bucer tied them more closely to the institutional structure of the visible church and its ministry. The keys were the justification for the disciplinary authority of the minister.

Bucer avoided as much as possible any discussion of the value of priestly absolution as an aspect of the power of the keys, since this was an issue on which the differences with Catholic theologians could not easily be resolved. Likewise he said very little about the value of private confession for individual instruction and consolation or the role of the minister as counselor in comparison to his earlier works. Bucer used Scripture, patristic works, and the example of the early church to support his understanding of the power of the keys and of penitential discipline. He was also willing to cite later scholastic theologians, although he did this to appeal to Catholic readers rather than because he accepted their authority.

Bucer's goal in both *Furbereytung* and *Defensio* was to persuade Catholic readers that the evangelical church was fully orthodox and had not "impiously introduced innovations in doctrine and ceremonies."[92] In contrast, his books addressed to the

---

[91] BDS 5: 346.16–347.4; cf. *Defensio*, C8r: "Eam autem agnoscimus esse Domini in suos dignationem, ut hi veris animi planctibus et carnis suae castigationibus, sanctis precibus, eleemosinis, et id genus alijs religiosis actionibus, eluere valeant, quae cum ipsi, tum pro quibus ad dominum intercedunt, mala meriti sunt. . . . Omnem tamen hanc vim vel propria vel aliena peccata per opera poenitentiae eluendi, sola niti misericordia domini, et merito Christi, ut credimus, ita testamur."

[92] *Defensio*, B1r: "ostendamque nos etiamnum cum omnibus Christo viventibus esse per omnia coniunctos, obedientiae Ecclesiasticae nulla in re nos subduxisse, nihil in dogmatis vel ritibus impie novasse: exceptoque eo solo, quod proh dolor non severiter satis et studiose vitam nostram iussis Dei conformem exhibemus, in nullo nos ab institutis Christi et Ecclesiae deflectere."

Münster Anabaptists dealt with the charge that the evangelical church had not gone far enough in its reforms. Bucer was especially sensitive to Anabaptist criticism that the magisterial church had no requirement for a public profession of faith which would recognize only the most dedicated Christians as members of the church. Already in 1531 he had suggested that the evangelical church introduce a public profession of faith following catechization. At the end of 1533, when he published an open letter to the Münster Anabaptists, entitled *Quid de baptismate . . . sentiendum*, he proposed a public ceremony as part of a larger system of instruction and discipline. He recommended that the ministers choose lay elders to assist them in instruction and discipline, using fraternal admonition and catechization. In addition, if the Münsterites wished to have some form of public profession of faith, they could restore the practice of the early church described by Jerome in which adolescents who had been catechized would profess their faith, after which the bishop would lay his hands on them and confirm them.[93] This ceremony would fulfill the same function as adult baptism in preserving the purity of the church.

A few months later Bucer addressed a second work to the Münster Anabaptists, *Bericht auß der heyligen geschrift*. In *Bericht* Bucer again proposed a confirmation ceremony for those baptized as children. The Münster Anabaptists taught that only those who had renounced "the old Adam, the devil and all the world" and who desired to live for Christ alone should be baptized, and they attributed the decline of the church to its adoption of infant baptism. Infants should be "brought to Christ" for prayer and blessing, since the gospel recorded that Christ had laid his hands on children and blessed them, but this passage could not be used to justify infant baptism.[94] Stating that the imposition of hands itself had sacramental value, Bucer ar-

[93]*Quid de baptismate*, F3a; this excerpt in TAE 2:224.5-17 (no. 4714). Bucer cited Jerome's *Contra Luciferianos*, MPL 23:164, although Jerome says nothing about individuals being instructed in the faith before the bishop's imposition of hands. Bucer was not the first reformer to suggest that confirmation should follow catechetical instruction; Zwingli had made the same suggestion in his *Schlußreden* a decade earlier, Z 2:122.20-123.9. In the Afterword to his Paraphrase of Matthew published in 1522, Erasmus had also proposed that children baptized as infants be instructed in the rudiments of the faith and then brought before the church to renew their baptismal vows publicly. Erasmus, however, never equated the reaffirmation of baptismal vows with the sacrament of confirmation; Payne, *Erasmus*, 171-174, 178-180. On the development of confirmation during the Reformation see Wilhelm Maurer, "Geschichte von Firmung und Konfirmation bis zum Ausgang der lutherischen Orthodoxie," in *Confirmatio. Forschungen zur Geschichte und Praxis der Konfirmation*, ed. Kurt Frör (Munich: Evangelisches Pressverband, 1959), 9-38; idem, *Gemeindezucht*, 44-53; Hareide, *Konfirmation*, 62-73; on the catechumenate in the early church, cf. Georg Kretschmar, "Konfirmation und Katechumenat im neuen Testament und in der alten Kirche," in *Zur Geschichte und Ordnung der Konfirmation in den lutherischen Kirchen*, ed. Kurt Frör (Munich: Claudius, 1962), 22-25. For a more detailed discussion of the Anabaptist influence on Bucer's confirmation ceremony, see Amy Nelson Burnett, "Martin Bucer and the Anabaptist Context of Evangelical Confirmation," *Mennonite Quarterly Review* 68 (1994):95-122.

[94]*Antwort auf den Ratschlag der Theologen zu Marburg*, in Robert Stupperich, ed., *Die Schriften der Münsterischen Täufer und ihrer Gegner*, vol. I: *Die Schriften Bernhard Rothmanns*, Veröffentlichungen der historischen Kommission Westfalens 32 (Münster: Aschendorff, 1970), 134-136; cf. *Bekenntnis von beiden Sakramenten*, ibid., 161-163; 168-169.

gued that the sequence of imposition of hands and baptism advocated by the Anabaptists should be reversed. Both practices symbolized acceptance into the church, but baptism fittingly came first as "the sacrament of rebirth."[95] Baptized children would be raised as Christians, and if they would not obey the church and ignored repeated admonition, they would be banned.[96] Infant baptism would not harm the purity of the church if its ministers were "zealous in teaching, admonishing and rebuking and in banning those who will not listen to the church."[97] If, beyond this, the Anabaptists still felt that a public profession of faith and renunciation of the devil was necessary, Bucer proposed that baptized children be instructed in the Christian faith and then confirmed in accordance with the practice described by Jerome.[98]

Bucer did express reservations about his proposal regarding confirmation, distrusting its emphasis on "the external renunciation and confession of men":

> If so much rests on human confession and renunciation, let us follow the custom of the fathers, and when the children have grown, let them make their profession and lay our hands on those who make this confession, the others will be excluded. But how many would not bring their child to this profession? And how would a person then have the right to exclude someone? Wouldn't the whole crowd claim to be Christian, just like now, when no one wants to apply the seriousness of Christian admonition and excommunication?[99]

In the final analysis, a confirmation ceremony could not guarantee the purity of the visible church; this was possible only through admonition and church discipline. Moreover, only those who had been baptized and thus incorporated into the church were subject to such admonition and discipline. Infant baptism was therefore necessary if children were to be raised to recognize the disciplinary authority of the church.

Bucer also discussed another method of preserving the visible purity of the church, the requirement of a precommunion examination. Theologians at Marburg had advised the Münster pastors to establish this type of examination, but the Anabaptists had rejected their idea as "papistic and unnecessary, where the true church otherwise exists."[100] This exchange prompted Bucer to defend the Marburgers and the practice they recommended. Bucer explained the rationale behind the suggested examination:

> No one on earth teaches that no one should be allowed to the Lord's table anywhere unless he has always first been questioned and examined. There could be some people in the church who are so well known and

---

[95]BDS 5:170.4-12, 20-24; 216.35-217.2, 22-24.
[96]Ibid., 218:27-35.
[97]Ibid., 175.26-30.
[98]Ibid., 175.39-176.9.
[99]Ibid., 217.10-21.
[100]Stupperich, ed., *Schriften*, 1:138.

proven that there is no reason for them to be examined. But we think that the Marburgers have established this law in general for the unlearned, untried crowd, who may truly be much improved where they are individ-ually spoken to and taught about God's ways. For this reason, such a Christian ordinance—which seeks nothing more than Christian instruc-tion of the unlearned, binds no consciences, and ladens no one with a useless burden as a form of tyranny, as happens with papistic confession—should not be mocked as papistic.[101]

Bucer stated that each person should examine himself to see if he was worthy to approach the Lord's Table, but no one could do this properly by himself.[102] For this reason no true Christian could complain about periodically receiving private instruc-tion in the faith from his pastor, "who must render account for his charges to God, who is constant in the practices of divine law and is therefore justly held to be more capable than others to teach and admonish to a Christian life." Bucer gave another reason why the pastor should be preferred above all others for such private instruc-tion, "so that the fellowship of the flock with their shepherd might increase and so that the shepherd of the flock could provide better care and counsel to them."[103]

Bucer's defense of the precommunion examination was based on his firm belief in the value of private instruction and individual counsel. Because he was defending the practices of others, he did not express his own reservations about whether such an examination should be required or merely encouraged. These reservations were more apparent in a letter he wrote to Thomas and Margareta Blarer in July of 1535 in re-sponse to their criticism that his support of the examination in the Bericht enabled the return of "papistic tyranny." Bucer protested that he did not think that those who had not confessed their sins should be kept from the Lord's Table, and at any rate, in the book he had been defending the Marburgers against the Münster "heretics," not argu-ing that such an examination should be required by all churches.[104]

Bucer's suggestions for preserving the purity of the visible church, for individual instruction, and for penitential discipline were first advanced against critics of the evangelical church. With the publication of his catechism in 1534, Bucer brought all of his ideas together in one work intended to teach the essentials of their faith to the inhabitants of Strasbourg, adults as well as children.[105] The catechism interpreted and expanded on the city's official doctrine as stated in the Tetrapolitan Confession

---

[101]BDS 5:255.8-17.

[102]Ibid., 255.18-29.

[103]Ibid., 255.31-256.6.

[104]Schieß 1:718, no. 614 (July 25, 1535).

[105]Ernst-Wilhelm Kohls calls it a "Laiendogmatik," "Martin Bucers Katechismus vom Jahre 1534 und seine Stellung innerhalb der Katechismusgeschichte," Zeitschrift für bayerische Kirchengeschichte 39 (1970):83-94; but as the editor of the catechism observes, the need in Strasbourg for a catechism which faithfully reflected the city's official doctrine as adopted at the synod, as well as later references to the catechism's use, demonstrate that the catechism was intended for children and adolescents as well, BDS 6/III:23-24 n. 39.

and the 16 Articles. Its discussions of the power of the keys and of church discipline are especially significant, given the vagueness of the city's church ordinance on these issues.

The section of the catechism devoted to the power of the keys restated the definition contained in *Furbereytung*, with two modifications. Bucer described the first type of loosing more clearly as admission into the church through baptism, and he stressed that it also applied to infants brought to the church by their parents.[106] This change was obviously aimed at the Anabaptists within Strasbourg. Bucer also combined the second and third types of binding and loosing into one category, "to refuse the fellowship of Christ's kingdom to those who have sinned, been reproved and sufficiently admonished to repentance by the proclamation of God's judgment but who will not repent, and promising the forgiveness of sins for the sake of our Lord Jesus to those who accept this reproof and devote themselves to reform, to absolve them and to re-accept them into favor."[107] According to this description, binding was the excommunication of an unrepentant sinner, while loosing was the absolution of a sinner who had demonstrated the sincerity of his repentance. The summary for younger children included with the 1534 catechism also made the distinction between two uses of the keys, although it did not expressly mention the keys: forgiveness came only through the church of Christ, "firstly, when I was accepted through baptism as a child of God by the church and afterwards, when I am punished for my sins and consoled with forgiveness from God."[108]

Bucer described the procedure for the second type of binding and loosing in great detail, following the pattern of Matthew 18. When a sinner refused to accept admonition he was to be pointed out to the elders of the church—"fearless, right-minded, reasonable, friendly men who above all are able to teach, reprove and admonish." These elders were to bear responsibility for the "Christian flock and are to tend it, that is, to lead it to improvement and to govern it with private teaching, admonition and reproof." Therefore, when someone should be reproved by the whole church, it was only fitting that such reproof be administered by these men.[109]

In a work written especially for the laity, Bucer emphasized the importance of lay participation in the process of admonition and discipline. One should not point out every sin to the elders and thus bring it to the attention of the church, he taught. Rather, where someone saw his brother sinning, he should first go to him in private; he should not bring the sin to the attention of others until he had done everything possible to bring the sinner to repentance. Admonition, whether given alone or with witnesses, was to be continued for as long as there was hope of reform. Moreover these

---

[106]BDS 6/III:84.23–25; 85.11–19.

[107]Ibid., 85.26–86.4.

[108]Ibid., 167.16–19. Bornert points out that this twofold definition of the power of the keys follows the tradition of the early church, which regarded penitential discipline as the "second repentance" which followed the "first repentance" of baptism, *Réforme Protestante*, 391.

[109]BDS 6/III:86.8–19.

admonitions, "because they are works of love, must also be tempered by love," a useful bit of advice intended to ward off overzealous, self-appointed censors.[110]

Only when the sinner obstinately refused to heed all admonition was he to be brought to the attention of the elders as representatives of the church. If the sinner refused to listen to their admonition, then he was "to be held as a heathen and reprobate sinner, as the publicans were regarded by the Jews." One was not to eat, drink, or have any other individual contact with him, so that he would be brought to shame and repentance. Even in this state "the sinner is not to be held as an enemy but still admonished as a brother as long as there is still hope of fruit." The catechism said nothing about the formal imposition or proclamation of the ban, but only that "those who absolutely refuse to listen and become dogs and pigs must be left to go their own way."[111]

Although Bucer accepted the principle that excommunication should include ostracism by the faithful, he took pains to avoid the complete separation advocated by at least some of the Anabaptist groups in Strasbourg. As in the church ordinance published later that year, the sinner was not to be denied any help or contact "which common citizenship or other relationship demands." On the other hand,

> where necessity does not require it, the children of God will have fellowship among themselves in the Lord and withdraw themselves from all those who have withdrawn themselves from Christ and live in a disorderly way. But to those who bear the name of Christ but do not want to obey his word, yet who are not totally wicked, they will always show somewhat more zeal and severity, since they are concerned for them, and they will have more hope for their reformation.[112]

Bucer added that the congregation was to pray for everyone unless assured by God that a person had sinned against the Holy Spirit, that is, that an individual had rejected a precept he knew to be true. But no one should be too quick to make this judgment, "which God does not reveal to everyone."[113] Bucer's solution again revealed his extreme reluctance to take the final step of declaring someone cut off entirely from the church and from all hope of repentance.

Bucer was explicit in stating who should be considered excommunicated: anyone who persisted in something that was manifestly and recognizably wrong and who scorned all admonition of his brothers and of the church. By the two criteria of manifest and recognizable he hoped to prevent the misuse of the ban where there was no sin involved or where the severity of the ban was not called for. In cases of obvious sin, where the sin was known to and offended the entire church, the series of private

---

[110]Ibid., 87.6–20.

[111]Ibid., 87.24–88.11.

[112]Ibid., 88.12–13, 25–89.1.

[113]Ibid., 89.1–5. This point refers to the provision in canon law that forbade prayer for an excommunicated person.

admonitions was dispensed with, and the church was to exercise its disciplinary power immediately. If the sinner repented by accepting the punishment, the church was not obligated to reaccept him immediately, however. God's grace was always to be promised to such a person, but he should be held for a time "in penance and discipline" in order to prove his repentance before he was granted complete reconciliation and readmitted to the Lord's Supper.[114]

Secret sins, on the other hand, were a different matter. These too were bound or loosed by the church, but only through the general preaching of God's judgment to those who persisted in sin and the preaching of forgiveness of sins to those who desired to reform. Where the church did not know of the sin, God had reserved its punishment for himself. A person who had sinned had to confess, since "forgiveness of sins can be promised only to those who desire to reform, which no one can do unless he confesses that he has done wrong and has sinned"; but secret sins need be confessed only to God. A general confession of sin to the church was sufficient for the church's general binding and loosing, since the Lord never commanded an enumeration of sins as occurred in auricular confession.[115]

With this statement the discussion moved more specifically to the issue of confession. Here Bucer summarized his previous statements on confession:

> Whoever has a genuinely stricken conscience and feels his sins, or is somewhat confused and does not know how he stands with God in his deeds but genuinely desires to please him and to serve him wholly, he will be driven to seek consolation and counsel from someone who can console and instruct him individually through God's word; with great desire he will also tell this person everything that makes him so anxious and why he needs advice; and he will much rather seek this from his pastor (*Seelsorger*) in so far as he knows that he is more able to give such consolation and advice and has more heartfelt trust in him, as with his father.[116]

This statement is important both for what it does and does not say. There are elements which have recurred in every discussion of the importance of confession: someone aware of his sins was almost compelled to confess, the confession was sought for the sake of consolation and counsel, and it was made to someone learned in God's word. Significantly, Bucer did not mention private absolution, referring instead to consolation and advice. Bucer preferred to teach his parishioners to rely on the counseling abilities of their pastor rather than on the words of absolution themselves. Although Bucer did not discourage confession to a layman, he felt that the pastor should be the preferred confessor.

Because these individual meetings between pastor and parishioner were voluntary, Bucer had to emphasize their beneficial aspects so that the practice would not

---

[114]Ibid., 89.6–90.4.
[115]Ibid., 90.4–91.1.
[116]Ibid., 91.1–10.

be abandoned completely. St. Paul praised its effectiveness, and each Christian could see for himself how it helped him in Christian deeds. At the same time Bucer warned against a false understanding of such meetings derived from Catholic practice. One did not need to confess all sins and should not put any confidence in one's own work by confessing. Where private confession was still practiced in a Christian way—a reference to the Lutheran precommunion examination—one should not complain about its use. But at the same time, even "more recent teachers" admitted that confession was instituted by the church, not by Christ or the apostles, and for it to be profitable, each person had to be drawn by his own contrition and repentance.[117]

Bucer then put his finger on the central problem of voluntary confession. Because it had to grow out of individual repentance, confession could not be required from everyone, but where it was not required, "one must also admit that considerable scandal has come from a situation where young people have no Christian discipline and individual teaching and admonition." Bucer's recommendation for this evil was to require instruction for the young, followed by a public confirmation ceremony, as was practiced in the early church.[118] Mandatory catechism instruction followed by confirmation thus became the replacement for mandatory confession or a precommunion examination. If Bucer had originally proposed the ceremony to meet the Anabaptists' desire for a public profession of faith, he also saw that it could be used as a way for the pastor to examine each child's understanding of his faith before admitting him to the sacrament for the first time. It would give him at least some control over who could be admitted to the Lord's Supper, thus preventing unworthy reception of the sacrament.

Bucer summarized his views on the power of the keys in the teacher's final exhortation to

> be diligent in attending catechism, the sermons and the sacraments, confess your sins without ceasing to God your Lord, with particular examination of your conscience, and do the same thing in church as often as general confession is made, and also confess to all whom you have offended, above all your parents, godparents and teachers whenever they punish you for doing wrong, and all who teach you self-control, respectability and sanctity and punish you for your transgressions. Above all, beware that you do not scorn any kind of reproof from anyone, whoever he may be. . . . Recognize the keys to the kingdom of heaven whenever someone reproves your sins and teaches you what is good, because although the ministers of the word are also the ministers of the keys, which is nothing other than the dispensing of the word and power of Christ, we are all members of one another and each person should always serve the others for edification in the Christian life.[119]

---

[117]Ibid., 91.14–92.6.
[118]Ibid., 92.6–20.
[119]Ibid., 92.22–93.15.

Bucer wished to impress on his readers the importance of mutual admonition and of submission to such admonition when it was given, the necessity of a sincere confession made to God and, where relevant, to any person affected by the sin, and respect for all those in authority. This is a far cry from the view on confession and the power of the keys which Luther had expressed in both his large and small catechisms, where the desire to confess and to receive absolution was the overriding theme. For Luther the consolation which came through absolution overshadowed all other reasons for meeting with the minister.[120] Bucer's catechism, on the other hand, emphasized the pedagogical value of confession—in it the Christian was taught from God's word by someone who was of sound moral character. Bucer saw confession as an opportunity to increase the trust and communication between pastor and parishioner. As he said, "truly, between the sheep of Christ and their shepherd, between the household of the Lord and the steward there should be much more fellowship in the things of Christ."[121] In essence Bucer stated the same view of confession's constructive side as he did in his first extended discussion of it in the Gospels commentary of 1527, and he argued just as strongly for the fact that it must remain voluntary, because repentance could not be compelled.

Bucer's statements in his catechism concerning fraternal admonition, excommunication, and ostracism, and mandatory catechization followed by public confirmation complement the Strasbourg church ordinance which was finally adopted and published at the end of 1534. The *Kirchenpfleger* could be identified with the elders described in the catechism, and the ordinance urged attendance at catechism instruction, although it stopped short of requiring it. With its statement that unrepentant sinners be "handed over to divine judgment" and its provisions regarding the degree of social ostracism, the ordinance recognized a limited and private form of excommunication, as outlined in the catechism. On the other hand, there was no mention of penitential discipline or a public confirmation ceremony. The church ordinance provided a broad framework for religious instruction and the exercise of church discipline. Within this framework the clergy worked to internalize the doctrinal and behavioral standards set forth in the catechism. Because the ministers had no coercive authority, they had to rely on the voluntary cooperation and submission of the laity. For this reason Bucer tried to encourage closer relations between pastor and parishioner and among the lay members of the church for the purpose of admonition and instruction.

In 1534 Bucer was still optimistic about the laity's willingness to cooperate with the pastors and to submit to their instruction and moral oversight. By virtue of their baptism, all of Strasbourg's inhabitants were members of the city's church; they were therefore all subject to the discipline of the church. In Bucer's opinion, this meant that they would all be taught the fundamentals of their faith, admonished when they

---

[120]Cf. "Ein kurze Vermahnung zu der Beicht," *Grosser Katechismus*, BSLK, esp. 729–732.

[121]BDS 6/III:91.17–20.

sinned, and disciplined to the extent that they refused to heed admonition. Religious instruction and admonition were therefore the most essential part of discipline, and the severe measure of excommunication was to be used only when the individual refused to acknowledge his sin and change his ways. In addition, a confirmation ceremony might be useful so that individuals would have a chance to profess their faith publicly. All Christians were to encourage one another, and the *Kirchenpfleger*, identified as elders of the church, were to assist the pastors in their responsibilities of oversight. The magistrate was to see that contumacious sinners and all who rejected the word of God did not harm the rest of the congregation or interfere with the ministers' task of building up the church. These remained the basic components of Bucer's programme of discipline.

But over the next few years, Bucer's optimism about the laity's acceptance of this programme began to fade. As a result, he modified his disciplinary system, placing more emphasis on the responsibility of the ministers and lay elders for instruction, admonition, and discipline. He derived the disciplinary authority of the ministers more explicitly from the power of the keys and expanded his definition of that power to emphasize its disciplinary function. Confirmation took on a new significance and became a key element of his comprehensive system of religious instruction, pastoral oversight, and church discipline. He now argued that this system was commanded by God's word and therefore absolutely essential for the well-being of the church. These elements emerge clearly in Bucer's works from the second half of the 1530s.

4

The Power of the Keys, Christian Discipline, and "True Pastoral Care," 1535-1538

During the later 1530s Bucer expressed his understanding of the power and use of the keys in three important works. In 1536 he published a third edition of his Gospels commentary, which contained significant modifications to his discussions of the power of the keys, absolution, and church discipline. Two years later he wrote his masterwork of pastoral theology, *Von der waren Seelsorge,* and at the end of 1538 he drafted a disciplinary ordinance for the Hessian church. The Gospels commentary, the pastoral treatise, and the disciplinary ordinance provide a basis for understanding the reformer's mature thought but, as with Bucer's earlier works, they cannot be divorced from the context in which Bucer wrote them. The Gospels commentary was published a few months after the signing of the Wittenberg Concord and reflected Bucer's new rapport with the Lutherans. He wrote *Von der waren Seelsorge* to convince his fellow Strasbourgers that discipline was necessary for the spiritual well-being of both the church and the individual Christian. The disciplinary ordinance was meant to win back to the Hessian church the many Anabaptists who criticized it for its neglect of church discipline. Each of these developments—Bucer's concord with the Lutherans, his experiences as a pastor of the Strasbourg church, and his appeals to the Hessian Anabaptists—contributed to the further elaboration of his understanding of absolution, discipline, and the power of the keys.

I. The Wittenberg Concord and its Consequences

The Wittenberg Concord was drafted at a meeting of South German theologians, led by Bucer, with Luther and his associates at Wittenberg in May 1536.[1] Although the Concord was primarily concerned with the interpretation of the Lord's Supper, it also contained a paragraph on the importance of private absolution. In the meetings which preceded the drafting of the Concord, Luther had brought up the disagreement over absolution and expressed his concern that the church have some

---

[1] For a description and evaluation of the events leading up to and ending with the Concord, see Bizer, *Studien,* 96-130; Köhler, *Zwingli und Luther* 2:432-455; Eells, *Martin Bucer,* 190-204; Greschat, *Martin Bucer,* 146-149.

means of instructing "the young and the unlearned" privately, of applying the consolation of the gospel individually, and of excommunicating those who taught or lived in a way opposed to God's word. As spokesman for the South Germans, Bucer acknowledged the value of private meetings between pastor and parishioner for admonition and instruction, but he held that such meetings had to remain voluntary, since they were not expressly commanded by Scripture. The sermons and the general absolution pronounced in public worship served to instruct and console the hearers, and the South Germans had established regular catechetical instruction for children. They recognized the need for private instruction and admonition but cited the difficulties they encountered from people "who, as soon as anyone speaks of such things, cry that we want to reintroduce confession and papal tyranny." Bucer stated that many cities had taken measures to punish vice, and he assured Luther, "we would not allow anyone to participate in the sacraments whom we know to live in sin and impenitence."[2]

Bucer's presentation satisfied Luther, and the two sides agreed on a carefully worded statement concerning absolution. The article used the term "absolution" equivocally to mean not only the words of forgiveness spoken by the pastor but also the entire *colloquium*, or meeting, between pastor and parishioner. It asserted that private absolution was to be retained in the church, since it provided opportunity for both consolation and private instruction, "for such a *colloquium* and examination is necessary for the unlearned." It then condemned the enumeration of sins required in auricular confession but stated that "the *colloquium* should be preserved on account of absolution and the institution of Christ."[3] The article could thus be interpreted to support the pedagogical and psychological function of the colloquium which Bucer emphasized as well as the objective effect of private absolution upheld by the Lutherans: the sinner believed he was forgiven not just because he heard the words of absolution but because through talking with the pastor he had come to understand more clearly the gospel of forgiveness of sins.

During the meetings at Wittenberg, Bucer had promised Luther that he would publicly retract his earlier criticisms of the Lutheran understanding of the Lord's Supper.[4] These retractions, along with several other important modifications, were incorporated into the third edition of Bucer's Gospels commentary. Bucer defended these changes in a dedicatory letter addressed to Edward Fox, the bishop of Hereford. He anticipated criticism because of the stronger connection he now made between the external elements of the sacraments and their internal, spiritual effects. Significantly, in describing his understanding of the sacraments, Bucer discussed not only baptism and the Lord's Supper but also absolution. He stated that his earlier writings on the sacraments had been written to counter the belief that the sacraments could transmit

[2]BDS 6/I:158.4–160.3.
[3]Ibid., 132.14–20 (Latin), 133.16–25 (German). The Latin version omits the phrase "of Christ."
[4]Ibid., 145.10–146.20.

salvation apart from true faith, for he feared that "too much of that which is Christ's is attributed to the external actions of the ministers."[5] These fears had been allayed as he had better come to understand that Luther and his followers not only attributed all salvation to faith in Christ, but that they also taught

> that by living faith we embrace [this salvation] offered and exhibited through the holy ministry of the church in words and symbols which the Lord instituted for this purpose: nor do they doubt that our Lord Jesus Christ is present for us in his church and that he himself forgives sins in heaven when the church by his order and through his ministry forgives sins on earth; that he truly washes away sins and regenerates those to whom it imparts baptism, which is a washing of regeneration, and that it truly gives his body and blood, that is himself, the true communion of his body and blood, when it dispenses the holy Eucharist. They also recognize this depends solely on the institution, virtue and work of the Lord, and not on the merit of any man, and that this is always presented whole, that is, not only by words or symbols, but together with the thing itself, and the gifts of God, which the words promise—that is, with absolution, the remission of sins, with baptism, regeneration and incorporation into Christ, and in the Eucharist the true body and blood of the Lord.[6]

With regard to the commentary as a whole, Bucer repeated the assertion he had made in his *Defensio*, that just as his views "rely on the word of God itself, so they differ very little from [those of] the orthodox fathers and from both the doctrine and practices taught long ago in the catholic church."[7] He acknowledged that "the authority of God" should always come first in matters of religion. But God had chosen to act through the saints of every generation, and it was therefore proper for Christians to heed

> those through whom he had ever spoken or acted, or today speaks and acts, and especially those speaking and acting through his church, that is

---

[5]1536 Gospels, fol. *4r: "Semper enim verebar ne externis rursus actionibus ministrorum id tribueretur, quod Christi est."

[6]Ibid., fol. *4v: "Per S. ministerium Ecclesiae in verbis, et symbolis quae ad id dominus instituit, oblatam et exhibitam, viva fide amplectimur: nec dubitant, Dominum nostrum Iesum Christum in Ecclesia sua nobis praesentem, ipsumque peccata remittere in coelis, dum Ecclesia eius iussu, et ministerio peccata remittit in terra: peccatis vere abluere et regignere, quibus illa baptisma, quod nimirum lavacrum regenerationis est, impertit, vere suum corpus, et sanguinem, hoc est, se ipsum nobis tradere, veram corporis, et sanguinis sui communionem, dum illa sacram dispensat Eucharistiam: denique agnoscunt haec sola domini institutione, virtute ac opere, et nullius hominis merito niti, eoque in Ecclesia semper praestari integra, hoc est, non verba modo, aut symbola, sed simul rem ipsam, et dona Dei, quae verba pollicentur, Absolutione, scilicet, remissionem peccatorum, baptismate regenerationem, et in Christum incorporationem, in Eucharistia ipsum verum Domini corpus, et sanguinem."

[7]Ibid., fol. *2r: "Nam in ea cuncta, quoad eius fieri potuit, sic exponere atque confirmare, maxime de quibus est hoc seculo aliquid controversiae, operam dedi, ut facile quivis cernat, ea sicut niti ipso verbo Dei, ita minime quoque dissidere ab orthodoxis patribus, et receptis pridem in Ecclesia catholica, cum dogmatis, tum institutis."

the consensus of all the saints, especially when it has lasted for so long. If nothing that is proposed in the name of God should be rejected, even if proposed recently by some individual, how much less should that be repudiated rashly which holy antiquity and the public consensus of believers through so many centuries commends to us?[8]

One example of this "rash repudiation," according to Bucer, was the rejection of "what they have handed on to us in the name of Christ before we have actually examined it and are convinced that it has nothing from the Spirit of Christ."[9]

Bucer maintained that his respect for patristic authority could not be interpreted as an attempt to restore "papal tyranny and superstition." He revered "the first, most holy fathers . . . because Christ lived, taught and wrote in them," but he sharply condemned the clerical hierarchy of the Roman church. He had no intention of restoring the "impiety and violence of the pseudo-bishops" but wished only to defer to "the ancient, truly holy fathers and pastors of the church in their holy writings and practices."[10]

Bucer's new appreciation of absolution, his increased emphasis on the ministry, and his greater respect for the example of the early church all left their mark on his discussion of Matthew 16 and the power of the keys. The new section was four times as long as that in the 1530 Gospels. Bucer not only added new material but also replaced large sections of the earlier passage, so that the 1536 edition differed markedly from its predecessor. The difference between the two editions is clear in the first few sentences. Whereas previously Bucer had defined the keys to the kingdom of heaven simply as the word of God, he now identified the keys with "the duty and power of administering the church of God, the republic of Christ, from the word of God."

Bucer went on to state more specifically what this power entailed:

---

[8]Ibid., fol. *2v: "In omni causa religionis solius Dei autoritatem valere debere, unamque hanc respiciendam esse. Verum dum sua placita Deus per cuncta filij sui membra profert, per sanctos omnium seculorum, agit siquidem spiritus Christi in omnibus membris Christi, huic spiritui Christi merito auscultamus, nostraque omnia accommodamus, per quoscumque ille unquam locutus est et egit, aut hodie loquitur, et agit, maxime vero loquenti, et agenti per ipsam Ecclesiam suam, hoc est, consensum sanctorum omnium, eumque tam diuturnum. Si enim nihil temere reijciendum est, quod Dei nomine offert, etiamsi id privatus aliquis et nuper adeo prodiens offerat, multo minus id repudiandum temere est, quod nobis commendat sancta vetustas et publicus credentium per tot secula consensus."

[9]Ibid., "Nihil volo recipi ideo, quia ipsi ita senserunt, docuerunt aut observaverunt: hoc autem gratiae Christi, quae in eis alias tam praeclare eluxit, dandum puto, ne quid eorum, quae illi nobis Christi nomine tradiderunt, repudiemus temere, hoc est, antequam certo exploraverimus et compertum iam habeamus id non esse a Christi spiritu profectum."

[10]Ibid., fol. *3r: "Eoque sicut priscos illos sanctiss. Patres summo in pretio habendos, et ijs quae vel docuerunt, vel observarunt singularem reverentiam deferendam iudico, quia Christus in eis vixit, docuit, et scripsit . . . me adhuc gratia Christi multum ab eo abesse, ut ulla in re connivendum modo putem impietati et violentiae pseudoepiscoporum, ne dum concedendum, aut ullam superstitionem revocandam, quamlibet multum deferendum censeam priscis illis vere sanctis Ecclesiarum patribus et pastoribus, sanctisque eorum cum scriptis, tum observationibus."

First, to receive into the church, with their sins forgiven and given the salvation of Christ, all who profess their faith in the gospel or who are offered to the church by believers. Second, to establish and govern these people so that they apply themselves wholly to the goal of this republic, that is, to live for the glory of God and the salvation of their neighbors, and by continually increasing in repentance and advancing in newness of life. To this latter task belong teaching, exhortation, admonition, correction, rebuke, punishment, the practice of prayer, the use of the sacraments, and the entire administration of the pastoral office. Beyond this, if any in the church do not wish to obey these holy admonitions and to live by the laws of this republic which require the penitential yoke—that is, the perpetual renewal of life pleasing to God—and if anyone commits that which openly opposes God's offshoots, it is part of this power to eject such a person from the republic of Christ and to exclude him from the communion of Christ and the saints. . . . In addition, it belongs to this power to forgive sins and to admit back into the church those who have been expelled and ejected from it due to their sin and their contempt for holy admonition and reproof, but afterwards have come to themselves and profess true repentance for their impiety, seek pardon for their sin and humbly ask to be readmitted into the flock of the Lord. Finally, it pertains to this power to designate public ministers of the church, doctors, pastors, governors and deacons, that is, dispensers of public alms and of whatever the republic of Christ needs to be most suitably and properly established and to promote the glory of Christ.[11]

This lengthy definition was much broader than what Bucer had written about the keys in his earlier works. There was now a marked jurisdictional emphasis not

---

[11]Ibid., 353B-354C: "At regnum coelorum, Ecclesia Christi est: claves igitur istae, id erunt quo Ecclesia Christ aliis clauditur, aliis aperitur. Id autem quid aliud est, quam munus et potestas administrandi Ecclesiam Dei, rempublicam Christi, ex verbo Dei. Cuius potestatis est primum in Ecclesiam recipere, condonatis peccatis et salute Christi addicta, omnes qui profitentur se Evangelio credere, aut offeruntur Ecclesiae Christi per credentes. Deinde in Ecclesia eosdem instituere et regere, ut ad finem qui est huic reipublicae, nempe, vivere in gloriam Dei et salutem proximorum, sese totos accommodent, hoc est, continuo magis resipiscant, et in novitate vitae promoveant. Ad id pertinet doctrina, exhortatio, monitio, correctio, increpatio, castigatio, precum usus, sacramentorum exhibitio, et tota officii pastoralis administratio. Praeterea si qui in Ecclesia sanctis monitionibus nolint parere, hoc est, legibus reipublicae huius non vivere, quae poscunt iugem poenitentiam, hoc est, vitae ad placita Dei perpetuam innovationem, et admittat quae aperte cum plantis Dei pugnent, potestatis huius est, talem rempublicam Christi eiicere, et communione Christi atque sanctorum excludere. . . . Ultra haec eiusdem potestatis est peccata condonare, et in Ecclesiam rursus admittere eos, qui eiecti Ecclesia fuerint ob peccata sua, et contemptum sanctae admonitionis atque correptionis: postea autem ad se revertuntur, veramque poenitudinem suae impietatis professi, veniam scelerum orant, et recipi rursus in gregem Domini suppliciter deposcunt. Postremo ad hanc potestatem attinet constituere publicos Ecclesiae ministros, doctores, pastores, gubernatores, diaconos, id est, dispensatores publicae eleemosynae, et quibuscunque opus est ad rempublicam Christi, quam commodissime et decentissime instituendam, et gloriam Christi provehendam."

present in the earlier editions of the commentary. Bucer emphasized this jurisdictional aspect of the keys by continuing his description of the church as the republic
of Christ. Just as in ancient Rome, where power belonged ultimately to the people
but the authority to exercise it belonged to the senate, so also in the church the power
of the keys was given to all, but the authority to use it belonged to the "presbyters and
bishops"—a direct denial of the Catholic claim that the keys were given to St. Peter
and his successors. Bucer cited John 20:22–23, where the Holy Spirit was given to
all the apostles, to make this point, and he argued that because the Holy Spirit and
the power of the keys were given at the same time, the latter could never be exercised
unless it was used in accordance with the Spirit.[12] Christ used the metaphor of the
keys, which signified the authority to admit or exclude, to signify the supreme power
in the church, the pastoral office. The most important function of this office, Bucer
stated, was "to grant the communion of Christ or to exclude from it, to accept into
the number of penitents to whom Christ comes as savior, or to keep them away from
it. Just as the first responsibility of public authority is to grant or deny citizenship."[13]

Here Bucer ended the first major change to his earlier discussion and took up
the question of papal primacy. In the last section of this passage, however, he returned to the question of confession and absolution, replacing the short paragraph
from 1530 with a full-page discussion of binding and loosing. In the earlier edition
he had stated bluntly that this passage "does not refer to that illusory absolution
which is made to those who confess," but rather to the preaching of pardon to those
who had faith and of condemnation to those who rejected Christ.[14] Now he avoided
any criticism of private absolution and vented his wrath instead on the Catholic requirement that each and every sin must be confessed to a priest. "Those who wish to
follow Scripture and the practices of the early church," he stated, "will admit that every loosing of sin done to adults requires a confession of sins; not, however, a list of

---

[12]Ibid., 354C: "Haec potestas penes Ecclesiam omnem est, autoritas modo ministerii
penes presbyteros et episcopos, ita ut Romae olim potestas populi fuit, autoritas senatus,
princeps potestatis huius, ut totius huius reipublicae Christus est, administri eius, qui eam ex
spiritu et verbo Christi administrant. . . . Ex quo liquet hanc potestatem omnem in Ecclesia
non nisi spiritu Christi rite geri posse."

[13]Ibid., 354D–355A: "Porro ista metaphora clavis, inde assumpta est, quod suprema
domus potestas, sicut et urbis penes cum est, cuius est suprema potestas clavium, hoc est,
cuius imperii est intromittere in aedes vel urbem, excludere aedibus vel urbe, quos vult. . . .
Clavium itaque nomine Dominus supremam potestatem intellexit in Ecclesia, munus pasto-
rale, illamque ab ea sui parte potissimum proposuit, qua peccata retinentur, et remittuntur,
qua homines vel vinciuntur reatu peccatorum, vel eo solvuntur. Quia primum in republica
Christi est, et praecipua portio muneris pastoralis, communionem Christi donare, vel ea excludere, in numerum poenitentium, quibus Christus servator venit, assumere, vel ab eo
arcere. Sicut primum est potestatis publicae, civitate donare, vel privare."

[14]1530 Gospels, 139B: "Etenim nequaquam hic de Absolutione illa, qua illusum confitentibus fuit, sed de praedicatione cum veniae poentitentibus et Christo credentibus fienda,
tum iudicii et condemnationis comminatione, qua impoenitentes et Christum reiicientes, ab
Ecclesia Christi repelli debent, hic agitur."

individual sins but rather acknowledgment that they are sin."[15] To support this claim, he described the penitential discipline of the early church more fully:

> Those who were bound again after having been loosed of sin through baptism were those who either had offended the church by their manifest sin or who did not want to heed the church calling them away from sin. These the ministers of the church and the holy senate bind with the guilt of their sins in the name and power of Christ and assign divine punishment, more severely for those whom they eject from the church, who have obstinately refused to listen to it, more gently for those who refrain from holy communion for a time until they have satisfied the church concerning their repentance by their attestation of true repentance. But neither of these can again be loosed without *exhomologesis*, that is, without public acknowledgment and confession of their sin.[16]

Bucer warned his readers that binding and loosing should not be done too quickly. No one could be loosed who had not first been bound, nor could those bound because of manifest sin or contumacy be loosed unless they had confessed that they had sinned. The church had no power to bind or loose secret sins except through the general absolution given daily to all penitents without private confession. The power of the church to forgive sins was a great consolation to the pious, he stated, but it was impossible to prescribe a never-fail method of confessing one's sins. Therefore, rather than requiring confession, Bucer advocated instead that people should be taught the law of God and true Christian behavior and be aroused to true repentance. With this in mind he recommended private catechization, following the example of the early church, "for what has been taught privately is more likely to move people's hearts." This private instruction, along with anything else which helped to build up the church, was a part of the power of the keys.[17]

---

[15]1536 Gospels, 359B–360A: "Etenim ex eo, quod hic Ecclesiae potestas tradita est ligandi et solvendi, effici id non potest, necesse esse ut homines quibuscunque peccatis nexi sunt, ea privatim sacerdoti exponant. . . . Qui ergo sequi volent scripturam, et observationem Ecclesiae veteris, ij fatebuntur ad omnem quidem solutionem peccatorum, quae adultis fiat, requiri confessionem peccatorum, eam autem non esse singulorum erratorum enarrationem, sed quod errata sint, agnitionem."

[16]Ibid., 360C: "Qui soluti peccatis baptismate iterum ligabantur, ij erant, qui aut manifesto flagitio vel scelere Ecclesiam offendissent, aut noluissent Ecclesiam audire a peccatis revocantem. Hos enim ministri Ecclesiae, et sacer senatus regni Christi nomine et potestate, quae totius Ecclesiae est, reatu peccatorum obstringebant, et divinae ultioni addicebant: gravius quidem illos, quos prorsus Ecclesia eijciebant, qui, scilicet, obstinate eam audire detractabant: mitius illos, quos ad tempus modo a sacra communione abstinebant, dum de sua poenitentia Ecclesiae verae poenitentiae attestatione satisfecissent. Neutri vero poterant iterum solvi sine exhomologesi, id est, sine publica agnitione et confessione peccati sui."

[17]Ibid., 360D: "Ligare et retinere peccata non temere praecedit. Nemo siquidem solvi potest non antea ligatus. . . . Inde ubi vera est Ecclesiae oeconomia, ligantur rursus qui in Ecclesia cum sunt, gravioribus flagitijs et sceleribus Ecclesiam offendunt, vel moniti etiam de mediocribus Ecclesiam contemnunt. Hi non, nisi profitentes poenitentiam, solvi possunt, ut ergo confiteantur se peccasse, ut ipsi se coram Ecclesia condemnent requiritur. Qui peccant

Bucer's new definition of the power of the keys and his increased respect for the authority of the church fathers also resulted in a revision of his interpretation of Matt. 8:4, Christ's healing of the ten lepers. In 1527 and 1530 he denied that the passage supported the practice of auricular confession. He now rejected the necessity of auricular confession, but not confession itself. He added that one should learn from the passage to value the ministry of the church, with its power to bind and loose. Bucer's new interpretation stemmed from his awareness of the passage's use by the church fathers, as becomes clear from his argument that it did not justify the enumeration of sins to a priest, "nor did any of the holy fathers derive that from this passage, when they piously and firmly taught about the discipline of the church, the confession of sins and the benefit of loosing, which is voluntarily accepted out of true repentance."[18] His new interpretation of the text took account of patristic authority on the issue of binding and loosing, particularly when he could use it to support his own position on church discipline.

In his discussion of confession, Bucer held the same views expressed six years earlier in the second edition of the commentary. He made many stylistic improvements to his discussion but only two changes of substance, both of which were linked to the ideas expressed in his passage on the power of the keys. Where previously he had condemned the requirement to confess to a specific person (one's parish priest) along with other aspects of Catholic confession, he now encouraged Christians to confess to "one who has the public duties of preaching the gospel and consoling consciences, such as bishops and pastors who properly perform their function."[19] And instead of criticizing the Lutherans for attributing too much value to private absolution as in the 1530 edition (a view which itself replaced the flat rejection of private

---

occulte, ut Ecclesia inde non offenditur, ita nec ligare tales Ecclesia potest, sique non ligat, neque solvere potest, nisi generali illa solutione quam quotidie affert in Ecclesia omnibus poenitentibus. . . . At quia maxime pijs solatio est haec in Ecclesia potestas remittendi peccata, eam requirunt magno desiderio omnes verae adflictae conscientiae, indeque ultro fatentur et indicant sua peccata, quantum huius ad id satis fuerit ut consolentur et erudiantur. Certam rationem vel enumerandi peccata, vel se illorum accusandi, nemo salubriter praescribet, sicut nec uspiam praescripta est. Urgenda est Lex Dei, inculcanda mors Christi, hincque excitanda vera vivaque resipiscentia. . . . Perutile autem esset, et ad exemplum priscae Ecclesiae, privatos quoque catechismos instituere. Quae nanque privatim traduntur, plus movere solent: possunt etiam ad captum hominum melius attemperari. . . . Haec et quaecunque ullo modo ad aedificationem facere possunt, in potestate clavium regni coelorum insunt."

[18]Ibid., 212D: "Explosi pridem sunt, quic hoc Christi dicto, necessitatem confessionis secretariae fundare conati sunt. . . . Id quidem ex hoc loco recte colligitur, ministerium Ecclesiae magni faciendum esse, et per id ligari, atque solvi oportere, qui sint in coelis ligati solutique habendi. Hoc enim Dominus in Ecclesia ita instituit, ut olim illud iudicium leprae. At ex eo posse construi, ut singula Christiani sacerdoti peccata enarrent, ni velint aeternum perire, id vero quivis videt, quam nulla ratione affirmatur. Neque id ullus sanctorum patrum ex hoc loco collegit, cum pie et solide hic monuerint de disciplina ecclesiae confessioneque peccatorum et solutionis beneficio, quae ultro, et ex vera poenitentia suscipiuntur"; for the earlier reading, cf. above, p. 34 n. 29.

[19]Ibid., 54D: "Docendi igitur sunt homines, Christiani quidem esse, et homini nonnunquam sua peccata confiteri, et maxime ei qui gerit publicum munus praedicandi evangelij et consolandi conscientias, uti episcopi et pastores sunt, suae functioni rite incumbentes. At confiteri certo tempore, et peccata singula, etiam cogitationum id humanam esse traditionem"; cf. above, p. 47 n. 62.

absolution in the 1527 edition), Bucer endorsed the value of private meetings between pastor and parishioner: "where there are those who rightly administer the keys of the kingdom of heaven, the gospel of Christ, who teach in good faith whence remission of sins may be sought, from whom the benefit of the keys will never be sought in vain, then this same meeting in the Lord will also be important for establishing piety."[20]

Bucer's emphasis on instruction was bound to be more acceptable to the Lutherans than his earlier implication that their position was sincere but misguided. By stressing that the confessor must "rightly" administer the keys and teach "in good faith," however, Bucer implied that it was the character and ability of the pastor, and not his office, which made the meeting beneficial. He avoided further conflict with the Lutherans by diverting attention from any disagreement over the value of private absolution as such and concentrating instead on the context in which the words of absolution were spoken, the private meeting between pastor and parishioner. In so doing he was justified by the equivocal use of the term "absolution" in the Wittenberg Concord.

As might be expected, the changes in Bucer's discussion of the power of the keys had ramifications for his discussion of church discipline. The passage devoted to Matthew 18 was almost twice its original length. Bucer added a brief exposition of the Ten Commandments, but the most important alterations to this passage came in his understanding of the phrase, "tell it to the church." Here he more clearly emphasized the importance of the ministry. The power of the keys, he stated, was given to "those who meet in the name of Christ in a fixed and orderly manner, and especially to those leaders whom the Holy Spirit has constituted as pastors and bishops in the church."[21] Bucer continued to oppose the use of public excommunication under present circumstances, recommending instead the practice of admonition and discipline among those "who have received Christ more fully." But among these more committed Christians Bucer now gave a greater role to the ministers, who were to admonish sinners in the name of the whole church. If the sinners refused to heed the final admonition, the ministers "are to excommunicate them from this same church in which they are especially well known and familiar and are not to admit them to the holy Eucharist." Bucer still hoped that God would restore "a just government and true censure" to the church, and he argued that its use would not be disruptive, as some feared: "up to the present the church's situation has been very confused and troubled, but if the ministers of the word wished to perform their duties

---

[20]Ibid., 55B: "At ubi sunt, qui claves regni coelorum, evangelium Christi rite administrant, qui unde petenda sit peccatorum remissio, bona fide docent, apud hos clavium beneficium petere suo fructu nunquam carebit, tum ipsum in domino colloquium suum quoque momentum ad instaurandam pietatem habebit. Hoc sane experiuntur pij . . ." cf. above, p. 47 n. 65.

[21]Ibid., 386D: "Deinde non est data ligandi et solvendi potestas, nisi convenientibus in nomine Christi, eoque certo ordine, et praeeuntibus ijs, quos spiritus sanctus constituit in Ecclesia pastores et Episcopos."

in good faith they would most easily restore Christian censure without any distur-
bance or division of the church."[22]

Despite his stronger emphasis on the need for some form of discipline among
more committed Christians, Bucer did not soften his condemnation of Anabaptist
separatism; this section remained unchanged from the previous edition. At the end
of the passage, however, he added a new paragraph in which he discussed Christ's
promise that a prayer agreed on by two or three would be answered.[23] This promise,
Bucer said, was what made private admonition and absolution fruitful, for if two people were to agree in praying for forgiveness, the sin had to be known and acknowledged as such by both people. The sinner could then have confidence in the
confessor's words of forgiveness: "since true prayer excludes doubt in the one seeking
[forgiveness], it is necessary that one brother reassures the other concerning the forgiveness sought and, by exhibiting it to him, makes him sure in the Lord."[24] Bucer
implicitly disassociated the promise of forgiveness with the power of the keys, however, by retaining his earlier statement that "the power of binding and loosing, that
is, of excluding from the church or receiving into it, whether at the beginning or after
sins have been committed," was to be found elsewhere, in the exegesis of
Matthew 16.[25] Bucer's interpretation of the passage thus differed in an important
way from Luther's. In *Von der Beicht* Luther had cited these verses together with the
standard passages on the power to bind and loose sins as assurance that a sinner received forgiveness through private absolution.[26] The promise of answered prayer gave
further support to the power of the keys—it was additional reassurance to the sinner

---

[22]Ibid., 386D–387A: "Ubi non datur, necesse est, ut qui plenius Christum receperunt,
sanctissimum hoc et saluberrimum Christi institutum inter sese reducant . . . ut contemptores monitiones deferant, quae Ecclesia illos si pergant contemnere, rem ad communes totius Ecclesiae ministros deferat, ut et illi nomine totius Ecclesiae illos moneant: et si pergant
verbum Domini contemnere, eos etiam excommunicent, vel illa ipsa Ecclesia, in qua noti illi
peculiariter sunt et familiares, tum ad sacram Eucharistiam eos non admittant, donec Dominus restituerit nobis iustam in Ecclesia politiam, veramque censuram. Utcunque autem per-
mixta perturbataque adhuc sunt omnia, tamen si ministri verbi suo muneri velint incumbere
bona fide, censurae Christianae facile plurimum restituent, citra ullam Ecclesiae perturba-
tionem aut sectionem, quam fidus minister Christi nullo pacto invehere sustinebit, qui novit
sibi omnem potestatem in Ecclesia datam ad aedificationem, non ad destructionem, et magis
muneris sui esse ad regnum Dei undique cogere, etiam caecos, surdos, atque debiles, quam
eo eijcere." Cf. above p. 38 n. 41 for the passage in the earlier editions of the commentary.

[23]Matt. 18:19–20; Bucer did not specifically discuss these verses in the earlier editions.

[24]1536 Gospels, 387B–388C: "Hic tamen potissimum loquitur Dominus de oranda venia ijs, qui peccarunt. Hinc ergo privata quoque et admonitionis et absolutionis fructus dis-
cendus est. Si nanque consentiant duo de venia peccati oranda, peccatum illud utrique
notum sit oportet, et ut peccatum agnoscatur. Hic ergo privata peccati eius vel monitio, vel
confessio intercesserit oportet. Iam cum oratio vera dubitationem excludit impetrandi,
necesse est ut frater fratrem etiam de impetrata venia confirmet, exhibendoque illi eam, secu-
rum cum in Domino reddat. Verum autem et illud est, Dominum hic promissionem de pau-
cis extulisse, ut doceret quam probet et amplectatur nos in ipso conspirare et convenire,
etiamsi minimo numero simus: magis ergo illi placemus, si plurimi inter nos in ipso conspire-
mus, innumeraque in nomine eius poterimus."

[25]Ibid., 387B: "De potestate vero ligandi et solvendi, hoc est, ab Ecclesia excludendi, vel
in eam recipiendi, sive ab initio, sive post admissa flagitia, supra 16."

[26]WA 8:177.35–178.22.

that his sin had been forgiven through the minister's spoken absolution. Bucer, however, seems to make a distinction between the power of the keys and the assurance which rests on Christ's promise of answered prayer. For Bucer, the promise of answered prayer gave assurance of forgiveness, while the power of the keys regulated the individual's relation to the church.[27]

The 1536 Gospels commentary demonstrates that despite the signing of the Wittenberg Concord, Bucer still did not completely share Luther's understanding of private absolution and the power of the keys. He had certainly moved much closer to the Lutheran position than he had been in the 1520s, but there remained important differences between them.[28] Bucer held private confession in great esteem because of its role in giving consolation and counsel, but he could not justify making such confession mandatory, no matter how beneficial. Likewise he could admit that the minister's words of absolution had great power to reassure individuals that they had been forgiven, but he did not derive this power directly from the minister's authority to bind and loose. Bucer eliminated polemical passages aimed at the Lutherans, to avoid giving unnecessary offense, but he did not fully accept the Lutheran position. He tried to minimize this disagreement by using cautious and at times ambiguous language. He discussed topics on which he and the Lutherans agreed, such as the consolatory function of the *colloquium*, and he avoided those topics where there was still disagreement. He made full use of the ambiguity contained in the Wittenberg Concord to obscure the differences of interpretation and emphasis that remained with the Lutherans.

Underlying Bucer's disagreement with the Lutheran position was his definition of the power of the keys. This definition had evolved as Bucer's appreciation for the visible church gradually increased. In the first edition of the commentary, where power of the keys was identified with preaching the word of God, Bucer considered only the initial entrance into the true, invisible church through faith in the word preached. In the Ulm church ordinance of 1531, Bucer expanded the power of the keys to include the minister's right to admonish sinners and direct the church. In *Furbereytung zum Concilio* of 1533 and his catechism of 1534 he described in more detail how the power of the keys gave ministers the authority to admit individuals to the church or to exclude them from it through preaching, baptism, church discipline, and excommunication. The 1536 Gospels commentary summed up these responsibilities as the minister's authority to administer the church from the word of God. The power of the keys was thus much broader than simply the authority to grant private absolution; it entailed the direction and guidance of the whole church.

[27]Cf. Roth's discussion of the scriptural basis used by Bucer and Calvin to justify private confession and of the role each assigned to the minister in hearing confessions, *Privatbeichte*, 134-138.

[28]In a study of the changes to Bucer's interpretation of John 6 in the three editions of his commentary, Irena Backus draws similar conclusions regarding Bucer's theology of the Lord's Supper, "Polemic, Exegetical Tradition and Ontology. Bucer's Interpretation of John 6:52, 53 and 64 Before and After the Wittenberg Concord," in David C. Steinmetz, ed., *The Bible in the Sixteenth Century*, Duke Monographs in Medieval and Renaissance Studies 11 (Durham, N.C.: Duke University Press, 1990), 167-180.

The power to bind and loose was, for Bucer, the most important aspect of the minister's authority. By preaching the gospel and baptizing those who responded to it, the minister brought people into the church; through public teaching and private instruction, whether catechization of children or individual *colloquia* with adults, he encouraged them to give themselves more completely to Christ and so built up the church; through excommunication he expelled contumacious sinners from the church to bring about their repentance and to prevent further scandal or harm to the church. In all these acts the minister exercised his authority to bind and loose, to forgive or retain sin.

Despite his emphasis on the jurisdictional authority of the ministers, Bucer avoided the medieval division of the power of the keys into *potestas ordinis* and *potestas iurisdictionis*. Instead he distinguished between the minister's role in bringing people into the church through baptism and his responsibility of aiding the growth and development of the individual Christian. This distinction underlay Bucer's two types of binding and loosing in his 1534 catechism. Bucer preferred this distinction between baptism and pastoral oversight to the Lutheran emphasis on the preaching of the word of God and the administration of the sacraments as the minister's primary functions.[29] Instead he listed several methods by which the word was proclaimed, such as teaching, exhortation, and admonition and gave these, as well as the administration of the sacraments, equal emphasis with the other aspects of the ministry. The overall effect of this approach was to stress the disciplinary authority of the ministers.

In one important respect, however, Bucer did show a greater openness to the Lutheran position, and that was his willingness to include absolution along with the sacraments of baptism and the Lord's Supper when discussing the role of the ministers in exhibiting and dispensing God's promise of forgiveness. While Bucer did not fully accept the Lutheran understanding of private absolution, his deeper appreciation for the connection between the external actions of the minister and the internal effects of those actions was a significant development which would in turn provide the basis for further evolution of his position on absolution and the power of the keys in the coming years.

Another equally important development in the commentary is Bucer's attitude towards the church fathers. Throughout his discussion of the power of the keys and church discipline Bucer referred to the teachings and practices of the early church. He used the church fathers in an apologetic fashion, as support for his own positions, but he also viewed the early church as a model to be followed in the exercise of penitential discipline and private catechization. As he stated in his prefatory letter, the

---

[29]Melanchthon retained the division between the *potestas ordinis* and *iurisdictionis* in his *Apology*, although the distinction is reinterpreted, so that the *potestas ordinis* is the authority to preach and to administer the sacraments, while the *potestas iurisdictionis* is the authority to exercise discipline; cf. Fagerberg, *Theologie*, 252–256. When Bucer did begin to use the Lutheran division of doctrine and sacraments, he added a third category, discipline. The triad of doctrine, sacraments, and discipline occurs with increasing frequency in Bucer's writings from the later 1530s and 1540s; for an early example, see the Hessian disciplinary ordinance, BDS 7:261.6–7; 265.3–4; 272.10–11; cf. below, p. 171 n. 34.

doctrine and practices of the early church were inspired at least to some degree by the Holy Spirit and should thus be taken seriously by all Christians. His respect for the fathers, expressed as early as 1533, had begun to assume a more prominent place and a more explicit justification. It would also play an important role in the development of Bucer's thought over the next decade.

II. The Strasbourg Church, 1535-1538

It was one thing for Bucer to set forth his ideas on admonition, religious instruction, and discipline in his commentary and quite another to see them carried out in the Strasbourg church. During the later 1530s Bucer continued his efforts to bring reality more into conformity with his ideals. His efforts focused on two areas—mandatory religious instruction, especially for children, and the exercise of church discipline, particularly the imposition of penance. This not only brought him into conflict with the city council but, judging from Bucer's attempts to forestall objections, met with opposition from the Strasburghers themselves.

The Strasbourg church ordinance was published at the end of 1534. Three months later, the city council reissued the *Constitution*, the disciplinary mandates which comprised the city's moral code. With these two documents the council gave the city's church an institutional framework and signaled its concern for the proper conduct of its citizens. Within a very short time, however, the pastors began to complain that the ordinances were not being enforced. In August of 1535 the pastors submitted a lengthy plea to the council, admonishing them to "take religion more seriously," so that piety was encouraged and public offense punished in the city.[30] The pastors complained that there were many in the city who neither attended the sermons nor allowed others in their household to do so. Among their proposals for reform, the pastors asked the city council to require that all children, along with their parents, attend the catechism services held four times a year and that the teachers be commanded to bring all their students to church. The council commission appointed to consider the pastors' complaints was reluctant to follow their recommendations, resolving only that citizens should be admonished to attend the catechisms with their children and servants, although it did recommend that teachers be authorized to take students who were ten years old or older to hear the sermons.[31] This was little more than a repetition of the provisions of the church ordinance and the *Constitution*.[32]

It is unlikely that the city council took even the few steps endorsed by the commission, for six months later the pastors appeared before them again, this time with more specific complaints and more strident calls for action.[33] The pastors described

---

[30]AST 84, fol. 92r-96v; summarized in Köhler, *Ehegericht* 2:440-442.

[31]AST 84, fol. 97r-98v.

[32]The church ordinance required parents, teachers with boarders, and householders with apprentices to send their charges to the catechisms but did not specify any action to be taken if these provisions were ignored; BDS 5:34.23-29; 35.1-5. The *Constitution* also urged diligent attendance at worship and catechism services; Röhrich, *Mittheilungen* 1:249-250.

[33]AST 84, fol. 99r-104v (March 1536); cf. Köhler, *Ehegericht* 2:442-444.

the desperate need for some kind of discipline for the city's children, who were growing up "wild and unruly, without any fear of God." All properly ordered churches had some form of private instruction, as confession had been under the papacy, they stated. While the gospel did not allow them to require confession, they merited God's punishment for not establishing a substitute for it. As they put it, the youth "learned to escape the papal yoke, but the yoke of Christ is not offered to them, at least with regard to external disciplinary ordinances. The gospel does not require that we destroy the pope's ordinances and not replace them with Christian ones." The most serious problem came from the children who were not in school and so were not taken to church by their teachers. The pastors asked that the council issue a mandate giving them the authority to instruct these children privately in the basics of the catechism—the Ten Commandments, the Creed, the Lord's Prayer, and the understanding of the sacraments. When the children had learned this, they could be admitted to the Lord's Supper.

Concerning the children in school, the pastors repeated their request that teachers bring their pupils to their parish church every Sunday. It did no good to require parents to take responsibility for their children's religious education. Many of them were too occupied with temporal goods and worldly reputation to be concerned with eternal things. Even when they did attend the sermons they left their children at home, as was obvious from the number of children playing in the streets and church squares during the services. There were many fatherless children and children whose fathers were unfit to raise them properly. When the teachers asked their pupils on Monday if they had been to church the day before, they found that "out of ten students, not even two have heard the Sunday sermon, and moreover some answer sarcastically and contemptuously." It was also useless, the pastors continued, to say that they had the right to summon negligent parents to remind them of their duties, because the parents regarded the summons as a joke and there was no way to compel compliance. The only solution the pastors saw was to require the teachers to take the children to church and to the weekly catechism classes every Sunday. If the teachers themselves were negligent in this, they were not fit to teach in a Christian city.

The city council obviously was not moved by as great a sense of urgency as the pastors, for over a year passed before it finally found time to debate even the modest proposals submitted by the new commission responsible for answering the pastors' renewed complaints.[34] The commission had acknowledged its desire that everyone attend the quarterly catechisms along with wife, children, and servants, but it continued to oppose mandatory attendance, "since the works of faith should not be compelled but [should be] voluntary." Instead, the pastors were to admonish parishioners

---

[34]AST 84, fol. 105r–108v, July 31, 1536; one of the marginal notes which record the council's decision regarding each proposal is dated May 2, 1537. Köhler, *Ehegericht* 2:444–445, assumes that this document is a synopsis of renewed complaints made by the pastors on July 31, 1536, but it is clearly a summary of the pastors' presentation of March 1536, along with the recommendations of the council commission charged with responding to the complaints submitted to the full council in July of that year.

from the pulpit to attend the quarterly catechism services and to send their children to church and to weekly catechism instruction, and the councillors were to encourage their fellow guildsmen in the same. In addition, teachers were required to bring the children both to the morning sermon and to catechetical instruction on Sunday afternoons; Thursdays were to be devoted to further religious instruction in the schools. Those who did not send their children to church or to catechism classes were to be referred to the council; the threat of being summoned by the council would carry more weight than that of being summoned by the pastors. The council apparently adopted these recommendations, but it tabled a proposal allowing the pastors to examine young people about their faith before admitting them to the Lord's Supper.

The pastors' two attempts to promote church attendance and catechetical instruction and the council's response on both occasions illustrate the areas where the pastors felt the church's needs most acutely. They also reveal the tensions developing between the magistrate and the clergy. The councillors agreed with the pastors that all children should be taught the essentials of their faith. Thus teachers were to see that children in their care attended catechism classes, and parents who failed to provide for their children's religious instruction could be called before the council. But the council was reluctant to require outright that everyone, including adults, attend worship or catechetical services. The pastors had no such reservations. In their opinion everyone without exception should be exposed to the teaching of the city's official faith.

The ministers' reference to confession shows their awareness that with its abolition they had lost a valuable method of private instruction. Regular catechetical instruction for children was the substitute they proposed. Confession could not be commanded, but the pastors saw nothing objectionable in requiring attendance at the catechetical services. The pastors were especially concerned about children who did not go to school and were not brought to church or to the weekly catechisms—in other words, those who had no other exposure to the gospel as it was preached in Strasbourg. They wanted to make sure that these children also had a proper understanding of the faith before admitting them to the sacrament for the first time. The church ordinance had contained a provision enabling the pastors to examine children before their first communion,[35] but this had apparently remained only a theoretical privilege. Now the ministers wanted a more specific mandate which would make clear that they had the right to instruct children in the catechism and to examine their understanding of it. The proposed examination before admission to the sacrament contained elements from both the Lutheran precommunion examination and the confirmation ceremony Bucer had suggested in his catechism of 1534. Like the precommunion examination, it would ensure that the individual had a basic knowledge of Christian doctrine, but unlike the Lutheran practice, it did not make any explicit provision for confession and absolution. Moreover, it would occur only once, before the individual received the sacrament for the first time. Unlike confirmation, however, it would not

---

[35]BDS 5:34.29-33.

be public. The council's opposition to this proposal meant that the ministers would have to find some other way to screen participants in the Lord's Supper.

It was perhaps in this context that the pastors drafted a three-point proposal "on how to establish church discipline."[36] It is striking that although the title refers to church discipline, the document itself was concerned with methods of pastoral supervision. It began with a justification for pastoral care: it was not sufficient to preach the gospel and administer the sacraments rightly, for many people rejected both preaching and the sacraments and gave no thought to the state of their souls. It was the responsibility of the church, and especially of her ministers, to seek after those lost souls and to act as shepherds and fathers towards all in their charge. So that the pastor would be able to carry out his responsibilities toward his sheep, it was necessary that bonds of "familiarity and fellowship" exist between them. Such fellowship could not exist, however, if the pastor did not know his sheep by name.[37]

The document proposed three measures to establish the necessary familiarity. First, each parishioner, with his entire household, should have his name enrolled in a parish register. This was not a burdensome requirement, the document stated, since the pastor could not impose any obligations or require obedience "beyond that which occurs in holy baptism." For this reason, those who were enrolled were first to be reminded of their baptismal profession, "since many people, after they have been baptized, seldom or never consider what they or others on their behalf promised to God and the church." Second, the document suggested that each individual be required to make a yearly confession of faith, consisting of "the chief articles of the Christian faith: the Ten Commandments, the twelve articles of the Christian faith, on the church and its sacraments, and absolution." The first confession of faith would be made publicly before the church by children who had reached the age of discretion, between ten and twelve years old, and was to be modeled after "the custom of the early church." This confession would thereafter be repeated privately each year to the pastor, so that individuals did not forget what they had previously learned and so that heresy, error, and false doctrine could be eliminated. Third, parishioners were to be required to seek out their pastors before participation in the sacraments and ceremonies of the church. Again, this custom "was observed in the early church and is still practiced in most churches." By means of these private meetings the laity could be better instructed in the significance of the ceremony. In meeting with prospective marriage partners, the pastors would have the opportunity to discover whether there were any legal hindrances to the match and to instruct the couple in their duties as husband and wife. Parents who desired to have their child baptized would be reminded of the sacrament's meaning and admonished not to choose "unbelieving, offensive

[36]AST 173 (V.E. VIII):166v–172v. Köhler, who briefly summarizes this document, "von Anrichtung einer Kirchenzucht," assumes that it belongs with the eight points concerning church discipline, written in Latin and dated 1548, which immediately precede it, *Ehegericht* 2:490. He does note, however, that "von Anrichtung" is more moderate in tone than other documents from 1548 and that it applies to the entire church of Strasbourg rather than to the establishment of "Christian fellowships."

[37]An allusion to John 10:14.

and bannable people" as godparents. Private instruction before the Lord's Supper, especially for the young and the "unlearned masses," would protect not only the recipient but also the dispenser from profaning the sacrament.

The document acknowledged that many people would see these proposals as an attempt to reinstate auricular confession and burden the church with useless and unnecessary laws. This concern, "which undeniably is propagated by the papists," only hindered the establishment of proper discipline in the church. The pastors' goal was to foster trust and fellowship between the pastors and "the sheep of Christ." They had no desire to examine "the secrets of the conscience," an examination which belonged to God alone, but rather would examine the individual's knowledge of Christian doctrine, so that sin and error could be eliminated. No one could be forced to confess hidden errors and sin, but the pastors could pass judgment on an individual's "external life and deeds."

The document is undated, but its proposals fit in well with the pastors' concerns during the second half of the 1530s. Its emphasis on the relations between pastor and parishioner, as well as its use of the shepherd and sheep metaphor, are themes which also occur in several of Bucer's writings from that period.[38] Bucer's increasing respect for the teachings and practices of the early church also dates from the later 1530s. The suggestion for a yearly confession of faith coincided with the pastors' concern for screening prospective recipients of the Lord's Supper. The first confession of faith, made publicly by children who had reached the age of discretion, was clearly a form of confirmation as Bucer had first suggested in his works of 1533-34. The document presumed that baptism laid certain obligations upon each Christian, a point Bucer made in his discussion of infant baptism in *Bericht* of 1534. On the other hand, the document also acknowledged that individuals needed to be reminded of the obligations assumed at baptism, which implies that perhaps the pastors were meeting some resistance from parishioners who did not want to conduct their lives in a manner acceptable to the clergy. When enrolling parishioners in the registers, pastors presumably would stress the consequences of baptism for the Christian's life, and the registers themselves would enable the pastors to keep closer watch over those within their parishes. The creation of special registers to improve pastoral supervision, the introduction of a public confirmation ceremony, and the practice of regular meetings between pastor and parishioner before participation in important church rites were ideas which the clergy continued to advocate for the city's church over the next several years. Over time, however, these proposals were modified and sharp-

---

[38]This is most notable in *Von der waren Seelsorge*, which is built around a pastoral metaphor, but references to shepherds and sheep and pastors knowing their flock also appear in the Ziegenhain disciplinary ordinance, cf. BDS 7:261.8-12 (returning errant sheep to the sheepfold); 271.30-272.27 (parents to meet with pastors before a child is baptized), both discussed below, and in the documents concerning the 1539 synod discussed in chap. 7. The synod articles also contained a provision urging frequent meetings between pastor and parishioners. Because the description of a public confession of faith makes no mention of a profession of obedience as well, I believe the document was written sometime before Bucer's stay in Hesse during the autumn of 1538, at which time he proposed a public profession of both faith and obedience as part of a public confirmation ceremony.

ened, assuming a new importance within Bucer's larger system of Christian discipline.

In the meantime, Bucer's concern for catechization led him to write a new catechism. Published in December 1537, the catechism was designed to be "of more use in teaching the younger and more simple children than the longer [catechism] which we published."[39] It was an abridgement of Bucer's earlier catechism, slightly more than one-third the length[40] and in general much more suited to children. The section on the use of the keys and church discipline in the new catechism reflected these general changes: it was shorter and more straightforward. It bore the title, "On the punishment and forgiveness of sins which should be exercised in the church," and it was accompanied by a woodcut of St. Peter bearing a key.[41] The opening question and its response spoke of the forgiveness which the Holy Spirit worked when, "through the ministry of the church he looses those who have sinned and devoted themselves to reform and consoles them with forgiveness."[42] By linking forgiveness to the intention to reform, Bucer betrayed his interest in the moral improvement of the sinner. Although Bucer acknowledged the consolatory power of absolution, it could be granted only when the sinner had demonstrated his repentance.

The catechism quickly moved on to the issue of church discipline and the ban, stating that those who had sinned and would not reform despite sufficient admonition were to be excluded from the church. Secret sins were privately rebuked, public sins were rebuked in public. As in his earlier catechism, Bucer interpreted "tell it to the church" to mean that those who would not heed individual admonition should be referred to the proper ministers of the church—the bishops, pastors, and elders who then admonished the sinner in the church's name and who banned the contumacious. Bucer drew two conclusions from this section. First, the child was to make use of the forgiveness of sins given through the church, "for it is a great comfort to all assailed consciences that the Lord has given his church the keys to heaven, the power to bind and loose, to forgive and retain sins." Second, he was to submit to the discipline of the church both in admonishing fellow Christians when they sinned and in accepting their admonition when he himself had sinned.[43]

Bucer emphasized the importance of fraternal admonition and the need to submit to such admonition, and by eliminating entirely his discussion of the role of the

<hr>

[39]BDS 6/III:177.11–15.

[40]48 leaves as compared to the 120 leaves of the 1534 catechism; Johann Michael Reu, ed., *Quellen zur Geschichte des kirchlichen Unterrichts in der evangelischen Kirche Deutschlands zwischen 1530 und 1600. Teil I: Quellen zur Geschichte des Katechismus-Unterrichts.* Vol. I: Süddeutsche Katechismen (Gütersloh: Bertelsmann, 1904; repr.: Hildesheim: Georg Olms, 1976), 6.

[41]BDS 6/III:188.The 1537 catechism contains 24 such woodcuts, which Ernst-Wilhelm Kohls attributes to the Strasbourg artist Hans Baldung Grien, "Holzschnitte von Hans Baldung in Martin Bucers 'kürtzer Catechismus'," *Theologische Zeitschrift* 23 (1967):267–284.

[42]BDS 6/III:191.33–35.

[43]Ibid., 194.1–27.

keys in baptism or admission to the church, he sharpened the focus on church discipline.[44] This emphasis came through even more clearly in the "brief instruction for the very young" appended to this section, where Bucer defined the office of the keys as "the admonition and punishment of sins, binding and banning those who do not wish to reform, loosing and reaccepting into God's grace those who dedicate themselves to reform."[45]

Bucer's concern for the exercise of church discipline came through even more clearly in his treatise *Von der waren Seelsorge*, published in the spring of 1538. As Bucer explained in the preface, he wrote *Von der waren Seelsorge* to describe "what [kind of] fellowship the church of Christ is, how Christ the Lord alone rules it, what ministry he uses for this, and how this ministry should be constituted and performed towards all those who are brought to the church of Christ and may be maintained and improved."[46] After describing the church and its ministers, Bucer devoted the majority of the book to a discussion of the five types of pastoral care exercised by the *Seelsorger*, the pastors and lay elders who were responsible for administering the church:

> The first: to lead to Christ our Lord and into his church those who are still alienated from him, whether through fleshly pride or through false worship. The second: to bring back those who were once brought to Christ and into his church but either through fleshly doings or false teachings were led out again. The third: to help back to true reformation those who remain in the church of Christ but have fallen and sinned gravely. The fourth: to strengthen again in proper Christian deeds and to make healthy those who stand firm in the fellowship of Christ and go astray in no particular or obvious way but are somewhat weak and sick in their Christian life. The fifth: to protect from all offense and heresy and lead to all good those not in serious sin and who are neither weak nor sick in their Christian deeds. These five works of pastoral care and of the shepherd's office the Lord has brought together in a very fine way by the metaphor of tending sheep when he says in Ezekiel 34:16, "I will seek the lost, and I will bring back the strayed, and I will bind the crippled and I will strengthen the weak, and the fat and the strong I will watch over."[47]

There are two emphases to Bucer's discussion. Under the theme of bringing the lost and alienated sheep into the fold—the first two types of pastoral care—he discussed the role of the magistrate in seeing that its subjects were brought to Christ.[48] Although Bucer vigorously advocated the right, or, as he viewed it, the God-given responsibility, of the magistrate to see that Christ's kingdom was furthered among its

[44]Cf. the 1534 catechism, ibid., 84.19-86.4.
[45]Ibid., 199.27-31.
[46]BDS 7:94.23-30.
[47]Ibid., 141.17-37.
[48]Ibid., 147.6-150.7; 156.27-35.

subjects, he nevertheless upheld a distinction between the office of the magistrate and that of the church: "the magistrate itself is not to preach the word or to dispense and administer the sacraments and discipline, for this is the particular ministry and office of the church." Instead, the magistrate was to oversee the ministers and ensure that they performed their pastoral duties faithfully and diligently, it was to establish schools so that children might be taught godliness, and it was to punish those who would hinder the ministry of the church or escape its jurisdiction.[49]

The second emphasis, described as healing the sick, helping the weak, and tending the strong sheep, concerned one aspect of pastoral duty, the exercise of church discipline. Bucer presented his justification for church discipline in the chapter on healing sick and wounded sheep, defined as those who were guilty of manifest, notorious sin against God or neighbor, who disobeyed those in authority, or who obviously led immoral and undisciplined lives. He drew three conclusions about church discipline from Scripture. First, all Christians were responsible for admonishing sinners, but those chosen as *Seelsorger* bore special responsibility for admonition. Second, attempts to heal and help such sinners were to continue as long as the sinner would allow. Finally, the "medication" used to heal wounded sheep was "to cause the sinner to recognize his sin so that he is sufficiently moved to true recognition, contrition and sorrow for his sin, and then to console him and strengthen him in hope of grace so that he will be most zealous and desirous for true amendment."[50] In cases of grave sin, this medicine included the imposition of public penance.

Bucer argued for the necessity of penitential discipline on the basis of Scripture and the church fathers. From the Old Testament he cited examples of individuals such as David and Ahab and the communal penance of the Israelite nation. He also used the provisions concerning sin and guilt offerings and the yearly Day of Atonement to support his claim that "the almighty, good God commanded this medicine for sin, the earnest and public humbling, discipline and penance" for his people under the Law. His chief example from the New Testament was the treatment of the Corinthian sinner, although he also referred to Peter after his betrayal of Christ, the repentant prostitute, and the publican in the temple. "Tertullian, Cyprian, Ambrose and all the old, holy fathers" described the penitential practices of the early church, while Ambrose's excommunication of the emperor Theodosius served as an example of how that discipline was applied.[51]

Bucer admitted that there was no express command for penitential discipline in the New Testament as there was in the Old, but he did not see this as a problem:

> Our Lord Jesus expressly prescribed very few external actions for us; and what he did prescribe, he encompassed in very few words. We have his written ordinances only for holy baptism, the Lord's Supper and penance,

[49]Ibid., 147.16–148.5.
[50]Ibid., 157.35–158.4; citation at 159.56–160.2.
[51]Old Testament: ibid., 161.8–18; 167.3–13; 168.20–169.8; citation at 169.9–11. New Testament: 165.9–166.34; 173.17–22, 26–34. Early church: 162.11–164.18.

and these only briefly described. . . . Concerning this present topic of penance we have no more than that the *Seelsorger* should forgive the sins of all the penitent and those who promise reform, and that what they bind on earth, shall be bound in heaven, and what they loose on earth shall also be loosed in heaven. . . . But the dear apostles, yes, the Holy Spirit in the apostles, then further established, for this ordinance and for others, what the work of Christ demands in this business, and what may make the work of God great, visible and acceptable.[52]

On this basis Bucer argued that the penitential practices of the early church were established "from God's command and the ordering of the Holy Spirit" as he worked through the apostles and their successors.[53] Bucer thus regarded penitential discipline as *de iure divino*, since it was not only prescribed by the apostles and practiced by the early church but instituted by Christ himself.

Bucer used examples from daily life to demonstrate that natural reason, "the light of nature," also taught the necessity of public penance.[54] A father disciplined his child, a lord his servant, and the magistrate its subjects, so that the offender could demonstrate his repentance and his desire to reform. Such discipline also made the sinner an example for others: "for with such punishment, disciplining and penance the people develop a genuine aversion to doing wrong, and if some penalty is imposed on them for their willfulness, others are deterred from sin."[55]

As in his earlier writings, Bucer identified the power of the keys with the minister's right to impose penitential discipline. The church could only loose and forgive sin when it recognized, insofar as it was able, that the sinner truly repented and intended to reform. Where grave sin was concerned, the sinner had to demonstrate his repentance with confession, lamentation, and weeping. The church could justly demand evidence of a person's contrition through a period of penance before he was readmitted to full fellowship, and it could consider the sinner bound until the penance had been performed. For this reason, the binding of the church consisted not only of the power to close heaven to unbelievers and the unrepentant, but also "to exclude believers from the heavenly fellowship of the church for a period and to hold them from the communion of Christians and to bind them to a period of penance."[56]

Bucer also described how penitential discipline should be exercised. He reminded his readers that public penance could only be imposed for grave sins which required drastic treatment. Lesser daily sins were confessed and repentance demonstrated in daily prayer and religious practices, "and when the *Seelsorger* encourage general daily

---

[52]Ibid., 169.27–170.5.
[53]Ibid., 170.17–171.5; 171.37–172.5.
[54]For Bucer's understanding of natural reason, see Koch, *Studium Pietatis*, 75–76.
[55]BDS 7:171.6–35.
[56]Ibid., 172.13–29; 205.18–29; citation 206.26–29.

confession, repentance and amendment through their faithful admonition, they heal the sheep of Christ of these lesser daily injuries." But there were some sins which required harsher measures. When the *Seelsorger* could not move those guilty of such sins to repentance through milder treatment, they had to follow Paul's example of severity and impose chastisement which, when performed, gave evidence of repentance and the intention to reform. The more serious the sin, the greater severity and zeal in imposing discipline and penance were required.[57]

Despite his passionate defense of penitential discipline, Bucer realized that it could sometimes cause more harm than good. There were people who might reject the church and its discipline because of the severity of the penance imposed. In such cases he recommended greater mildness, since little repentance and only limited reform were better than no repentance or reform at all. But where a person had sinned and refused to accept any discipline and show any repentance, the *Seelsorger* could not loose him from his sin, since Christ had commanded that those who did not listen to the church were to be treated as heathens.[58] Penitential discipline could also be harmful if its severity caused the sinner to despair of forgiveness.[59] The greatest danger associated with penitential discipline, however, arose when it was imposed without proper oversight and performed only as an external practice without genuine repentance. Echoing his earlier statements, Bucer attributed this problem to the bishops' neglect of their pastoral duties and their concern with secular affairs. As a consequence of this "perversion of discipline," Bucer charged, public penance had become a pompous ceremony rather than a medication for the soul. "And even this has almost disappeared, so that nothing is left of penance but the imposition in confession of a few prayers, masses, pilgrimages, and some fasts and almsgiving"; there was little concern for "true, believing contrition." Bucer contrasted this negligent practice with the wisdom of the church fathers in matching the penance imposed to the person and particulars of the sin and in prescribing length and degree of penance to help both the sinner and the church become more opposed to sin and more zealous in good works.[60]

Bucer anticipated several objections which might be raised to the reintroduction of penitential discipline. Public penance was necessary even if the sinner had already repented, he argued, for its purpose was not to obtain forgiveness from God but to instill greater hatred of sin and to prevent future sin.[61] Bucer defended the temporary exclusion of sinners from the Lord's Supper, stating that only those who had been fully reconciled with the church should be allowed to receive the sacrament, which was the highest degree of communion with God and with other Christians. More-

---

[57]Ibid., 175.4–176.34.
[58]Ibid., 177.3–17.
[59]Ibid., 179.30–180.8.
[60]Ibid., 177.18–178.12.
[61]Ibid., 180.36–183.22. Bucer again gave the definition of satisfaction taken from Gennadius of Marseilles (falsely attributed to Augustine) which he had used in both *Furbereytung* and *Defensio*, this time without specifically mentioning his source; see above p. 76 n. 90.

over, the ministers of the church had the right to demand that penitents demonstrate their sincerity before reassuring them of forgiveness through the Lord's Supper. Admitting sinners to the sacrament without evidence of repentance only strengthened the godless, misled the people, and aroused God's wrath.[62]

The existence of a Christian magistrate which punished sins did not eliminate the need for penitential discipline. Bucer granted that the magistrate had "the highest physical power over all souls," but the elders of the church had to have the power to discipline so that the children of God might be brought to true repentance. Moreover, when Christ instituted such discipline in the church, he did not say that it should be abolished when the civil authority was Christian; rather, the Old Testament showed clearly that church discipline existed alongside punishment by a "God-fearing magistrate."[63]

Bucer also addressed the charge that the church's disciplinary power gave rise to "clerical tyranny." It was the responsibility of the Christian magistrate to prevent the elders of the church from misusing their authority and to ensure elders were chosen who would not be prone to such misuse. More importantly, Bucer attributed the emergence of "clerical tyranny" to the bishops' entanglement with secular responsibilities rather than to their exercise of spiritual discipline. As he summarized, such tyranny was due not to the clergy's use of church discipline but rather to its refusal to apply such discipline to its own members.[64]

Bucer bluntly dismissed the argument that church discipline could not be established for fear that it would drive people away from the church. The Holy Spirit had guided the practice of penitential discipline in the early church at a time when the churches were as large and contained as many nominal Christians as the Strasbourg church, and so it did no good to argue that the reestablishment of discipline was simply not feasible under present conditions.[65] The discipline which he advocated was nothing more, and nothing less, than what Christ had commanded, "and where the Lord's order and command is, there is also his Spirit and help, and everything, through his help, will be possible and will lead to reformation." Moreover, the ministers had no intention of introducing the use of penitential discipline suddenly and without warning but would establish it gradually, as people came to recognize it as a "salutary medicine."[66] In the final analysis, Bucer believed that all true Christians were obliged to support the establishment of penitential discipline in the Strasbourg church:

We must once and for all decide whether we want to be Christians. If we want to be Christians and the sheep of the Lord, we must truly hear his voice. . . . We must ascribe the hindrances to Christian discipline and

[62]Ibid., 183.23–188.30.
[63]Ibid., 188.31–191.34.
[64]Ibid., 198.20–203.11.
[65]Ibid., 194.15–198.19.
[66]Ibid., 192.17–35.

repentance not to the times, not to papal destruction, not to the preaching against papal tyranny and of Christian freedom, but to our unbelief
and false hypocrisy, we who boast much but have very little Christian
faith and who have very little desire that everything be established according to the right manner of faith.[67]

Although Bucer presented the chief components of church discipline under the
heading of "healing sick and wounded sheep," he had not exhausted his discussion
of pastoral care. Pastors were "to strengthen the weak sheep"—those with a weak faith
or too little fear of God—by means of the word of God through public preaching and
private instruction, the administration of the sacraments, and urging participation in
the collective practices of the church such as prayers, almsgiving, and hymn-singing.[68]
The "strong and healthy sheep" could also profit from this type of care, but in discussing this final category Bucer focused on another aspect of church discipline, "the
exclusion and separation of false goats." As he observed, a mangy sheep could quickly
devastate an entire flock. Both divine law and "the light of nature" taught that those
who did not live according to the rules of a community were to be excluded from it.[69]
For this reason the pastor or *Seelsorger* was to exclude all those who would not listen
to the church and who persisted in their sin. The pastor was not to give up on such
people but was to continue his admonitions to repent when he had the opportunity.
Like a shepherd, a *Seelsorger* did not completely eliminate a mangy sheep that had
been separated from the flock until he had tried all types of medication, but he applied this medication in a separate place and did not allow the sick sheep any contact
with the healthy flock.[70]

Bucer distinguished excommunication from penitential discipline, which was applied to penitents who were willing to reform. Those who would not repent were
completely cut off from the church, not just separated for a period of time. Others
could pray for them and admonish them when they had the opportunity, but otherwise unrepentant sinners were left to go their own way. As in his 1534 Catechism,
Bucer drew a fine line regarding the degree to which excommunicates were to be
shunned. Christians could not withdraw or refuse any necessary aid or assistance, but
they had to demonstrate to the sinner that they were offended by his "godless deeds."
All voluntary contact was to be broken off, but civil or family ties and responsibilities
towards the sinner were still to be fulfilled.[71] Bucer illustrated how to maintain this
balance:

> Respectable people and friends have dealings with those they otherwise
> avoid in the things which civil society or common human necessity

[67]Ibid., 193.23–194.7.
[68]Ibid., 206.31–212.19.
[69]Ibid., 219.23–220.4.
[70]Ibid., 220.5–28.
[71]Ibid., 220.29–221.19.

require, and they do with them what has been imposed on them all by the magistrate, and so, for example, they eat with them and do other things, work, buy and sell, and help them in need. But beyond this they do not accept them, have nothing to do with them, avoid their company and in all things demonstrate their aversion and indignation at their wanton and dishonorable life. Christians should act in the same way towards those who have been excluded from God's church.[72]

In addition to social ostracism, which was intended to shame the sinner and bring him to repentance, Bucer saw a role for the magistrate: "Where there is a proper, God-fearing government, the imperial statutes and old Christian practices towards those banned from the church will be enforced also in their civil relationships, as they have deserved, and through civil exclusion and avoidance which the magistrate brings about they will be brought to reformation. For heathens among Christians should be held as heathens."[73] Excommunication was not a civil punishment per se, but in Bucer's eyes it should have civil consequences imposed by the magistrate after the church had pronounced its sentence.

Bucer also described how family and household should treat an excommunicated sinner. They could not and should not shun him or her, but they were to do their best to bring about repentance by showing their own sorrow at the sin, by frequent admonition to repentance, and by their own example of a virtuous life. Where the excommunicate was under the authority of another, as a wife to her husband, children to their parents, and servants to their masters, the one in authority should try to encourage repentance through harsher treatment and, if possible, moderate use of shunning.[74]

Although Bucer was fairly explicit about the purpose and consequences of excommunication, he expressed the hope that it would not often be necessary. It was the task of the Seelsorger to use temporary exclusion of sinners to protect the "healthy sheep" from infection; they were to teach, preach, and admonish "in public and in private, in the churches, in homes and wherever they are able" so that faith and repentance increased.[75] For such a system to work, two things were necessary: conscientious shepherds and an obedient flock. Bucer devoted the remainder of the book to these two topics and closed with the prayer that the Lord would cause this "so salutary and necessary work of true pastoral care" to be better recognized and desired by all.[76]

---

[72]Ibid., 221.23-33.

[73]Ibid., 222.12-17.

[74]Ibid., 222.18-223.33. In describing the obligation of family members towards an excommunicate, Bucer followed the provisions of medieval canon law, which exempted wife and household from the penalty of minor excommunication normally incurred through association with an excommunicate. The canon law provisions were much debated among canonists, however, and in practice the families of excommunicates continued to be excommunicated themselves; Vodola, Excommunication, 60-67.

[75]BDS 7:223.34-224.7.

[76]Ibid., 240.37-241.3.

At the heart of Bucer's lengthy defense of penitential discipline and excommunication in *Von der waren Seelsorge* was his interpretation of the power of the keys. If the authority to bind and loose given by Christ included the right to impose penance on the repentant and to excommunicate the unrepentant, then the church's pastors, defined as both ordained ministers and lay elders, had to be able to exercise this authority. Indeed, they could not properly fulfill their responsibility as caretakers of souls if they were not able to bind sinners either with penance or with excommunication. In arguing for the use of penitential discipline, Bucer gave the example of the early church almost as much weight as Scripture in arguing for the use of public penance. This accorded with his statement in the 1536 Gospels commentary that the church fathers also had the Spirit of Christ and therefore their words and example could not be dismissed lightly. Bucer set the practices of the early church alongside the Law of the Old Testament, the institution of Christ, and the apostolic prescriptions of the New Testament as arguments for the necessity of penitential discipline.[77]

Bucer devoted very little attention in his book to fraternal admonition, which he had earlier stated was the most important component of discipline. He described admonition and private instruction as a part of the care given both to the "weak and sick sheep" and to the "strong and healthy sheep," but they received little more than passing mention, especially in comparison with the lengthy treatment of both penitential discipline and excommunication. In a book concerned especially with the church and its ministry, Bucer wished to focus on those elements of discipline and pastoral care that were the special responsibility of the pastors and elders. He noted in passing that all Christians should aid and give counsel to each other, each according to his ability, and that those in positions of authority were to be especially diligent in warding off harm and promoting what was beneficial to their charges, but since the book was concerned primarily with pastoral care, he would restrict his discussion to those passages of Scripture which described the responsibility of the elders of the church.[78] *Von der waren Seelsorge* can therefore be seen as a lengthy plea for extending the authority of the pastors and lay elders in the Strasbourg church. As a consequence, the argument for fraternal admonition was of secondary importance.

At about the same time that he was writing *Von der waren Seelsorge*, Bucer preached a series of sermons, based on the text of Matt. 11:28–30, in the village of Benfeld, near Strasbourg. Bucer devoted his second sermon to an explication of the yoke of Christ. That yoke, he stated, was "nothing other than [Christ's] government and discipline which he carries out in his holy church."[79] Bucer further defined this "government and discipline of the church" as

---

[77]Bucer used similar criteria for judging whether church practices are obligatory in a letter written to Louis du Tillet a few months later: those ceremonies instituted by Christ, recommended by the apostles, and practiced by the early church were required to be observed in the church; Bornert, *Réforme protestante*, 295; on Bucer's exchange with du Tillet, cf. Pollet, *Correspondance* 2:528–33.

[78]BDS 7:214.20–29.

[79]Ibid., 41.14–16.

the power and use of the keys to heaven, the proper spiritual and godly government among the faithful, through which all the elect, by the Holy Spirit and the heavenly power of Christ with his word, where they still stray in false worship or arrogant life, are brought to Christ our Lord, the arch-shepherd, and into the sheepfold of his church through true faith, and are preserved and reformed in the same through daily instruction, admonition, punishment and discipline, so that they continually die to all evil and constantly grow and increase in the life of Christ, that is, in all good works. And where anyone does not want to be shown how to reform or allow himself to be disciplined, to exclude that person from the church of Christ.[80]

This description of the "government and discipline of the church" was a restatement of the definition of the power of the keys from the Gospels commentary, phrased in the same pastoral language as *Von der waren Seelsorge*. Bucer went on to stress that acceptance of this discipline involved an act of the will: "to take the yoke of Christ upon you is to commit yourself to the obedience of Christ in his church and to its discipline," or, as he also phrased it, "to commit yourself to the discipline and government of Christ, which he exercises in his church."[81] Bucer did not mention confirmation in this context, but he was clearly moving towards the view of confirmation which would be codified in the disciplinary ordinance which he wrote for the Hessian church a few months later.

III. The Hessian Church Ordinances of 1538/1539

In August of 1538, Landgraf Philip of Hesse asked Bucer to come to Hesse in order to help counter the spread of Anabaptist teachings in his territories.[82] Bucer willingly agreed to the Landgraf's request and arrived in Hesse at the end of October. His assignment was twofold: to attempt to win back to the church several Anabaptist leaders who were imprisoned in Marburg, and to act as an advisor at a synod to be held at Ziegenhain in November. Bucer was the chief author of the disciplinary ordinance which resulted from the synod. The ordinance reflected the ideas which he had advanced in *Von der waren Seelsorge* as well as the concerns of the Anabaptists—particularly the followers of Melchior Hoffman—who were such a threat to the Hessian church.

---

[80]Ibid., 44.5-17.

[81]Ibid., 41.24-26; 42.5-7.

[82]Bucer's acceptance of the Landgraf's invitation in Lenz 1:45, no. 14; for background on the Hessian church and the spread of Anabaptism there, see Lenz 1:317-326, Beilage I; Walter Sohm, *Territorium und Reformation in der hessischen Geschichte 1526-1555*, 2nd ed., ed. G. Franz, Veröffentlichungen der historischen Kommission für Hessen und Waldeck XI/ 1 (Marburg: Elwert, 1957), 130-150, 158-161; John C. Stalnaker, "Anabaptism, Martin Bucer, and the Shaping of the Hessian Protestant Church," *Journal of Modern History* 48 (1976):601-643; Werner O. Packell, "The Melchiorites and the Ziegenhain Order of Discipline, 1538-39," in *Anabaptism Revisited: Essays on Anabaptist/Mennonite Studies in Honor of C. J. Dyck*, ed. Walter Klaassen (Scottsdale, Pa.: Herald, 1992), 11-28.

The important role played by the question of church discipline was apparent from the public debate which Bucer held with the imprisoned Anabaptists. Much of the debate focused on the proper use of the ban. Bucer held that it was the responsibility of the pastor, acting in the name of the church, to ban sinners. If the pastor neglected this duty, individual Christians could reprove and warn the sinner privately, but they could not exercise the ban themselves by separating from the congregation. Such separation was a condemnation not of the sinners in the church but of the church's ministry and of the church itself.[83] Bucer was sympathetic when one of the Anabaptists stated his disillusionment with the Hessian church because it had not introduced the ban, but he also pointed out that there would always be both good and bad in the church. It was the church's goal to reform the bad through its teaching and discipline. Exclusion from the church was done for two reasons, so that the excommunicate would be shamed into repentance, and so that he would not lead others astray.[84]

The emphasis the Anabaptists placed on excommunication coincided with some of Bucer's deepest concerns. Although he opposed their separation from the church, he was sensitive to their criticisms. As he wrote to the Landgraf, "the most obvious objection of these people, unfortunately, is that we administer [the church] so badly, and with this argument they lead many people astray. May the Lord help us to eliminate this argument of the Anabaptists and the papists, and even of our own consciences and of the Lord." Already Bucer was formulating a plan by which he hoped "to achieve reformation of the church, for the sake of the Anabaptists and others," which would be discussed at the upcoming synod.[85]

Events were to give further shape to Bucer's plan. Peter Tasch, one of the most important of the Anabaptist leaders in Hesse, had been present at the debate and had secretly sought Bucer out afterwards for private conversation.[86] Tasch wished to be reconciled with the official church and to help ease the return of other Anabaptists "who were now convinced that they had created much offense and no reformation by their separation." The suggestions which Tasch gave, and which Bucer summarized in a letter to the Landgraf on November 3, meshed nicely with positions Bucer already held.[87]

---

[83]Günther Franz, ed., *Urkundliche Quellen zur Reformationsgeschichte Hessens*, vol. 4: *Wiedertäuferakten, 1527–1626*, Veröffentlichungen der historischen Kommission für Hesse und Waldeck XI/4 (Marburg: Elwert, 1951), 215–217. The excerpt from this debate translated into English by Franklin Littell, "What Butzer Debated with the Anabaptists at Marburg: A Document of 1538," *Mennonite Quarterly Review* 36 (1962):256–276, contains some egregious translation errors.

[84]Franz, *Quellen*, 234.

[85]Ibid., 238–239, no. 79.

[86]On Tasch (or Tesch), see Werner Packull, "Peter Tasch en de Melchiorieten in Hessen"; *Doopsgezinde Bijdragen* 12–13 (1986–1987):107–138; idem, "Peter Tasch: From Melchiorite to Bankrupt Wine Merchant," *Mennonite Quarterly Review* 62 (1988):276–295.

[87]Franz, *Quellen*, 239–241, no. 80.

Tasch saw two potential hindrances for Anabaptists wishing to be reconciled to the church. First, preachers would not be zealous enough in their pastoral duties and, through neglect of discipline, would create new offense. Second, once they were no longer persecuted, the former Anabaptists would again become caught up in "worldly and fleshly doings." For both these reasons, an effective form of discipline was necessary. Tasch also suggested that "re-converted" Anabaptists not be required to receive the Lord's Supper immediately upon return to the church. Although they accepted the reformers' teaching on the sacrament, they did not want to receive the sacrament in churches where there was no ban and hence "no differentiation between the people" who could partake of the Lord's Supper. Furthermore, there should be no requirement for public recantation, for this would only cause other Anabaptists to regard them as backsliders and harden them in their own beliefs.[88]

The suggestions attributed to Tasch are so similar to Bucer's own thoughts that one wonders whether the reformer perhaps read his own ideas into Tasch's words. At any rate, the Ziegenhain disciplinary ordinance incorporated provisions similar to those in the Strasbourg ordinance which would make easier the reintegration of former Anabaptists into the church. The disciplinary ordinance was divided into an introduction and five sections of unequal length. The first section emphasized the responsibility of the superintendents to see that all churches were served by ministers able to preach, teach, admonish, and discipline and "do all that pertains to the care of souls."[89] The second section provided for the appointment of lay elders, including both government officials and representatives from the congregation, who would have oversight of the pastors, the authority to judge doctrinal disputes, and the right to administer church affairs. Together with the pastors, they would also be responsible for pastoral care in each congregation, which included the admonition and discipline of anyone whose beliefs or conduct needed correction.[90]

The third section required that all children be sent to catechism instruction, which was to be held in every parish at a time convenient for all. It also introduced a confirmation ceremony for those children who had learned their catechism and were ready to be admitted to the Lord's Supper for the first time. The ceremony was to be performed on the principal church holidays—Christmas, Easter, and Pentecost—in front of the gathered congregation and in the presence of elders and godparents. The children were to answer the pastor's questions concerning "the chief elements of the Christian faith" and then "submit themselves publicly to Christ and the church." The pastor prayed for them, placed his hands on them, and "confirmed them in the name of the Lord to Christian fellowship." Finally, the children were admitted to the Lord's Table with an admonition to remain faithful to the gospel and to obediently accept "Christian discipline and reproof from each and every Christian and especially from their *Seelsorger*."[91]

---

[88]Ibid., 240.
[89]BDS 7:261.19–262.9.
[90]Ibid., 262.10–263.23.
[91]Ibid., 263.24–264.28.

The liturgical ordinance for the church of Kassel, also drafted by Bucer, included an order for the confirmation ceremony which explained in more detail what submission to the church entailed. As part of the profession of faith, the children stated that the fellowship of the church included obedience to God's word, the acceptance of reproof from the elders or other Christians and readiness to reprove other Christians when necessary, willingness to bring contumacious sinners to the attention of the pastors and elders, and acknowledgment that anyone banned by the pastors and elders would be regarded "as a banned heathen."[92] Although one child could make this confession of faith for all of the confirmands, each child was asked, "do you believe and confess, and will you also commit yourself into the fellowship and obedience of the church of Christ, as you have now heard that this child believes and confesses and commits himself to the church of Christ?" In addition, each child was to make the prescribed confession of faith privately to the elders and pastors in the week before the public confirmation ceremony.[93] The ceremony thus provided an opportunity for children not only to demonstrate their knowledge of and intellectual assent to Christian doctrine, but also to state their willingness to recognize the disciplinary authority of the church's leaders—"to commit themselves to the obedience of the church."[94]

The fourth section of the Ziegenhain disciplinary ordinance specified in greater detail how discipline was to be exercised. In a manner reminiscent of the Strasbourg church ordinance, Bucer distinguished the form of discipline applied according to the type of behavior subject to discipline. In response to the Anabaptists' concerns about the neglect of church discipline and the ban, the Hessian ordinance was more explicit in this area, but its differentiation between groups was similar to the Strasbourg ordinance. The Hessian ordinance described three groups subject to admonition: those who had separated themselves completely from the church, those who attended the church services but would not partake of the Lord's Supper, and those who received the sacrament but who did not live in a manner appropriate for a Christian and therefore were an offense to the entire church. The first goal was to persuade anyone completely separated from the church to attend the preaching services. To this end, one of the elders or anyone else who might have influence with the individual was sent to speak privately with him. The elders could also summon the separatist to appear before them, a recommendation especially in the event that he would not heed private admonition. If the individual persevered in his contumacy, despite repeated admonition, he was "left to God and the magistrate" and avoided by other Christians. Bucer repeated the provisions from the Strasbourg ordinance specifying that civil obligations to the sinner were to be performed, and as in *Von der waren Seelsorge* he attempted

---

[92]Ibid., 311.29-43.

[93]Ibid., 312.17-33.

[94]On the significance of this public commitment to the church and the influence of the Hessian Anabaptists on the confirmation ceremony, see Burnett, "Martin Bucer."

to balance the degree to which he was to be ostracized with the familial or other responsibilities due him.[95]

Those who attended the sermons but did not receive the Lord's Supper were also to be admonished by the pastors and elders. If any in this second group avoided the sacrament because of error rather than out of contempt for it, they were to be instructed in a gentle way and regarded as catechumens, "namely, as disciples of Christianity to which, however, they have not yet completely committed themselves." Such people could not be completely cut off from the church, but neither could they be regarded as full members of it. Those who did hold the sacrament in contempt, on the other hand, were admonished for as long as there was hope of reform. Continued contumacy was to be countered with avoidance by other Christians. Again, as was the case with separatists, such ostracism was to be tempered by the performance of familial or civil responsibilities and continual admonition to repent.[96]

Finally, individuals who had not separated from the church in any way but had committed grave sins were admonished, again by the pastors and elders. If admonition proved fruitless, the sinner was "denied the fellowship of the Lord's table and considered as a heathen." Such people could not be reaccepted into the church until they had demonstrated their repentance through their actions and had sought pardon from the elders; in other words, until they had submitted to penitential discipline. The sins for which a person could be excommunicated are listed; they follow the Ten Commandments and range from teaching false doctrine, defined as anything opposed to the Augsburg Confession, to "showing mad, bestial immoderation in eating, drinking, and other external actions." Those who persisted in such sins despite admonition were to be excluded from the church so that they were brought to shame and repentance and did not destroy other Christians.[97]

To prevent abuse, no one could be excommunicated without the knowledge of the superintendent, who was also to give the final admonition and, if there was no repentance, to pronounce the excommunication in the presence of the pastors and elders of the sinner's church. Only under unusual circumstances was the excommunication to be imposed publicly,

> because we do not believe at this time that it would bring any improvement to ban anyone before the congregation, unless it was such a grave and notorious sin in which the person defiantly perseveres, such as public blasphemy against God, perversion of Christian doctrine or such gross, vile obstinacy against all good that God in his law commanded such people to be executed. In addition, [news of] this banning, even if it is done only before the elders, will spread sufficiently among the congrega-

[95]BDS 7: 265.1–266.30.
[96]Ibid., 266.31–267.26.
[97]Ibid., 267.27–269.30.

tion so that each godly person will know how to act towards the one who has been banned.[98]

Imposition of the ban was accompanied by a reminder of the power to bind sins in heaven given to the church by Christ. The ordinance specified that even if the excommunicate had already been punished by the magistrate for sins such as murder or adultery, he still had to perform the penance imposed by the elders and be kept from the Lord's Supper for a period until his repentance had been recognized and he was reconciled with the church.[99]

The consequences of excommunication included more than simply exclusion from the Lord's Supper and social ostracism. Since he was to be regarded as a heathen by other Christians, the excommunicate could not stand as godparent at a baptism, and his own children were to be presented in baptism by friends or by people appointed by the elders. He could not hold governmental office or act as representative of the government. If he died before being reconciled with the church, he was denied a church burial.[100] These latter provisions were the most controversial of the disciplinary ordinance, and the Landgraf himself expressed reservations about having the children of excommunicated persons baptized. He also required that the ban be introduced initially only in those cities such as Kassel and Marburg which had "the most capable and learned pastors." This no doubt weakened the appeal of the disciplinary ordinance to Anabaptists somewhat but, as Philip astutely observed, not all pastors had "the same gifts of learning, understanding and Christian discretion, and . . . among the unskilled pastors there could occur much human passion, hatred, envy and ill-will, which would not be good and would bring great detriment to the evangelical cause."[101] This limitation delayed the establishment of the ban, but it did not lead to any changes in the disciplinary procedure as such.

The fifth and final section of the ordinance dealt primarily with the sacraments, baptism and the Lord's Supper. Parents and godparents were to be admonished concerning their religious duties when their children were baptized, and the pastors were to see that suitable godparents were chosen.[102] All who wished to partake of the Lord's Supper were to be examined and instructed by the pastor beforehand. This precommunion examination was not to be regarded as a burden imposed by man, "since one could never be sufficiently examined, instructed, admonished or consoled concerning the Lord's promises."[103] Finally, the pastors were to preach diligently

---

[98]Ibid., 270.1–22.

[99]Ibid., 270.23–28; 271.4–13.

[100]Ibid., 270.29–271.3, 14–29.

[101]Franz, *Quellen*, 245–247 (no. 84, Dec. 1, 1538).

[102]These provisions were reinforced in the Kassel church ordinance of early 1539, which contained more specific provisions regarding the administration of the sacraments and other church ceremonies, BDS 7:283.13–22.

[103]Ibid., 273.6–9.

against drunkenness, blasphemy, and other sins which were common among the people.[104]

The Hessian disciplinary ordinance can be seen as the most complete statement of Bucer's views on Christian discipline. It contained all the elements Bucer regarded necessary for a well-ordered church. There was regular mandatory catechetical instruction for children and adolescents, along with the opportunity for each child to make a confession of faith and a profession of obedience to the church in a public confirmation ceremony. The Hessian church was provided with elders who would assist the clergy in the tasks of private admonition and pastoral oversight. These *Seelsorger* had the authority to impose penitential discipline on the repentant and to excommunicate contumacious sinners. The ordinance was intended to help win the Anabaptists back to the Hessian church, but its provisions were not simply a response to the Hessian situation. Bucer had advocated many of its policies long before his arrival in Hesse. For example, he incorporated one of Tasch's suggestions into the ordinance when he allowed those unwilling to receive the sacrament to be considered as catechumens, but the Strasbourg church ordinance of 1534 had contained a similar provision, and Bucer had made the comparison with catechumens as early as his *Grund und Ursach* of 1524. Likewise, the ban outlined in the disciplinary ordinance met the criteria Bucer had outlined in his debate with the Anabaptist leaders. It was imposed by the proper church authorities rather than by the individual Christian, it was preceded by admonition, and its goal was the protection of the congregation and the repentance of the sinner. But these were also common themes in Bucer's earlier works.

Like the Ulm church ordinance, the Hessian disciplinary ordinance has often been regarded as an example of what Bucer wanted to establish in Strasbourg but which the city's magistrate forbade. In their provisions regarding discipline, however, the two ordinances are very similar, both in entrusting congregational oversight to a body of laymen and in distinguishing between the three groups subject to discipline. Both ordinances prescribed a nonpublic form of the ban. The chief difference between the two ordinances on the issue of excommunication is one of detail. Bucer's draft ordinance for Strasbourg implicitly gave the pastors and *Kirchenpfleger* the right to decide when an individual should be excommunicated. The Hessian ordinance also implicitly gave to pastors and elders the authority to excommunicate dissidents and those who "persevered in their contempt for the Lord's Supper";[105] but it was more explicit concerning the excommunication of contumacious sinners. In this respect the ordinance took account of the size and existing structure of the Hessian church. Hesse was a large, heterogeneous territory; since 1531 it had been divided among six superintendents who were responsible for oversight of ecclesiastical affairs. Bucer accepted this structure and acknowledged the authority of the superintendent by giving him the right to admonish a contumacious sinner for the last time before

[104]Ibid., 271.30-275.22.
[105]Ibid., 267.15.

declaring him banned.[106] Even in this case the Hessian ordinance discouraged the public proclamation of excommunication. The ordinance's justification for this limited publicity was most likely intended to mollify Anabaptist critics who advocated a more stringent use of church discipline.

A more significant difference between the Strasbourg church ordinance and the Hessian disciplinary ordinance, the public confirmation ceremony, was the result of further development in Bucer's ideas between 1533 and 1538.[107] At the time that he drafted the Strasbourg ordinance, Bucer was only beginning to see how confirmation could fit into a more comprehensive system of discipline. In the intervening years, he increasingly emphasized that Christians should not only know the essentials of their faith but that they should also willingly accept the admonition and spiritual guidance of the *Seelsorger*, the pastors, and elders. The confirmation ceremony prescribed for Hesse provided an occasion on which the confirmands could publicly confess their faith and also promise their obedience to the *Seelsorger*. The solemnity of the ceremony , including the prayers of the congregation and the quasi-sacramental sign of the imposition of hands, would impress on the children the serious nature of their submission to the church and their responsibilities as Christians.[108] This ceremony now became an essential part of Bucer's system of Christian discipline, and his later writings all stress its importance.

Bucer's emphasis on the need for confirmation and penitential discipline reflected his growing disillusionment with the inhabitants of Strasbourg, both children and adults. At the time he wrote the Strasbourg ordinance Bucer was still confident that fraternal admonition and discipline, rightly applied, would be welcomed by all who called themselves Christians. In the *Bericht* of 1534 he argued that, since they had been incorporated into the church through baptism, all children should be raised as Christians and subjected to the pastors' disciplinary authority. This confidence dissolved in the face of opposition from both magistrate and laity in Strasbourg. The pastors' frequent complaints to the council about the unruliness and indiscipline of the city's youth demonstrate that Bucer's expectations in the area of catechization were not being fulfilled. Neither the children nor their parents seemed overly con-

---

[106]Sohm, *Territorium*, 76–77. The provision requiring a precommunion examination is another example of how Bucer incorporated existing practices in Hesse into his disciplinary ordinance. The examination had been established by the church ordinance of 1526. Stalnaker also points out the similarities of the Strasbourg and Hessian ordinances and attributes their differences to the contrasting political and administrative circumstances found in a free imperial city and in a large territorial state, "Anabaptism," 633–638.

[107]Historians of confirmation have made much of the Hessian disciplinary ordinance, since it prescribed the first Protestant confirmation ceremony; cf. Wilhelm Diehl, *Zur Geschichte der Konfirmation. Beiträge aus der hessischen Kirchengeschichte* (Giessen: J. Ricker, 1897), 10–13; Maurer, *Gemeindezucht*, 78–81; idem, "Geschichte," 28–31. Hareide's analysis of Bucer's theology is superseded by Hammann, *Entre la Secte*, 297–303, but Hareide is correct in his statement that the primary goal of the Hessian ordinance was discipline broadly defined, *Konfirmation*, 140–144.

[108]On the quasi-sacramental nature of the imposition of hands, see above, pp. 78–79; Hammann, *Entre la Secte*, 197–199.

cerned with the type of pastoral care which Bucer wanted to establish. Bucer responded to this public apathy by sharpening his rhetoric. Submission to the church and its pastors, what Bucer referred to as "the yoke of Christ," was "voluntary" in the sense that it was a choice made by the individual, but it was also commanded by God and therefore required of all Christians.

Over the next decade Bucer became even more strident in urging the acceptance of the yoke of Christ. Within Strasbourg he continued to advocate a comprehensive system of discipline including religious instruction, submission to the church, moral oversight, penitential discipline, and excommunication. He advocated the same system of discipline outside of Strasbourg as well, but here he had to take account of the larger religious and political situation of the German empire. In particular, his involvement in the religious colloquies and ecumenical dialogue with the Catholics, as well as the attempt to reform the archiepiscopal territories of Cologne, had ramifications for the further development of his system of discipline.

5

Christian Discipline in Confrontation with Catholic Theology, 1539-1549

Bucer's reputation as the "apostle of concord"[1] rests not only on his unflagging efforts to bring Lutherans and Zwinglians together on the issue of the Lord's Supper but also on his repeated attempts to bring about a reconciliation between Protestants and Catholics. From the late 1530s Bucer became actively involved in the religious colloquies intended to reunite the German church. He also became one of the major figures in the attempt to reform the archiepiscopal territories of Cologne. In both these areas, Bucer hoped that Protestants and Catholics would find a common basis for reform in the standards of the early church as reflected in Scripture, the fathers, and the oldest church canons.

Bucer's ideas on discipline brought him into conflict with Catholic doctrine on several points. As part of his disciplinary system, he had reinterpreted the Catholic sacrament of confirmation, modifying the ceremony and giving it a new significance. He had also rejected mandatory auricular confession and the scholastic definition of satisfaction, both integral parts of the sacrament of penance, and advocated instead the reintroduction of patristic penitential practices. Moreover, he denied that confirmation and confession were sacraments, although he did give them a special place among the rituals of the church. If Bucer's attempts to reunite the German church were to succeed, he either would have to persuade his Catholic counterparts to accept these views or else he would himself have to accept an interpretation closer to Catholic teaching.

An important precondition for Bucer's discussions with the Catholics was his own theological evolution from his earlier Zwinglian orientation to a more Lutheran position on the sacraments and private absolution.[2] Equally important, Bucer's hu-

---

[1]Hubert Jedin, A History of the Council of Trent, vol. 1: The Struggle for the Council, trans. Dom Ernest Graf, O.S.B. (St. Louis: Herder, 1957), 362 n. 2.

[2]Bullinger and his fellow pastors in Zürich continued to condemn private confession and reject any form of private absolution. Regarding Melanchthon's Concilium to Francis I, Bullinger wrote to Johannes Zwick in March 1535, "Et de confessione auriculari retinenda perverse videntur sedulo disputare. . . . Isti vero ad exemplum veteris, hoc est papisticae confessionis, nescio quas feces subinde in impuro vase cogitant retinere," Pollet, Correspondance

manist training gave him a point of contact with reform-minded Erasmian Catholics, who were sensitive to criticism of the practices associated with both penance and confirmation. His emphasis on the teaching and practice of the early church was likely to agree with their own prescriptions for church reform. Finally, Bucer used both the church fathers and the oldest provisions of canon law to argue that his disciplinary system was more in accord with the early church than were the current practices of the Roman church.

Bucer's desire to bring reform to Catholic territories dated from relatively early in his career,[3] but his first direct involvement in efforts to reunite the church came in August of 1534. At the instigation of the French minister Guillaume du Bellay, Melanchthon had written a memorandum for Francis I describing how Catholics and Protestants could reach agreement on disputed questions of doctrine and practice. Bucer was also asked to draw up a memorandum with his own suggestions concerning the reconciliation of the churches.[4] Bucer's statements about penance were optimistic but deliberately vague. He was confident that "those who compared the present form of confession with the practice of the church fathers and who sought to establish that which brings about amendment rather than what causes greater harm" would quickly reach an agreement regarding confession. The enumeration of secret sins was not required by divine law, but confession itself helped bring about genuine repentance and calmed consciences. Unlike Melanchthon, Bucer said nothing specifically about private absolution or the power of the keys.[5]

2:523.37-524.7; cf. a letter written in April 1541, by the Zürich pastors to Farel condemning the precommunion examination, Herminjard 7: 74 (no. 960), and the account of Bullinger's *Gutachten* to the Siebenbürgen reformer Johannes Honterus in 1543, in Roth, *Privatbeichte,* 13-17.

[3]For instance, in his Psalms commentary of 1529 he attempted to present evangelical doctrine in a way that would win Catholic readers, especially those in France, to the cause of the Reformation; see Marijn de Kroon, "Bemerkungen Martin Bucers über das Abendmahl in seinem Psalmenkommentar von 1529," in *Bucer und seine Zeit, Forschungsbeiträge und Bibliographie,* ed. Marijn de Kroon and Friedhelm Krüger, Veröffentlichungen des Instituts für europäische Geschichte Mainz 80 (Wiesbaden: Franz Steiner, 1976), 88-89; above, p. 40.

[4]Karl Josef Seidel, *Frankreich und die deutschen Protestanten. Die Bemühungen um eine religiöse Konkordie und die französische Bündnispolitik in den Jahren 1534/1535,* Reformationsgeschichtliche Studien und Texte 102 (Münster: Aschendorff, 1970), is the most detailed account of French efforts for religious concord. He gives a summary of the memoranda written by Melanchthon, Bucer, and Kaspar Hedio, 16-46. See also Pollet's introduction to Bucer's memorandum, *Correspondance* 2: 488-509; Robert Stupperich, *Der Humanismus und die Wiedervereinigung der Konfessionen,* Schriften des Vereins für Reformationsgeschichte 53/2 (160) (Leipzig: M. Heinsius, 1936), 32-35, and Eells, *Martin Bucer,* 166-172. Marijn de Kroon discusses Bucer's memorandum as an example of the reformer's desire to bring about the reunification of the church, *Studien zu Martin Bucers Obrigkeitsverständnis. Evangelisches Ethos und politisches Engagement* (Gütersloh: G. Mohn, 1984), 57-69.

[5]Pollet, *Correspondance* 2: 512.4-10; cf. Melanchthon's memorandum, CR 2: 747-748. Hedio was less conciliatory in his opinion on confession, stating that theologians had mixed together the three forms of confession: privately to God, publicly to the church, and privately to one's brother. Hedio stressed the importance of confession for counsel and instruction. This definition of confession was the one given by Bucer in his Gospels commentary and

Bucer's memorandum evoked sharp criticism from both Constance and Zürich,[6] but it brought to the fore some of the themes which would recur over the next several years, such as the church's need for private catechization and confession, the rejection of mandatory confession of all sins, and the importance of the early church's example. In particular, the writings of the church fathers assumed an increasingly important place in Bucer's writings during the later 1530s. Already in the aftermath of the memorandum's publication, Johannes Zwick expressed his fear that Bucer was allowing the authority of the fathers to supplant the word of God.[7] Bucer defended his use of the fathers in the preface to his 1536 Gospels commentary, in part to allay such fears. By 1539 Bucer was urging the establishment of both penitential discipline and a public profession of faith and obedience because these were required by Scripture, established by the apostles, and observed by the early church.[8]

Bucer's respect for the authority of the church fathers provided a natural point of contact when he became involved in direct negotiations with Catholic theologians concerning the reunification of the German church. In early January 1539, he participated in a colloquy at Leipzig arranged by the chancellor of ducal Saxony, Georg von Karlowitz, with Elector Johann Friedrich and Landgraf Philip.[9] The colloquy reached an impasse when the Protestant participants refused to recognize as binding the doctrines and practices of the early church up through the fourth century, but they did agree to a debate with Georg Witzel, a former Lutheran pastor, who had returned

---

was ultimately derived from Melanchthon; above, p. 31-32. There is a certain irony in the fact that it was Hedio, rather than Bucer or Melanchthon, who gave this definition. Seidel, in summarizing Hedio's position, points to it as "an instructive example of a basic problem of all efforts for concord: that the parties agree on the use of a term but give it a completely different meaning." Seidel, *Frankreich*, 44. Eells aptly states that Bucer's *Concilium* was "formulated so as to minimize, if not conceal, the importance of the basic differences on doctrine and practice," *Martin Bucer*, 168.

[6]For an account of the opposition to the memorandum, Seidel, *Frankreich*, 88-122.

[7]Letter to Joachim Vadian, (May 25, 1535, no. 818); E. Arbenz and H. Wartmann, *Vadianische Briefsammlung 1508-1540*, Mitteilungen zur vaterländischen Geschichte 24-30a (St. Gallen, 1884-1913), 5: 222: "Totus est in lectione veterum. Hinc veremur, ne verbo Dei paulatim successurae sint patrum auctoritates."

[8]See below, p. 166.

[9]On the Leipzig colloquy see Cornelis Augustijn, *De Godsdienstgesprekken tussen rooms-katholieken en protestanten van 1538-1541* (Haarlem: F. Bohn, 1967), 16-24; Ludwig Cardauns, *Zur Geschichte der kirchlichen Unions- und Reformbestrebungen von 1538 bis 1542*, Bibliothek des königlichen preussischen historischen Instituts in Rom 5 (Rome: Loescher, 1910), 1-24, with the text of the reunion proposal drafted at Leipzig, 85-108; Peter Fraenkel, *Einigungsbestrebungen der Reformationszeit. Zwei Wege · Zwei Motive*, Institut für europäische Geschichte Mainz, Vorträge 41 (Wiesbaden: Steiner, 1965), 6-36; Robert Stupperich, *Humanismus*, 2-49; Günther Wartenberg, "Die Leipziger Religionsgespräche von 1534 und 1539. Ihre Bedeutung für die sächsisch-albertinische Innenpolitik und für das Wirken Georgs von Karlowitz," in *Die Religionsgespräche der Reformationszeit*, ed. Gerhard Müller, Schriften des Vereins für Reformationsgeschichte 191 (Gütersloh: Gerd Mohn, 1980), 35-41. In addition to Bucer, the Hessian chancellor Johann Feige represented the Landgraf, Melanchthon and the Saxon chancellor Gregor Brück represented the Elector. Duke Georg was represented by Karlowitz, the Leipzig theologian Ludwig Fachs and Georg Witzel; Lenz 1: 63-68, no. 23; cf. Brück's report to the Elector, CR 3: 624ff.

to the Catholic church and was now employed by the duke. Witzel, an enthusiastic admirer of Erasmus, had advocated using the early church as a norm for doctrine and practice in his *Typus ecclesiae prioris*, written for Karlowitz in 1538 but not published until 1540.[10] Melanchthon and Brück eventually withdrew from the meetings on the elector's instructions, but Bucer and Witzel continued their discussions and finally reached agreement on fifteen points set forth in a document which Bucer published six years later with the title, *Ein Christlich ongefährlich bedencken, Wie ein leidlicher ane-fang christlicher vergleichung in der Religion zu machen sein möchte.*[11]

The Leipzig articles were concerned not with doctrine but with practice. Some of the most controversial questions—transubstantiation and the sacrificial nature of the mass, the number of the sacraments, and other issues—were not mentioned, and the largest share of the document focused on questions of church order.[12] This generalization held true for the third article, "on the penitence of those who are baptized and already in the church." The article stated that since all Christians sinned daily, they were to be aroused to true contrition through the law of God, consoled with forgiveness through the gospel, and led to seek forgiveness, consolation, and strength in the church "through the word and power of the keys, which is the proper (*ordenlich*) absolution." Those who had committed more serious sins were to confess to their pastor (*Seelsorger*) and perform satisfaction to the church as demonstration of their contrition and amendment. The article rejected set penances for each sin as having no basis in God's word and stressed that in imposing penance, the pastor was to steer between the extremes of discouraging the sinner and giving him a false confidence in the value of his own works, so that all incentives to sin were eliminated and the individual desired to change his ways. Those who had seriously offended the church were excluded from the Lord's Table "according to the ordinance of the early church" during the period of their penance, while those who rejected the church's penance and persisted in their sin were held as heathens and non-Christians until they repented and submitted to penance. The article concluded that penitence consisted of

---

[10]Magnus Ditsche, "Das 'Richtscheit der Apostolischen Kirche' beim Leipziger Religionsgespräch von 1539," in *Reformata Reformanda, Festgabe für Hubert Jedin zum 17. Juni 1965,* ed. Erwin Iserloh and Konrad Repgen (Münster: Aschendorff, 1965), 1: 466-475, esp. 469-471; on Witzel see Friedrich W. Kantzenbach, *Das Ringen um die Einheit der Kirche im Jahrhundert der Reformation. Vertreter, Quellen und Motive des "ökumenischen" Gedankens von Erasmus von Rotterdam bis Georg Calixt* (Stuttgart: Evangelisches Verlagswerk, 1957), 176-202, esp. 194-197; Winfried Trusen, *Um die Reform und Einheit der Kirche. Zum Leben und Werk Georg Witzels,* Katholisches Leben und Kämpfen im Zeitalter der Glaubensspaltung 14 (Münster: Aschendorff, 1957).

[11]Stupperich #79. In *Ein Christlich ongefährlich bedencken* Bucer claimed to be the author of the articles, and almost twenty years later Witzel acknowledged that Bucer had drawn up the greater part of the agreement, *Warer Bericht von den Acten der Leipischen und Speirischen Collocution,* ARC 6: 18. Regardless of who actually wrote them, the fact that Bucer was the first to publish the articles is evidence that he endorsed their contents; cf. Hubert Jedin, "An welchen Gegensätzen sind die vortridentinischen Religionsgespräche zwischen Katholiken und Protestanten gescheitert?" in idem, *Kirche des Glaubens/Kirche der Geschichte. Ausgewählte Aufsätze und Vorträge* (Freiburg: Herder, 1966), 1: 363; cf. also Fraenkel's remarks in *Einigungsbestrebungen,* 13-14 n. 19.

[12]Fraenkel, *Einigungsbestrebungen,* 14-23, summarizes what the articles do, and do not, discuss.

contrition, confession, and satisfaction. But confession was made first to God, and then to men, "to receive instruction, counsel and consolation from the pastor or another Christian" or to be reconciled with an individual who had been offended, or to the church as public testimony of repentance. Likewise, satisfaction was performed towards the individual or the church which had been injured, but not towards God, since Christ was our only satisfaction.[13]

Cardauns interprets this article, with its emphasis on the punishment of public sin and the use of excommunication, as "still standing on the ground of Catholicism" and sees Witzel's influence reflected in it,[14] but the underlying theology and the views expressed accord much more closely with Bucer's understanding of confession and church discipline. Although it retained the basic elements of contrition, confession, and satisfaction, it redefined the latter two to accommodate the Protestant position, and its description of confession echoed the three types discussed by Bucer in his Gospels commentary. The article defined the power of the keys only loosely as absolution; it did not discuss whether confession was required by divine law or whether all sins were to be confessed, and it implied that confession did not have to be made to a priest. The article mentioned the consolatory power of absolution only indirectly, placing more emphasis on absolution as restoration of fellowship with the church than as assurance of forgiveness.

Article 6, on confirmation, reflected the views which Bucer had developed on confirmation since 1534. Ultimately derived from apostolic practice, confirmation arose from the custom in which bishops laid hands on and prayed for those baptized as infants "after they had been sufficiently instructed in the Christian faith and had given themselves in obedience to the church."[15] Perverted through the negligence of more recent bishops, this "ceremony and custom" should be reformed, so that through catechetical instruction, "the fellowship and obedience of the church may very suitably be furthered" and the common people would be less attracted by Anabaptist "errors."[16]

In both articles Bucer returned to the technique which he had used in his 1529 Psalms commentary of avoiding controversial issues and concentrating on possible areas of agreement.[17] The practices of the early church in both penitential discipline and confirmation were held up as models for both parties. Although Bucer had rejected the suggestion that the early church serve as a binding norm in all areas for the

---

[13]Cardauns, Reformbestrebungen, 88-90.

[14]Ibid., 11, 13.

[15]The manuscript copy of the articles uses the term gegeben; Bucer's edition of the articles, published six years later has the word ergeben.

[16]Cardauns, Reformbestrebungen, 96-97. The reference to confirmation as a means of combatting Anabaptist errors is revealing, because Bucer had written the Hessian ordinance, with its confirmation ceremony, only a month earlier.

[17]In this sense, Articles 3 and 6, like the first two articles on the place of works in salvation and the freedom of the will, can be characterized as Erasmian; cf. Fraenkel, Einigungsbestrebungen, 14.

colloquy's participants, he had himself argued for a restoration of patristic practice with regard to discipline and confirmation. The model of the early church had a further advantage in Bucer's eyes, since it allowed him to ignore later developments in medieval scholastic theology concerning the sacraments of penance and confirmation.

The Leipzig articles were circulated among both Protestants and Catholics over the next several months, but they met with criticism from both sides.[18] At the two major colloquies sponsored by the emperor in 1540, held at Hagenau and at Worms, the participants instead used the *Augsburg Confession* as the basis for discussion. At Worms, Bucer became involved in secret meetings with Johannes Gropper, a lawyer and self-taught theologian in the employ of the Archbishop of Cologne, and the imperial secretary Gerhard Veltwyk.[19] The result of these meetings was the book which the emperor would present a few months later to the delegates at the Regensburg colloquy as a new basis for discussion.

The extent to which Bucer was willing to compromise with his Catholic counterparts during this period becomes clear from the *Concilium theologicum* which he wrote to an unnamed individual discussing "whether, and to what extent, Christians living in churches still burdened by papal tyranny are able to participate in its rites and ceremonies."[20] In the *Concilium theologicum*, Bucer described a hierarchy of ceremonies within the Catholic church. The first category was comprised of ceremonies instituted by God; along with the sacraments of baptism and the Lord's Supper, Bucer also included in this category the exercise of church discipline, ranging from private admonition through public rebuke to excommunication and the imposition of penance for grave sin.[21] The second category consisted of ceremonies which were introduced by the fathers for various reasons. Among those established "in imitation of the Lord and the apostles, though without their express command," Bucer listed the confirmation of children after they had been instructed in their faith.[22] Other patristic practices "arose and were accepted out of an excess of pious emotion"; included in this sub-category was the private confession of sins, which had been introduced to reassure troubled consciences but which was in reality a form of private catechization.[23] The third type of ceremony Bucer dismissed as abuses or misuses of ceremo-

---

[18]Cardauns, *Reformbestrebungen*, 1, 4-18.

[19]On the secret meetings see Eells, *Martin Bucer*, 278-289, with details to be corrected by Stupperich, *Humanismus*, 75-94; the primary source of information on the meetings are Bucer's letters to the Landgraf written from Worms, Lenz 1: 273ff., nos. 101ff. On the authorship of the so-called "Regensburg Book," see Robert Stupperich, "Der Ursprung des 'Regensburger Buches' von 1541 und seine Rechtfertigungslehre," ARG 36 (1939): 88-116.

[20]This is the subtitle of the work; cf. the description of this document by Peter Matheson, "Martyrdom or Mission? A Protestant Debate," ARG 80 (1989): 154-172; Pierre Fraenkel, "Bucer's Memorandum of 1541 and a 'lettera Nicodemitica' of Capito's," *Bibliothèque d'humanisme et renaissance* 36 (1974): 575-587; as well as the latter's introduction to the critical edition in BOL 4. The document was probably written in 1540.

[21]BOL 4: 13, par. 49-51, 55.

[22]Ibid., 13, par. 56-57.

[23]Ibid., 15, par. 64-65.

nies introduced by Christ or the saints; the sale of indulgences and the doctrine of satisfaction on which indulgences were based belonged in this category.[24]

Bucer believed that Christians should repudiate those ceremonies which fell into the third category. The ceremonies of the first category, however, were holy and should not be rejected, even if they contained abuses. Ceremonies of the second category fell between these two extremes. Some could be reformed and restored to their original purity; others had been so "contaminated by superstition" that they should be abolished. The responsibility for reform lay with the authorities of the church and the state, however. Where neither took steps towards reforming the ceremonies, Christians were still to participate in them, rejecting superstitious abuses and reminding themselves and others of how they could piously be used. As Bucer repeated throughout the *Concilium theologicum*, "to the pure, all things are pure."[25]

Bucer then described how an evangelical Christian living in a Catholic territory was to regard each of these ceremonies. He lamented the degeneration of church discipline into private confession and deplored the use of excommunication for secular ends, but he also stressed that Christians were not to reject church discipline entirely; rather they were to point out abuses and teach its proper exercise.[26] The ceremony of confirmation was acceptable, Bucer stated, if it was administered in imitation of apostolic practice, so that it followed catechetical instruction, included a public profession of faith, and was accompanied by prayer and the imposition of hands. If, however, the confirmation ceremony consisted only of the chrism and the recitation of Latin phrases which the people could not understand, then Christians were not to participate in it. On this point Bucer was willing to make a further concession: if the Christian offended his neighbors by seeming to reject a sacrament, Bucer counseled him to accept the "remnants of patristic practices" inherent in confirmation and to condemn the perversions only where this would edify.[27] Christians could make use of private confession because it combined individual instruction and the absolution of sins, but they should reject the associated "superstitions" such as trust in external works. Furthermore, they should ask the priest to impose a form of satisfaction "which was fitting for Christians," such as fasts, prayer, and almsgiving. Bucer reminded his reader to choose as confessor a wise priest "and one not ignorant of spiritual matters (such as is common among the mass priests [*sacrificulorum*]), since the scholastic doctors also ordered singular selection made from those to whom you confess your secret sins."[28] Bucer reserved his harshest criticism for indulgences and the scholastic doctrine of satisfaction. The power of the keys, he stated, pertained to the forgiveness of sin, not to the punishment imposed as a form of penance. Once sin

---

[24]Ibid., 15, par. 67, 69.
[25]Ibid., 17, par. 78–82; cf. Titus 1:15.
[26]Ibid., 65, par. 302–305.
[27]Ibid., 70–71, par. 307–311.
[28]Ibid., 82–83, par. 343–349, citation par. 348.

was forgiven, the penance which sinners performed was intended as a remedy against sin and a deterrent to others.[29]

Bucer's *Concilium theologicum* reflected the fundamental convictions which he would maintain in his discussions with Catholic theologians concerning penance, confirmation, and church discipline. Admonition, penitential discipline, and excommunication were divinely commanded and therefore necessary for the church. Confirmation had a lesser status. The Catholic ceremony was to imitate apostolic practice by including both a public profession of faith and the imposition of hands; otherwise it had no purpose. Finally, the essence of private confession was individual instruction and consolation, and if it was to be of any value, it had to be made to a wise and pious confessor. In all of his subsequent efforts to reach agreement with the Catholics, Bucer would continue to advocate these positions as the basis for consensus.

Bucer's first public opportunity to defend these positions came during the Regensburg colloquy, which began in late April 1541.[30] For a little over a month the Protestant and Catholic collocutors debated over the articles contained in the Regensburg Book, the result of Bucer's talks at Worms with Gropper. It was clear to the participants that not all of the book's articles were of equal importance, and in order to facilitate discussion of the major issues, the Protestants were willing to pass over any disagreements on secondary issues.[31] One of these secondary issues was the interpretation of confirmation. The Regensburg Book defined confirmation as a sacrament, although one which was not necessary for salvation, and it traced the rite's origin to the apostolic imposition of hands. The article on confirmation recommended that children should be instructed in the faith before being confirmed, at which time they were to profess their "faith in Christ and obedience to the church," as canon law provided.[32]

More important for the fate of the colloquy were the issues of transubstantiation and the authority of the church; here the discussion broke down, for the collocutors could not reach agreement. The article on penance proved to be yet another stumbling block. The Regensburg Book derived this sacrament from Christ's words granting the power to bind and loose sins in Matt. 18:18 and John 20:23. It urged the confession of sins which burdened the conscience to a priest, who could console and encourage the penitent; it was "just and holy" for individuals to submit to the pastoral care of a priest at least once a year, so that he could examine their faith and morals and apply a "salutary medicine" for their sins. Those who had been thus absolved

---

[29]Ibid., 104, par. 422-425.

[30]On the Regensburg colloquy and its aftermath, see Augustijn, *Godsdienstgesprekken*, 73-130; Stupperich, *Humanismus*, 94-104; Jedin, *Trent* 1: 379-389; Peter Matheson, *Cardinal Contarini at Regensburg* (Oxford: Clarendon, 1972), 97-144. The spokesmen for the Protestants were Bucer, Melanchthon, and Johannes Pistorius; for the Catholics, Gropper, Eck, and Julius Pflug.

[31]This is how Melanchthon later described the colloquy and the Protestant position on confirmation; CR 4: 417.

[32]Ibid., 216. The article referred to De Consecratione, dist. 5, cap. 6, a decree of the council of Orléans; Friedberg 1: 1414.

could be assured of their reconciliation with the church and the forgiveness of the sins which they had confessed.

The Catholic collocutors objected to this article because it implied that mortal sins could be forgiven without the mediation of a priest in the sacrament of penance, and they insisted that the article clearly state that individuals must confess all mortal sins of which they were aware. They also added a paragraph stating that although satisfaction for sin was to be attributed to Christ alone, nevertheless canonical satisfaction as imposed by the pastor and rightly used was beneficial in removing the causes of the sins committed, in healing the effects of sin, in lessening or eliminating the temporal punishment for sin, and in serving as an example for others.[33]

The Protestants in turn protested against the Catholics' insistence on the confession of all mortal sins and on the validity of satisfaction, which they based on "the authority of the fathers and the church."[34] As leader of the Protestant delegation, Melanchthon drafted the counterarticles giving their objections to the Catholic position. He repeated the Lutheran view that private absolution was to be retained, but that the enumeration of sins was neither necessary nor commanded by divine law, and that such a requirement only burdened consciences.[35] In a lengthier statement of the Protestant position he acknowledged the usefulness of requiring confession of all mortal sins as a means of preserving external discipline, but he argued that the despair felt by the pious who were unsure if they had confessed every sin made such a requirement more detrimental than beneficial. The Protestants were able to preserve discipline through a precommunion examination and private absolution without the harmful effects to individual consciences which resulted from the mandatory enumeration of sins. Furthermore, although the church had the authority to judge manifest sin through the use of public penance as described by the church fathers, it had no authority over secret sins and thus could not require them to be revealed in private confession.[36]

A second counterarticle stated the Protestant position on satisfaction. Canonical satisfaction had once been imposed by the church to test the sincerity of a notorious sinner's repentance, but over the years these works of satisfaction had wrongfully been accorded some ability to atone for sin, thus obscuring the free forgiveness of sin through Christ. In the Protestant churches the magistrate punished notorious sin, hence there was no need to restore the penitential rites of the early church which had only led to error. It was the magistrate's responsibility to take action against grave sin, and its punishment was more effective than was canonical satisfaction.[37]

---

[33]ARC 6: 69.25–71.6; cf. CR 4: 217–218.

[34]See the report of the Saxon chancellor Friedrich Burckhardt to Elector Johann Friedrich, CR 4: 291 (no. 2230).

[35]Ibid., 354–355 (no. 2254).

[36]Ibid., 355–363 (no. 2254).

[37]Ibid., 364–367 (no. 2254).

The collocutors finally set aside the article on penance along with the Protestant counterarticles and proceeded to the next issue. However, their disagreement over penance had revealed the fatal weakness of the Regensburg Book and of the policy of conciliation which it advocated. As originally worded, the article on penance was a carefully balanced statement of positions accepted by both sides, such as the consolatory effect of absolution based on the power to bind and loose sins and the importance of submitting to the priest's pastoral care. It was silent on many of the issues which were disputed. Although the article contained statements which made it less than completely satisfactory for either side,[38] it was intended to present a common ground which both Catholics and Protestants would be willing to accept. The article's attempt to avoid controversy failed, however, when the Catholic collocutors amended it to require the confession of all mortal sins. The Protestant collocutors reacted to the Catholic position by stating more strongly their own view that the enumeration of sins could not be compelled. Once the battle lines were drawn, there was no room left for compromise or ambiguity on the issue of confession.[39] Moreover, the impasse concerning the major issues, such as the sacrament of penance, caused the reluctant consensus on secondary issues such as confirmation to evaporate. While the Protestants were willing to compromise on the issue of confirmation for the sake of concord, after it became clear that concord was impossible they quickly asserted their own position.[40]

[38]For example, during the secret negotiations which resulted in the original text of the Regensburg Book, Bucer had reported to the Landgraf that the parties still disagreed about the requirement of yearly confession, although he held out hope for agreement since his Catholic counterparts did not insist on the detailed listing of every sin and believed that only "older, proven men should be appointed" to hear confessions; Lenz 1: 288-289 (no. 106; Dec. 31, 1540).

[39]The disagreement over satisfaction was not so clear-cut. From Melanchthon's counterarticle it is obvious that he saw no merit in endorsing the use of canonical satisfaction or penance. Bucer, however, was apparently more willing to compromise, according to the Saxon chancellor's report to Elector Johann Friedrich (CR 4: 291, no. 2230). Bucer's conviction that the church had the right to expect evidence of repentance before granting absolution and his advocacy of penitential discipline gave him a natural point of contact with the Catholics on the imposition of satisfaction. This explains his greater openness to the paragraph on satisfaction. On differences between Bucer's and Melanchthon's attitude towards the colloquy, see Cornelis Augustijn, "Die Religionsgespräche der vierziger Jahre," in Die Religionsgespräche der Reformationszeit, ed. Gerhard Müller, Schriften des Vereins für Reformationsgeschichte 191 (Gütersloh: G. Mohn, 1980), 43-54; cf. Wilhelm Neuser's analysis of Bucer's position on transubstantiation and the reservation and veneration of the consecrated host at Regensburg, "Bucers Programm einer 'guten, leidlichen reformation' (1539-1541)," in Horizons Européens de la Réforme en Alsace. Das Elsass und die Reformation im Europa des XVI. Jahrhunderts, Aufsätze zum 65. Geburtstag von Jean Rott, ed. Marijn de Kroon and Marc Lienhard, Société Savante d'Alsace et des Régions de l'Est, Collection "Grandes Publications" 17 (Strasbourg: Istra, 1980), 231-233.

[40]Cf. Melanchthon's criticism of the article on confirmation, CR 4: 489-490; German version, 503-504: catechization followed by the public profession of faith, accompanied by congregational prayer and the imposition of hands, was commendable but it was not a sacrament.

At the end of May the Regensburg Book, along with the dissenting articles of the Protestants, was presented to the emperor. Both the Catholic and Protestant estates resisted imperial pressure to accept those few articles of the book on which the collocutors had reached agreement. Bucer, however, did not give up hope that the Regensburg Book could still bring about the reconciliation and reform of the German church. Instead, he campaigned aggressively for the recognition by both parties of the articles which had been accepted. At the end of 1541 he published the German text of several of the documents submitted at the colloquy, accompanied by his comments on them.[41] His commentary had two goals: to defend the Protestant position, and to attack the Catholics who in his opinion had sabotaged the colloquy by refusing to accept those articles which had been endorsed by both parties. The first goal was most evident in Bucer's account of the actual colloquy. He described the disagreement over the article on penance and upheld the Protestant position, stating that since God's word said nothing about confession of sins "beyond those in which a person needs counsel or consolation," they could not bind consciences by requiring the enumeration of sins. Likewise, they opposed the Catholic position on satisfaction because it was worded in such a way that the old abuses of satisfaction could easily recur.[42] Bucer reminded his readers, however, that there remained a great deal of agreement between the two parties. There were Catholic authorities "such as Panormitanus and others" who taught that the enumeration of sins was commanded by man rather than by God. The book had properly stressed Christ's satisfaction for sin, and in rejecting the article the Protestants did not in any way reject Christian discipline.[43]

The second, more polemical goal was most obvious in Bucer's comments on the official letter in which the Catholic estates rejected the Regensburg Book. The Cath-

[41]*Alle Handlungen vnd Schrifften, zu vergleichung der Religion . . . zu Regensburg verhandlet* (Stupperich #69c). He had already published the documents, in Latin but without commentary, the previous August under the title *Acta Colloqvii in comitiis imperii Ratisponae habiti* (Stupperich #69).

[42]*Alle Handlungen*, fols. 70v–71r: "Als dann die Collocutoren des anderen theils aber hert hielten / ob dem schluoß des vorgemelten Concili / jnn welchem auch begotten wurdt / das jeder Christ järlich / zuom wenigsten eynmal / alle sein sünd seinem Priester beichten solle . . . haben wir doch die gewissen / on Gotlichs wort / nierget an gewisset zuo binden / oder lassen hingohn / das eyn schein solches hette / Wie dann die erzelung der sünden / weiter dann jeder raht vnnd trost bedarffe / auß keynem Gottes wort erzwungen werden mage. . . . Des gleichen haben wir auch von der Satisfaction gethon. . . . Da wir dann besorget / das etliche leut die wort im Buoch gesetzet / dahin ziehen möchten / die alten mißbräuch / so bei der Satisfaction / der kirchen eyngefüret seind / zuoferben / und wider einzuofüren"; cf. fol. 136v.

[43]Ibid., fols. 213r–v: "Nun sind auch Paepstliche Lerer / alß Panormitanus vnnd andere / die halten / das dise erzelung allein ein menschen gepott seie / iuris positivi wie sie sagen. Sunst ist auch diser artickel aller dingen verglichen worden. . . . Der buoß halben ist gar nichs im streit bliben / also auch nit von der Satisfaction / welches alle die wol erkennen werden / die des so hievon imm Buoch / vnd in vnseren artikculen deshalben eingeben / gesetzet ist / recht gegen einander halten wöllen. Dann wie vor gesagt / das Buoch die genuogthuoung für die sünde / allein den todt Christi erkennet / so verwerffen wir keine Christliche vnd besserliche züchtigung/ Bekennen auch das der Herre denen / die solche züchtigung imm rechten glauben an jn auffnemen / offt die zeitliche straff milteret vnd hinnimmet."

olics had stated their desire to remain faithful to "the old religion" contained in Scripture, the writings of the fathers, and the decrees of church councils.[44] In response to this assertion, Bucer compared the "old religion" of the early church with the practices of the "new religion," the Roman church. In the early church the bishops "with all the elders, the whole clergy, and also all Christians" were quick to help those who had sinned through Christian reproof and admonition. The unrepentant were banned and not readmitted to the church until they had sufficiently demonstrated their repentance, while those guilty of manifest sin but repentant were temporarily kept from the sacrament, bound by some penance, and absolved publicly by the elders when the church had been satisfied by the sinner's repentance. The Catholics, on the other hand, merely imposed a few prayers or pilgrimages or, if the sin was regarded as serious, such as disobedience to some papal requirement, the sinner was told to buy an indulgence or was sent to the bishop's penitentiary or even to Rome for absolution. Excommunication was imposed only as a means of collecting money and not for bannable sins like drunkenness or immorality. In confession the priest showed little concern that the sinner demonstrate genuine contrition and amendment of life.[45]

Bucer also compared the practice of confirmation in the early church with contemporary Catholic ritual. In the early church confirmation had been administered by a bishop who laid his hands on children after they had been instructed in the Christian faith and were ready to profess their faith and obedience to the church themselves; this was done "so that the obedience and discipline of the church could be better and more firmly maintained." In the present-day church, however, confirmation was a mockery performed in open violation of the church canons and apostolic practice.[46] Bucer had not abandoned his hopes for reconciliation, but his harsh criticism of his Catholic opponents implicitly acknowledged that further negotiations would be futile.

On a more positive note, Bucer included in his book a memorandum in which he described how ecclesiastical abuses could be eliminated and a "Christian reforma-

---

[44]CR 4: 528 (no. 2314).

[45]*Alle Handlungen*, fols. 200r-201r.

[46]Ibid., 198v-199r: "[Die firmung] ist bey den alten ein bestätigung im glauben deren gewesen / die nach dem sie inn der kindheit geteüffet / hernaher aber / da sie des alters halben fähig worden / des Christlichen glaubens vnnd lebens also vnterricht gewesen sindt / das sie iren glauben / vnd gehorsame der Kirchen / selb haben mögen / vnd wöllen bekennen / vnnd versprechen. Dise besetigung hatt der rechte ware Bischoff gethon / mitt gemeinem gebett / vor allem volck / vnd dem hend auflegen . . . [damit] die gemeyne kirchen gehorsame vnd zucht / desto bass vnd steiffer erhalten wurde. . . . Was gotlosen schimpffs aber vnd zauberwercks / haben die Weihbischoff darauß gemacht? Sie sitzen da nach mittag / das wider die Canones außtrucklich ist / haben jren diener neben jnen stohn mit eym beckin / darein er das gelt empfaha. So sie dann das kind vor jnen haben / sprechen sie ettliche wort zuo latein / streichen damit dem kind das öl an die stirn / vnd schlahens an eyn backen / damit lacht man / vnd verbind das kindt / vnd geht dahin / vnd meynet diß werck sei sehr krefftig / das kind vor allem vngemach zuobewaren / Ist nuon das die alte Religion vnd Apostolische haltung?"

tion" accomplished in Germany. Part of his programme included the reestablishment of Christian discipline among the laity, which began with the catechization of children followed by a confirmation ceremony in which children would publicly profess their faith and obedience to the church.[47] Bucer advocated the use of admonition and penitential discipline, arguing that the "Christian ban must again be brought into its proper use according to God's word . . . and not imposed for debts and other worldly things" as was the practice of the ecclesiastical courts.[48] Not surprisingly, Bucer's recommendations accord with the system of discipline he established through the Hessian church ordinances of 1538. He attempted to introduce this same system in the archiepiscopal territories of Cologne during the ultimately unsuccessful reformation from 1542 to 1545.

The failure of the Cologne reformation left its mark on Bucer's subsequent efforts to bring about the reconciliation and reform of the German church. These efforts were the outgrowth of further political and religious developments within the empire, particularly the possibility of a national council called by the emperor. The recess of the Diet of Speyer in June of 1544 called for the religious question to be discussed at a Diet to be held in Worms before the end of the year. The decisions resulting from this Diet would be subject to the approval of a future general church council. Originally scheduled to begin in October 1544, the Diet of Worms did not get underway until March 1545.[49] The delay in proceedings at Worms gave Bucer the opportunity to publish several works defending the emperor's right to call a national council, arguing that the pope was unfit to undertake the reform of the church, and presenting his own proposals for reconciliation and reform. Although he continued to argue that sincere and pious Christians could easily reach agreement on the essentials of the Christian faith, the works contained bitter polemical attacks against all who claimed that only the pope could undertake the reformation of the church.[50]

As in his earlier works, Bucer generally avoided the discussion of doctrine, concentrating instead on church practices. However, where he did touch on doctrinal is-

---

[47]Ibid., 116r-v; Melanchthon also recommended that children be catechized but he did not propose a confirmation ceremony, CR 4:542-543 (no. 2317).

[48]*Alle Handlungen*, 116v: "Auch so jemandt wider abtretten wolte/ durch Christliche straff vnnd Ban / vor dem fahl verhütet / oder zuor buoß wider auffgericht. . . . Also würdt man auch den Christlichen Bann / wider nach gottes wort / in sein rechten prauch richten müssen / Damit der wider die ofenbarn lastern / heylsamlich gebraucht / vnd nit schulden einzuoziehen / vnnd zuo andern weltlichen dingen / oder gegen den lastern alleyn vmb zeitliches genieß willen / vnnd nit die laster abzuotreiben / wie inn den vermeynten Sendten beschehen / mißbraucht werde."

[49]Paul Heidrich, *Karl V. und die deutschen Protestanten am Vorabend des Schmalkaldischen Krieges. 2. Teil: Die Reichstage der Jahre 1544-1546*, Frankfurter Historische Forschungen 6 (Frankfurt a.M.: Joseph Baer, 1912), 50-57.

[50]Bucer's antipapal polemic was also influenced by the long-awaited general council which was to convene in Trent in March of 1545; the council did not open until the end of that year. Horst Rabe, *Reichsbund und Interim. Die Verfassungs- und Religionspolitik Karls V. und der Reichstag von Augsburg 1547/1548* (Cologne: Böhlau Verlag, 1971), 36-56, gives a good short summary of papal and imperial relations leading up to the opening of the Council of Trent; a lengthier and more detailed treatment in Jedin, *Trent* 1: 491-544.

sues, he endorsed standard Protestant views, emphasizing the value of private confession for instruction and consolation but rejecting the compulsory enumeration of sins.[51] Absolution and confirmation were listed along with ordination as ceremonies in which the imposition of hands was used as a sign of benediction. In absolution the imposition of hands symbolized the reconciliation with the church of those who had confessed their sins and demonstrated their repentance and desire to reform; in confirmation it followed the public profession of faith and submission to obedience of those who had been baptized as infants.[52] Bucer also advocated the exercise of discipline by ministers and elders who were charged with the oversight of all Christians; they were to admonish sinners and bind with penance all those guilty of public sin; contumacious sinners were banned and excluded from Christian fellowship until they repented.[53]

In all these works Bucer referred back to the practices of the early church as justification for his views. He also stated that agreement on church discipline would be easily attainable on the basis of "the word of God, the apostolic traditions and ordinances which we have abundantly in the writings of the holy fathers and in the canons of the holy councils and also in the laws of the Christian emperors."[54] He listed specific passages from canon law and the fathers to support this assertion.[55] Cyprian

---

[51]For example, when he published the Leipzig articles from 1539 as *Ein Christlich ongefährlich bedencken*, Bucer appended a "report to the Christian reader" in which he defended the positions set forth in the articles; cf. fols. G4 r-v: "Es sollen aber doch beide / die guothertzigen die der menschlichen beicht vnd satisfaction tyrannei billich schewen / vnd die buoß vnd zuchtflüchtigen / die alle ware buoß vnd besserliche zucht hassen / wol auff alle wort sehen / vnd vermercken / das alles / so wir in artickel von / Beycht / Satisfaction / vnnd absolution der kirchen / von wegen der groberen vnnd bekantlicher sünden gemeldet / gentzlich gestellet vnd gemeßiger haben / auff das der H. Paulus davon geleret hat, j. Cor. v, ii. Cor. ii. vij. vnd xij. Dann weder mehr noch weniger hab ich in disem Artickel zuogeben / wie es die wort klarzeugen / gedencke auch nimmer mehr weiters zuo zuogeben. So vil dan die besondere beycht belanget . . . ist solliches alles gestelt vnd gemessiget auff besserliche vnderweisung / rhat / vnd trost / den die leut damit bey jren seelsorgren suochen vnd entpfahen mögen vnd sollen / Item auff versünung der verletzten brüder vnnd besserung gemeyner kirchen. Da sie dem menschlichen zwang / die sünde dem menschen vergeblich / ja den mehrern theyl mit schwerer ergernüssen zuo erzelen / keyn thür auff gethon / Noch davon etwas weitter gesetzet / dann so vil die notturffrige vnnd besserliche vnderweisung (deren aber vil mehr bedörffen / dann es erkennen wöllen) auch Christlicher rhat vnnd trost der gewissen erfordret."

[52]*Wie leicht vnnd füglich Christliche vergleichung der Religion . . . zu finden vnd in das werck zuo bringen*, Stupperich #84, 26-27;*Wider vffrichtung der Messen, anderer Sacramenten vnd Ceremonien vnd des Papstumbs*, Stupperich #87, fols. D3v-D4v, E1 r.

[53]*Wie leicht vnnd füglich*, 28-30.

[54]Ibid., 28: "So vil die kirchenzucht vnd geistlich regiment belanget / würdt die Christliche vergleichung auch on alle mühe zuo finden sein / wan man nach dem Gottes wort / die Apostolischen Traditionen vnnd ordnungen / die wir in schrifften der H. Vätter / in den Canonibus der heyligen Concilien / vnd auch in den Legibus Christlicher Keyser überreichlich haben / wille gelten lassen."

[55]Ibid., 40-41; on confirmation, the decree of the Council of Orléans used in the Regensburg Book and the decree from a council of Meaux which immediately follows it in the Decretum (de consecratione, dist. V, c. 6-7; Friedberg 1:1414); on absolution, Cyprian's letters (Lib. 1, Epist. 3; Lib. 2, Epist. 12; Lib. 3, Epist. 12; he also cited these letters on the topic

was also called to witness regarding the practices of penitential discipline and excommunication, as were "the books of the dear fathers written about penitence."[56]

In only one work of the period did Bucer directly discuss the theology underlying the sacraments of confirmation and penance. *Der newe glaub, von den Doctoren zu Louen . . . furgegeben* contained a scathing critique of 32 doctrinal articles drawn up by the theology faculty of Louvain in 1544. In his discussion of confirmation and penance, Bucer made little attempt to find common ground with the Catholics. He rejected the assertion that confirmation was a sacrament instituted by Christ, "for where has the Lord . . . commanded any word about striking anyone on the cheek, which they perform on children in place of confirmation?" True confirmation included the imposition of hands in imitation of Christ's example and apostolic practice, and it was performed after children had been catechized and had professed their faith, a ceremony "which has been re-established in our churches."[57] Bucer characterized the four articles on penance as in part obscure and misleading, in part entirely against God's word. While he acknowledged the fathers' use of penitential discipline and absolution, he charged that this penitential discipline had long since vanished from the papists' church.[58] True contrition resulted in confession to God but did not have to include the intention to confess to a priest and to perform the satisfaction he imposed.[59] Bucer condemned the assertion that all mortal sins had to be confessed to a priest and that only those sins which had been confessed were forgiven. The granting of absolution was primarily the responsibility of ordained ministers who acted in

---

of absolution in his Florilegium, BOL 3:52–53) and sermon *de lapsis*, as well as a canon from the third council of Carthage (Causa XXVI, Q. VI, c. 14; cf. Friedberg 1:1041, also listed in the Florilegium, BOL 3:52) and the ancient formulas of absolution.

[56]*Wie leicht vnnd füglich*, 41: "Der Christlichen buoßzucht vnd Bans halben hatt man uberflüßig vil / bey allen alten Vätteren / vnd in Canonibus. Vnd besonders in vermeldten Epistolen Cypriani / vnd in den büchern der lieben Vätter von der Buoß geschriben."

[57]*Der newe glaub*, Stupperich no. 82, B1v–B2r: "Dann wa hat der Herre von jren ölebest- reichen an den stirnen? Vnd von jrem backen schlagen / das sie mit den kinderen an statt der Firmunbg treiben ie ein wort befolhen? Die hende hat er wol den kindlin augffeleget [sic] / jnen seinen segen also mitzuotheilen / So haben die Apostel den geteufften mit dem hend aufflegen den h. Geist gegeben. . . . Dem nach haben die alten ware Bischoue die ienigen so in kindheit geteuffet waren / nach dem sie den Catechismum gelernet / vnd jren glauben selb bekennet / in Christlicher gemeinschafft der Kirchen bestettiget / Welches auch wider in vnseren Kirchen angerichtet ist."

[58]Ibid., B4v–C1r: "Hierinn ist auch ein theil dunckel / vnnd ein theil dem wort Gottes widerwertig. . . . Die Alten haben die so in schweren sünden ergriffen / oder sich selber haben angegeben / nach bewerter rewe / vnd versprochner vnd bewisner besserung / von den sünden mit dem hend aufflegen absoluieret / vnd zur gemeinschafft Christi wider auffgenomen. . . . Dise buoszucht aber vnd handlung ist bei den Päpstlichen Priestern lengist verspulget. Dem wort Gottes ist widerwertig / das sie dis jr Sacrament / des wesenliche stuck sie auch jre beicht vnd gnugthun sein wöllen / zuor seligkeit von nöten machen."

[59]Ibid., C3r: "Dan ob wol ware rewe selb ein Beicht der sünden gegen Got ist / vnd das war bebennen [sic] der sünden gegen menschen / wa es bessert / gewißlich mit sich bringet / des gleichen auch ein ernstes casteyen des fleyschs / vnd eyfer zuo allen guotten wercken / So bringet sie doch gar nit ein solichs erzelen der sünden / vor dem Priester / wie dise Doctoren jre Beicht forderen / Noch vil weniger einigen gedancken des Volthuns / damit die rewenden solten die verdienten straffen wöllen bezalen."

the stead of the entire church, but he stated that Christ had given all his members the authority to bind and loose sin.[60] Finally he denounced the article on satisfaction for teaching that works of penance were necessary as the punishment which remained after sins had been forgiven. Christ alone was the satisfaction for sin, and Scripture, apostolic tradition, and the writings of the earliest fathers said nothing about the transformation of eternal punishment into temporal punishment through the power of the keys.[61]

By the time *Der newe Glaub* was published, efforts to reunite the church through peaceful means had ended. Charles V had already begun negotiations with the pope to obtain financial support for war against the Protestants. The long-threatened war began in the summer of 1546 and ended with the emperor's final victory over the Schmalkaldic League in April of 1547. Charles V's triumph brought him one step closer to his goal of returning the Protestants to the Catholic fold. In order to stabilize the situation in the German church until the religious question could be dealt with by a general council, he hoped to devise an interim settlement acceptable to both Protestants and Catholics at the Diet of Augsburg which opened in September 1547.[62] Bucer was once more drawn into the process of formulating a statement of doctrine that could serve as the basis for the reconciliation and reformation of the German church. In the spring of 1548 he was called to Augsburg by the electors of Brandenburg and the Palatinate to critique the proposed Interim text which the emperor had given them.[63]

Bucer spent two days examining a German translation of the proposed Interim and then submitted his comments in a letter to the electors. He was well aware of the precarious situation of the Protestants as he examined the proposal. The Interim was the final attempt to reconcile the German church by imposing a settlement on both the Catholic and Protestant estates from above. The Protestants were in no position to oppose its provisions. Bucer's annotations were intended to make more palatable

[60]Ibid., C3v-D1 r: "Diser Articul hat drei ding / die dem wort Gottes widerwertig seind / Das ein / das sie sagen / der Beichten solle / seie schuldig / wesenlichen fleiß vnnd ernst zuthuon / dem Priester alß seinem Richter alle seine tödliche sünden zuo offenbaren / auch die im hertzen verborgen sein. Diß hat Gott nie gefordert/ die alte Kirch auch nie gehalten. . . . Das ander / so in disem Articul dem wort Gottes widerwertig ist / das sie deuten / als solten die von jren sünden nitt mögen geabsoluieret werden / die sie dem Priester nitt erzeleten. . . . Das dritt in disem Articul wider das Gottes wort ist / das sie die Absolution jren geweyheten Priesteren allein zueignen. Die ordenlichen Diener der Kirchen sollen disen dienst wol fürnemlich verrichten von wegen der gemeinden Christi / Daneben aber lebet / lehret / tröstet der Herre Christus die war rewenden / in allen seinen gliederen."

[61]Ibid., D1 r-D3v.

[62]On the background to the Augsburg Interim, see Rabe, *Reichsbund*, 260-272, 407-449.

[63]PC 4: 903-921 (nos. 747-752) and BDS 17: 346-438 (Documents 1-7 on the Augsburg Interim with their introductions) are the chief sources of information on Bucer's stay in Augsburg. Werner Bellardi describes Bucer's reactions to the Interim from his first reading of it to his final expulsion from Strasbourg after its introduction in the city, "Bucer und das Interim," in de Kroon and Lienhard, ed., *Horizons Européens*, 267-294.

those statements in the Interim which, unchanged, were unacceptable to the Protestants.[64] Under pressure from both electors to endorse the Interim, Bucer could give only a very qualified approval, speaking for himself personally and not as a representative of his church. Of course Bucer was concerned with the text of the Interim as a whole, and his comments on the chapters dealing with the sacraments of confirmation and penance were brief in comparison to his criticisms of the provisions regarding the sacrifice of the mass, the invocation of the saints, the commemoration of the dead, and the restoration of Catholic ceremonies. Nevertheless they revealed the extent to which Bucer was willing to compromise on the issues of confirmation and penance and which provisions he could not accept without modification.

Bucer protested against the Interim's assertion that the church had seven sacraments, suggesting instead that it accept St. Augustine's view that only baptism and the Lord's Supper were sacraments. He accepted the statement that unworthy priests could validly administer the sacraments, but, in accordance with both Scripture and "all the old canons," he recommended adding that the church should not allow obvious sinners to administer the sacraments.[65]

With regard to confirmation, Bucer was willing to base the ceremony on Christ's promise of the Holy Spirit, but he rejected its identification with the apostles' imposition of hands as recorded in the New Testament. Instead it was a ceremony established in imitation of apostolic practice, attested to by St. Jerome. He also protested against the statement that the chrism, applied with the sign of the cross, was an element of the rite which dated from the time of the apostles. Unless the Catholics could produce evidence to support this assertion, he felt that it would be better if the ceremony consisted only of congregational prayer and the imposition of hands. Bucer's rejection of the apostolic origin of confirmation and of the chrism was the more vehement since the article stated that anyone who rejected its position on confirmation denied that "the universal church is the pillar and foundation of truth." Bucer emphasized his esteem for confirmation, pointing out that he had himself helped to establish a ceremony in some churches in which children "professed their faith and promised their obedience to the Lord and to the church" and were then confirmed with congregational prayer and the imposition of hands before being allowed to the Lord's Supper. The draft had suggested that children receive catechetical instruction so that they could profess their own faith at confirmation, as the Council of Orléans required, but it stated that even small children could receive the sacrament of confirmation. In line with his own view of confirmation, Bucer emended this paragraph to require catechetical instruction before confirmation. Finally, in opposition to the

---

[64]Cf. Bucer's later criticism of the final form of the Interim that although there were large sections which were acceptable, those sections were nullified by a few provisions: "Twenty of the choicest courses of a meal can be made lethal with the smallest amount of poison, and how often a short phrase keeps one from accepting a contract which otherwise has many other sections which one would gladly accept," BDS 17: 540.21–24.

[65]BDS 17: 367.14–22; cf. ARC 6: 322.1–13.

draft's assertion that only bishops could administer confirmation, Bucer argued that Innocent III had held that bishops could entrust this duty to priests.[66]

Bucer accepted the draft's definition of the sacrament of penance as absolution administered in accordance with the power of the keys given to priests by Christ. However, he proposed several alterations regarding the confession of secret sins. The article on penance stated that the priest had received the power both to bind and to loose but could not exercise that power unless he knew which sins should be remitted or retained, knowledge which could only be gained through auricular confession and the enumeration of sins. Bucer objected that binding to penance, which occurred when an individual confessed his secret sins, had to be voluntary as it had been in the time of Cyprian. No one should be compelled to confess secret sins, for "we cannot assume for ourselves any more power over consciences than has been given us by the Lord."[67] The article commended confession as a remedy for sin and specified that Christians should be taught to be neither too careless nor overly scrupulous in preparing to confess. Bucer made more explicit the pedagogical nature of confession by adding that private instruction and the imposition of penance were necessary along with the words of absolution, "for otherwise the listing of sins would be of no use." He also added a sentence on the need for pious and experienced confessors, as taught by Origen and required by canon law.[68] Finally, he proposed adding a phrase specifying that through an individual's penance the church was satisfied that his repentance was sincere.[69]

Bucer's suggested alterations underlined his fundamental pedagogical and disciplinary concerns. Children had to be instructed in their faith and have the opportunity publicly to profess their faith and obedience to the church. While sinners were assured of forgiveness through priestly absolution, private confession was also a pedagogical device used to bring about the sinner's amendment through instruction and the imposition of penance. To achieve these goals, it was necessary that the confessor be able to instruct the penitent and that satisfaction be understood as demonstration of genuine contrition. The priest had no authority over the consciences of others. Rather, individuals had to be free to choose to submit to the binding of the priest. Implicit in this view was the belief that mortal sins could be forgiven outside of the sacrament of penance. The themes which appeared in some of Bucer's earliest discussions of penance and confirmation proved to be his dominant concerns in this

---

[66]BDS 17: 368.11-370.5.; cf. ARC 6: 323.23-324.22.

[67]BDS 17: 370.7-12.

[68]The editor of Bucer's *Briefmemorandum* cites Ambrosius' *de poenitentia*, but the reference is to Origen's sermon on Psalm 37, MPG 12: 1386, and the section of the Decretum pertaining to confessors, *de poenitentia*, dist. 6; Friedberg 1: 1242-1244. Bucer had used this passage in the *Bestendige Verantwortung*, 216v, where he mistakenly identified the Origen sermon as Psalm 57; cf. Bucer's miscitation of Origen's sermon on Psalm 57 in his memorandum on the Interim written for the Strasbourg city council, BDS 17: 516.3-5.

[69]BDS 17: 370.13-371.7.

last effort to formulate an article on the sacraments which would apply to both Catholics and Protestants.[70]

Bucer's proposed alterations to the draft Interim were his last attempt to reconcile the German church. The Interim became imperial law through its incorporation into the final resolution of the Diet of Augsburg in June, but it applied only to the Protestants, for the Catholic estates had rejected it, and the emperor gave way before their resistance.[71] Thus one of the chief reasons for Bucer's personal and carefully circumscribed acceptance of the Interim no longer existed, and he led the ministers' resistance to its introduction in Strasbourg.[72] In two separate memoranda on the Interim written for the Strasbourg city council, Bucer repeated the same objections that he had made to the electors. He criticized the provisions allowing confirmation to be administered to small children and condemning those who did not accept the Catholic view of the sacrament. He also disputed the claim that confirmation was established by the apostles, since the apostles themselves neither required confirmation nor practiced it themselves. The imposition of hands recorded in the New Testament was a miraculous sign, and not the basis of confirmation.[73] He endorsed instead his own view of confirmation: the public profession of faith and obedience, accompanied by congregational prayer and the imposition of hands, was "the genuine, ancient confirmation which brings reform, which has also long been established in some of our churches—but this is completely unknown to our opponents."[74]

Regarding penance, Bucer pointed out that individuals should confess their sins "in so far as it helped their pastors to bring them to repentance and amendment and to console them with absolution," but auricular confession and the enumeration of sins were not necessary for salvation.[75] For private confession to be beneficial, it had to be made to pious and proven ministers. Finally, the binding to penance was applied primarily for sin which was either manifest or attested to by witnesses.[76]

Bucer's final statements on confirmation and penance reflect the basic evangelical convictions which ultimately undermined all of his attempts to reach agreement

---

[70]The Interim's articles on confirmation and penance were criticized from the Catholic side because they reflected Protestant views. Valentin von Tetleben specifically identified its positions with Bucer: "It desires that infants be confirmed once they are adults who with their own mouth can attest and profess their faith . . . and this is the formula of Bucer, against the rite of the church"; likewise, "it makes no mention of contrition and satisfaction but magnifies absolution, according to the opinion of the Lutherans, Zwinglians and Bucer"; ARC 6: 346.

[71]Rabe, Reichsbund, 436–442.

[72]Bucer stated that he would have been willing to accept a version of the Interim and to make concessions in rituals and ceremonies if its provisions, particularly those concerning the doctrine of justification, had been imposed on the Catholic estates as well, but because the Catholics were allowed to persist "in their obvious idolatry and abuses," there was no reason for the Protestants to compromise their practices, BDS 17: 496.27–497.14.

[73]Ibid., 447.21–448.14.

[74]Ibid., 514.7–515.8.

[75]Ibid., 449.9–13.

[76]Ibid., 515.10–516.10.

with his Catholic counterparts. In his discussions of penance and confirmation with the Catholics, he employed three separate but related methods of argumentation in order to gloss over the fundamental conflict between evangelical and Catholic theology. The first method was simply to avoid discussion of controversial issues. Bucer used this tactic in the locus on confession in his Psalms commentary of 1529 as well as in his *Concilium* written for Francis I. This was the technique which Erasmus used in discussing confession, although the Dutch humanist never went so far as to deny the authority of the church to require the enumeration of sins. This approach was especially useful when, as in Leipzig, the collocutors agreed to focus on church practices rather than on doctrine.

When doctrinal conflict did arise, Bucer resorted to his second method of argumentation, citing the authority of the fathers and of canon law in addition to Scripture in order to challenge developments in scholastic theology since the days of the early church. Although Bucer used this type of argumentation in his Psalms commentary, it became increasingly important from the end of the 1530s. The Leipzig articles of 1539 also reflected this approach. Encouraged by Karlowitz' original proposal to use the early church as a norm for reuniting the German church, Bucer redefined the sacrament of penance so that it conformed more closely to the penitential discipline of the early church. This allowed him to bypass those issues relating to penance which had been developed by medieval theologians, such as the priest's role as judge and the necessity of confessing all mortal sins. Moreover, it coincided nicely with Bucer's own disciplinary concerns as evidenced by his advocacy of penitential discipline in *Von der waren Seelsorge*. Likewise, confirmation was modeled after the practice described by Jerome; there was no discussion of its divine institution or sacramental nature. The appeal to the prescriptions of the earliest canons and the example of the church fathers seemed to Bucer to be one of the most effective ways to win Catholics to his idea of reform.

Despite Bucer's optimism, however, it did not prove so easy to ignore the developments of medieval theology. At Regensburg the Catholic collocutors upheld the sacramental character of penance and confirmation, championed the scholastic doctrine of the power of the keys, and argued that mortal sins had to be confessed to a priest in order to be forgiven. This last issue proved to be the Achilles' heel of compromise, for it was a position which neither Bucer nor the other Protestant theologians could accept. Bucer continued to advocate the model of the early church in the years after Regensburg, but his proposals could appeal only to other Protestants, for he refused to acknowledge the validity of the medieval theological tradition.

After the failure of the religious colloquies and the attempted reformation of Cologne, Bucer harshly criticized Catholic teaching and practice. In these later works Bucer employed his final method of argumentation, charging that the Catholic church did not enforce its own canons and decrees. There was still hope for reconciliation if the Catholic hierarchy would abide by the teachings and traditions of the early church as reflected in the writings of the church fathers and in the oldest parts of canon law. Bucer's attacks on the leaders of the Catholic church could hardly be called dialogue, but by this time, despite his protestations of sincerity, there was little realistic hope of reuniting the churches. Instead, by pointing out the abuses and shortcomings of the propapal party when judged according to the standards of the early church, Bucer hoped to win reform-minded German Catholics to the evangelical side. In this respect, although they comprised only a small part of his writings, Bucer's polemical attacks on the scholastic doctrine of penance and the Catholic practice of confirmation were perhaps the best indicator of his motives for discussion with the Catholics and his reaction when those discussions failed. By persuading his Catholic counterparts to accept a "catholic reformation" based on the teaching and example of the early church, Bucer hoped to pave the way for a fully Protestant Reformation in doctrine and practice, and when his efforts failed, he vented his anger on those Catholics who had refused to be enticed by his proposals.

But Bucer's interchanges with Catholic theologians, whether ecumenical or polemical, were only one part of his efforts to bring reformation to the German church. In addition to his role in the theological and theoretical discussions of the 1540s, he was also a key figure in the attempt to reform the territories under the secular jurisdiction of the archbishop-elector of Cologne and his cathedral chapter. The church ordinance which Bucer wrote for the archiepiscopal territories and the works in which he defended the proposed reformation illustrate his practical concern for the restoration of Christian discipline.

6

Christian Discipline and the Attempted Reformation of Cologne, 1542–1545

From the end of 1542 through 1545 much of Bucer's energy was directed towards the reformation of the archiepiscopal territories of Cologne.[1] The reformation attempt presented a unique challenge to Bucer for several reasons. The reformation was not primarily a popular movement but was imposed by the territories' secular ruler, who recruited Bucer to preach and to write a church ordinance for his lands. The fact that the ruler, Hermann von Wied, was one of the three archbishop-electors of the Holy Roman Empire made the reformation extremely unusual and meant that its success would have far-reaching political as well as religious consequences.

In his preaching and teaching Bucer presented an evangelical view of the sacraments of penance and confirmation, and in the church ordinance he wrote with Melanchthon's help he outlined a system of Christian discipline to be established throughout the archiepiscopal territories. Because the territories were still Catholic, he expressed his ideas as much as possible within a traditional framework, at the same time giving a theological defense of his evangelical position which he hoped would win support for the reform. Attacked by Catholic polemicists who accused him of heresy, he defended the orthodoxy of his views by comparing them with the practice of the early church. Bucer's ordinance and his writings defending it give perhaps

---

[1]The standard work on the attempted reformation of Cologne is still Conrad Varrentrapp, *Hermann von Wied und sein Reformationsversuch in Köln. Ein Beitrag zur deutschen Reformationsgeschichte* (Leipzig: von Duncker & Humblot, 1878); biographies of the major figures all contain accounts of the attempt, cf. August Franzen, *Bischof und Reformation. Erzbischof Hermann von Wied in Köln vor der Entscheidung zwischen Reform und Reformation*, Katholisches Leben und Kirchenreform im Zeitalter der Glaubensspaltung 31 (Münster: Aschendorff, 1971), 57–106;Walter Lipgens, *Kardinal Johannes Gropper (1503-59) und die Anfänge der katholischen Reform in Deutschland*, Reformationsgeschichtliche Studien und Texte 75 (Münster: Aschendorff, 1951), 132–159. J. V. Pollet, O.P., *Martin Bucer, Études sur les relations de Bucer avec les Pays-Bas, l'Électorat de Cologne et l'Allemagne du Nord, avec de nombreux textes inédits*, 2 vols., Studies in Medieval and Reformation Thought, 33-34 (Leiden: E.J. Brill, 1985), 1:83–234 and 2:35–162, examines the affair with particular reference to Bucer's involvement and publishes several relevant documents. Bucer's letters to Philip of Hesse, Lenz 2:113–158, give a running account of events during the reformer's stay at Bonn.

the clearest example of how he hoped to reform the Catholic church by means of Christian discipline.

At the close of the Diet of Regensburg, the emperor had charged the Catholic estates to undertake a "Christian reformation" in their lands in anticipation of the long-promised general council of the church. The archbishop of Cologne, Hermann von Wied, took this admonition to heart, and in February of 1542 he invited Bucer to discuss the prospects of reform with his theological advisor Johannes Gropper and the suffragan bishop Johann Nopel. Bucer had first met the archbishop and Gropper at the Hagenau colloquy, and after the failure of the Regensburg colloquy Bucer and Gropper had remained in contact. The Strasbourg reformer sent Gropper a copy of his Latin edition of the documents from the colloquy published in the fall of 1541, and the two theologians had exchanged friendly letters. It was therefore not unnatural for the archbishop to assume that the two men would be able to work together on the reformation of his territories. The archbishop was sorely mistaken, however, for Gropper was adamantly opposed to Bucer's involvement in the reformation attempt.[2]

In September the archbishop asked the Strasbourg city council to grant Bucer a leave of absence to assist in the reformation of his lands. Bucer arrived in Bonn, where he was to spend the next several months, in mid-December of 1542, and took upon himself a demanding schedule of preaching and teaching. Almost immediately the clergy in Cologne, led by Gropper, submitted an official protest against Bucer's calling to Bonn and his activities there,[3] which led Bucer to publish a summary of his teachings in defense of his ministry, *Was im namen des Heiligen Euangeli . . . gelehret unnd geprediget würdt.*[4]

In Bonn, as in Strasbourg and elsewhere, Bucer advocated a system of religious instruction, fraternal admonition, and church discipline. Children baptized as infants were to be catechized, so that they could profess their own faith and obedience to the church, after which they would be confirmed with prayer and the imposition of hands.[5] Every Christian was to admonish all those he saw in sin, but the leaders of each congregation had the particular responsibility of seeing that each individual was admonished according to need. Those who had committed serious sin were kept from the Lord's Table until they had demonstrated their repentance, while any who refused to repent were excluded from the church entirely until they too had repented and demonstrated this satisfactorily to the church.[6] This system of penitential discipline was to exist along with public preaching and private confession. For private con-

---

[2]Bucer later printed Gropper's letters to him as evidence that his bitterest opponent in Cologne had once held him in great esteem. Pollet discusses the relations between the two men as well as Gropper's attitude towards the reformation attempt, *Relations* 1:161–177.

[3]Varrentrapp, *Hermann von Wied*, 142 n. 2; a summary of the charges made against Bucer on 143–146.

[4]Stupperich #75; cf. W. Rotscheidt, "Martin Butzers Rechtfertigung seiner Wirksamkeit in Bonn 1543," *Monatshefte für rheinische Kirchengeschichte* 37 (1943):10–23.

[5]*Was im namen*, d₃r–v.

[6]Ibid., f₂v–f₃v.

fession to be fruitful, however, it had to be made to men who knew how to console and instruct sinners so that they rightly recognized and truly repented of their sin. True confession did not consist in recounting all the evil one had done, "which arrogant men often do over their wine," but in recognizing that all our actions merited only eternal condemnation. Only those penances which were appropriate to and which necessarily accompanied "genuine, believing contrition," such as fasts and prayer, were to be imposed. Finally, the forgiveness of sins pronounced in confession rested not on any aspect of the confession itself or on any work of the priest, but solely on God's promise to forgive those sins in heaven which had been forgiven through the ministry of the church.[7]

Bucer presented his views in a positive way and for the most part avoided criticism of Catholic doctrine. Given the circumstances in Bonn, Bucer feared that any polemics would only harm the progress of the reformation.[8] This conciliatory tone did not deter Bucer's opponents, however. Eberhard Billick, the Carmelite Provincial and a professor at the university, wrote a sharp response to Bucer's defense, criticizing each article of doctrine and attacking Bucer personally as well.[9] Billick's pamphlet did not long go unanswered. In early July, only two months after Billick's work appeared, Bucer published a self-defense of over three hundred pages, *Die ander Verteydigung vnd erklerung der Christlichen Lehr*. In this book Bucer defended his view that children should be catechized and then called to profess their faith and obedience publicly, after which they would be "confirmed into the full fellowship of Christ" with the imposition of hands and the prayer of the congregation.[10] Billick had criticized Bucer because he did not include confirmation among the sacraments, did not limit its administration to bishops, and omitted the anointing with the chrism. Bucer responded to these complaints by charging his opponent with placing too much emphasis on externals while neglecting God's command. He dismissed the first issue as merely a quarrel over terminology, noting that the fathers had called even the sign of the cross a sacrament.[11] He referred to Jerome's account of confirmation, which was indeed

---

[7]Ibid., f₃v-g₁r.

[8]Cf. his statement to the Landgraf that he had purposely moderated the tone of *Was im Namen*, Lenz 2:137 (no. 162; Mar. 24, 1543).

[9]Varrentrapp, *Hermann von Wied*, 165-168. The full title of Billich's work was *Judicium Cleri et universitatis Coloniensis de doctrina et vocatione Martini Buceri ad Bonnam*. I have used the German translation of the work, *Urteil der Universitet und Clerisie zu Cölne von Martin Bucers Lerung vnd ruffung gen Bonn, uß Latynischer sprach trewlich verteutsch, durch Jaspar von Gennep, Bürger zu Cölne*, 1543.

[10]*Die ander Verteydigung*, Stupperich #76, 90v-91r: ". . . Wie die Seelsorger die kinder . . . den Catechismum . . . lehren / vnd darinn vben / Vnd wenn sie den gefasset / thuon ihren glauben in der versamlung Gottes bekennen / vnd sich in die gohorsame Christi vnnd seiner Gemeinen selb begeben / vnd sie darauff mit dem gebett / vnd hendt aufflegen / in die gantze Gemeinschafft Christi vnd seiner Gemeinden bestetigen."

[11]Ibid., 91r: "Da sehe / vmb den namen / nitt vmbs werck, vmb die eussere larven des dieners / nitt vmb den dienst/ vmb der menschlichen anhang / nitt vmb den befelch Gottes / streyten diese leuth. Nu des namens halben / were das werck wider recht im schwanck / solte es ein geringe disputation haben. Weyl doch die H. Vätter / auch das zeychen des creutzes ein Sacrament heyssen"; cf. the marginal note, "Des namen halben solle man nitt zancken wann manns werck hat."

administered by a bishop, but he pointed out that Jerome himself had stated that this was done to give honor to the episcopal office, not from legal necessity. Lastly, although he admitted that the chrism was an ancient custom, it was not necessary. In the process of refuting Billick's charges, Bucer was not above engaging in scathing polemic against the contemporary Catholic ceremony, which he described as "an abomination in such lofty, divine things."[12]

Billick's criticism of Bucer's preaching on penance focused on two issues, the confession of specific sins and the meaning of satisfaction. Bucer not only dismissed the idea that confession of specific sins was necessary, Billick charged, but he made a mockery of confession by emphasizing the pedagogical value of confession and ignoring the importance of absolution. Billick also accused Bucer of perverting God's word and the statements of the church fathers on the issue of satisfaction. To be sure, Christ's death was the payment for our reconciliation with God, but in his mercy God had also allowed us to pay for our misdeeds and sins through our works.[13] In response, Bucer protested that he neither ignored the importance of absolution nor scorned the recounting of specific sins in confession, as he had been accused. Confession served both for instruction and for the consolation of absolution. But it was not necessary to confess all sins, since God had not commanded it, and a complete confession of sin was impossible. The detailed enumeration of specific sins was useful only to the extent that it produced true contrition. This contrition, especially for serious sin, necessarily and voluntarily resulted in prayer, almsgiving, and other works of penance, but such works were never regarded as satisfaction for sin, since satisfaction was reckoned to Christ alone. To Billick's charge that he had distorted the meaning of Scripture, Bucer argued that his opponent had done the same in attempting to prove the necessity of confessing every sin. He promised that in a future Latin work he would prove that he had correctly cited the fathers.[14]

The Latin work which Bucer hoped to write fell victim to the larger project which occupied him during the first half of 1543: the writing of a church ordinance for the archiepiscopal territories.[15] Bucer used as models the Brandenburg-Nürnberg ordinance of 1533, the 1539 Saxon and the 1543 Schwäbisch-Hall ordinances, as well as

---

[12]Ibid., 91v–92v; "dieser greuwel in so hoher Göttlichen sachen."

[13]Billick, *Urteil der Universitet und Clerisie*, D$_1$a–D$_3$a.

[14]*Die ander Verteydigung*, 135r–136r.

[15]Bucer did, however, discuss his interpretation of the term satisfaction in his *Bestendige Verantwortung*, described below. There is no complete modern critical edition of the Cologne ordinance, but it is available in two reprinted forms: Aemilius Ludwig Richter, ed., *Die evangelische Kirchenordnungen des sechszehnten Jahrhunderts, Urkunden und Regesten zur Geschichte des Rechts und der Verfassung der evangelischen Kirche in Deutschland*, vol. 2, *Vom Jahre 1542 bis zu Ende des sechszehnten Jahrhunderts* (Weimar: Landes-Industriecomtoir, 1846; repr.: Nieuwkoop: de Graaf, 1967), prints large sections of the ordinance, while Hermann von Wied, *Einfältiges Bedenken: Reformationsentwurf für das Erzstift Köln von 1543*, ed. and trans. Helmut Gerhards and Wilfried Borth, Schriftenreihe des Vereins für Rheinische Kirchengeschichte 43 (Düsseldorf: Presseverband der evangelischen Kirche im Rheinland, 1972), is an edition of the entire ordinance in modern German.

the ordinance he had written for Hesse in late 1538. Philip Melanchthon, who had come to Bonn to assist Bucer in the reformation attempt, wrote part of the doctrinal section, but Bucer was the ordinance's main author.[16]

The church ordinance contained an interwoven system of penitential and eucharistic discipline which began with regular catechetical instruction and reached its most drastic form in the full exclusion from the church. The ordinance specified that catechetical sermons were to be preached either in the early morning or the evening service on Sundays and feast days, with additional catechetical instruction at least once a week between March and November.[17] When children had been instructed in their faith they were to make a public profession of faith and pledge their obedience to the church, then be confirmed with the imposition of hands and the prayers of the congregation. The ordinance justified this form of confirmation with references in the Psalms to a public profession of faith as well as by the practice of the imposition of hands before admission to communion in the early church. As it stated,

Because there can be no confession of faith and voluntary commitment into the fellowship and obedience of Christ at baptism when it is administered to infants, the manner and character of true faith and of fellowship in Christ requires that the young make this confession of faith and commitment into the fellowship and obedience of Christ after they have been instructed in the faith and have recognized what has been given them in holy baptism and into what kind of fellowship they have been received.[18]

The ordinance acknowledged that confirmation had been the responsibility of suffragan bishops, but it stated that the territories were too large for the suffragan to visit each congregation within it every year. Therefore it authorized those conducting the yearly visitation to confirm children of the appropriate age. In the week prior to the visitation, the pastor and his helpers were to meet with the children to practice with them the proper responses to questions on the Apostles' Creed, the sacraments, and the responsibilities entailed by membership in the church.[19] Each child was to make a profession of faith and obedience to the pastor at this time. During the actual ceremony conducted by the visitors, one child made the proper responses for the entire group and the others were asked if they agreed to the same profession of faith and

---

[16]CR 5:148–149, no. 2730; cf. Varrentrapp, *Hermann von Wied*, 176–177; Mechthild Köhn, *Martin Bucers Entwurf einer Reformation des Erzstiftes Köln. Untersuchung der Entstehungsgeschichte und der Theologie des "Einfältigen Bedenckens" von 1543*, Untersuchungen zur Kirchengeschichte 2 (Witten: Luther Verlag, 1966), 51–57, 67–71.

[17]Children were to be spared from attending these early morning catechetical services on work days "during the harsh winter months"; Richter, *Kirchenordnungen* 2:36; *Einfältiges Bedenken*, 115–116.

[18]Richter, *Kirchenordnungen* 2:40; *Einfältiges Bedenken*, 132–133. Cf. Köhn's analysis of the theological rationale for confirmation. She concludes with Diehl that the confirmation in the Cologne ordinance accords with the ceremony Bucer established four and a half years earlier in the Hessian church ordinances, *Entwurf*, 137–139; Diehl, *Geschichte*, 44–48.

[19]Richter, *Kirchenordnungen* 2:40–41; *Einfältiges Bedenken*, 133–134.

pledge of obedience. The ordinance also made provision for the possibility that none of the children were able to give the proper responses from memory: the visitors were allowed to read the answers and have the children respond with a simple "yes." In any case both pastors and visitors were admonished to ensure that the children understood the sense of what they were saying rather than to insist upon the perfect recitation of the words themselves.[20]

Only those who had "demonstrated that they were Christ's disciples" should receive the sacrament. To ensure that they did not "cast pearls before swine," the pastors were to allow no one to the sacrament who had not previously confessed his sin and been absolved.[21] This confession could be made after the preparatory Vespers service on Saturday evening or before the communion service on Sunday morning.[22] Although individuals were to confess their sins in order to receive absolution, Bucer was at pains to differentiate this practice from Catholic auricular confession:

> For the sake of absolution, confession will remain, but in such a way that henceforth no one will be compelled to enumerate his sins. Nevertheless, each person should make a humble confession that he has sinned and that he is genuinely sorry for having offended God; that he has the heartfelt intention and desire to amend his life and . . . live without causing further offense. Moreover each individual should confess to the priest those sins which especially oppress and burden the conscience, desiring counsel and consolation from the word of God and then requesting absolution.[23]

During this meeting the pastor was to examine the penitent's knowledge of the Creed and the Ten Commandments, "so that the people would learn what sin was." The examination was thus a form of catechetical instruction, "especially for the young or unlearned." The pastor could deny absolution if he ascertained that the sinner was not truly penitent or did not intend to amend his life. Even where absolution was desired and reform promised, the pastor could postpone absolution until the sinner no longer lived in manifest sin.[24]

The ordinance also contained further provisions regarding unrepentant sinners. As always, the procedure followed the pattern of Matthew 18. Those guilty of manifest sin or who had been convicted of sin by several witnesses were to be admonished to repent and be reconciled with God and the church by their pastor and "those who

---

[20]*Einfältiges Bedenken*, 138-139; Richter omits this section. The obvious preference for understanding and concurrent deemphasis on perfect memorization of the words indicates that Gerald Strauss is perhaps too categorical in stressing the importance of rote memorization of the catechism, at least when generalizing this view to cover the entire sixteenth century, *Luther's House of Learning: Indoctrination of the Young in the German Reformation* (Baltimore: Johns Hopkins University Press, 1978), 170-175.

[21]*Einfältiges Bedenken*, 150.

[22]Ibid., 154.

[23]Richter, *Kirchenordnungen* 2:45; *Einfältiges Bedenken*, 168.

[24]Richter, *Kirchenordnungen* 2:45; *Einfältiges Bedenken*, 168-169.

have been appointed to this duty in every city and village."[25] This admonition was considered successful if the sinner ceased from sin, made any necessary restitution, confessed to the pastor, and asked for absolution. Where the sinner refused to acknowledge three successive summons to confession, or if he did appear but refused to reform, the matter was brought to the attention of the superintendent. The superintendent together with the pastor and the appointed elders was to summon the sinner one final time, and if he did not repent and promise to reform, he was pronounced banned by this assembly. The ordinance did not specify the public proclamation of the ban, but it did describe the consequences of excommunication. The excommunicate was excluded from the Lord's Supper, forbidden to witness baptisms or weddings, and could not be given a church burial if he died. He was not, however, to be excluded from hearing sermons but rather was encouraged to attend them in the hope that this would lead to repentance.[26]

It was the secular government's responsibility to punish manifest vice with fines, imprisonment, banishment, or even death, and the pastors' responsibility to remind the government to do its duty. Nevertheless, ecclesiastical and secular penalties were to be clearly differentiated, and if the secular government allowed the excommunicate to retain his civic rights, other Christians were to continue to do business with him, although they were to avoid any unnecessary contact and were to show by their demeanor their offense at the sin. If and when the excommunicate repented, reformed, and made any necessary restitution, he was reaccepted into the church. First, however, he was to confess both the original sin and his sin of disobedience in ignoring the admonition of the church. This done, he was reconciled by the pastor before the altar in the presence of the appointed elders.

The ordinance specified that the extreme penalty of excommunication was to be applied only in cases of public sin for which the sinner would not repent, and not for secular offenses such as debt. It was the duty of the pastors to teach their congregations to fear the ban and to regard it as God's rejection of obstinate sinners. The ecclesiastical courts would be given another means of compelling compliance to their decrees so that the true spiritual significance of the ban would not be distorted by the courts' misuse of it.[27]

The provisions of the ordinance, especially those requiring confession and absolution before communion, reflect Bucer's sensitivity to the reception of the reformation in the archiepiscopal territories. In a letter to his Strasbourg colleagues, Bucer reported that one of the most damaging charges made against him at Bonn was that the Strasbourg church allowed those who had not been examined beforehand to receive the Lord's Supper. In the archiepiscopal territories, "where the authority of the pastors is great and the people are marked out by their obedience in ecclesiastical mat-

---

[25]There is no further mention in the ordinance as to how these men were to be appointed or what other duties, if any, they were to have; however, they can be compared to the *Kirchenpfleger* in Strasbourg and the elders of the Hessian church ordinance.

[26]Richter, *Kirchenordnungen* 2:45–46; *Einfältiges Bedenken*, 169–170.

[27]Richter, *Kirchenordnungen* 2:46; *Einfältiges Bedenken*, 170–171.

ters," it created great offense that in Strasbourg few people received the sacrament, and those who did were not examined beforehand.[28] He could rightfully accuse his adversaries of impiety, superstition, and hypocrisy, Bucer wrote, but at the same time he had no answer to sincere Christians who asked why those who called themselves reformers did not restore "what was necessary for religion," such as participation in the sacrament and the public profession of faith and obedience to the church by each individual.[29]

Prominent throughout the ordinance is Bucer's use of the church fathers and the practices of the early church to justify its provisions, particularly where they deviated from medieval practice. For instance, the ordinance specified that pastors and preachers were to teach that "those who were not worthy to receive the sacrament because they knowingly remained in sin" were not to be present at the celebration of the Lord's Supper. On the other hand, all who were present in the church were admonished to receive the sacrament. Bucer defended this requirement by referring to the early church which, "when it still followed the apostolic ordinance completely," had even excommunicated those Christians who attended the eucharistic service but who did not receive the sacrament.[30] Bucer was realistic, however, admitting that under current circumstances this practice would be difficult to implement, since it would require that those who were not allowed to receive the sacrament or who did not wish to do so would have to leave the church after the sermon and before the beginning of the communion liturgy. Furthermore,

> there are many good-hearted people who are not yet able completely to
> understand this mystery and the proper use of this holy sacrament, who

---

[28]Bucer's complaint that too few people received the Lord's Supper is borne out by the parish registers; cf. Lorna Jane Abray, *The People's Reformation: Magistrates, Clergy and Commons in Strasbourg, 1500–1598* (Ithaca: Cornell University Press, 1985), 195.

[29]TB 14:24r-25r (February 18, 1543): "Gravissimum crimen quod hostes contra me apud bonos objicere possunt est quod inexploratos incognitos admissam Domini admittimus quod illam plerique nostrum in totum negligunt. . . . Nemo autem mediocriter Christianus in hac praesertim provincia in qua magna est pastorum auctoritas et plebis insignis in ecclesiasticis rebus obedientia, non abhorret, in Republica et Ecclesia bene constituta multos et magnos esse, qui non communicant sacramentis Christi. Deinde ad communionem admitti plane ignotos non exploratos. . . . Sed quia per se adeo repugnat religioni multos sacramentis non communicare, et tam paucos exploratos et cognitos communicare, id vero me pudefacit, illud me dejecit et apud optimos quosque obmutescere facit. Si enim recriminari adversarios velim, apud quos scilicet omnia perversa sunt, impietate, superstitione, hypocrisi, audio a non malis: At vos reformatores mundi estis qui nihil debetis non restituere, quod ad religionem est necessarium ut est sacramentis communicare et singulos fidem suam apud Ecclesiam profiteri, seseque in obedientiam Ecclesiae tradere." The lack of a precommunion examination in Strasbourg had been publicized by Count Christoph von Gleichen (Bucer identified him as "monoculus a Glichen"), a member of the cathedral chapters of both Strasbourg and Cologne and therefore well acquainted with practices in the reformer's home church; cf. Varrentrapp, *Hermann von Wied*, 130-131. A short time later Bucer asked Philip of Hesse to intervene with the count in order to stop his slanderous statements about Bucer, Lenz 2:142, no. 164.

[30] *Einfältiges Bedenken*, 148; Bucer cited the writings of Pope Pelagius I and John Chrysostom.

can still pray together with the congregation and be greatly improved through the teaching, admonition and other things done during the Lord's Supper, and they may daily be instructed and led to complete understanding of and blessed use of the sacrament.

Pastors therefore were not to be hasty in expelling from the communion service those who would not receive the Lord's Supper but who had not committed notorious, grave sin or whose refusal to participate did not reflect a deliberate rejection of the sacrament.[31]

The conservatism of the archbishop of Cologne and the constraints he placed on Bucer regarding the provisions of the ordinance are undoubtedly reflected in its final form. Nevertheless, the system of instruction, admonition, and discipline which it contains is faithful to the ideas which Bucer had consistently expressed from the mid-1530s.[32] Working in a Catholic territory, Bucer was able to shape medieval practices such as confirmation, auricular confession, and excommunication to fit his vision of the purified and restored church in a way that he could not do in Protestant areas where those practices had been rejected in the early years of the Reformation. Having himself become more conservative over the years with regard to retaining traditional practices, Bucer was now better able to adapt the institutions, after giving them a new theological basis, to the needs of the evangelical church.

This new theological basis did not escape the notice of Bucer's Catholic opponents in Cologne. When the ordinance was presented to a diet of the territorial estates in July, representatives of the cathedral chapter asked for two to three weeks to study the ordinance and to draw up their response to it. This response, *Christliche und Catholische Gegenberichtung*, was written by Johannes Gropper in the name of the chapter and sent to the archbishop in early October.[33] Bucer began a response to the

[31]Richter, *Kirchenordnungen* 2:41; *Einfältiges Bedenken*, 147-149; citation at 149. Although Bucer did not use the term catechumen, he clearly considered these "good-hearted people" to be in the same category as those he had compared to catechumens in his earlier ordinances. His reluctance to use the term catechumen in this case may have been due to the fact that in the early church the catechumens were required to leave the church after the prayers of the church and before the eucharistic liturgy began.

[32]In her analysis of the Cologne ordinance, Köhn also concludes that it accurately reflects Bucer's thought and is not merely a copy of the various ordinances he used as models. The sections which rely on the Brandenburg-Nürnberg church ordinance of 1533, such as the requirement of a precommunion examination and the warning to sinners to abstain from receiving the Lord's Supper, are modified to accord with Bucer's chief concerns. Other sections of the ordinance, for instance the confirmation ceremony, follow the practice of the Strasbourg church or the Hessian ordinances which Bucer had written. Cf. Köhn's discussion of the warning to sinners to abstain from the sacrament, *Entwurf*, 121, the precommunion examination, 142-144, and confirmation, 137-139. The Brandenburg-Nürnberg ordinance contained no provision for excommunication; on that ordinance's silence concerning the ban, see the introduction to the Brandenburg-Nürnberg ordinance of 1533, in Sehling, *Kirchenordnungen*, 11/1:118-121.

[33]Varrentrapp, *Hermann von Wied*, 205-208; 223-225. The *Gegenberichtung* is also known by the name of its Latin translation, *Antididagma, seu christianae et catholicae religionis . . . propugnatio.*

Gegenberichtung soon after he received a copy in the fall of 1543.[34] His lengthy manuscript, the *Bestendige Verantwortung*, took about a year to write and was finally printed in Bonn in the first part of 1545.[35]

The *Gegenberichtung* was a thorough, critical examination of the reformation ordinance which used frequent and lengthy citations of the church fathers and the decrees of both regional and general church councils to argue that the doctrines and practices contained in the ordinance contradicted the teaching and tradition of the universal church. It followed a fixed pattern in its critique of the reformation ordinance. Taking up each section of the ordinance, it began with a statement of the position held by the "universal church," supported by passages from the fathers, conciliar canons, and Scripture. Then, set off by a different typeface, Gropper cited provisions of the ordinance which deviated from the position of the universal church. These citations were often followed by a criticism of the provisions. Bucer closely followed the pattern of the *Gegenberichtung* in refuting its charges. He also proceeded section by section, first summarizing the criticisms of the ordinance and then responding to every point, taking up each patristic citation from the *Gegenberichtung* in the process. The resulting work, over twice the length of the *Gegenberichtung*, was Bucer's most complete defense of the doctrines taught by the reformation ordinance.

Gropper's liberal use of patristic authority to support his position compelled Bucer to confront those statements of the fathers which seemed most to contradict evangelical doctrines. This approach, however, only gave Bucer the opportunity to support his assertions made over the past decade that the evangelical church was more faithful to the early church in doctrine and practice than was the contemporary Catholic church. On the issues of penance and church discipline, Bucer argued that the passages from the fathers used by Gropper either did not pertain to the practice of auricular confession, were cited out of context, or actually supported the provisions of the ordinance.[36] Moreover, Bucer often charged his opponents with misrepresenting or deliberately distorting passages of "the book of the reformation." The ordinance did not oppose the teaching and practice of the catholic and universal church, as the author of the *Gegenberichtung* claimed. Rather, the opponents of the ordinance

[34]As Bucer wrote to Bullinger, "the confutation is being confuted"; Lenz 2:225 (Dec. 28, 1543).

[35]Köhn, *Entwurf*, 60–63. Lipgens, *Gropper*, 148 n. 2, says there were two German editions of the *Bestendige Verantwortung*, the first published in 1544 by the same printer responsible for the 1545 edition, but none of the Bucer bibliographies or secondary works on the Cologne reformation attempt mentions a 1544 edition. From Bucer's letter to Albert Hardenberg, one of the archbishop's theological advisors who oversaw the publication of the *Bestendige Verantwortung*, it appears that the book was not published before February 1545; Pollet, *Correspondance* 1:210.4–211.3 (Jan. 28, 1545).

[36]For instance, on confession: "Wer auch der Vätter schrifften, welche die Gegengelehrten anziehen, recht ansehen will, der muß bekennen, daß das Buch aller ding gleicher meynung ist mit den H. Vättern," *Bestendige Verantwortung*, 214v; cf. Bucer's discussion of the abolition of the office of penitentiary in Constantinople, 217v–218r, and his summary of patristic teaching on confession, 218v–219v.

had created false distinctions between the contents of the ordinance and the teaching of the church in order to mislead Christian readers.[37]

One of the disagreements between the reformation ordinance and the *Gegenberichtung* concerned the number of sacraments. Gropper objected that the ordinance recognized only two sacraments, while the universal church, both eastern and western, had always acknowledged seven sacraments.[38] In the *Bestendige Verantwortung* Bucer discussed the nature and number of the sacraments as a direct response to Gropper and then dealt with the sacramentality of confirmation and penance or absolution when defending provisions of the ordinance directly concerning them. Given his opponents' definition of a sacrament as a visible sign of divine grace established by Christ himself, Bucer maintained that only baptism and the Lord's Supper could be called sacraments, as Augustine and other fathers agreed. As a third "quasi-sacrament" Bucer recognized the imposition of hands as used by Christ, although Christ had never commanded his apostles to use this sign in the same way as he had the water of baptism and the bread and wine of the Lord's Supper. The imposition of hands was used in ordaining ministers in the New Testament. It was also practiced by the early church when confirming those baptized as children after they had professed their own faith and obedience to the church, and when absolving penitents and reconciling them to the church. In these cases particularly the imposition of hands served as a visible sign of God's gracious acceptance, and in this sense it could be called a sacrament. Christ had indeed commanded a confession of faith and obedience as well as the absolution of the genuinely contrite, but there was no explicit command in Scripture that the imposition of hands be used in conjunction with the practices of confirmation or absolution. Thus it could not be regarded as having the same stature as baptism and the Lord's Supper.[39]

Bucer also argued that neither penance nor confession could be considered a sacrament. As he pointed out, both Scripture and the fathers used the word *poenitentia* to mean not a visible sign but rather genuine contrition and sorrow for sin. Even Peter Lombard had described penitence as a virtue or grace through which one lamented past sin and resolved to avoid it in the future.[40] Nor could absolution be called a sacrament, for it was not a sign but a work of the church's ministry and the care of souls. Bucer did not dispute the institution of absolution by Christ, and he himself cited the Corinthian sinner as an example of how the power to bind and loose was exercised. He even allowed that, in accordance with the testimony of Cyprian and other fathers concerning the use of imposition of hands when absolving the penitent, one could speak of a sacrament of absolution. Or if one used the term "sacrament" in the same sense as the Greek word "mysterium," then both penitence and absolution

---

[37]On issues such as the ordinance's requirement that repentant sinners be assured of forgiveness, ibid., 224r, its provisions regarding satisfaction, 225r-v, and excommunication, 228r-229r.

[38]*Gegenberichtung*, 24v-26v.

[39]*Bestendige Verantwortung*, 64r-65r.

[40]Ibid., 65v; *Sentences* IV, dist. XIV, 3,1.

could be called sacraments. But penance could be described as a sacrament only according to these broader uses of the word.[41] Likewise, confirmation was neither a sacrament nor necessary for salvation. Bucer claimed that scholastic theologians taught that the chrism was only a sacramental, not a sacrament. Moreover, the anointing with oil, although an ancient custom, had not always been a part of confirmation the way that the imposition of hands was. The confirmation ceremony was meant to preserve people within the church through their own confession so that they would not be misled by Anabaptists who pointed to passages in Scripture requiring each individual to confess his faith for himself.[42]

The *Gegenberichtung* had found three major faults in the reformation ordinance's provisions on repentance, confession, and church discipline. The ordinance, it stated, did not require secret confession of all one's sins to a priest, it did not teach the importance of works of satisfaction as a demonstration of true repentance, and it made the ban too mild a penalty, since it allowed the excommunicate to remain in civil society and it prohibited the imposition of excommunication for certain sins. Gropper cited an impressive array of patristic sources to uphold the priest's power to grant absolution and impose penance, and to demonstrate that the church had always taught the necessity of confessing secret sins. In light of this authority, the ordinance seemed to mock the significance of confession and absolution by stating that sinners could be absolved after making only a general confession of sin.[43]

Bucer responded to this accusation by arguing that the ordinance in no way opposed the teachings of the church fathers. It allowed only those who had first confessed and been absolved to receive the sacrament, it encouraged individuals to confess those sins which were especially burdensome, and it instructed the pastor to examine the penitent and give any needed catechetical instruction. No one was to be absolved who was not willing to turn from his sin and amend his life. The fathers themselves had never demanded more than this, and any attempt to prove the necessity of confessing all sins from their writings was only an attempt to mislead people.[44] Bucer supported this assertion by taking up, one by one, the patristic citations quoted in the *Gegenberichtung*. A number of the citations, such as those from Tertullian and Cyprian, concerned public confession and penance, not private confession. Those fathers—Origen, Jerome, Ambrose, Augustine, and others—who wrote about private confession taught that God had given priests the authority to forgive sins, and that individuals should seek them out as doctors for their souls and should not be afraid to reveal their sins to them. They regarded private confession highly because through it the pastor could more easily move people's hearts to true repentance. "Nevertheless, because neither the Lord nor the apostles commanded or ordained this secret confession . . . so none of the old, holy fathers required it as necessary but rather left

---

[41]*Bestendige Verantwortung*, 213v–214r.
[42]Ibid., 108v–110r.
[43]*Gegenberichtung*, 114v–120r.
[44]*Bestendige Verantwortung*, 214v–215r.

it voluntary and faithfully urged its use, and this for each individual as much or as little as he realized it would be of greater or lesser use."[45]

Bucer also pointed out that the reformation ordinance made use of private confession to further a proper understanding of sin and repentance, since it required such confession before reception of the Lord's Supper. The requirement to confess was not burdensome, since an enumeration of sins was not necessary, while those who needed special consolation or instruction would have the opportunity to receive it. Bucer maintained that the confession of all sins required by *Omnis utriusque sexus* must be interpreted to refer only to those sins whose confession would better enable instruction and amendment, "for otherwise the canon would not be useful nor would it be possible to obey."[46]

Bucer then responded to the specific criticisms of the reformation ordinance made in the *Gegenberichtung*. He first took up the claim that individuals were to confess each and every sin to a priest.[47] This position, Bucer charged, derived from a misunderstanding of the power of the keys. Bucer's description of this power is a restatement of what he had written elsewhere. Binding and loosing were not restricted only to sins committed after baptism, since those who were baptized had their sins forgiven and those who refused baptism had their sins retained. Beyond this initial binding or loosing, priests had the authority to bind sinners either with penance or with the ban, and to loose them and restore them to Christian fellowship if they saw genuine repentance accompanied by amendment of life. To make this judgment it was not necessary that the priest know the nature and number of each sin committed; it was sufficient if he saw the penitent's faith and heartfelt contrition. Moreover, the church had the right to bind only publicly known sins, as in the case of the Corinthian sinner, or when individuals voluntarily revealed their hidden sins in order to submit to penance.[48]

The *Gegenberichtung* had also found fault with the ordinance's provision that confessing sinners were not to be left in doubt but were to be assured of God's forgiveness. This, Gropper asserted, gave the power of granting absolution to the one confessing rather than to the priest, who was required to absolve the sinner even if he did not know what sins the person had committed.[49] In response, Bucer accused his opponent of deliberately misrepresenting the ordinance's contents. The provision that repentant sinners were to be reassured of divine forgiveness accorded with Am-

---

[45]Ibid., 218v-219v; citation at 220r: "Nicht desto weniger aber weyl weder der HERR noch die Apostolen diese heymliche Beycht gepotten oder verordnet . . . so haben diß werck auch keine der alten H. Vätter als notwendig erforderet sonder es frey gelassen vnd allein getrewlich darzu vermanet Vnnd doch diß ein jeder so vil mehr oder weniger nach dem er dessen nutz mehr oder minder erfaren hat."

[46]Ibid., 220v-221r; citation at 221r: "dann wo anders möchte diese ordnung weder nutzlich noch möglich sein."

[47]*Gegenberichtung*, 114v.

[48]*Bestendige Verantwortung*, 221v-223v.

[49]*Gegenberichtung*, 119v-120r.

brose, who taught that no one was able to do penance properly unless he hoped to be forgiven. Moreover, the ordinance expressly stated that priests were to make sure that the persons confessing were truly contrite and intended to reform, "so that they did not cast pearls before swine." In addition, absolution was to be postponed until any restitution had been made or the sinner reconciled with anyone he had harmed or offended. Thus it was the priest and not the penitent who determined if and when absolution was to be granted; the sinner could not demand absolution after making only a superficial general confession. Last but not least, Bucer turned the argument against his critics. They had no basis to accuse the reformation ordinance of allowing for easy absolutions when their own priests were guilty of absolving people who showed no faith or contrition and no intention of abandoning their life of sin. Requiring the endowment of masses, a pilgrimage or repetition of the Lord's Prayer instead of genuine reform was no real penance. His opponents insisted that everyone go to a priest and tell him about every evil thought, word, and deed and then perform whatever penance was imposed, but this was not the confession or penance which God commanded or the fathers taught.[50]

This brought Bucer to the issue of satisfaction. The *Gegenberichtung* had described two types of satisfaction taught by the universal church: the satisfaction which imparted forgiveness of sins and was ascribed to Christ alone, and the canonical satisfaction imposed by the pastor. This latter type of satisfaction uprooted the causes of sin, removed or softened the temporal punishment of sin, and satisfied the church offended by the sin. The *Gegenberichtung* claimed that the reformation ordinance rejected works of satisfaction and simply required the pastor to announce forgiveness to all after he had heard only a general confession of sin.[51] Bucer responded to this charge by accusing his opponents of finding disagreement where there was none.[52] Indeed, Gropper's definition of satisfaction sounds remarkably similar to Bucer's own earlier descriptions of penitential discipline. Nevertheless, to forestall any suspicion that the reformation ordinance opposed the teachings of the fathers, Bucer devoted several paragraphs to the proper understanding of canonical satisfaction. He began by referring to an earlier section of the *Bestendige Verantwortung* in which he discussed at length the fathers' use of the word *satisfacere*. In proper Latin usage, the term meant "to be reconciled or to be restored to favor with someone whom a person has angered, and not a payment or settlement of something where someone has previously lost someone's favor or done something wrong"; restoration to divine favor came only through genuine repentance and confession. The fathers expected such satisfaction or *exhomologesis* to include a public demonstration of repentance through lamentation, mortification of the flesh, and almsgiving.[53] Nevertheless, although

---

[50]*Bestendige Verantwortung*, 224r–226r.

[51]*Gegenberichtung*, 120r–122v.

[52]*Bestendige Verantwortung*, 226r–v.

[53]Ibid., 226v–227r; citation at 226v: "Im Artickel von der Gnugthuung ist hie oben dargethan, das die elteren Lehrer der kirchen das wort Satisfacere vnd Satisfactionem gebrauchet haben, welches auch die rechte art der Lateinischen Sprach vermag für sich versünen vnnd

Bucer obviously approved of patristic penitential practice, he pointed out a problem in citing the fathers on the subject: "in their admonitions (and in order to emphasize that to which they admonished) the dear fathers sometimes used overly enthusiastic language and exalted the matter with their words more than it should in itself be exalted." This use of hyperbole was more suited to admonition than to teaching, and when Bucer's opponents used such patristic statements to teach they misled the people. For this reason the sayings of the fathers were always to be compared with Scripture.[54]

Bucer also rejected the automatic imposition of certain types of penance for specific sins. The manner and length of penance imposed for any given sin could not be prescribed beforehand, and the development of such set penances for certain sins was a perversion of the early church's practice. Indeed, the harsh nature of public penance meant that an individual must be free to accept or refuse its imposition if hypocrisy was to be avoided.[55] Bucer repeatedly accused his opponents of neglecting the practices of the fathers and ignoring the penitential canons of the early church; they therefore had no right to criticize the provisions of the reformation ordinance concerning the use of penance.[56]

The final section on excommunication was the most polemical part of the discussion on penance and church discipline. In his discussion of excommunication Gropper seemed purposefully to have distorted certain provisions of the ordinance in order to discredit it in the eyes of his readers. Bucer responded by charging his opponents with obvious lies, misrepresentation, and disrespect for the archbishop as patron of the ordinance. His own criticism of Catholic practice was much harsher as he compared their use of excommunication—or rather, in his opinion, their misuse of it—to the practices prescribed in the ordinance. Gropper had argued that there were two types of excommunication, the first based on Matthew 18 and used in cases of private injury in which the sinner was denounced to the proper authorities, and the second based on I Corinthians 5 and imposed in cases of obvious sin committed not

---

wider zu gefallen darstellen dem, den einer erzürnet hatt, vnnd nicht für ein bezalen oder vergleichen deß, das man vor verschütt oder vnrecht gethan hatt. Vnd weyl wir vns mit Gott anders nit versünen noch vns ihm zu gefallen wider darstellen mögen, so wir gesundiget vnd jhn erzurnet haben, dan mit rechter rew vnd Beycht der sunden vnnd bitten vmb gnad durch vnseren HERREN Jesum Christum"; cf. 37r.

[54]Ibid., 35v-39v; citation at 39v: "Die lieben Vätter haben in vermanungen (die sachen dazu sie ermanet damit zu grössen) etwan vberschwenckliche rede gebrauchet, vnd die sachen mit worten höher gehebt, dan sie an jn selb zu erheben sein, so man einfeltig leren soll. Dan solche Hyperbolae, vbertreffende reden sich zum ermanen besser reimen, dan zum lehren. Nun aber bringen die Gegengelehrten vnd jrs gleichen solche Hyperbolas .i. vberschwenckliche reden ein, als einfeltig mässige reden des lehrens, vnd machen den Leuthen damit ein gespenst für den augen, das sie das liecht Göttlicher schrifft nit mehr recht anschawen können. Darumb ist von nöten, wan diß leut solche sprüch der Vätter fürbringen, das die Christen als bald bedencken vnd sehen, ob auch der H. Geist in seiner schrifft also rede, vnd so sie das nit finden, sollen sie sich solch reden als menchen reden nit jrr oder kleinmütig lassen machen."

[55]Ibid., 227v-228r.

[56]Ibid., 35r-36v; 226v; 228v.

just against one's brother but against God. The ban described by the fathers allowed for absolutely no contact with the excommunicate in either spiritual or secular affairs. Where such severity was not observed the ban was liable to lose its potency. Gropper found fault with several of the ordinance's provisions regarding the imposition of the ban: the requirement that no one, not even notorious sinners, be excommunicated without previous private admonition, the role of the appointed elders in private admonition, the proclamation of the ban by a superintendent rather than by the bishop and in the excommunicate's home church rather than from the episcopal seat, the express limitation of the ban to ecclesiastical affairs with no concurrent civil penalty, and the prohibition of imposing excommunication for debt and other secular offenses.[57]

In response, Bucer argued that there was only one way to use the ban, and that was "to exclude the sinner from the fellowship of the body of Christ through the proper authority of the church in the name of the Lord and by his Spirit with the agreement of the congregation of God for sin that is either publicly known or of which the individual has been convicted." There were, however, two degrees of excommunication. Obstinate sinners were excluded from all fellowship with Christians, while those who promised to reform were excluded only from the Lord's Supper "and some of the other more holy ceremonies of the church in so far as this serves [to bring] them to reforming humiliation." Christians were to admonish their brothers whenever they became aware of any sin, and it was therefore wrong to distinguish between private injury and public offense when imposing the ban.[58]

Bucer responded sharply to the specific procedural criticisms of the Gegenberichtung. It was uncharitable to condemn the use of private admonition in case of public sin, nor did the requirement of private admonition mean that no further action was to be taken against those in manifest sin. The use of appointed elders was defended by the existence of such elders in both the Jewish synagogue and the New Testament church. If the bishops could delegate the authority to the officialis of ecclesiastical courts, then a superintendent, who performed the work of a bishop but did not have the title, should have the authority to exercise this "episcopal task" of excommunication.[59]

Gropper had distinguished between three degrees of excommunication: exclusion from the Lord's Supper alone, exclusion from all of the sacraments for those on

---

[57]Gegenberichtung, 122v–126r.

[58]Bestendige Verantwortung, 229r–v; citation at 229r: "Vnd ist die selbige einige weiß vnd der einige weg, ratio et via una excommunicandi, das ist zu bannen, das der Sünder durch den ordentlichen gewalt der Kirchen im namen des HERREN vnd auß seinem Geist auch mit gehelle der Gemeinde Gottes von gemeinschafft des Leibs Christi außgeschlossen werden, es seie von offner oder von vberzeugter sünden wegen. . . . Das ist aber war, inn dem bannen vnnd außschliessen sollen vnderscheidliche grad behalten werden, das nemlich etlich gar von aller gemeinschafft des Volcks vnsers HERREN Christi außgeschlossen werden, als die in sünden verharren, Etliche aber nicht von aller gemeinschafft Christi, als die sich zu besserung erbieten, welche man allein vom Tisch des HERREN vnnd etlichen anderen heiligeren hendlen der Kirchen, so nemlich jnen zu besserlicher demütigung dienstlich sein mag vnd nit gantz von aller gemeinschafft der Religion außschliessen solle."

[59]Ibid., 230r–231r.

whom public penance had been imposed, and major excommunication or anathema in which all contact with the sinner was forbidden.[60] Bucer acknowledged in theory the Christian's right to impose the anathema, which he defined as "the recognition and damnation of someone as completely and eternally cut off and separated from Christ our Lord," but such a sentence could only be pronounced over those who had sinned against the Holy Spirit, and knowledge of this type of sin came only through "the special revelation of the Holy Spirit." For all practical purposes anathema pertained only to false doctrine, not to individuals.[61] The proper differentiation of the ban made in Scripture was between the temporary exclusion of the penitent, which the fathers had further subdivided according to the seriousness of sin and depth of repentance, and the more complete exclusion and ostracism of the impenitent. The sinner's repentance was always to be the goal of such shunning, and Christians were to treat the excommunicate in such a way that he neither underestimated the offense caused by his sin nor despaired entirely of forgiveness. In addition, where the ruling authority allowed excommunicated sinners to remain in public office or to retain other rights of citizenship, Christians were to continue to do business with them.[62]

Bucer asserted that his opponents had no right to find fault with these provisions regarding treatment of the excommunicated, since they themselves did not adhere to their own laws and canons regarding excommunication. Their clergy especially were guilty of simony, immorality, involvement in secular affairs, and neglect of their ministry, offenses which were grounds for excommunication, yet, as Bucer stated, his opponents "not only want us to have fellowship with them in both spiritual and secular affairs but also want us to trust body and soul to them and neither believe nor do anything other than what they prescribe."[63]

Bucer also rejected as "obvious falsehood" the *Gegenberichtung's* charge that the penalty of excommunication prescribed by the reformation ordinance was too mild. Gropper had claimed that excommunication in the ordinance entailed only exclusion

---

[60]*Gegenberichtung*, 124v–125r.

[61]*Bestendige Verantwortung*, 231r–v: "Dan ein Anathema machen ist jhn erkennen vnd verdammen, als von Christo vnserem HERREN gentzlich vnd ewiglich abgeschnitten vnd gesündert. Welches vrtheyl der mensch wol vber falsche lehr aber vber keinen menschen zu fellen hatt, dan allein die, so zu dem Todt sündigen vnd den H. Geyst lästern. . . . Nun aber kein mensch dem andren im hertz sehen kan . . . dan allein durch besondere offenbarung des H. Geysts."

[62]Ibid., 232r–v.

[63]Ibid., 232v–233r: "Sie klagen, das Buch lasse zu, mitt den Verbanneten gemeinschafft zu haben in Burgerlichen sachen, vnd sie haben gemeinschafft wöllen, auch das jederman die habe mit den Verbanneten in allen Geistlichen vnd Burgerlichen sachen. Dan die Clerici, so offentliche Simoniaci seind, verbottene weiber bey sich haben oder sich sonst mit der fornication vbersehen, die jre Kirchendienst nit trewlich verrichten, die sich vngeschickt trincken, die sich mit weltlichen geschefften beladen, verbannen die Canones mit der H. Schrifft vnnd gepeut der HERR durch seinen lieben Apostel vnd alle alte Vätter, das die Gleubigen mit solchen vberal kein gemeinschafft haben sollen. Die Gegengelehrten wöllen aber, das wir mit solchen nit allein gemeinschafft haben, beyde in Geistlichem vnd weltlichem, sonder wöllen auch, dass wir jnen leib vnd seel vertrawen vnd anders nit gleuben noch leben dan sie vns fürschreiben."

from the Lord's Supper and from attendance at baptisms and weddings,[64] but Bucer pointed out that this was merely one aspect of excommunication. In actuality the ordinance allowed the excommunicate to hear sermons, but he was not to participate in any other ecclesiastical activity. Bucer claimed that his opponents could not criticize the provision concerning the retention of rights of citizenship by excommunicates, since this decision belonged to the civil authority. The ordinance only laid down guidelines concerning the treatment of the excommunicate when the secular authority allowed him to retain his civil rights, and Bucer added, realistically but with perhaps a touch of bitterness, "where is the magistrate who does not do this?" His opponents should be criticizing the secular authorities; but in the meantime Christians had to be taught how to act towards those in government positions who had been excommunicated. The magistrate violated imperial law when it did not impose the civil ban for publicly known sins. Nevertheless, when the magistrate neglected its duty and allowed the sinner to retain his civil rights, Christians could not refuse to submit to its authority, for this refusal to submit would soon lead to revolt such as had happened in Münster. On the other hand, Christians were to avoid any unnecessary association with the excommunicate. Only in matters required by the secular authority or by the physical needs of the excommunicate were Christians to have contact with him.[65]

The final criticisms of the ordinance concerned the use of the ban by ecclesiastical courts. Gropper had interpreted the ordinance to mean that the ban could not be imposed for deception in trade or the refusal to repay a debt. In addition, he had cited canons which specified that an excommunicate could not be absolved unless penance had been performed or a fine paid, and he charged the ordinance with deviating from this requirement.[66] Bucer replied that the prohibition of the ban "in secular affairs" was another way of stating that it could not be imposed for sin which was not publicly known. But since refusal to fulfill secular obligations was obvious sin, the ban could be applied in such cases. The ordinance actually increased the scope of the ban by applying it to all cases of manifest sin, such as simony, usury, and sexual immorality, while his opponents imposed it only for cases of debt or other litigation in their courts. As far as requiring penance or payment of a fine before absolution, the ordinance stated that an excommunicate was to reform, be reconciled with those he had injured, and confess his sins before being absolved, and this was a more genuine penance than the fines demanded by its opponents.[67]

The provisions of the reformation ordinance and their defense in *Bestendige Verantwortung* demonstrate how Bucer integrated the theory and practice of confirmation, confession and absolution, and church discipline. His evangelical theological presuppositions are obvious: neither confirmation nor penance was a sacrament; private confession had to remain voluntary; it was not necessary to confess each and ev-

[64]*Gegenberichtung*, 125r–v.
[65]*Bestendige Verantwortung*, 233r–v.
[66]*Gegenberichtung*, 125v–126r.
[67]*Bestendige Verantwortung*, 233v–234r.

ery sin. Nevertheless Bucer attempted to appeal to reform-minded Catholics. He allowed that both confirmation and absolution could be regarded as "sacramental" ceremonies if accompanied by the imposition of hands. He specified that confirmation should follow religious instruction and that it entailed the confirmand's public submission to the disciplinary authority of the church.

Bucer also endorsed wholeheartedly the statements of the fathers praising the value of private confession, and in the reformation ordinance he referred to absolution as the voice of the gospel. Although he held that mandatory confession only created hypocrites, he did not hesitate to require confession before participation in the Lord's Supper. He justified this requirement on two grounds. First, confession was linked with individual catechization, whereby the pastor had the opportunity to instruct his parishioners on the true nature of sin and do what he could to evoke repentance. Catechization was not to replace confession; rather, it was to lead to more genuine and heartfelt contrition and confession. Second, the purpose of the precommunion examination was the granting of absolution, and this was not to be automatic. The minister's right to delay or withhold absolution until there was evidence of repentance and reform placed him in the role of judge. Bucer gave as much attention to the power to bind sin as he did to the power to loose it, and his fiercest criticism of Catholic practice was that priests were too ready to grant easy absolution to those who were not truly penitent. The priest's right to deny absolution, combined with his obligation to examine and instruct each individual in the Creed, the Ten Commandments, and the nature of sin, was the means by which Bucer hoped to avoid hypocrisy and insincere repentance. His defense of a principle which he had vigorously condemned in one of his earliest works illustrates the extent of his disillusionment concerning the religious sensibilities of the average layperson.

Bucer's ideas on penitential discipline and excommunication were the most elaborate part of the system. He presented a wide range of disciplinary measures ranging from the refusal to grant absolution and thus exclusion from the Lord's Supper to the complete exclusion from the church and ostracism by other Christians. The penalty's severity was determined by the gravity of sin and the degree of repentance, if any, demonstrated by the sinner. The provisions requiring reformation of life and reconciliation with the injured party before the granting of absolution followed the practice of the early church, in which penance had to be performed before the sinner could be reconciled with the church. The nature of this form of penance, for so Bucer regarded it, depended on the nature of the sin: if the offense was public knowledge, then the change in behavior and the elimination of the offense had to be publicly demonstrated as well. The severity of the disciplinary measures imposed on the penitent also varied according to the individual case. Ideally, none of those who had been excommunicated was to remain in the church during the communion service, although Bucer admitted that this ideal would be very difficult if not impossible to achieve. Beyond that it was apparently left to the ministers to decide how best to discipline a repentant sinner guilty of grave offense. Bucer specifically mentioned exclusion from other church ceremonies, such as baptisms and weddings, and some degree of ostracism by other Christians, but repentant sinners could attend prayer services as well as sermons and could be restored to full fellowship with the church at the point of death. Exclusion and ostracism were taken to their extremes in the case of an obstinate sinner, and deathbed absolution was denied to the unrepentant.

Except for very rare cases, Bucer rejected major excommunication if, as in the *Gegenberichtung*, it was equated with the anathema. In other respects, however, the consequences of excommunication were similar to those prescribed by canon law. Bucer also distinguished between the penalties imposed by the church and those imposed by the magistrate. While he believed that the secular government should act against notorious sinners, he was obviously pessimistic about the magistrate's performance of its duties. Nevertheless he did not want the distinction between church and state blurred by having one perform the responsibilities of the other. Pastors were to admonish the civil authority to perform their God-given duty to punish public sin, but that was all. The magistrate's failure to act against sinners should not affect the way pastors and laity interacted with those sinners beyond the overriding command of submission to the magistrate's authority.

While the system of instruction and discipline outlined in the Cologne ordinance was similar to that which Bucer prescribed for Hesse, it also reflected the fact that it was to be imposed on a Catholic territory. Bucer retained the practices of confirmation, confession, and excommunication, purged of abuses and reformed in accordance with evangelical doctrine. In the *Bestendige Verantwortung* he defended the reformation by arguing that the reformed practices agreed with the teaching of the church fathers, and he accused the Catholics of perverting the institutions of the patristic church. Nevertheless, just as he had failed to win the Catholic collocutors to his vision of reform, Bucer was also unable to persuade his Catholic opponents in Cologne to accept his reformation of penance and Christian discipline. The retention of outward forms did not hide the evangelical justification given them in the ordinance. Backed by the emperor's military dominance in northwest Germany, the Catholic forces of Cologne succeeded in thwarting the reformation attempt. Hermann von Wied was excommunicated and removed from office by the pope. With the emperor's victory over the Schmalkaldic League, the estates of the archiepiscopal territories had no choice but to recognize Hermann's Catholic successor in January of 1547.[68] The Reformation attempt ended in failure.

The outcome of events in Cologne magnified Bucer's growing pessimism about the state of the evangelical church in Germany. He attributed the worsening political position of the Protestant estates to their lack of repentance and their neglect of Christian discipline.[69] But his pessimism was also fed by the frustrations and failures which he experienced throughout the 1540s in attempting to establish a system of Christian discipline in his own church. It is time to examine Bucer's efforts to impose "the yoke of Christ" on his fellow Strasburghers.

---

[68]Franzen, *Bischof*, 105–106.

[69]Bucer to Philip of Hesse, Lenz 2:489 (no. 249, March 25, 1547); to Ambrosius Blarer, Schieß 2:623 (no. 1438, May 13, 1547).

7

A Prophet without Honor? Bucer and Christian Discipline in Strasbourg, 1539-1546

Bucer's career in Strasbourg during the 1540s was marked by efforts to establish a functioning system of Christian discipline. Pastoral and pedagogical concerns dominated in the system which Bucer called "the yoke of Christ." To accomplish his goal Bucer had to win the support of the magistrate, his fellow clergymen, and the laity for the various components of discipline and pastoral care—catechization, confirmation, fraternal admonition and pastoral oversight, penitential discipline and excommunication. Bucer had argued at length for the use of penitential discipline and excommunication in *Von der waren Seelsorge*, but he did not stop there in his efforts to establish a disciplinary system in the Strasbourg church. During the decade of the 1540s he urged the acceptance of "the yoke of Christ" in memoranda submitted to the city council, instructions and accords drawn up for the *Kirchenkonvent*, and popular theological works intended for the laity. Although most of the clergy supported his attempts, Bucer's plan for Christian discipline received only lukewarm support from the magistrate and laity. The problem which Bucer faced in Strasbourg was not so much one of outright opposition to his vision of Christian discipline but rather the indifference of the laity to measures which were voluntary combined with the unwillingness of the magistrate to give the clergy any coercive authority over the city's inhabitants.

The problems encountered by the clergy in their attempts to exercise Christian discipline are illustrated by the fate of the proposals which resulted from the second Strasbourg synod held in May of 1539. The ministers drew up several proposals concerning administration of the sacraments, the use of discipline, uniformity of ceremonies, and supervision of ecclesiastical affairs, and then presented them to the council for approval. The council's discussion of these proposals stretched over the next three years.[1] Even after the council concluded its deliberations in November 1542, it needed

---

[1]The introduction to the synodal documents, BDS 6/II:195-199, gives a resumé of each council session in which the synodal decrees were discussed.

further prodding from the pastors before the articles were published in final form. On August 14, 1544—well over five years after the synod was held—the articles were officially presented to the pastors and *Kirchenpfleger*.[2]

The decrees drawn up at the synod reflected the ministers' perceptions of the shortcomings of the Strasbourg church and their suggestions to remedy these failings, while the version finally adopted by the city council demonstrated the magistrate's reservations about giving the clergy too much authority in the church. The proposed decrees would have established a mechanism for pastoral care as set forth in *Von der waren Seelsorge* by giving official recognition to the ministers' responsibility for pastoral supervision. By modifying or rejecting several key proposals, the council set limits to that responsibility and reasserted its own ultimate control over the city's church.

The pastoral emphasis appeared already in the first chapter of the decrees, "on doctrine and preaching." It exhorted the ministers to diligence in overseeing and looking after their parishioners, "to see what kind of fruit their preaching and teaching brings to each one." They were to be faithful in holding weekly catechetical instruction for children and gentle in admonishing and reproving so that they would be more trusted and respected by their flock and "their ministry would bear more fruit."[3] This general statement of pastoral responsibility was all the clergy could wring from the council. A provision which would have given the ministers the authority to summon their parishioners individually for admonition and correction was tabled when the council discussed this section.[4]

The same concern for instructing and admonishing parishioners underlay the requirement that preparatory Vesper services be held in each parish church on the Saturdays before the celebration of the Lord's Supper. After the service the pastor was to be available for private instruction for those who desired it, and he could even ask those who he thought were in need of such counsel to meet with him if they did not seek him out themselves.[5] But again the city council placed a limit on the pastor's authority: in their first discussion of the synod articles, they set aside for further consideration a provision which would have allowed pastors to reject unworthy communicants.[6] A committee of councillors drafted an alternate proposal but this too was rejected. In an attempt to mollify the pastors, the council did allow them to warn the people from the pulpit "to consider the salvation of their souls and repent."[7] The one

[2]RP 1544, August 11, fols. 370r, 373r; TAE 4:108 (no. 1387).
[3]BDS 6/II:235.3-10.
[4]RP 1540, May 18, fols. 182r-v; excerpt and summary TAE 3:331.13-18 (no. 920).
[5]BDS 6/II:243.15-244.7.
[6]RP 1540, May 18, fols. 182v.; TAE 3:331.24-27 (no. 920). During this time the pre-communion examination was required in at least one church—the French-speaking congregation pastored by Jean Calvin. In a letter to Farel written in May of 1540, Calvin defended his requirement that those wishing to receive the Lord's Supper were to appear before him, stating that the examination gave opportunity to instruct, admonish, and console, CO 9:41 (no. 218).
[7]RP 1542, November 16, fols. 460r; TAE 3:332.24-27 (no. 920).

exception to this general refusal to allow pastors to reject unworthy communicants concerned people from nearby villages that had remained Catholic. In such cases the pastor was to instruct the individuals beforehand and not admit them to the sacrament unless they showed signs of having "truly reformed, so that no one is lightly admitted who later returns to the papist abomination, with grave offense."[8] This provision was only a pale reflection of the authority desired by the pastors.

If the pastors were thwarted in their attempts to screen participants in the sacrament of communion, they did have somewhat more success regarding the selection of godparents. The ministers had long been concerned about the problem of unworthy godparents, and the 1534 church ordinance had stated that parents should choose "proper, God-fearing people . . . not for their money or some other worldly reason."[9] The memorandum "on how to establish church discipline" had also stressed the need to ensure that suitable godparents were chosen.[10] The synodal articles gave the minister the right to reject anyone who was obviously unworthy: "those who publicly speak against and mock our Christian religion, or who have been banned by the church and live publicly in sins punishable with the ban."[11] The city council also adopted three articles "on the misuse of the ban" restricting the publication of sentences of excommunication imposed by the episcopal courts which still operated in Strasbourg.[12] Significantly, there is no evidence that the pastors sought or the council deliberated on any use of excommunication beyond these "abuses" by the ecclesiastical courts.

On the other hand, the magistrate refused to consider the synod's proposals regarding confirmation. In its first discussion of the synodal articles, the city council tabled a section concerned with confirmation, and nothing more was said about it.[13] The most the pastors could obtain was the requirement that children be examined by the ministers before they were allowed to receive the sacrament for the first time. This provision was merely another repetition of the clause of the 1534 church ordinance, which implies that the earlier requirement was still ignored. To aid the ministers in their responsibility for pastoral care, the people were admonished to receive the Lord's Supper in their own parishes; this way each pastor would know his own parishioners and be better able to admonish and instruct them.[14]

---

[8]BDS 6/II:245.34-246.4.

[9]BDS 5:32.8-14; cf. similar provisions which Bucer incorporated into the Hessian disciplinary ordinance, BDS 7:272.7-17.

[10]See above, pp. 102-103.

[11]BDS 6/II:236.6-20.

[12]BDS 6/II:246.5-21. For a description of the episcopal court and its workings, see Karl Stenzel, "Die geistlichen Gerichte zu Straßburg im 15. Jahrhundert," *Zeitschrift für die Geschichte des Oberrheins* 68 (N.F. 29) (1914):365-446; 69 (N.F. 30) (1915):52-95; 201-253; 343-383. The Strasbourg pastors protested directly to the bishop concerning the court's use of the ban in January 1540, ARC 4:148.43-150.6.

[13]TAE 3:331.19-23 (no. 920). The editors of TAE suggest that the council was reluctant to take any action on confirmation in view of the upcoming religious colloquy at Hagenau.

[14]BDS 6/II:244.8-13.

Bucer was certainly aware of the council's reluctance to endorse a public confirmation ceremony; it was perhaps in an effort to sway one or more of the council members that he wrote his strongest defense yet of confirmation, as part of a memorandum concerned primarily with the uniform administration of the sacraments in the city's churches.[15] Where he had earlier only suggested the confirmation of children, he now saw it as something required by Scripture: "the almighty God demands in New and Old Testament that every believer, when he reaches the appropriate age, should himself confess his faith in the church and give himself to the Lord." For this reason the early church had confirmed those baptized as infants after they had learned their catechism, at which time they professed their faith and "gave themselves into the obedience of Christ." Bucer's double emphasis on both the confession of faith and the public profession of obedience was deliberate: "[Christ] ordered that each person deny himself and take his yoke upon him. For this reason all the apostles held that no one who has reached the age of reasoning should be accepted into Christian fellowship who has not himself confessed his faith and given himself to the Lord."[16] Confirmation had assumed a new importance, and as a ceremony expressly commanded in God's word and practiced in the early church, it was to be reestablished in the Strasbourg church.

The synodal decrees as they were finally approved illustrate the city council's cautious and rather ambivalent attitude towards the pastors' ideas concerning Christian discipline. On the one hand it was willing to support the clergy in their attempts to admonish and instruct the citizens in Christian doctrine, piety, and morals, and so

---

[15]Ibid., 203–212. The dating of this document is problematic. The editors assume the memo was written in 1538, but the heading, "post peregrinationem Matt. Zellij. Anno 1538 factam," is a *terminus post quem*, based on a reference to Zell's journey to Wittenberg contained in the document, rather than a firm date. Bucer was in Strasbourg for only a few months after Zell's return in the summer of 1538. He spent part of September in Basel (Lenz 1:45, no. 15, Sept. 20, 1538), and he left for Hesse on October 10 (Schieß 2:7, no. 821, Oct. 8, 1538). He went from Hesse to Wittenberg in November to arrange for the colloquy sponsored by Karlowitz (Lenz 1:52–53, no. 20, November 17, 1538); he returned to Hesse, then traveled directly from there to Leipzig for the colloquy in January. He arrived back in Strasbourg in mid-January (TAE 3:305, no. 885, Jan. 29, 1539), but left again for Frankfurt on February 9 for a meeting of the Schmalkaldic League (BDS 7:9); he did not return home until the end of April, one month before the synod was held (Schieß 2:24, no. 840, Apr. 30, 1539). In light of the brief period between Zell's homecoming and the beginning of Bucer's travels, and given Bucer's involvement in developments outside of Strasbourg, it is doubtful that he would have had much time to devote to the liturgical ordering of the Strasbourg church during the second half of 1538. On the other hand, the views expressed in the memorandum reflect concerns that would have been discussed at the synod; this is particularly true of the reference to Zell's willingness to give a brief admonition concerning reception of the sacrament after his sermon, "if it were incorporated into a general (church) order," BDS 6/II:208.19–209.3. For this reason I believe the memorandum was written sometime between the synod in May 1539, and the discussion of confirmation by the council in May 1540. On the importance of the 1539 synod for attempts to reconcile Melchior Hoffman and his followers with the Strasbourg church, see Packull, "Peter Tasch: From Melchiorite"; for Bucer's new emphasis on the Scriptural justification for confirmation in conjunction with the synod, see Burnett, "Martin Bucer."

[16]BDS 6/II:203.3–204.13.

it approved provisions which stated more explicitly the pastors' responsibilities towards their charges and even gave them some authority over their parishioners beyond the power of persuasion. A pastor could meet with an individual for private examination or instruction after the preparatory service for communion if he believed that the individual was in need of such instruction. But the city council was careful to put limits on the ministers' authority. Thus a pastor could not turn individuals from the congregation away from the Lord's Supper, and he did not have the authority to summon for questioning any and every parishioner if he believed it necessary.

The synodical articles demonstrate that the chief conflict between city council and clergy was not over the right to excommunicate sinners so much as over the authority to summon parishioners for admonition and reproof. The council had refused to give this authority to the pastors in the 1534 church ordinance. In January of 1539 it had issued a mandate which reiterated that summoning was the responsibility of the *Kirchenpfleger* alone,[17] and it did not alter its position in its consideration of the 1539 synodal decrees. The authority to summon parishioners was a more basic issue than the power of excommunication, for in Bucer's view of church discipline, admonition was always to precede excommunication except in extraordinary cases. The right to excommunicate concerned the pastors' jurisdiction only over unrepentant sinners, while the authority to summon for admonition enabled the pastors to exercise what Bucer considered as the scriptural mandate to provide pastoral care for all Christians. Insofar as they were not given the express authority to summon their parishioners, Bucer and the other ministers could see the 1539 synod as a failure.[18]

At about the same time that the city council finished its deliberations on the synodal articles, the Strasbourg clergy themselves reached an agreement among themselves on the uniform celebration of the worship services and administration of the sacraments in all the parish churches. In many ways the *Concordia Sacri Ministerij* of 1542 supplemented the synodal articles regarding the administration of the sacraments. Concerning baptism, the *Concordia* was explicit about the qualifications of godparents: only those individuals "with whom we can partake of the Lord's Supper with a good conscience" were acceptable; those who "scorned the gospel or lived impiously" were to be rejected. Children who had not yet been examined by their pastor and then admitted to the Lord's Supper were not allowed to stand as godparents, nor were Catholics, "who condemn our religion and proclaim it to be false and heretical, and who neither bring their children to our baptism nor attend our worship services."[19]

The *Concordia* also attempted to regulate admission to the Lord's Supper. It briefly described the preparatory Vespers service to be held before communion,

---

[17]TAE 3:308-309 (no. 890), the so-called "mandat vom fürbeschicken."

[18]Cf. the remarks in the introduction to the synodal decrees which compare them to the Hessian disciplinary ordinance, BDS 6/II:199-200.

[19]Ibid., 229.2-14. Protestants were also forbidden to stand as godparents at Catholic baptisms; not that Catholic baptism was regarded as invalid, but "so that it would not seem that we assent to their abominations," ibid., 229.15-18.

stressing that individuals wishing to receive the sacrament should be examined concerning their understanding of it. During the communion service itself the pastors were to warn their parishioners that only the truly penitent were worthy to receive the sacrament, and that in the early church those who were guilty of grave sin, even if truly penitent, were kept from the sacrament "until they had satisfied the church for a set period of time."[20] Given the city council's refusal to give the pastors the authority to exclude individuals from the sacrament, the ministers had to rely on such admonitions in the hope that their parishioners would voluntarily submit to this type of eucharistic discipline.

If discipline could only be carried out on a voluntary basis, then it was even more necessary to see that everyone involved in the disciplinary process understood the importance of discipline and how it was to be exercised. During the next two years Bucer set forth his views on the purpose and necessity of church discipline and the church's ministry of binding and loosing in two works, one for church leaders—the *Ratio examinationis canonicae* —and one for the laity—a new catechism.

The *Ratio* was part of a plan for the reformation of the chapter of St. Thomas which Bucer drew up in 1542 or 1543.[21] The reformation, which was never adopted, was Bucer's attempt, as he put it, to restore the chapter to the original form and purpose intended by the canons of the church.[22] Key to his proposal was control over who was admitted to the chapter. No one was to be accepted who had not been properly examined and approved.[23] For this reason Bucer included in his proposal a model of the examination questions which were to be used to determine the candidate's suitability for ministry in the church, whether as pastor or teacher.

The examination included several questions on church discipline and the power of the keys together with their expected responses. The discussion of church discipline grew out of the questions concerned with baptism. Baptism was not to be given immediately to all who requested it but was to be preceded by catechization. As in the early church, adults were to make a public profession of repentance and faith and of obedience to Christ before they were baptized.[24] Those who had been baptized as

---

[20]Ibid., 231.8-14.

[21]Gustav Knod, *Die Stiftsherren von St. Thomas zu Straßburg (1518-1548). Ein Beitrag zur Straßburger Kirchen- und Schulgeschichte,* Beilage zum Programm des Lyceums zu Straßburg (Strasbourg: C. F. Schmidt, 1892), 11-12; a Latin translation of the proposal is printed in SA 192ff. The chapter of St. Thomas was the only one of the city's four chapters to accept the evangelical faith. Bucer was elected to the chapter following the death of Wolfgang Capito in November 1541, and in 1544 he was named dean.

[22]*De reformatione collegii canonici,* SA 192.

[23]Ibid., 192, 222. The Municipal Statute of September 9, 1539, required that all candidates nominated or elected to the city's chapters submit to an examination "as required by sacred Scripture, the holy canons and imperial law." The content of this examination was not specified, but Knod believes that candidates for prebends in the chapter of St. Thomas were required to accept the Tetrapolitan Confession. At any rate the examination was certainly not as detailed as the one Bucer envisioned in his *Ratio;* Knod, *Stiftsherren,* 6-9. The Municipal Statute is printed in BDS 7:572-575.

[24]This insistence on a public profession of faith before baptism was not mere rhetoric but the actual practice of the Strasbourg church; cf. complaints made to the city council in September 1539, that Bucer had conducted the baptism of a ten-year-old Anabaptist child

children were to be instructed in the catechism and were then to make their own public profession of faith and obedience, after which they were confirmed "in this same faith and obedience to Christ and the church with the imposition of hands."[25] Obedience to Christ and the church included acceptance of "the teaching, exhortation, admonition and correction of Christ in the church, both publicly and privately." This meant that "if the church binds us or others to penance according to Christ's command or ejects anyone from the fellowship of Christ, or again absolves from these bonds and receives back into the communion of Christ, we accept this judgment and act in accordance with it as the judgment of Christ."[26] Individual submission to admonition and discipline by the church was presented as an essential element of the Christian life.

This response highlighted the two facets of discipline, fraternal admonition and public penance including excommunication. These two aspects were brought together in a later question which described the disciplinary procedure of Matthew, chapter 18. Individuals were to admonish one another about sin which was unrecognized by the sinner. If the one admonished repented, he was to be assured of God's pardon; if he did not repent he was to be publicly admonished by the church and excommunicated. Excommunication was justified only in cases of contumacy. Penitents guilty of grave sin were not excommunicated but were bound to penance and kept from receiving the sacrament. The presbyters, acting with the agreement of the church, were responsible for admonition, for excommunication, for withholding the sacraments, and for absolving repentant sinners after they had satisfied the church with fruits of their repentance.[27] The church required satisfaction of this kind since it had the power to forgive the sins of those whom it judged to be truly penitent, but this judgment had to be made with great caution, since "a little bit of yeast from someone not truly repentant will spoil the whole dough of the church."[28] Bucer justified

---

"in such a way that the Anabaptists were more strengthened than deterred." The council gave their support to Bucer, stating that it was the custom of the early church to question adults whether they wished to be baptized before performing the baptism itself. TAE 3:365.25-366.8 (no. 953).

[25]SA 228, no. 63-64.

[26]Ibid., 229, no. 65: "In quo est sita communio et obedientia CHRISTO et ecclesiae? R. Vt . . . doctrinam, exhortationem, admonitionem, et correctionem CHRISTI in ecclesia publice et privatim nobis impertitam, cupide audiamus et amplectemur. . . . Sique ecclesia nos vel alios iuxta mandatum Christi, ad agendam poenitentiam ligaverit, vel consortio Christi plane eiecerit, sive rursus his vinculis absolverit, et in communionem Christi receperit, iudicium hoc ratum habeamus, et ei, ut Christi iudicio obtemperemus."

[27]Ibid., 230, nos. 78-79, 81-83. Bucer later described two types of presbyters, those who administered the gospel, the sacraments, and discipline, and those whose only responsibility was the exercise of discipline—in other words, pastors and lay elders, 231, no. 93.

[28]Ibid., 230, no. 85: "Quare requirit ecclesia a poenitentibus huiusmodi satisfactionem? R. Quia mandatum habet peccata eis tantum remittendi, et ad consortium CHRISTI eos modo admittendi, quos peccatorum suorum vere poenitere iudicare queat: eiusmodi iudicio, quod non dubitat a CHRISTO approbatum iri, et dignum sit fideli dispensatione donorum Dei: ac religione cavendi, ne paulem fermenti non vere poenitentium, massam ecclesiae corrumpat: aut ne quis etiam seipsum inani poenitentia fallat." The allusion is to I Cor. 5:6.

the need for public penance with many of the same Old Testament passages he had earlier used in *Von der waren Seelsorge*.[29] He emphasized that the church could neither require penance at certain times nor prescribe set penances for specific sins, since all penance was imposed so that sin was better recognized and avoided, which in turn depended on the individual sinner.[30]

The questions in the *Ratio* were not limited to public penance. Bucer also endorsed the private binding and loosing of sins, which he said was particularly useful when an individual did not sufficiently recognize his sin or needed to be reassured of God's forgiveness. No law could require that individuals confess and seek absolution from their minister, but the people should be taught to hold confession and absolution in high regard. This type of private binding and loosing was necessary in the sense that when an individual admonished his brother to repent, he ought to bind him to penance and abstention from the sacrament if he was unrepentant and absolve and console him if he repented. Bucer upheld the principle that any individual could bind or loose his brother, but as in his Psalms and Gospels commentaries, he stated that the penitent should prefer to seek such absolution from a presbyter as one who was more skilled in the use of binding and loosing.[31]

Bucer specified that all those who attended the communion service and "are not bound to penance or kept from the sacrament by the church" were to partake of the sacrament. This statement was obviously aimed at dissenters who rejected the evangelical interpretation of the Lord's Supper and voluntarily abstained from it, and at Catholics accustomed to attending the mass but not receiving the sacrament. The position that all who were able should partake of the Lord's Supper had a side effect in making more obvious, and thus marking out for social stigmatization, those who were unable to participate. The communion service was a visible sign of the unity of the congregation, and those who did not participate were shown to be outside of that community.[32] Finally, Bucer added that because the sacrament ought to be given only to Christ's disciples and not to the unworthy, no one who was completely unknown or unexamined should be admitted to it.[33]

Bucer's catechism of 1543 is an interesting counterpart to the *Ratio*. Roughly contemporary with the *Ratio*, the catechism differed markedly in structure and emphasis from Bucer's earlier catechisms. Although other sections of the new catechism were abridged versions of the 1537 edition, Bucer no longer treated the sacraments

---

[29]For instance, Exod. 33:4; Lev. 16.29; 1 Sam. 7:6; cf. BDS 7:167.3-13; SA 230-231, no. 86.

[30]SA 231, no. 87.

[31]Ibid., no. 88-90.

[32]This point foreshadows the section of the Cologne reformation ordinance, written in early 1543, in which Bucer also stated that everyone present at the celebration of the Lord's Supper should receive the sacrament; cf. above, pp. 150-151. Although Bucer still opposed the idea that those present at the communion service should be required to receive the sacrament, he had clearly lost much of the patience towards individuals who abstained which he showed in *Grund vnd Ursach*, written during the early years of the Reformation.

[33]SA 229-230, no. 77-78.

and absolution in the context of the third article of the Creed but rather discussed them separately in a special section covering thirty-two of the catechism's total of sixty pages. The new section contained three parts. The first paragraph dealt with the ministry of the church and the first of its components, the preaching of the word; the second part was comprised of paragraphs on the sacraments in general, on baptism and the Lord's Supper; and the third part covered other church practices.[34] These practices were themselves divided into two categories, "special exercises and acts"— confirmation, penitential discipline, the ordination of church ministers, and the benediction of marriages[35]—and "general church practices"—public worship, congregational prayer, hymn-singing, fasting, and almsgiving. The section closed with a fervent plea that the readers consider what was required by God's covenant with his people.

As in his earlier catechisms, Bucer endeavored to make his discussion of penitential discipline practical. Citing Matthew 18 he described three types of discipline, each more severe than the previous stage: private admonition, the reproof of the church, and the church's power to bind and to loose. Bucer stressed that private admonition was to be given with humility and kindness and with care that the person's reputation was not harmed.[36] Reproof by the church was the responsibility of the ministers and the *Kirchenpfleger* towards all who ignored private admonition and had offended the church by their sin. In addition, the elders of the church were to admonish each and every individual as they believed this would bring about moral improvement. Bucer reminded his readers that the purpose of such rebuke was not to shame the sinner before the entire church but to bring him to true repentance.[37] Under the topic of binding and loosing, Bucer repeated his familiar argument for exclusion from the sacrament combined with a period of penance for those guilty of grave sin. His explanation of binding was a self-conscious defense of the imposition of penance. Likewise his definition of loosing focused on the lifting of penance after the sinner

[34]Bucer's division of the ministry into the three parts of word, sacraments, and discipline appeared already in the 1537 catechism, where he stated that "edification in faith and all good" was brought about "through the word of teaching and admonition, the holy sacraments, church discipline together with the other holy church practices," BDS 6/III:189.10–12; cf. Bucer's draft of a presentation by the Strasbourg pastors to the bishop of Strasbourg, written in the fall of 1542, where he argued that "the right Christian appointment to and oversight of the Christian church consists of the pure doctrine of the holy gospel, the right use of the holy sacraments, the holding to church discipline with the goal of reform and the proper appointment to and performance of the common ministries of the church," ARC 4:169.9–12; his letter to Ambrosius Blaurer in which he described the three ministries of the church as doctrine, sacraments, and discipline, Schieß 2:226 (Dec. 22, 1543, no. 1055). Mention of the threefold ministry of doctrine, sacraments, and discipline occurs in other works of the 1540s as well; cf. for example *Alle Handlung* (1541), 22v, 111r; *Wider Vffrichtung* (1545), fl 4.

[35]There is a clear parallel with the sacraments of the Catholic church; the seventh sacrament, extreme unction, was subsumed under communion for the sick in the section on penitential discipline.

[36]BDS 6/III:248.22–249.5.

[37]Ibid., 249.5–25.

has demonstrated genuine contrition. No one was to be loosed from sin who had not first proven his repentance and changed his ways. The power of binding and loosing was to be exercised when the congregation was assembled and with its approval, but a pastor could also exercise this power in private when he became aware of secret sins, by telling the unrepentant to abstain from the sacrament or, if the person had repented, by absolving, consoling, and readmitting him to the sacraments.[38] Those who were sick were also to be absolved "privately and before those who were with him," if they were truly repentant and "desired God's grace."[39]

Although Bucer's ideas on penitential discipline were expressed at length in this section, his view of discipline's central role in the church emerged in his references to it in other sections. For instance, he stated that fasting was appropriate when one had fallen into grave sin.[40] Likewise, he underscored the importance of the "common practices" of the church such as public worship and congregational prayer by stating baldly that those who did not attend worship on Sundays and on special days of prayer and had no justifiable excuse for their absence should be excluded from the church.[41] In accordance with his views on church discipline and its role in pastoral care, Bucer several times exhorted obedience to the ministers and submission to their use of discipline and admonition.[42]

Obedience to the church and its ministers was also emphasized in the section on confirmation. The confirmation Bucer described in his catechism was similar to

---

[38]Ibid., 249.26–251.19.

[39]Ibid., 251.19–24. Bucer's new appreciation for private absolution of the sick was reflected in the Order for Visiting the Sick included in the SA. This order, apparently written before Bucer went to England, differs markedly from the Order included in Strasbourg's liturgical books from the 1530s and reprinted in Friedrich Hubert, ed., Die Straßburger liturgischen Ordnungen im Zeitalter der Reformation nebst einer Bibliographie der Straßburger Gesangbücher (Göttingen: Vandenhoeck & Ruprecht, 1900), 119–127. Unlike the earlier order, the later ceremony discussed the circumstances in which the sick could be privately absolved and allowed to receive the Lord's Supper, and it included a brief liturgy for confession and absolution. The order cautioned that the sick were not to be absolved and given the sacrament unless they were perceived to be genuinely penitent and in danger of death. If recovery seemed likely, they were not to be absolved until they had recovered from their illness. The ministers were to ask sick persons "whether they have been forbidden to partake of the sacraments, and if so by whom, and whether it was done in the name of the whole Church or at least through particular ministers," SA 359. If the individual had been "publicly excommunicated by the church," he was also to be absolved by "the council of the chief ministers of the Church," presumably the Kirchenkonvent. Those who showed no sign of repentance were to be "committed to the judgment of the Lord"; if they died they were not to be buried with other Christians "and even after death are to be regarded as excommunicated and excluded from the Church," SA 360. In dubious cases, it was better to absolve those who might recover or who might not be genuinely repentant than to allow a potentially repentant individual to die unabsolved. In any case, absolution was "always to be imparted to them as a corporate act of the Church and therefore not without the presence of the rest of the gathering to represent the Church of Christ, and only after a confession of sins has been publicly recited to them and they have made a public petition for grace," SA 361; English translation taken from D. F. Wright, ed. and trans., Common Places of Martin Bucer, The Courtenay Library of Reformation Classics 4 (Appleford, England: Sutton Courtenay Press, 1972), 434–437.

[40]BDS 6/III:259.1–14.

[41]Ibid., 256.24–30; cf. 255.9–13.

[42]Ibid., 243.19–20; 245.26–29; 248.17–20; 254.1–2.

the one prescribed by the Hessian and Cologne ordinances. It was a public ceremony in which children professed their faith and "committed themselves in obedience to the church," accompanied by the prayers of the congregation and the minister's imposition of hands.[43] In the catechism, as in the *Ratio*, the confirmation ceremony served as a public testimony of the individual's acceptance of the covenant made with him in baptism, an acceptance which was demonstrated, among other things, by submission to church discipline.

Despite his advocacy of Christian discipline, Bucer had very little success in seeing such a system officially adopted in Strasbourg. The catechism, the canonical examination, and the resolutions of the second synod reveal what Bucer wished to establish in Strasbourg. Bucer's complaints to the city council about the lack of a functioning system of discipline, as well as the complaints of other Strasburghers to the council about the pastors' attempts to exercise discipline tell the other side of the story: the resistance of magistrates and citizens to the clergy's imposition of "the yoke of Christ."

In August 1540, Bucer appeared before the city council, accompanied by Wolfgang Capito and Kaspar Hedio, to complain about the magistrate's tardiness in their deliberations on the results of the synod held more than a year before.[44] The situation of the Strasbourg church was deplorable, he declared: no one made any attempt to reform, they did not receive the sacrament, neither young nor old came to hear God's word, many led offensive lives. Bucer stressed that the lack of discipline was not simply an internal matter for the Strasbourg church; it was a potential hindrance to a settlement of the religious question in Germany. The city claimed to be faithful to God's word, but its opponents saw that in Strasbourg "we are not concerned about the affairs [of God], we do not hold God before our eyes, further his word and reform ourselves." Bucer was sensitive to charges that the Protestants had no form of church discipline, and he wanted to be able to respond truthfully that the Strasburghers "had indeed thrown off the pope's yoke and abolished his ceremonies but had established good order and Christian discipline in its place." A functioning system of discipline was necessary if the Protestants were to have any credibility at future religious colloquies held in Germany.[45] To this end the pastors preached that those who lived in manifest sin were to be ostracized. In defense of their actions, they argued that they were obliged by the Scriptures to preach such a ban. They did not intend to be overzealous in its use but would patiently admonish and instruct sinners before excommunicating them. According to Bucer, this was "not a papistic ban, but a true Christian ban by which those chosen from the church and each parish (i.e. the *Kirchenpfleger*) may admonish, reprove and desire to see each individual reform." Bu-

---

[43]Ibid., 247.17–248.20.

[44]RP 1540, Aug. 13, fols. 302r–304v; excerpts printed in TAE 3:424–426 (no. 1052).

[45]This concern for Strasbourg's reputation among the Catholic estates and its implications for the possible reconciliation of the German church appears frequently in Bucer's writings from this period. At the time he appeared before the city council, he had just returned from the colloquy at Hagenau and was anticipating the upcoming colloquy at Worms.

cer reminded the council that the clergy were not seeking sole authority in the church, since the *Kirchenpfleger* were also responsible for seeing that the church ordinance was enforced. The council heard Bucer out, then it resolved to proceed with its consideration of the synodal decrees. Bucer's linkage of discipline and the larger political situation may have had its intended effect, for the council did not forbid any further sermons on the ban.

Bucer claimed that the disciplinary process was administered both by the pastors and the *Kirchenpfleger*, but in fact the pastors had great difficulty persuading the *Kirchenpfleger* to carry out their responsibilities in this area. Moreover, the parishioners themselves were unwilling to heed pastoral admonition and to accept the *Kirchenpflegers'* right of moral and pastoral oversight. In June of 1541 the city council had to arbitrate between two of its members—Claus Kniebis, who was a *Kirchenpfleger* from Bucer's parish of St. Thomas, and Jakob Wetzel von Marsilien. A few days earlier Kniebis had called together residents of his parish to read them the ordinances granting the *Kirchenpfleger* the right to summon parishioners for admonition. Wetzel von Marsilien had protested against Kniebis' actions, claiming that only the magistrate had the authority to summon Strasbourg's inhabitants, and their disagreement was brought before the city council. After some debate, the council decided in favor of Kniebis and told the other *Kirchenpfleger* to follow the example set in the parish of St. Thomas.[46] The conflict between Kniebis and Wetzel revealed the weak link in the disciplinary structure of the Strasbourg church: it depended on the willingness of the individual *Kirchenpfleger* to see that discipline was exercised. When pastors and *Kirchenpfleger* in a parish were zealous and committed to the cause of oversight and admonition, as at St. Thomas, they had at least the lukewarm backing of the council. On the other hand, the council did not concern itself overly if the *Kirchenpfleger* did not seem to be fulfilling their duties. Its final motive in admonishing other *Kirchenpfleger* to imitate the practice in the parish of St. Thomas was not preoccupation with the enforcement of discipline but the fear that different practices in the various parishes could lead to turmoil and unrest.

There are few records that reveal whether the city council's decision to support Kniebis and, by implication, to encourage the *Kirchenpfleger* to summon individuals had much effect. In December of 1542, three councillors, including Kniebis, reported to the council that the *Kirchenpfleger* had summoned Wolfgang Schultheiss to appear before them "because of his unseemly talk and arguments such as that Christ our Lord is not necessary for salvation," but Schultheiss had not appeared.[47] This incident implies that the *Kirchenpfleger* were perhaps being more conscientious in the use of their power to summon dissidents, but Schultheiss was a former pastor suspected

---

[46]For details on this dispute, see Amy Nelson Burnett, "Church Discipline and Moral Reformation in the Thought of Martin Bucer," *Sixteenth Century Journal* 22 (1991):439–456, esp. 449–450.

[47]TAE 3:548–549 (no. 1232).

of Spiritualist tendencies who had been dismissed from his post by the council, and was therefore hardly a typical parishioner.[48]

A clearer view of the practice of summoning and the exercise of discipline in the church comes from another petition submitted to the city council by the clergy in August 1542.[49] The pastors included the usual complaints that the Sabbath was not being properly observed and that people continued to walk around in the cathedral during sermons and baptisms; then they brought up problems with the exercise of discipline. It caused "not a little offense" that people who were considered banned by the Strasbourg church had their marriages solemnized and their children baptized in Catholic churches outside the city. The *Kirchenpfleger* were not summoning or taking action against these people as they had been commanded to do by the magistrate. The pastors cited the case of one woman in particular who had recently attended a (Catholic) church service outside the city, "defiantly scorning our church." They asked that the woman, who had been summoned by the *Kirchenpfleger* but had refused to appear, be declared "an open enemy of our church, so that she does not come to our baptisms or stand as godmother." If this were not done, the pastors threatened publicly to refuse to let her participate, "as they were obliged before God to do."

The woman was a member of the prominent and well-connected Schenckbecher family,[50] and the magistrate could not allow the clergy to refuse participation in a public event to such a person, so in this case they gave way to the pastors' demand. When a committee appointed to consider the list of grievances presented their report three months later, the council resolved to summon the woman and forbid her to participate in any baptisms. The councillors clearly wanted to retain the final authority and would not allow the pastors to take action against the woman themselves. At the same time they decided to summon the steward of the chapter of Old St. Peter to rebuke him for sending his wife outside the city to have her baby so that the child could be baptized in a Catholic church.[51]

The pastors' complaints and the city council's response illustrate the workings—and the limitations—of pastoral oversight and church discipline in Strasbourg in the

---

[48]Schultheiss was one of a group termed "Epicureans" who opposed Bucer during the Synod of 1533; Werner Bellardi, *Wolfgang Schultheiss. Wege und Wandlungen eines Straßburger Spiritualisten und Zeitgenossen Martin Bucers*, Schriften der Erwin von Steinbach-Stiftung 5 (Frankfurt a. M.: Erwin von Steinbach-Stiftung, 1976).

[49]RP 1542, August 23, fols. 333r–334v; the document is AST 84, fols. 125r–130r (no. 39).

[50]The pastors do not give the woman's first name; on the Schenchbecher family, see Julius Kindler von Knobloch, *Das goldene Buch von Straßburg* (Vienna, 1885–86), 2:318. The family's prominence is reflected by the positions held by its members. Laurentius Schenckbecher, the provost of the chapter of St. Thomas from 1525 to 1537, was a zealous Protestant, according to Knod, *Stiftsherren*, 21–22. His father-in-law, Andreas Drachenfels, served several times as Ammeister before resigning from the Senate in 1524; Thomas A. Brady links him with the group of Catholics which resisted the introduction of the Reformation in Strasbourg; *Ruling Class, Regime and Reformation at Strasbourg 1520–1555*, Studies in Medieval and Reformation Thought 22 (Leiden: E.J. Brill, 1978), 211–212, 305–306.

[51]RP 1542, Nov. 8, 448v.

1540s. The pastors considered some of the city's inhabitants to be excommunicated. Some of these were loyal Catholics who did not accept the teachings and ceremonies of the new church. The pastors were clearly frustrated with such people, particularly when their social standing gave prominence to their rejection of the evangelical church. They advocated some degree of social ostracism so that stubborn Catholics would be forced to conform, or at least prevented from defying the Strasbourg church publicly. The case of the Schenckbecher woman also illustrates why the pastors felt they needed the authority to screen prospective godparents, as described in the *Concordia* and in the synodal articles which were being debated by the council at this time.[52]

The magistrate's actions did little to eliminate the pastors' complaints that the *Kirchenpfleger* were not being diligent enough in summoning refractory parishioners or to change their view that they were conscience-bound to reject unworthy godparents. In February 1543, the city council discussed complaints that the *Kirchenpfleger* of St. Thomas were summoning citizens with their families and servants, and that the pastor of St. Thomas had refused to baptize a child. The council took a conciliatory position: the summoning of young and old could continue, but no one could be forced to answer the summons. The councillors also decreed that the pastors should meet with proposed godparents before the baptism to determine their suitability rather than break off the ceremony if the pastor believed the godparents were unacceptable.[53]

This compromise did not lead to any great improvement in the Strasbourg church, and in February of 1545, Bucer, Hedio, and Zell appeared before the city council yet again, this time to justify themselves in the face of complaints that in their sermons they had criticized the magistrate for not punishing sins and had even implied that the magistrate's laxity gave rise to sin.[54] The pastors took the occasion to point out that many people in the city had no respect for religion, the church, or the pastors themselves, were adherents of various sects, and disregarded with impunity the provisions of the city's moral code.

As usual, the city council appointed a commission to respond to the pastors' charges. The commission proposed that, in addition to drafting a more stringent moral code and improving enforcement of existing provisions, the pastors in each parish be empowered to summon their parishioners, examine their faith and morals, and admonish them concerning the proper understanding and use of the sacraments. If the

---

[52]BDS 6/II:235.21–236.20; cf. *Concordia*, ibid., 229.2–14. The final discussion on baptism and the Lord's Supper in the city council took place a week later, BDS 6/II:198. F. J. Fuchs describes other complaints made about Catholics in the city, "Les Catholiques Strasbourgeois de 1529 à 1681," *Archives de l'Eglise en Alsace* 22 (1975):141–169.

[53]RP 1543, Feb. 12, fols. 51r–51v; TAE 4:16–17 (no. 1260). "Die zu St. Thoman" most likely means the *Kirchenpfleger*, since the controversy was not over who did the summoning but over who was being summoned. This would not have been the case if the pastors had been summoning; cf. the attempts to give them this authority.

[54]RP 1545, Feb. 4, fols. 35r–37v; a short extract in TAE 4:125–126 (no. 1421).

parishioners opposed the clergy, they were to be referred to the *Kirchenpfleger*. Those who refused to heed the *Kirchenpfleger* were to be referred to the council.[55]

This proposal was presented to the full council in May 1545, but instead of discussing the report the council appointed a new committee member and charged the panel with drafting a new plan.[56] The second version was presented to the council several months later.[57] The second draft also contained the provision authorizing the pastors to summon their parishioners, but the proposal was again rejected. Instead, the council reasserted the right of the *Kirchenpfleger* to summon any who opposed the gospel, although they allowed that a minister could be present at the examination if his expertise was needed. As they put it, the responsibility of dealing with those who opposed the gospel in word or deed "belongs to the *Kirchenpfleger* and the council and not the pastors, as the *Kirchenpfleger* ordinance shows."[58]

The city council's decision regarding summoning followed the same pattern that had emerged in all of its dealings with the pastors over the course of the decade since the adoption of the church ordinance. Although the councillors may have acknowledged the justice of the pastors' concerns and were willing to take some steps to rectify the situation, they would not give the pastors the full authority that they wanted either to admonish or to discipline their parishioners. Attendance at church and catechism was encouraged but not required, pastors could examine and instruct but not bar from the Lord's Supper, *Kirchenpfleger* could summon but citizens need not appear. In the final analysis it was the city council, not the pastors or even the *Kirchenpfleger*, who exercised control in church affairs, and the councillors did not intend to share this authority with anyone.

The gap between what Bucer wished to establish and what the city council would allow was particularly glaring with regard to the practice of pastoral oversight and summoning for admonition. Ideally, the pastor, his assistants, and especially the *Kirchenpfleger* of each parish would together be responsible for the exercise of discipline. All residents of a parish would be subject to this discipline, since the *Kirchenpfleger* had the authority to summon whomever they wished for admonition and instruction. In reality, however, since the pastors were denied any power to summon and the *Kirchenpfleger* neglected their disciplinary responsibilities, only those parishioners who wished to receive the Lord's Supper could be disciplined. Even then the pastor was officially limited to private admonition and instruction, for he had no statutory right to exclude the recalcitrant from the sacrament.

---

[55]AST 84, no. 42; excerpt in TAE 4:136.19-29 (no. 1439).

[56]RP 1545, May 30, fol. 215r; TAE 4:137 (no. 1440).

[57]AST 84, no. 40; excerpts in TAE 4:173.34-174.6 (no. 1488).

[58]RP 1545, Jan. 6, 1546, fols. 529r-530r, TAE 4:174-175 (no. 1489). Werner Bellardi has mistakenly assumed that the discussion described in the *Ratsprotokolle* concerned Bucer's book, *Von der Kirchen mengel vnnd fähl*, BDS 17:157-158; cf. *Geschichte*, 22-25. Hammann, in giving the book a later date, correctly points out the connection between the committee report allowing the pastors the right of summoning and the council's debate of Jan. 6, *Entre la Secte*, 431-433.

This does not mean, of course, that the pastors made no attempt to exclude grave or obstinate sinners from the Lord's Supper. The *Concordia* shows that they agreed on the importance of such exclusion, and Bucer's catechisms taught that grave sinners were to be kept from the sacrament for a time. But the pastors had no mechanism to enforce obedience and had to rely on their parishioners' voluntary compliance. Bucer's emphasis in all of his works of this period on the importance of submitting to the authority of the church's pastors and elders is a reflection of the fact that in Strasbourg the acceptance of church discipline was essentially voluntary.

A voluntary system of church discipline would be effective only to the extent that the laity respected the pastor's authority and would obey him when told to abstain from the sacrament or to demonstrate their repentance by performing some kind of penance. It was in order to encourage submission to pastoral authority that Bucer had introduced a public confirmation ceremony in Hesse. The confirmands were expected not only to confess their faith but also to acknowledge their obedience to the disciplinary authority of the pastor and elders. Although there is no firm evidence of public confirmation in the Strasbourg church prior to 1551, René Bornert has suggested that such a ceremony was established in Strasbourg in 1538 or 1539.[59] In various works dating from the 1540s Bucer himself mentioned his role in establishing an evangelical confirmation ceremony.[60] These statements could refer to the Hessian rather than the Strasbourg church. On the other hand, both the *Ratio* of 1542 and the catechism of 1543, each written for the Strasbourg church, describe a public confirmation ceremony in which children were confirmed after they had professed both their faith and their obedience to the church.[61] In a letter to Ambrosius Blarer written at the end of 1543, Bucer stated that it was the responsibility of the *Hausvater* to see that those within his household were catechized and then individually professed their faith in Christ and their obedience to the church.[62] If the Strasbourg church did have a confirmation ceremony, participation in the rite, as in most of the other elements

---

[59]*Réforme protestante*, 365–369. Bornert suggests that the Hessian confirmation ceremony was modeled after existing practice in Strasbourg, but I argue elsewhere that Bucer first proposed the confirmation ceremony in Hesse and then tried to introduce it officially in the Strasbourg church during the 1539 synod; see Burnett, "Martin Bucer."

[60]*Der newe glaub*, B₂r (published in 1545); and in his critique on the draft Interim in April 1548, BDS 17:369.19–24; see above, pp. 136, 138, 140.

[61]In a letter to Jean Calvin dated August 29, 1545, Juan Diaz referred to the custom of the Strasbourg church "to admit no one to the Lord's Table unless he has first given a confession of his faith in an assembly of the church," CO 12:151 (no. 688). This public confession of faith may have occurred within a confirmation ceremony, but from Diaz' account it seems more likely that his public confession of faith was an individual one. The synodal articles of 1539 gave pastors the right to refuse the Lord's Supper to those who came from Catholic areas unless they were satisfied with their evangelical orthodoxy; such a provision would have applied in the case of the Spaniard Diaz.

[62]Schieß 2:227; TB 15:3r: "Ut ergo singuli patres familias suam familiam et Christo junctos liberos, Christo instituant, ut ad Ecclesiam et catechismum adducant, ut singuli suo tempore solenniter profiteantur fidem Christi, communionem et obedientiam Ecclesiae."

of Christian discipline, would have been voluntary; the pastors could do no more than exhort their parishioners to see that their children were confirmed.

This voluntary or noncoercive system of discipline had another serious drawback for the pastors. Given their legal inability to summon their parishioners for admonition and the failure of the *Kirchenpfleger* to use their authority to do so, the pastors had the most trouble disciplining the people who they believed were in most need of it: those who would have nothing to do with the official church, whether because they were still faithful to the Catholic church, were adherents of some Anabaptist sect or, as Bucer put it, had rejected "the papal yoke" but refused to accept "the yoke of Christ" in its place. To such individuals exclusion from the Lord's Supper meant nothing, since they had no desire to identify with the evangelical church. The only means of dealing with such people was by encouraging the magistrate to act against those who openly opposed the church, by teaching parishioners to avoid them, and by preventing them from performing any ecclesiastical function, such as standing as godparent, which would seem to lessen the severity of their offense in rejecting the official church. Such ostracism was a measure which the magistrate opposed, however, and when the pastors started preaching that excommunicated sinners were to be avoided, the city council objected. Nor did the council look kindly on the pastors' threats to bar persons they considered excommunicated from participation in church functions. The pastors' attempts to discipline those unwilling to submit to their authority eventually came to the attention of the magistrate, and invariably the council used the opportunity to reinforce its own authority over both pastors and church.

Nevertheless, despite the resistance of both magistrate and laity to the clergy's proposals for Christian discipline, it cannot be said that Bucer was "a prophet without honor in his own country." There were council members who believed that the pastors should have the right to summon their parishioners, and there were *Kirchenpfleger*—particularly in Bucer's own parish—who apparently took their responsibilities seriously. It was these men, along with Bucer's followers among the laity, who made possible the introduction of the best-known of Bucer's many projects for the establishment of Christian discipline: the "Christian fellowships."

8

The "Christian Fellowships" in Strasbourg, 1546–1549

As a result of the limitations placed on their freedom to exercise what they saw as their pastoral responsibilities, Bucer and his fellow ministers grew disillusioned with the situation of the Strasbourg church over the course of the 1540s.[1] Faced with the magistrate's firm refusal to grant the pastors the authority to summon their parishioners for admonition or discipline, Bucer proposed a new plan which would allow the ministers to carry out the disciplinary responsibilities which he believed God required of them. His new plan was the creation in each parish of a "Christian fellowship,"[2] an institutional structure which would give the pastor the right to discipline those who formally agreed to submit to him and which provided for the appointment of lay elders to assist in the exercise of Christian discipline when the *Kirchenpfleger* could not be relied upon to perform their duties.

Most discussions of the "Christian fellowships" have relied on the pioneering account by Werner Bellardi which traces their genesis, development, and demise between the years 1546 and 1550 on the basis of documents preserved in the Strasbourg archives. Although Bellardi gives a brief summary of the Strasbourg clergy's efforts to exercise church discipline before the establishment of the "fellowships," he does not discuss the relationship between the "fellowships" and the other components of Bucer's disciplinary system.[3] A more serious drawback of Bellardi's study is his assumption that regular gatherings of lay members of the "fellowships" were al-

---

[1]Cf. Bucer's frequent complaints over the lack of discipline in his letters to Ambrosius Blarer over the course of 1542; Schieß 2:107 (no. 931), 128 (no. 948), 131–132 (no. 951), 152 (no. 971).

[2]The term "Christian fellowship" (*christliche Gemeinschaft*) is somewhat misleading. Scholars have used the term in a concrete sense as the name for the disciplinary structure Bucer proposed to establish in each parish. Bucer used it in a more abstract sense, as for instance when he wrote of pastors "admonishing to Christian fellowship" or elders "maintaining Christian fellowship"; BDS 17:184.16–20; 185.11–13. Even when he used the word in a more concrete sense, he generally referred not to a specific group of people but more importantly to the bond which united the individuals within that structure, as in "voluntary commitment to the fellowship of the church," ibid., 193.18–19. I therefore use the term with quotation marks to signify the nuance of meaning.

[3]Bellardi, *Geschichte*, 10–22.

ways an integral part of the movement.[4] These gatherings, however, were not a part of Bucer's original proposal but were a later development, and the attention paid to them has distorted both the goals of the "fellowships" and their significance.[5]

Bucer first proposed the establishment of these "fellowships" in a treatise entitled *Von der Kirchen mengel vnnd fähl*, probably written in late 1546 but never published.[6] In *Von der Kirchen mengel vnnd fähl* Bucer explained the power of the keys in popular form and advocated measures by which that power could be restored to the church for its further reform and edification. As in his 1536 Gospels commentary, Bucer interpreted the power of the keys broadly to mean the church's authority to govern its members. He summarized the spiritual responsibilities of the church under five headings: the proclamation of the pure gospel, the administration of the sacraments according to Christ's command, the granting of private absolution, the exercise of excommunication, and the proper ordering of the external ceremonies "by which these above-mentioned points may be retained among the people with more fruitfulness and usefulness to the church."[7]

Bucer described the shortcomings of the Strasbourg church in each of these areas, beginning with the preaching of the gospel. Although the pastors had been faithful in proclaiming God's word, there were many in the city who did not live in accordance with the gospel. Bucer complained about the Catholics who had separated from the city's church, the Anabaptists who had split into numerous sects, and the Epicureans who had cast off the "papal yoke" and now lived godless lives. Moreover, the magistrate had not fulfilled its responsibility to use its sword to eliminate such harmful influences on the church.[8]

Likewise, the proper use of the sacraments had been restored to the church, but the sacraments themselves were not treated with due reverence. Bucer painted a bleak picture of the spiritual indifference demonstrated by the Strasburghers. Parents were

---

[4]This assumption can be traced to the late seventeenth century, when Philipp Jakob Spener first published Bucer's "Mehrung götlicher gnaden" to defend the orthodoxy of his Pietist conventicles; *Geschichte*, 1–6. Bellardi's mentor Gustav Anrich also assumed that the lay gatherings were a central part of the "fellowships" from their inception; "Ein Bedacht Bucers über die Einrichtung von 'christliche Gemeinschaften'," *Festschrift für Hans von Schubert zu seinem 70. Geburtstag*, ARG Ergänzungsband 5 (1929):46–70. This is an abridged version of Bucer's *Von der kirchen mengel vnnd fähl*. Each of these works by Bucer is discussed below. Bellardi used the records of the "fellowship" meetings in the parish of St. Wilhelm from the latter half of 1549, after Bucer's departure from Strasbourg, to describe how the "fellowships" operated. He published this *Gemeinschaftprotokoll* as an appendix to his work, *Geschichte*, 167–198.

[5]To cite only the most recent examples, Euan Cameron, "The 'Godly Community' in the Theory and Practice of the European Reformation," in *Voluntary Religion*, ed. W. J. Sheils and Diana Wood, Studies in Church History 23 (Oxford: Basel Blackwell, 1986), 131–153; Gottfried Hamman, *Entre la Secte*, 363–386..

[6]Bellardi believes that the work was written at the turn of 1545/1546, *Geschichte*, 22–24, while Hammann dates it from the summer or early autumn of 1546, *Entre la Secte*, 431–433; cf. the discusion of dating in TAE 4:200–202 (no. 1526). Following the arguments of TAE, I believe that a date of late 1546 is most likely.

[7]BDS 17:163.3–14.

[8]Ibid., 164.29–167.9.

negligent in having their children baptized, or they chose unacceptable godparents. The majority of the city's inhabitants received the Lord's Supper only rarely or not at all, either because they regarded it as unnecessary for salvation or because they did not want to give up their sinful way of living. Others abstained because they were offended that all people were admitted to the sacrament without distinction. Because there was no precommunion examination and absolution, many young people and some adults received the sacrament without having been properly instructed. In addition, many unrepentant sinners partook of the Lord's Supper because they did not want to be seen as "heathens and non-Christians."[9]

Bucer also decried the disappearance of individual absolution and excommunication, which he identified as the "true core" of the power of the keys.[10] He rejected the claim that the general absolution pronounced after public confession during the worship service fit this narrow definition of the power of the keys. Rather, general absolution was a form of preaching the gospel, in which forgiveness and condemnation were proclaimed in general terms. The ministers could only loose the sins of those who repented and promised to reform. Similarly, the power of the keys could not be applied to those who had not heard or understood the gospel: these people did not seek out forgiveness of sins, nor were they a part of the church so that they could be excluded from it. The practice of the Strasbourg church, in which absolution was spoken to the whole congregation, "the majority of whom were unworthy," could not be called true absolution, which always required that the individual recognized his sin and desired forgiveness through the gospel from the church.[11]

Bucer stated that individual absolution could be granted either publicly or privately. As an example of public absolution, he cited the example of the early church, which required catechumens to confess their sin and profess their desire to receive forgiveness through admission to the church. After congregational prayer, these individuals were confirmed by the minister with the imposition of hands, and, through the absolution which was spoken, they were made members of the church and admitted to the sacraments. Those baptized as infants also had to profess their faith and "give themselves into the obedience of God and his church" before being admitted to the Lord's Table. This absolution and voluntary submission to obedience had

---

[9]Ibid., 167.10-171.5.

[10]Ibid., 171.10-13.

[11]Ibid., 171.28-173.5. Bucer's view of general absolution in the Sunday service recalls Osiander's opposition to general public absolution and his conflict with the Nürnberg city council and his fellow ministers over the value of public absolution; cf. Dietrich Stollberg, "Osiander und der Nürnberger Absolutionsstreit," *Lutherische Blätter* 17 (1965):153-168. The conflict began in 1533 and dragged on for several years. In July 1533, Osiander wrote to Bucer giving his view of the conflict, Pollet, *Correspondance* 2:115-118; see also Pollet's description of the affair and accompanying documents, 124-128, 131-136. Bucer's position on general absolution expressed in *Von der kirchen mengel vnnd fähl* is closer to that expressed by the Wittenbergers in their attempt to resolve the strife than to Osiander's rejection of general absolution as "harmful and Satanic"; Stollberg, "Absolutionsstreit," 158-161. For both Bucer and the Wittenbergers, the absolution pronounced in public was a form of preaching the gospel and worth preserving; WABr 6:527-534 (nos. 2052-2054).

completely disappeared, and Bucer warned that if it was not restored, "we can expect nothing so surely as the final downfall and destruction of the whole church."[12]

Bucer also praised private absolution, "which was especially established in the church as an eternal and sure medication for tormented and afflicted consciences and hearts, in order to console and strengthen them at any time."[13] Because of human frailty and weakness, Christ had established certain external signs, such as holy baptism, the Lord's Supper, and absolution, "through which as an instrument the holy gospel which is preached publicly can be applied and surely appropriated by each person individually."[14] A person burdened by sin who had confessed and been absolved by a minister of the church could have as much confidence in this absolution as if he had heard the voice of God from heaven. All true Christians, he asserted, should desire to confess their sins, to talk with their pastor and be instructed by him when necessary and, finally, to receive absolution as assurance for their faith.[15]

Just as Christ established absolution as consolation for the terrified conscience, so he established excommunication as a medicine for sin. Under the heading of excommunication Bucer included the fraternal admonition and reproof which a Christian gave to his brother or sister so that he or she did not become hardened in sin. The fear of public punishment or humiliation served as a deterrent to sin, as did the knowledge that an individual must account for his actions not only to God but also to those who had pastoral oversight. When done according to Christ's command, exclusion from the church, pronounced when there was no more hope of repentance, was a fearful sentence since it signified God's wrath towards the sinner. The use of admonition and discipline not only prevented sin but also fostered the virtues of humility, obedience, and patience. With its disappearance, no one was willing to endure admonition or reproof, and notorious sin was allowed to go unpunished.[16]

Finally, Bucer argued, church ceremonies should be properly ordered and the church provided with faithful ministers to preach the gospel, deacons to gather and distribute alms, and elders who, along with the pastors, had oversight over the church, saw that children attended catechism, and ensured that fraternal correction was rightly used. But in Strasbourg the sermons were only sparsely attended, no one took the days of prayer seriously, and there were more children playing in the streets during the time of the catechism services than there were inside the church. The Kirchenpfleger who were to oversee the church often proved more of a hindrance than a help because some of them did not attend the pastors' meetings, receive the sacrament, or even go to church.[17]

---

[12]BDS 17:174.3-28.
[13]Ibid., 174.32-175.3.
[14]Ibid., 176.2-6.
[15]Ibid., 176.12-25.
[16]Ibid., 177.32-179.7.
[17]Ibid., 179.8-180.13.

The defects which Bucer lamented were for the most part the same complaints which the pastors had repeated to the city council over the last two decades. But in addition to the familiar complaints about sects and unpunished sinners—children avoiding catechism and adults avoiding the Lord's Supper—and the lack of proper discipline and excommunication, Bucer added a new complaint, the disappearance of individual absolution. His discussion of public absolution is striking because he linked it not with baptism but with the ceremony which preceded baptism and marked the end of the catechumenate in the early church.[18] Moreover, his description of private absolution reveals how close he had come to adopting the Lutheran position. From the time of the Marburg colloquy Bucer had acknowledged the consoling power of absolution, but through the 1530s this facet of private confession was always of secondary importance in comparison with its pedagogical function. During the early 1540s, however, he increasingly emphasized the importance of individual absolution,[19] and in *Von der Kirchen mengel vnnd fähl* the emphasis of his earlier works was reversed. Bucer now depicted the psychological torments of the soul weighed down by sin and praised the assurance such a person received from the words of absolution. He mentioned only in passing the instruction the individual received when he went to a pastor to confess his sins and receive absolution. Bucer echoed the *Augsburg Confession* in calling absolution "the voice of God from heaven."[20]

Bucer's emphasis on individual absolution was the logical outworking of his interpretation of the power of the keys. Individuals were loosed first when they were admitted into the church through baptism and when they were again reconciled to it after having been excluded from the sacraments or completely excommunicated.[21] In each case the individual had to confess his sin and profess his acceptance of the gospel before he could be loosed.[22] Bucer held that infants could be loosed through baptism, but from the end of the 1530s he had argued that these children also were to make a public profession of faith and obedience in order to become full members of the church. In *Von der Kirchen mengel vnnd fähl* he carefully avoided any mention of baptism, particularly in connection with a confession of sin or profession of faith, probably because of his fear that his words would be used by various Anabaptist

---

[18]In the *Florilegium patristicum* which he compiled during the 1540s, Bucer cited Augustine's description of "the sanctification of catechumens through the sign of the cross, prayer, imposition [of hands], and the communion of sacred bread" in *de peccatorum meritis et remissione*; BOL 3:166. On the rites which marked the end of the catechumenate, see "Catéchuménat," DTC 2/II:1983-1985.

[19]Cf. his discussion of private absolution in the 1543 Catechism and in the Order for Visitation of the Sick; above, p. 172 n. 39.

[20]BDS 17, 176.17-18; cf. CA XXV, BSLK, 97.

[21]On loosing in baptism, cf. *Furbereytung zum Concilio*, BDS 5:306.3-7; 1534 Catechism, BDS 6/III:84.23-85.25; after penance or excommunication, BDS 5:306.36-307.3; 308.12-17; BDS 6/III:85.26-86.4.

[22]In his Florilegium, Bucer also cited Augustine and Cyprian as stating that those baptized were asked "if they believed in the remission of sins and eternal life through the holy church"; BOL 3:19.

groups in Strasbourg to support their own position on adult baptism. Bucer himself placed the emphasis on the confirmation of those baptized as infants. This, rather than adult baptism or the rites marking the end of the catechumenate, was the patristic ceremony which he regarded as the more appropriate model for the Strasbourg church. The public profession of faith made in confirmation and the private confession of sin made to the pastor each allowed for the individual response required for the loosing of sin in absolution.

Bucer's complaints about the failings of the Strasbourg church comprised only the first half of his treatise. The heart of the work was his proposal to restore the power of the keys to the church. Bucer freely admitted that the use of the ban would not establish proper discipline in the church, since it would have to be exercised not only on the common man but also on some of the city's most prominent citizens, "unless we want to strain out gnats and swallow camels." But this would only create factions and unrest in the city and lead to further harm for the church.[23] Fortunately, Bucer stated, Christ, the apostles, and their successors used another means to build up the church. He proposed to follow the example of those who "preached the gospel to all but recognized as members of God's church, as their brothers and sisters, only those who had freely given themselves to such fellowship and had been baptized; with these alone did they practice fraternal reproof and warning and the dispensation of the sacraments."[24]

Bucer then outlined a formal procedure by which Strasbourg's inhabitants would voluntarily agree to accept church discipline. The procedure would be implemented in several stages. First, the pastors would preach on the aforementioned shortcomings of the church and warn their hearers that the wrath of God would be kindled if there was no improvement. They would also explain to their congregation the need for close relations between the pastor and individual members of his flock. Then each pastor would visit or summon before him his "most zealous and God-fearing" parishioners to instruct them individually about the characteristics of "true Christian fellowship." When this had been accomplished, the pastor would call together all these parishioners to explain once more the importance of such fellowship and to answer questions. At this meeting two or three men would be elected to carry out the responsibilities of pastoral oversight together with the ministers and *Kirchenpfleger*. These elders were to be chosen, Bucer stated, "so that when the *Kirchenpfleger* from the magistrate, whether because of secular business or for other reasons, cannot or will not be present during the subsequent church acts (*kirchen vbung*), the pastors would have these same [elders] at hand and—what has been necessary for the church at every time—would know how to act with the help and counsel of these same [elders]." In any case nothing would be undertaken in the church unless the *Kirchenpfleger* had first been informed, since "we want the *Kirchenpfleger* to retain the full

[23]BDS 17:181.11-18.
[24]Ibid., 181.22-182.4.

measure and form of their office and authority as has been laid on them by the magistrate."[25]

The pastor and the newly elected elders were each to make confession of their
faith and public submission to the admonition of the church.[26] Together with the
Kirchenpfleger they were then to begin a systematic examination of all those who had
attended this initial meeting, either by summoning the entire household, including
domestic help, or, where this was not feasible, by visiting each house. The head of
the household would be examined about doctrine and sacraments as set forth in "our
confession of faith submitted to the emperor and estates of the empire in Augsburg,"[27] while wife and children were questioned from the catechism. The household
would then be instructed about "what they should and must do, and also what they
should flee, avoid and cease doing if they want to live blessedly in this fellowship";
this was an admonition to attend church, receive the sacraments, submit to discipline,
give alms, and avoid sin.[28]

All who agreed to this system of oversight and discipline were to promise their
obedience to the pastors and elders, and their names would be recorded in a special
register. The pastors and elders would visit the homes of these families once a year
to remind them of their commitment. Those who did not wish to enroll in this "fellowship" would still be welcome to attend the sermons; their marriages would be solemnized, their children baptized, and their sick visited. But if they wished to receive
the Lord's Supper although they "lived in obvious sin and led an unchristian life,"
they would be admonished by the pastors and elders either to reform or to abstain
from the sacrament "until God the Lord in time better illumines their heart."[29]

Bucer confidently asserted that this plan would remedy the defects of the Strasbourg church: it would provide opportunity for private instruction in the city's faith
for each individual according to his or her need; it would prevent the unworthy from
receiving the Lord's Supper; it would ensure that children and servants learned their
catechism and publicly submitted to the church's authority. Individuals would seek
out their pastor several times a year in order to receive absolution before partaking of
the Lord's Supper, fraternal admonition could be used to strengthen the weak, and
the church would have pious and God-fearing elders to assist the pastors in building
up the church.[30] To forestall possible opposition to his proposal, Bucer argued that

---

[25]Ibid., 183.11–184.36

[26]Ibid., 184.36–185.14.

[27]It is unclear whether the Tetrapolitan or the Augsburg Confession was intended. However, the chief points of doctrine which Bucer listed—original sin, law and gospel, good works,
Christian liberty, baptism, the Lord's Supper, and absolution—seem to fit better the outline
of the Augsburg Confession than they do the Tetrapolitan Confession. Moreover, Bucer's own
discussion of absolution in Von der kirchen mengel vnnd fähl accorded more with the statement of the Augsburg Confession than with the Tetrapolitan Confession; cf. above, pp. 50–51.

[28]BDS 17, 184.15–187.28.

[29]Ibid., 187.28–188.18

[30]Ibid., 188.19–189.19.

the pastors had no wish to challenge the authority of the magistrate but were merely attempting to perform their ministry faithfully through the exercise of Christian discipline.[31] There was no need to fear that the plan would lead to divisions within the church, since all those who enrolled in a "fellowship" would at all times obey the pastors who had been confirmed by the magistrate and who taught the city's official doctrine.[32]

The proposal laid out in *Von der Kirchen mengel vnnd fähl* was in essence a means of institutionalizing the disciplinary procedures which Bucer had advocated over the last decade. As he envisioned it, the plan would give the parish pastors coercive power to admonish and discipline all those who voluntarily agreed to accept their authority. Although Bucer insisted that the church governed with the authority of the Holy Spirit, voluntary submission and moral persuasion were obviously ineffective tools for directing or controlling the behavior of the Christians in Strasbourg. In order to discipline unacceptable conduct and foster appropriate behavior, the ministers needed some form of coercive power. The institutional structure Bucer described would give the pastors the authority they needed to direct the lives of their parishioners along the desired path.

Von der Kirchen mengel vnnd fähl did not mention any meetings of those who had enrolled in a "fellowship." Only the pastors and elders would meet, in order to accept prospective members or to summon those already enrolled for admonition or rebuke. In effect, the pastors and elders together functioned as a consistory. The *Kirchenpfleger* were to be present at the meetings of the pastors and elders, but they would not be directly involved in the disciplinary process. Bucer at no time denied the magistrate's right to supervise the church as represented by the presence of the *Kirchenpfleger*, but he acknowledged the futility of his earlier expectation that the *Kirchenpfleger* would function as lay elders, since many of the *Kirchenpfleger* had proved unwilling to perform the duties of that office. One senses a veiled reproof in Bucer's mention of *Kirchenpfleger* who "cannot or will not" attend the meetings of pastors and lay elders.

The most striking feature of the proposed "fellowships" was the requirement for a public profession of faith after which the individual's name was enrolled in a special register. This requirement combined several elements first proposed in the document *Von Anrichtung einer Kirchenzucht*, such as the use of parish registers and an initial public profession of faith, followed by a yearly private examination by the pastor.[33] Such a procedure seems to imply that the "fellowships" were restricted groups set apart from the larger city church, despite Bucer's assertions that they were not separatistic. The "fellowship" registers were not intended to separate members from nonmembers, however, but rather to help the pastors keep track of those who had agreed

---

[31]Ibid., 189.20-191.21.
[32]Ibid., 191.22-195.2.
[33]See above, pp. 102-103.

to submit to their pastoral care. In this sense they served the same purpose as the parish registers were intended to do in the earlier proposal.

Bucer stated in *Von der Kirchen mengel vnnd fähl* that the plan of the "fellowships" had been discussed with the *Kirchenpfleger* and approved by "all who loved the gospel."[34] By the end of 1546 there was apparently enough support for the plan in the city council that the pastors could proceed with its implementation. Bucer reported to Ambrosius Blarer in mid-December that the Strasbourg pastors were trying a new method of exercising discipline and that he would explain in more detail if the plan succeeded.[35] Two months later a complaint was made to the city council that the pastors of St. Thomas (Bucer) and New St. Peter (Paul Fagius) were "summoning people individually and attempting to establish the ban for themselves." The council's response, that the pastors were to proceed with more moderation in "preaching, visitation of households, the ban and baptism," implies that the council was aware of the plan and had given its tentative approval.[36] There is at any rate no indication that the council was surprised by the report, and it did not forbid the pastors to continue.

Nevertheless, Bucer was called before the city council in April 1547, to address some concerns which had arisen about the parish "fellowships."[37] The pastors had been accused of separating from the city's church and of trying to exercise the ban, but Bucer explained that they had merely reached an agreement to practice mutual admonition with those pious citizens who were willing. No one was compelled to enter into this agreement, nor did the pastors visit any home against the wishes of its occupants in order to gain their assent to the disciplinary procedure. Moreover, they desired that the *Kirchenpfleger* help in the establishment of the parish structures.

At the same time the pastors submitted a lengthy memorandum advocating measures to improve the city's disciplinary code. One of their recommendations revealed the close connection between their previous attempts to enforce Christian discipline and the newly established "Christian fellowships." Supporting themselves with several passages from the Old Testament, they described "the ways and means which God the almighty has commanded" to ensure that all baptized were taught to obey his commandments. First, the young were to be taught all of God's requirements and commandments. At appropriate times, God's law was to be proclaimed "in all earnestness" before all the people, both young and old. Finally, "a promise [to obey] the divine law was required from each individual with all earnestness." In accordance with this last practice, the early church had required "the use of question and answer" when adults were baptized, children confirmed, and sinners absolved and reconciled

----

[34]BDS 17:193.9-17.

[35]Schieß 2:547 (no. 1381, December 17, 1546). It is possible that Bucer wrote *Von der kirchen mengel vnnd fähl* shortly after December 1546, and that some of the pastors had already begun to form "fellowships" in their parishes by that time.

[36]RP 1547, Feb. 21, 64r-65r; TAE 4:215 (no. 1542).

[37]RP 1547, Apr. 11, 182r-v; TAE 4:218 (no. 1548a). Bellardi summarizes Bucer's oral and written defense to the city council, *Geschichte*, 30-32.

with the church.[38] The pastors urged that these measures be enforced in the Strasbourg church. The city's inhabitants should be required to send their children to catechetical instruction. With the help of the parish baptismal registers, the pastors could monitor children who had reached the appropriate age and would admonish parents if they were not sending their children to the weekly catechisms.[39] Servants and apprentices, especially those who came from Catholic areas, were also to be instructed in the catechism and required to attend the quarterly catechisms held especially for domestic help. Their names were also to be recorded in parish registers. Finally, so that the ministers could better carry out their pastoral responsibilities towards adults, they recommended that the parish boundaries be clarified. Individuals were free to attend the preaching services "wherever they thought it would do the most good," but the solemnization of marriages, baptisms, visitation of the sick, catechetical instruction, and the "preservation of Christian fellowship with adults" were all to be restricted by parish.[40]

The pastors did not specifically discuss either a public confirmation ceremony or the enrollment of adults in a "Christian fellowship." Nevertheless their recommendations for catechization and their defense of a public vow seem to assume that the logical end of catechetical instruction was a public profession of faith and obedience. Likewise, the clear demarcation of parish boundaries was necessary if pastors and lay elders were to know who fell under their disciplinary authority. Furthermore, the pastors used parallels from both civic life and military activity to defend the requirement of a public oath of submission and enrollment in a register. Citizens of a well-ordered city, they argued, were divided among various guilds, and each member accepted his guild's statutes and regulations and pledged his obedience to them. His name was recorded and he was periodically called to assemble with his fellow guild members to hear the guild articles and to renew his promise of obedience. Likewise armies had their own officials and regulations, and the commanders had lists giving the names of those under their authority. The memorandum implied that since such regulations were used in ordering transitory human activity, there should be no qualms about using the same methods within the church to order activities having eternal significance.[41] Since the plan for parish discipline proposed in *Von der Kirchen mengel vnnd fähl* required a public vow of obedience and enrollment in a parish register, it seems likely that the comparisons were chosen to defend the "Christian fellowships" against charges of novelty.

The pastors' recommendations concerning catechization and parish organization thus demonstrate the place of the parish "fellowships" within the comprehensive plan of pastoral care and Christian discipline that Bucer envisioned for the entire city.

[38]BDS 17:213.22-215.15.

[39]At least two of the city's seven parish churches had baptismal registers by the 1540s; still extant are those from Old St. Peter for the years 1544-1545 and St. Wilhelm, beginning in 1543.

[40]BDS 17:215.29-218.9.

[41]Ibid., 218.17-219.6.

Mandatory attendance at the weekly catechisms for children and at the quarterly cat-echisms for servants ensured that all would be taught the basics of the evangelical faith. Both confirmation and the vows made upon admission to the parish "fellow-ships" gave the pastors the right to act more decisively in disciplining individual sin-ners. Scripture was cited specifically to justify the solemn vow of obedience and the registration of those making the vow. Neither the memorandum nor the oral presen-tation describe the adult "fellowships" as providing opportunity for those enrolled to meet together.

A similar picture of the "fellowships" emerges from the report of the commission appointed to consider the pastors' memorandum.[42] The commission was guardedly positive about the Christian "fellowships":

> Regarding [the pastors'] undertaking and their use of the ban: we have been told and reassured, by officials from the government and council-men who were present during such actions [handlungen], that they were held and regarded as an arrangement whereby if someone saw any fault or defect in another, he would speak with him in a friendly way, telling him to cease from offense and evil and would admonish him to act rightly, and that they hold and regard it [as something] to help each other to good, and do not want to exclude, avoid or shut out anyone; and so we will allow it. If, however, it should lead or threaten to lead to divisions, separations or factions and sects or other ills, and there is concern that harm will arise from it, then the council will have to have proper supervi-sion so that such evil will be prevented and avoided.[43]

Bellardi interpreted the commission's description of the movement as referring to gatherings of those enrolled in fellowships,[44] but the "actions" which the council-lors observed were more likely the regular meetings of pastors and elected elders pre-scribed by Von der Kirchen mengel vnnd fähl. If the plan had included regular gatherings of lay members, it is unlikely that the commission would have approved of it. Such assemblies by "fellowship" members separate from the city's church could very easily have been regarded as "leading to . . . factions and sects," which would

---

[42]Bellardi discusses these provisions in the context of the new disciplinary ordinance which the city council was considering, Geschichte, 33–37.

[43]TAE 4:219.11–23.

[44]This view is fostered in part by the document's discussion of the "Convocationen," which Bellardi mistakenly assumes to mean the assembly of "fellowship" members. It is clear from the city council's review of this provision the following December, where it is called the "convocatzen der predicanten," that the commission was discussing the Kirchenkonvent, the biweekly meeting of the pastors and their assistants; RP 1547, Dec. 25, 681r. The com-mission recommended that the Kirchenpfleger were to attend the meetings of the Kirchenkon-vent on a rotating basis, with instructions that if they saw anything that could lead to "quarrels, harm or other disadvantage," they were to bring the matter before the city council; cf. the rotation prescribed by the 1534 church ordinance, where the Kirchenkonvent is also termed the Convocatz, BDS 5:30.31–31.27.

justify the intervention of the council.[45] The commission also recognized that the proposal was not concerned primarily with excommunication; rather, the heart of the plan was the mutual admonition which "fellowship" members agreed to give and to accept from others.[46] Their description of the proposal faithfully reflected Bucer's view that admonition, not excommunication, was the most essential part of discipline.

On a related topic, the commission supported the ministers' demand that children be required to attend catechism instruction. The pastors could summon those parents who did not send their children to catechism services and admonish them to better performance of this parental duty. If their admonition had no effect, they were to refer the parents to the *Kirchenpfleger*, who were to ask them why they ignored their children's religious education. Parents who opposed the city's doctrine or who were otherwise negligent were reported to the city council for further disciplinary measures. However, the commission shied away from requiring servants to attend the quarterly catechisms, since, as it argued, faith could not be produced by such compulsion. More practically speaking, the commission feared that apprentices who came from outside the city would leave rather than submit to such a regulation, to the city's disadvantage. Nevertheless, masters could admonish their servants and apprentices to attend the catechisms.[47] The pastors were advised to use discretion in examining those who came, asking only those questions to which the individual knew the answer so that he or she was not "terrified or humiliated." Finally, the commission agreed on the clarification of parish boundaries, so that ministers would be better able to exercise their responsibilities of oversight and pastoral care and the parishioners would know to which pastor they should go for baptisms and weddings. However, each individual was to remain free to hear sermons and to receive the sacrament in any of the city churches.[48] This last provision concerning reception of the sacrament was a serious weakening of the plan for parish discipline.

The city council accepted the commission's recommendations, but only after altering them to strengthen their own authority. The councillors clearly did not wish to allow the pastors much independence of action and wanted their representatives, the *Kirchenpfleger*, to participate in every step of the disciplinary procedure. The pastors were allowed to summon parents and godparents only in conjunction with the *Kirchenpfleger*. The city council emphasized again that membership in the parish "fellowships" was to be voluntary. In addition it decreed that when an individual was

[45]Cf. the reaction of the city council to such meetings when they are first mentioned in November 1547, and Bucer's defense of the gatherings in which he argued that they would not lead to schism, discussed below.

[46]Hammann observes that the magistrate was not opposed to the organization of the "Christian fellowships" per se, only to any attempt to exercise the power of excommunication, *Entre la Secte*, 334–335.

[47]This was essentially a reiteration of the city council's position on mandatory catechism attendance expressed a decade earlier; see above, pp. 99–101.

[48]AST 84, 249r–251v (no. 45).

subjected to church discipline on account of a sin condemned by the city's moral code, the case was to be reported to the city council and the sinner punished.[49]

The city council's decision regarding voluntary membership in the "fellowships" continued the policy of cautious approval expressed in February. In addition, its endorsement of mandatory attendance at catechism instruction for children and the redrawing of parish boundaries demonstrated that the councillors were not entirely deaf to the pleas of the clergy. However, the council resolved not to publish any of its decisions until the entire draft of the new disciplinary code had been discussed and approved, a task which was not completed until January of 1548.[50]

In the meantime, the pastors proceeded with the establishment of parish "fellowships" on their own. In August 1547, a formal description of the commitment made by new members to a parish "fellowship" was drawn up. Presumably the formation of "fellowships" in several of the parishes had progressed to the point where there was a need for a written statement of what was expected from new members. The description is an expanded version of the same section in *Von der Kirchen mengel vnnd fähl*, but it is careful to note that when a "fellowship" member fell into open sin, he was summoned by the *Kirchenpfleger* as well as the pastors, "in accordance with God's command . . . and also the ordinance of our synod accepted by the city council"; reconciliation of repentant sinners was also performed by the pastors with the advice and consent of the *Kirchenpfleger*.[51]

At the end of October a complaint was brought before the city council that the pastors were causing schism by pressuring the people to attend special gatherings—some parishioners obviously felt they were being forced to enroll in a "fellowship."[52] The council resolved to tell the pastors to suspend their procedures until deliberation on the disciplinary code revision was finished. In the meantime, it asked the pastors to consider how discipline could be administered as the responsibility of the magistrate and not the clergy. A week later it was reported to the city council that "the pastors were still summoning their people," causing further unrest among the city's inhabitants.[53] The city council repeated its earlier decision to have the pastors discontinue their efforts and appointed three councillors to deliver the message in

[49]RP 1547, May 24, 267v. Again, the city council was concerned with pastoral oversight rather than lay assemblies.

[50]The earlier-approved sections were reviewed and approved at the end of December, RP 1547, 681r-682r; 684r, and the printed copies to be distributed to the guilds were approved in late January, RP 1548, 22v; cf. Bellardi, *Geschichte*, 36-37. Contra Bellardi, I find nothing in the city council minutes to imply that "the city council's decision regarding the pastors' exercise of the ban was reversed." This statement most likely stems from Bellardi's mistaken interpretation of "Convocatz" to apply to the parish "fellowships" rather than the *Kirchenkonvent*.

[51]BDS 17:248-255, citation 254.12-18; cf. 185.15-187.33. The paragraph in *Von der kirchen mengel vnnd fähl* gives the responsibility of summoning to the pastors and elders and does not mention the *Kirchenpfleger*, 187.25-28.

[52]RP 1547, Oct. 31, 579v, 580v-581r.

[53]Ibid., Nov. 7, 596r-v.

person. This conflict between pastors and city council was complicated by a new development. For the first time the records mention a meeting of lay "fellowship" members, held in Paul Fagius' church of New St. Peter. On November 8, the day after the council issued its second warning, Fagius attended a gathering of his parishioners in defiance of the council's prohibition.[54]

The next day Bucer, Fagius, and two other pastors were cited to appear before the city council to answer charges that they had acted against the city council's command by establishing "conventicles in which everyone must confess his faith." They were also accused of setting themselves up as an independent authority and creating divisions within the city by refusing to give the sacrament to those who did not join such "conventicles."[55] Bucer responded with an impassioned defense of the pastors' actions. They were only carrying out that which God's word and the desperate situation of the church in Strasbourg compelled them to do, he asserted. The Lutherans did not admit anyone to the Lord's Supper unless he had first been examined by his pastor, and their pastors had the right to summon individuals if necessary. In Strasbourg, on the other hand, the sects and Epicureans had such a hold that many people never came to hear the sermons, others never received the Lord's Supper, and many people reached marriageable age without even knowing how to pray. Since the magistrate seemed unable to do anything to improve the situation, the pastors, in accordance with God's command, had begun to instruct the people and "to lead them into Christian fellowship." They summoned their parishioners and admonished them to commit themselves to Christian fellowship, and "there were very few who had not recognized this plan as Christian." As to those who maintained that the pastors were pressuring people to give account of their faith and piety, Bucer stressed that they acted only with individuals who gladly accepted their admonition and they were compelling no one.

In response to the charge of disobeying the magistrate's command, Bucer claimed that they had never been forbidden to summon individuals to speak with them. On the contrary, they had the command of God to do so. Moreover, the magistrate in its printed ordinances had specified that the pastors should omit nothing in seeing that people were brought into Christian fellowship. Bucer admitted that this responsibility was especially given to the *Kirchenpfleger*, "but it was not forbidden to

---

[54]Bellardi, *Geschichte*, 40–41. Bellardi and other scholars who follow his account assume that this meeting of the New St. Peter "fellowship" is only the first mention of gatherings which had always been part of the "fellowship" ideal. This is, however, a case of reading later developments into earlier ones, since, as has been pointed out, the documents prior to November 1547 say nothing about such gatherings, and Bucer's defense of the "fellowships" focuses primarily on their disciplinary and pastoral nature. Only from November on is there any discussion of lay assemblies for purposes other than initial enrollment in the "fellowships."

[55]The RP used the term *Bruderschaft*, the first time this word occurs in any of the documents concerning the "fellowships"; RP 1547, Nov. 9, 600r–605r; cf. Bellardi's account of Bucer's oral presentation and written justification, *Geschichte*, 41–48. The other two pastors who appeared with Bucer and Fagius were Johann Marbach, pastor for the parish of St. Nicholas, and Johann Lenglin, pastor for the parish of St. Wilhelm.

the pastors, who also wanted to see the *Kirchenpfleger* carrying out their duties." The pastors had no desire to "grasp after the sword." They wanted to support the authority of the magistrate, but they were at the same time responsible for performing the ministry established by Christ. The other three pastors each added their own support to Bucer's presentation, stressing the fact that they also felt conscience-bound by the word of God to carry out their pastoral responsibilities.

The city council heard out the pastors' defense and then stated that it did not have the time to respond at length. It noted rather laconically that it recognized the ordinances it had issued, but "it couldn't recall that the provisions were quite so far-reaching." Still, it did not want to disobey the word of God. The matter needed further consideration, and until the city council had reached a final decision, there were to be no further gatherings.

The pastors did not limit the defense of their actions to an oral presentation. They also submitted to the city council a justification of the "fellowships," written by Bucer, describing how they exercised discipline through them and refuting objections to their existence. Some of the arguments echo points made in the memorandum submitted to the city council the previous April, but there is a new polemical tone. Bucer maintained that the public confession of faith and submission of obedience to the church was a principle taught in both Old and New Testaments. Again, he stressed that the early church required such confessions from adults before they were baptized and from those baptized as infants before they were admitted to the Lord's Supper. Likewise, he cited the comparison between commitment to "Christian fellowship" and to civic society: whenever men wished to place special emphasis on the entrance into any group, such as joining a guild or obtaining citizenship in a city, they marked the occasion with special ceremonies and made solemn vows so that membership was recognized to be important.[56]

Bucer also defended the selection of lay elders responsible for individual instruction and admonition of all Christians.[57] The *Seelsorger*—pastors and lay elders—were to use the Ten Commandments as a model in helping their charges recognize sin and grow in Christian virtue, although "they are not immediately to demand the highest perfection from each and every person but are to begin with the first most basic and necessary points of doctrine."[58]

He then summarized the disciplinary procedures practiced in the "fellowships." Those guilty of secret sins were admonished according to the three stages of Matthew 18, with the goal of bringing them to repentance. Only in cases of contumacy was the sinner brought before the elders. Those who had been banned were not admitted to the prayers or the Lord's Supper, although they were not excluded from sermons. Christians were not to have any communication with them beyond

[56]BDS 17:262.30–264.9.
[57]Ibid., 264.10–267.6.
[58]Ibid., 271.21–26.

that required by domestic or civic ties. Shunning was to be used as "a necessary medication for the soul" and in such a way that the excommunicate recognized his sentence as God's judgment. Those who had sinned openly and offended their neighbors were to be punished publicly as a deterrent to others. These were also to be called before the *Seelsorger* for admonition and were regarded as "heathens and publicans" if they did not repent or if they refused to appear. This sentence could only be imposed for sins which excluded from the kingdom of Christ—the deliberate mortal sins "with which faith in Christ cannot co-exist"—such as teaching false doctrine, blasphemy, perjury, and the like. Bucer's enumeration again followed the Ten Commandments. Only for such serious sins could an individual be called before the *Seelsorger*, or representative of the whole church.[59]

If the sinner repented and promised to reform, the *Seelsorger* could require him to perform penance and to abstain from the Lord's Supper for a period, especially if they questioned his sincerity or if the sin was notorious. If his repentance was genuine, the pastors prayed for him and "loosed him from the bond of exclusion." The individual was to be admitted to the next celebration of the Lord's Supper after there had been a public confirmation of his absolution and reconciliation with the church. This reconciliation, Bucer suggested, could be performed during the preparatory service held the evening before the Lord's Supper was celebrated, since all who had committed themselves to the "fellowship of Christian discipline" should be present at this service.[60]

The *Kirchenpfleger* were to be present at all meetings of the *Seelsorger*, which were held every Sunday and "whenever the work of Christian discipline requires." Those who desired to commit themselves to the "fellowship" were to appear at these Sunday meetings as well, so that they could be properly instructed and could make their confession of faith and promise of obedience and have their names entered in the register.[61]

Women also belonged in the "fellowships," but to maintain proper order in the church, they were subject to special conditions. Male members of a "fellowship" were to instruct their wives and daughters at home and make the confession of faith and promise of obedience for them before the elders. If necessary the *Hausvater* could ask an elder to instruct his wife, daughters, or maids. The women were to oversee and admonish one another, and where one would not accept the admonition of her sisters, husband, or *Hausvater*, one or two elders were called in for admonition in the presence of the *Hausvater*. If this was unsuccessful, she was brought before the gathered *Seelsorger*, and the disciplinary procedure was then the same as for men.[62] Bucer evidently wanted to reassure the city council that in exercising discipline, patriarchal

---

[59]Ibid., 272.3-275.19.
[60]Ibid., 275.20-276.30.
[61]Ibid., 277.1-21.
[62]Ibid., 277.22-279.6.

authority would be preserved and nothing would be done that would undermine the hierarchical structure of society.

The objections which Bucer refuted were similar to those discussed in *Von der Kirchen mengel vnnd fähl*. The number of people willing to commit themselves to "the fellowship of Christian discipline" was unimportant: the pastors were obligated to obey God's command by teaching and admonishing, and God himself would draw people to submit to discipline.[63] If the "fellowship" members created schism by boasting of their superiority, they would be disciplined, and the presence of the *Kirchenpfleger* at all meetings held for the purpose of discipline would ensure that nothing untoward happened.[64] Those who would not publicly commit themselves to Christian fellowship but regularly received the sacrament would be allowed to continue, although they were to be encouraged to make the public commitment, and if any were guilty of gross sin they were not to be admitted to the Lord's Supper. Those who refused to receive the sacrament and who scoffed at individuals who submitted to discipline were simply to be endured.[65]

To the fear of a "new papacy," Bucer argued that the past perversion of a good institution did not mean the institution should be abandoned but rather reformed and rightly established. The Strasbourg pastors hoped to preserve the sound practice of discipline by involving the laity and, insofar as possible, representatives from the magistrate.[66] Finally, Bucer rejected the view that discipline was either unnecessary because the magistrate punished sin or impossible to establish given present circumstances. The magistrate was responsible for seeing that the church had faithful ministers but, just as it did not preach or administer the sacraments, neither was it to exercise Christian admonition and discipline directly. And the same Holy Spirit who commanded and established discipline in the apostolic church would also establish discipline in the Strasbourg church.[67]

At the request of the city council and *Kirchenpfleger* Bucer also drew up a report justifying the pastors' right to summon their parishioners based on the provisions of several of the city's mandates and ordinances.[68] It is clear from his arguments that he

---

[63]Ibid., 280.1–27.
[64]Ibid., 281.4–27.
[65]Ibid., 282.8–19.
[66]Ibid., 284.3–285.30.
[67]Ibid., 286.14–289.14.
[68]"Verzeichnis des so aus m. g. herren Kirchenordnung zu beforderung christlicher gemeinschafft zuvermercken ist, aus bevelh vnser gepietenden herren, vnd Kirchenpfleger zu S. Thoman verzeichnet," AST 16, no. 47; excerpts in TAE 4:191–192 (no. 1510), where it is dated May/June 1546. The document seems to fit more logically in the wake of Bucer's presentation to the city council in November 1547, however, in which Bucer's citation of the city's ordinances to support the pastors' authority to summon was viewed with scepticism by the council. Moreover, some of the points made in the document reflect concerns about the "fellowship" proposal expressed at this time; cf. n. 74. The document is not explicitly attributed to Bucer, but the fact that it was intended in part for the *Kirchenpfleger* of Bucer's parish of St. Thomas, as well as its reference to the practice of summoning in that parish, make his authorship fairly certain.

had copies of the cited ordinances and mandates before him as he made his points. Bucer claimed that the city council's first directive at the beginning of the reformation, that pastors and preachers should faithfully carry out their ministry and neither add to nor subtract from the word of God, in itself gave license to the pastors to see that every Christian in each parish was built up in his or her faith.[69] He cited the church ordinance of 1534, which stated that along with the *Kirchenpfleger* the pastors and their assistants were to see that their parishioners dedicated themselves wholly to Christ.[70] Likewise, the resolutions from the second synod charged the ministers with seeing that the sermons produced fruit in the lives of the people, "which cannot happen if the pastors and their assistants do not have genuine Christian knowledge of and fellowship with young and old."[71] To those who protested that the ordinance on summoning specifically limited this authority to summon to the *Kirchenpfleger*, Bucer answered that in the parish of St. Thomas, the summoning was always done through the *Kirchenpfleger*, then added that although the ordinance referred only to the *Kirchenpfleger*, it did not forbid the ministers to use this authority as well. Moreover, the 1534 church ordinance virtually endorsed the clergy's power to summon when it stated that the ministers should use every means necessary to establish their parishioners in genuine Christian fellowship.[72]

Bucer also gave the reason why the 1534 church ordinance emphasized the responsibilities of the *Kirchenpfleger* and not of the pastors to summon: at the time the ordinance was drafted, it had seemed necessary so that the *Kirchenpfleger* would be empowered to act when the pastors and helpers were not present. Moreover, the sectarians had so alienated the people from their pastors that it was thought perhaps the *Kirchenpfleger* would have more influence. Bucer continued that even though relations between people and pastors had not improved in the intervening years, "the pastors cannot neglect forever the duties laid upon them by God and the magistrate." He rejected the argument that the pastors had no right to exercise "this most necessary and salutary work of Christian fellowship and of building the body of Christ" without the specific authority of mandate or ordinance; those who held this view committed the same error as the papists who claimed that the responsibility for Christian reformation rested only with the pope, bishops, and councils, not the Christian mag-

---

[69]A reference to the mandate from December 1, 1523, commanding that the pure word of God be preached. This mandate was reissued along with several others as part of the *Constitution* in 1535, Röhrich, *Mittheilungen* 1:260-262.

[70]"Verzeichnis," AST 16, no. 47, p. 1; cf. the Strasbourg church ordinance, BDS 5:37.4-10; cf. also no. 2 of the "Verzeichnis" with BDS 5:38.9-14.

[71]AST 16, no. 47, pp. 1-2, no. 4; cf. BDS 6/II:235.3-10.

[72]AST 16, no. 47, p. 4, no. 9-10. This is a reference to the 1539 mandate on summoning which itself repeated provisions from the 1534 church ordinance. The 1539 mandate clearly stated that the *Kirchenpfleger* were to do the summoning and the pastors were not even mentioned in it, but Bucer (rather optimistically) interpreted the mandate's reference to the earlier church ordinance to mean not only the passages it quoted directly but also the general introduction of the section on discipline, which mentioned the responsibility of the pastors together with the *Kirchenpfleger*; TAE 3:308-309 (no. 890), and BDS 5:37.4-34.

istrate or the people. The pastors could not be forbidden to do all that they could to bring about true reformation, particularly when the magistrate and people were negligent in their responsibility to foster true Christian love and fellowship.[73]

Bucer's final point in this defense dealt with the concern that over time that which had started out well would "be the occasion for offense and give rise to immorality as happened under the papacy, or to evil sedition as is evident among the Anabaptists." It was wrong to ignore the good that God had commanded because of fear that it would allow for evil, he argued. He described the precautions taken by "the magistrate and all Christians" that

> Christian fellowship is sought out, established, preserved and exercised according to God's word and ordinance, as we now intend to establish it; we will deal with the heads of households in public places set aside for such divine matters, and we will not be in contact with servants except in the presence of the household heads, so that no one will have reason to be offended by this plan.[74]

In his presentation to the council and the documents which he submitted in conjunction with it, Bucer emphasized the disciplinary nature of the "fellowships." What had upset the council, however, was not the exercise of discipline per se but rather the gathering of lay members in Fagius' parish of New St. Peter and the fear that the pastors were encouraging the formation of conventicles (Brüderschaften). Bucer took note of this concern in a letter summarizing his council presentation for four of his fellow ministers who had not been at the council session.[75] In the letter he outlined the procedure followed in creating the "fellowships" and defended Fagius' meeting with his parishioners. Almost in passing, he described the gathering: the pastor began with an admonition to "Christian fellowship and discipline" on the basis of a Scripture text that was read, then asked if anyone had particular questions about doctrine, desired counsel, or had anything to share "for the common edification"; finally he closed the assembly with prayer.[76] Bucer also argued that in addition to hearing public preaching, each Christian should have the opportunity for "friendly meetings" in which he could discuss his particular concerns and "share with his brothers what

---

[73]AST 16, no. 47, pp. 4-6, no. 12-14.

[74]This statement reflects concerns which occur in other documents defending the movement written at this time and provide further support for dating the "Verzeichnis" in November 1547, rather than May/June 1546; cf. Bucer's assurance that meetings with the heads of households would be held only in public places, BDS 17:296.15; 303.3-7; the concern for propriety and contact with servants only through the head of the household is also reflected in the description of how female members of the parish "fellowships" were to be disciplined.

[75]Cf. Bellardi's description of the letter and of the circumstances surrounding its composition, Geschichte, 48-50. The letter was sent to Matthis Zell, pastor of the cathedral parish, Johann Steinlin of St. Aurelien, Theobald Negri of Old St. Peter, and Kaspar Hedio, the cathedral preacher.

[76]BDS 17:304.20-24.

the Lord had given him."[77] It was disgraceful to allow gatherings on Sunday for the purpose of gambling, shooting, and "all other activities that blaspheme God and offend the church" but to forbid gatherings in or by the church for prayer and instruction.[78]

Kaspar Hedio also submitted a lengthy memorandum to the city council commission charged with investigating the lay gatherings and the "fellowship" movement from which they had developed.[79] Most of Hedio's memorandum was a theoretical defense of church discipline, with little attention given to the practical details of its exercise. This is to be expected, since Hedio was the cathedral preacher and not a parish pastor; thus he was not responsible for the care of souls and played no direct part in the "fellowship" movement. One of Hedio's chief concerns was preventing the unworthy from receiving the Lord's Supper, and he referred approvingly to the Lutheran precommunion examination, a practice "which some pastors would like to have here, but this would have been more possible when we first got rid of the papacy."[80] Hedio supported the basic framework of the "fellowship" movement, stating that negligent Kirchenpfleger should be replaced by men who would perform their duties more zealously and urging the appointment of lay elders to assist with the exercise of discipline.[81] He opposed the gatherings of lay "fellowship" members, however. These meetings were not evil in themselves, he stated, but they could create offense and added nothing to what was already taught in public sermons (a not very surprising opinion, coming from the cathedral preacher). Those individuals who desired additional instruction, counsel, or consolation were always free to approach their pastor in private.[82]

By now it was becoming clear to Bucer that the council's opposition to the lay gatherings threatened the entire "fellowship" structure, and with it the exercise of Christian discipline. Therefore he wrote yet another memorandum at the end of November specifically defending the regular meetings of laity enrolled in a parish "fellowship."[83] In his memorandum Bucer took account of Hedio's views, particularly his reservations concerning the meetings of the laity. He defended these "Christian gatherings and discussions" on the basis of both Scripture and reason,[84] and then addressed twelve objections raised against the gatherings and the "fellowship" movement as a whole. Obviously the greatest opposition was due to the fear of schism and

---

[77]Ibid., 301.9-12.

[78]Ibid., 303.3-12.

[79]The memorandum has been edited by Werner Bellardi, "Ein Bedacht Hedios zur Kirchenzucht in Straßburg aus dem Jahre 1547," in Marijn de Kroon and Friedhelm Krüger, eds., Bucer und seine Zeit, Forschungsbeiträge und Bibliographie, Veröffentlichungen des Instituts für europäische Geschichte Mainz 80 (Wiesbaden: Steiner, 1976), 117-132. Bellardi points out the similarity between Bucer's and Hedio's positions, Geschichte, 52-57.

[80]Bellardi, "Bedacht," 130.

[81]Ibid., 128-129.

[82]Ibid., 131-132.

[83]"Mehrung götlicher gnaden;" this was the document published by Spener in the seventeenth century. Bellardi describes the memo, Geschichte, 57-58.

[84]BDS 17:319.13-321.24.

the divisive effect that the gatherings would have on the church; five of the twelve objections reflect this fear in one way or another. Bucer argued that the "fellowships" were not elitist, since enrollment was open to all who claimed to be Christians. "Fellowship" members who belied their identification as Christians "by word or deed" would be admonished to repent and, if they remained contumacious, expelled from the "fellowship" as they deserved.[85] Members in good standing would show Christian forbearance towards those who mocked them as self-righteous; thus there was no reason to fear potential divisions among Strasbourg's inhabitants.[86] Factors such as the size of the "fellowship" or the conduct of its members towards nonmembers did not override the pastors' obligation to teach the baptized to obey their Lord's commands.[87] The gatherings were to be scheduled at a time when they would not interfere with parish worship services or the noon sermon at the cathedral.[88] God's word provided no other way for the pastors to perform their ministry faithfully without "this private discussion and catechism of adults," and the majority of the theologians and ministers in the city agreed that the gatherings were necessary.[89] Unlike the Anabaptists, who encouraged people to avoid public worship services, the pastors held their gatherings publicly and taught correct Christian doctrine as expressed in the city's confession of faith.[90]

Bucer also rejected criticism of the gatherings as an unnecessary innovation. Christians needed to encourage one another in godliness, especially "the weaker members who have great need for such edification."[91] Even if God moved the city council to reissue its disciplinary ordinances and the *Kirchenpfleger* to do their duties, Christians would still need a means to help them grow in mutual love and obedience to God's word.[92] In Lutheran churches, the pastors had the authority to summon their parishioners for admonition. Through the precommunion examination they could instruct their charges in the faith, absolve them of sin, and prevent the unworthy from receiving the sacrament. This type of discipline, Bucer stated, would be even less acceptable to the Strasburghers than the proposal "to practice the catechism of Christ only with those adults who are willing."[93] Nor was the idea of an adult cate-

[85]Ibid., 323.26–324.6
[86]Ibid., 326.1–5.
[87]Ibid., 324.20–325.17.
[88]Ibid., 327. 21–328.29.
[89]Ibid., 330.19–331.14.
[90]Ibid., 334.23–335.20.
[91]Ibid., 329.1–11.
[92]Ibid., 335.24–336.20.
[93]Ibid., 332.10–333.4. Walther Köhler dismisses the references to the Lutheran practice as an attempt to obscure the fact that the precommunion meeting with the pastor "was something completely different from Bucer's 'fellowship' in its organic structure as Bucer outlined it"; *Ehegericht* 2:479, but Köhler himself overlooks the fact that the Lutheran practice and the Strasbourg "fellowships" were meant to achieve the same purposes: to allow the pastor the opportunity to instruct, console, and counsel parishioners and to screen prospective participants in the Lord's Supper to prevent its unworthy reception.

chism new. Bucer referred to works "published 16 and 20 years earlier" in which he had stated the need for Christian instruction and admonition. The ministers had tried several times to put their ideas into practice, but a few of the ministers and most of the *Kirchenpfleger* and parishioners had always opposed them. Now, however, the majority of the parish pastors were committed to the plan and the three who had not created "fellowships" in their parishes agreed in principle, although they were physically unable to carry out the plan.[94] Those who opposed the pastors' intentions did so either out of ignorance of God's word, the concern—due to lack of faith—that something harmful could come from God's command, or the fear that the result would be "the extension of Christ's kingdom which would hinder them in their unchristian deeds."[95]

The command of God's word was a sufficient response to arguments that the gatherings would be impossible to establish at the present time or under the present conditions in the Strasbourg church.[96] Likewise, the fear of something's misuse did not justify its disuse.[97] But to ensure as much as possible that "Christian fellowship and discipline" was established and maintained in the best way possible, Bucer recommended a number of practical measures. The parish boundaries should be firmly fixed so that the inhabitants of each parish could be summoned in small groups to be taught about the "fellowships" and given the opportunity to enroll. Those who agreed to commit themselves to the "fellowship" would be divided into groups according to the streets they lived on, and individuals would be chosen on each street to be responsible for oversight.[98] These individuals would meet weekly with the pastors and *Kirchenpfleger*. All those committed to the "fellowship" would meet every four to six or at most eight weeks for admonition, instruction, and the public profession of new members.[99] Bucer suggested that these meetings be held at the time of the Sunday vesper service after the children's catechism "so that these Christian discussions cause less suspicion on account of their seeming novelty." The city council was to choose members of the *Schöffen*, the large advisory council comprised of guild representatives, to be present at these gatherings when the *Kirchenpfleger* were unable to attend, so that the magistrate would be assured that temporal or governmental matters were not discussed. No gatherings could be held without the presence of these

[94]BDS 17:329.16-330.8. The pastors had pleaded poor health and lack of assistants as reasons why they had not established "fellowships"; cf. the report of the commission which met with these pastors, AST 84, no. 52.

[95]BDS 17:331.15-332.1.

[96]Ibid., 322.9-16.

[97]Ibid., 336.25-337.2.

[98]This proposal was first made by Hedio, cf. "Bedacht," 129.

[99]Bellardi, *Geschichte*, 58, assumes that prior to this time lay gatherings had been held weekly, but earlier documents speak only of regular meetings of the pastors and lay elders as part of their supervisory and disciplinary responsibilities, not of meetings for all enrolled members. The manner in which Bucer describes the plan for periodic lay assemblies gives the impression that such assemblies are an innovation, not a modification of existing practice.

representatives of the magistrate. Finally, the *Kirchenpfleger* were to perform their office faithfully in summoning all who avoided word or sacrament or dishonored both by their sinful lives.[100]

Despite the barrage of written justifications for the "fellowships," the city council proved hard to convince. A commission appointed by the council met at least twice during the month of December to investigate the pastors' actions, and at its second meeting it reaffirmed the council's command that the pastors were to take no further action.[101] From the end of 1547 until after Bucer's departure for England in 1549 the parish "fellowships" disappear from view. The city council's suspicions regarding the lay assemblies proved to be well-founded, however. In the tense political and religious situation of 1548, the "fellowships" continued to evolve in character, now functioning more as centers of resistance to the threatened imposition of the Augsburg Interim than as a mechanism for the exercise of discipline.[102] This transformation was actually encouraged by the city council's ban on further disciplinary activity within the "fellowships," a policy which Bucer lamented in a letter to Ambrosius Blarer in November 1548. After a promising beginning to the establishment of discipline had been made in four parishes the previous year, he wrote, the attempt had been forcibly suppressed. He noted with bitterness that many of those who had especially opposed the attempt had now left the city out of fear that it would be placed under the imperial ban for its resistance to the Interim.[103]

Bucer's efforts to erect a system of discipline through the parish "fellowships" ultimately failed. What then is the significance of the movement? Some scholars have argued that the proposal for the "fellowships" was a complete break with Bucer's past ideas on church discipline,[104] but it would be more accurate to describe them as yet another attempt to create an institutional structure for Christian discipline in its broadest sense, as Bucer had described since his 1527 Gospels commentary and had sought to establish in Strasbourg throughout his long career. The "fellowships" provided for religious instruction both before and after enrollment, a public profession of faith and obedience, mutual admonition of all members, and the right of the pastors and lay elders to impose public penance or excommunication if necessary. The

---

[100]BDS 17:337.39–339.21.

[101]AST 84, no. 52 and AST 176, 424r (p. 873). Contra Bellardi, *Geschichte*, 59, I found no mention of a discussion of Bucer's "Mehrung" at the second meeting.

[102]Both Bellardi, *Geschichte*, 63–67, and Hammann, *Entre la Secte*, 385–386, stress the changes in the character of the "fellowships" as the city was put under increasing pressure to accept the Interim. Bellardi describes meetings of a group of people opposed to the introduction of the Interim in Fagius' church of New St. Peter during the late summer and fall of 1548. The magistrate allowed this group to continue meeting on the condition that no new members were accepted into it and that controversial questions were not discussed. The group proved to the the nucleus for the "fellowships" which reemerged in 1549.

[103]Schieß 2:762 (no. 1594).

[104]Most notably Walther Köhler, who describes Bucer's proposal as "a completely new plan," *Ehegericht* 2:470. Köhler's entire discussion of the "fellowship" movement (467–494) is distorted because he does not see Bucer's distinction between secular moral discipline and pastoral church discipline or the complementary functions of magistrate and church.

details of how the "fellowships" were to be administered are strikingly similar to the provisions of the Hessian disciplinary ordinance of 1538. Lay elders were responsible for exercising discipline with the pastors. Discipline consisted of private admonition and the summoning of contumacious or notorious sinners before the assembled *Seel-sorger*. The list of excommunicable sins was based on the Ten Commandments,[105] the ban was not limited to exclusion from the Lord's Supper but also included shunning modified by the performance of household or civic duties, and the imposition of penance was followed by absolution and reconciliation with the church.

The procedure for enrolling in a "fellowship" also paralleled the provisions concerning confirmation in the Hessian ordinances. The public profession of faith and obedience which preceded enrollment was similar to that required of confirmands; in both cases this profession marked the entrance of the individual into the full communion of the church. Moreover, both enrollment in a "fellowship" and the public confirmation ceremony were intended to impress on the individual his duties of submission to pastoral authority and the responsibilities of full fellowship in the church. Bucer accorded to confirmation a quasi-sacramental character by using the imposition of hands, which was not an element of the enrollment procedure, but the enrollment was nonetheless seen as an occasion of great solemnity and was intended to have the same goal of deepening commitment to the church as manifested by submission to the pastor's authority. Both it and confirmation were justified by a comparison with the public vows made by new citizens or guild members.

The various descriptions of the "fellowships" reveal why the city council was concerned and the citizens alarmed at their establishment. Despite Bucer's repeated assertions that no one was forced to answer a summons and come to an assembly for enrollment, the average layman must have been under some social pressure to appear. This would have been especially true in the parishes where the *Kirchenpfleger* were involved with the summoning procedure, since they represented the city council's authority.[106] While the pastors may not have explicitly invoked the provisions of the 1539 mandate on summoning with regard to these gatherings, it is likely that parishioners felt threatened by the summons. It would have been even more difficult to refuse to be enrolled as a member of the parish "fellowship" for those who did attend. Bucer implicitly acknowledged this pressure when he wrote that "without doubt the devil would sow weeds in this acre [i.e., the "fellowships"]. Our gatherings, like those of the Lord and the apostles, will not be free of the devil's children."[107] Moreover, discipline lost its voluntary nature entirely for those individuals who had enrolled in a "fellowship." Once they had publicly pledged their obedience to the church, they were placed under the moral supervision of the pastors and lay elders,

[105]Compare the list in the Hessian ordinance, BDS 7:268-269, with that in the *Kürtzer Vnderricht*, BDS 17:274-275.

[106]When summoning parishioners to appear before them to discuss enrolling in a "fellowship," the pastors invoked the authority of the Kirchenpfleger; BDS 17:296.12-15; 309.1-2.

[107]Ibid., 323.20-22.

and they could not avoid the consequences of nonconformity with the pastors' inter-pretation of orthodox faith and morals. Enrollment thus marked the individual's ac-ceptance of the clergy's coercive authority in admonishing and disciplining sinners.

Bucer's defense of the lay assemblies reveals how the pastors' undertaking had evolved from the plan outlined in *Von der Kirchen mengel vnnd fähl*. Originally the laity had met only initially with the pastors and elders, so that the pastors could ex-plain to them the importance of discipline and how it would be exercised and could enroll new members in the "fellowship." As Bucer described the summoning proce-dure, it was similar to the assembly called by the *Kirchenpfleger* in the parish of St. Thomas which had led to the conflict between Claus Kniebis and Jakob Wetzel von Marsilien in 1541. By 1547, however, the pastors played a much more prominent role, and they made clear to those summoned that their disciplinary authority rested not on the city council's mandates but upon the word of God.[108] Even more signif-icantly, the structure of the "fellowships" changed as lay members began to meet to-gether with the pastors in order to ask questions or to encourage their fellow Christians. Aside from allowing discussion of troublesome theological issues such as infant baptism, the regular gathering of the lay members provided a potential forum for opposition to the magistrate and a possible threat to the city council's authority. This was one of the aspects of the assemblies which caused the city council to halt the further development of a movement which it had tolerated since the previous spring.

Although by the end of November Bucer was vigorously asserting the necessity for regular meetings of lay members of the "fellowships," it is doubtful that he was the actual instigator of such meetings. The credit (or blame) for such assemblies should rest with Paul Fagius. The first documented gatherings were not held until late October or early November 1547, and they met not in Bucer's parish of St. Thomas but in Fagius' parish of New St. Peter. Bucer did not discuss any meetings of those enrolled in the "fellowships" in any of the memoranda from the first part of 1547, although he vigorously defended the meetings after it became clear that they were jeopardizing the entire "fellowship" movement. Two additional bits of evidence from a slightly later date also point to Fagius as the original sponsor of the "fellowship" gatherings. In June of 1549, several elders from the parish of New St. Peter described the founding of their "fellowship" to a meeting of the *Kirchenkonvent*. In response to several years of sermons on the necessity for church discipline and fraternal fellow-ship, they stated, some members of the church had approached their pastor, Paul Fagius, and his assistant, Georg Fabri, and asked to meet with them for catechization and discussion of God's word.[109] Not quite a year later, John Burcher, an English

---

[108]Cf. the lengthy list of Scripture passages Bucer cited in defense of "true spiritual fel-lowship among the members of Christ and with their minister" and of the use of fraternal admonition; Ibid., 296.20-297.12.

[109]The presentation and its circumstances are described in Bellardi, *Geschichte*, 76-78. It is possible that the elders were referring to the meetings held in the fall of 1548 rather than to those discussed in November 1547. It is worth noting that Fabri (or Schmid) was a former

exile living in Strasbourg, described the "fellowships" as he saw them in a letter to Heinrich Bullinger. He also attributed the creation of these "conventicles," which he soundly criticized, to Fagius.[110] While neither of these statements is conclusive proof, they offer evidence that the regular gatherings of lay "fellowship" members were organized by Fagius, not by Bucer.

It should be stressed, however, that the development of regular meetings of the laity for instruction and admonition was a natural outgrowth of the ideas inherent in the proposals for "Christian fellowship." Given Bucer's constant emphasis on individual instruction, it is not surprising that "fellowship" members would begin to meet together. In a city where private confession was regarded with deep suspicion as "papistic," regular gatherings of those enrolled in "fellowships" seemed like an acceptable alternative to private meetings with the pastor for the purpose of individual instruction and counsel. Moreover, it is likely that devout laymen, inspired by the example of the Anabaptist conventicles or former Anabaptists themselves, would want to initiate similar meetings within the official church. In this sense Fagius was only bringing Bucer's principles to their logical conclusion, a fact which Bucer certainly recognized in his defense of the lay gatherings.[111]

The parish "fellowships" are often compared to Luther's "third type of Christian worship" described in the preface to his German Mass of 1526,[112] but Luther's plan differed fundamentally from Bucer's. The Wittenberg reformer described gatherings of "those who earnestly desire to be Christians" for the purpose of "prayer, reading, baptizing, reception of the sacrament and other Christian practices."[113] Bucer did not originally envision such gatherings. The informal statutes provided that "fellowship" members regularly attend public worship and receive the sacrament in their parish churches, and in the earliest proposals regarding the "fellowships," there was no mention that those enrolled met as a group. The "fellowships" were first and foremost a disciplinary structure, and when members did begin to meet together, part of

---

Anabaptist who had been reconciled with the church; his appointment as assistant at the church of New St. Peter in 1540 had caused some complaints among the parishioners; TAE 3:404.11-26 (no. 1015). Werner Packull has drawn attention to the charges that the conventicles consisted of former Anabaptists, "Peter Tasch: From Melchiorite," 292.

[110]Hastings Robinson, ed., *Original Letters Relative to the English Reformation*, The Parker Society (Cambridge: Cambridge University, 1847) 2:662-664 (April 20, 1550, no. 211). Given Burcher's negative opinion of Bucer evident from the same letter, it seems likely that if Burcher had thought Bucer was responsible for the gatherings he would have been more than happy to lay the blame at Bucer's feet; this implies that by 1550 Fagius was commonly believed to be responsible for them. Martin Greschat also emphasizes Fagius' role in the formation of the "fellowships"; *Martin Bucer*, 221-222, although he gives no specific evidence for his view.

[111]Hammann, following Bellardi's assumption that regular lay assemblies were always a part of the "fellowship" movement, discusses how such gatherings fit into Bucer's ecclesiology. His analysis is still persuasive even if the idea for such gatherings did not originate with Bucer, and it helps explain why Bucer would support the assemblies so enthusiastically, *Entre la Secte*, 371-379.

[112]See, among others, Anrich, "Bedacht," 66-67; Bellardi, *Geschichte*, 108-109; Hammann, *Entre la Secte*, 384.

[113]WA 19:75.3-30.

the justification was the opportunity for mutual admonition. Moreover, the sacraments were always to be celebrated in public, not privately among "fellowship" members. For Bucer the "fellowships" were not so much an opportunity for more committed Christians to gather separately, as a core from which reform could spread through the entire church as more people were brought under the disciplinary authority of the pastors and admonished to progress in piety.[114]

It would be more accurate to compare the structure of the "Christian fellowships" with the Genevan consistory under Calvin.[115] The aspects of the "fellowships" which have drawn the most attention of scholars, particularly the assemblies of "fellowship" members, have obscured the basic similarities in purpose and procedure between the "fellowships" as Bucer first proposed them and the consistory which Calvin was able to establish. As in Geneva, the Strasbourg pastors and elders, whether Kirchenpfleger or laymen chosen from the parish, were to meet weekly to carry out their responsibilities of church discipline and moral supervision. They were to have the authority to summon for admonition those whose sins had become known to them, and ideally they would have the right to excommunicate the contumacious and reconcile the repentant with the church.

The "fellowships" probably operated on a somewhat less formal basis than the Genevan consistory, since no records were kept of those who were summoned for admonition, although this may also be due to the brevity of their existence or the loss of the relevant documents. They also differed from the Genevan consistory in that the jurisdiction of the pastor and elders was limited, in the first instance to those in their own parish and in the second instance to those who agreed to accept their right of supervision and discipline. Bucer's often-repeated view that the "the pastor should know his sheep" justified the existence of a "fellowship" for discipline within each parish rather than one disciplinary authority responsible for the entire city church as was the case in Geneva. The more restricted jurisdiction of the ministers and elders as well as the emphasis on mutual admonition among parishioners gave the "fellowships" a more expressly pastoral rather than a disciplinary character.

The Strasbourg city council was not deceived by Bucer's attempts to put the same old proposals for giving the pastors disciplinary authority in the new guise of the parish "fellowships." It held to its position that church discipline and the supervision of morals was the responsibility of the Kirchenpfleger, and no amount of assurance by the pastors could convince it that the formation of "fellowships" would not usurp the Kirchenpflegers' authority. In addition, the city council was concerned by the prospect

---

[114]Van 't Spijker compares Bucer's suggestion of a gathering of "more fully committed" Christians in the 1527 Gospels with Luther's "third type" of voluntary worship; he rightly observes that for Bucer this proposal was only a temporary measure to be followed until "the holy law of Christ" was accepted by the majority, Ambten, 314-315.

[115]On the Genevan consistory, see Robert M. Kingdon's, "The Control of Morals in Calvin's Geneva," in idem., Church and Society in Reformation Europe (London: Variorum Reprints, 1985), VIII:8-16; E. William Monter analyzes cases brought before the consistory at a slightly later date, "The Consistory of Geneva, 1559-1569," Bibliothèque d'Humanisme et Renaissance 38 (1976):467-484.

of civil discord aroused by the "fellowships": division between residents of parishes with "fellowships" and of parishes without them, between members and nonmembers, between *Hausväter* and those under their authority. When the assembly of "fellowship" members threatened to turn that prospect into reality, the council acted quickly to stop the pastors' project.

In the end the disastrous course of events which had spurred Bucer to establish the Christian "fellowships" prevented him from bringing that plan to fruition. The threat to the city's evangelical church posed by the Augsburg Interim soon demanded all of Bucer's attention. In January 1548, he left Strasbourg to be within closer range of the imperial Diet at Augsburg, and he did not return to the city until the end of April. Until his exile from the city a year later, he devoted his energies to combatting the Interim. It was in this context that Bucer published his last work in Strasbourg, "A Summary of the Christian Doctrine and Religion Taught in Strasbourg over the Last 28 Years." Among the Summary's twenty-eight articles are statements on the importance of catechization and public confirmation, the need for private admonition and public penance, excommunication and absolution, and the responsibility of each Christian for his brother and of the pastors and elders for all.[116]

The city's final settlement with the bishop required the council to relieve Bucer of his pastoral duties in Strasbourg, and he was forced to leave the city in the spring of 1549 for exile in England. Although some of the parish "fellowships" still existed, their purpose and structure were altered by conditions in the city after the introduction of the Interim, and Bucer had no more influence upon them from his new home. But for Bucer, England was a new field of ministry. His last two years of life were devoted to promoting the success of the Reformation under Edward VI. The restructuring of the English church provided him with his final opportunity to elaborate his ideal system of Christian discipline.

---

[116]*Ein Summarischer Vergriff*, published in July of 1548, BDS 17:133.3-17; 134.9-14; 136.25-138.9.

9

The Ministry of Discipline in England, 1549-1551

Bucer arrived in England at the end of April 1549.[1] Until his death two years later he devoted himself to the reform of the English church, becoming involved in debates with Catholic opponents, trying to heal divisions within the Protestant ranks over issues such as the Lord's Supper and the use of vestments, and offering his suggestions for the reform of the liturgy. In his treatise *De Regno Christi*, written for King Edward VI, he presented his plan for the reformation of the English church and society both in general and in several chapters of specific recommendations. He also made full use of his position as Regius Professor of Theology at Cambridge to pass on to his students his vision of a reformed church and ministry.

As it had been in Germany, Christian discipline was a vital component of Bucer's proposals for reform. His English works made frequent mention of the three-fold ministry of doctrine, sacraments, and discipline. Bucer had used these three elements to describe the ministry of the church since the late 1530s, but he gave them particular prominence in his last major works.[2] Their importance is clear from his definition of the church, identified as the kingdom of Christ:

---

[1] On Bucer's life and influence in England see A. Edward Harvey, *Martin Bucer in England* (Marburg: Bauer, 1906); Herbert Vogt, *Martin Bucer und die Kirche von England*, Ph.D. diss., Westfälische-Wilhelms-Universität (Münster, 1966); Constantin Hopf (Hope), *Martin Bucer and the English Reformation* (Oxford: Blackwell, 1946); Wilhelm Pauck, *Das Reich Gottes auf Erden. Utopie und Wirklichkeit. Eine Untersuchung zu Butzers De Regno Christi und zur englischen Staatskirche des 16. Jahrhunderts*, Arbeiten zur Kirchengeschichte 10 (Berlin: de Gruyter, 1928), 68-114. Shorter accounts of Bucer's activities include Constantin Hope (Hopf), "Martin Bucer und England. Sein Beitrag zur englischen Reformationsgeschichte," *Zeitschrift für Kirchengeschichte* 71 (1960):82-109; Basil Hall, "Bucer et l'Angleterre," in *Strasbourg au coeur religieux du XVIe siècle. Hommage à Lucien Febvre, Actes du Colloque international de Strasbourg (25-29 mai 1975)*, ed. Georges Livet and Francis Rapp, Société Savante d'Alsace et des Régions de l'Est, Collection "Grandes Publications" 12 (Strasbourg: Istra, 1977), 401-429.

[2] For example, in Book I of *De Regno Christi*, Bucer described how the kingdom of Christ was to be administered through the dispensation of doctrine, sacraments, and discipline; his lectures "on the power and use of the sacred ministry," delivered at Cambridge from November of 1550 until the onset of his final illness in February 1551, were structured around the categories of doctrine, sacraments, and discipline.

The Kingdom of our Savior Jesus Christ is that administration and care of the eternal life of God's elect, by which this very Lord and King of Heaven by his doctrine and discipline, administered by suitable ministers chosen for this very purpose, gathers to himself his elect. . . . He rules and governs those who have been incorporated into himself and his Church, purging them daily more and more from sins and establishing them in all piety and righteousness and hence eternal life. He also shapes and perfects them, using for this purpose the ministry of his word and sacraments through fitting ministers, in public, at home and in private, and also by the vigilant administration of his discipline, not only of penance, but also of ceremonies and of the entire life.[3]

Bucer did not use the phrase "the power of the keys" because his focus was on Christ as ruler and governor of the church rather than on the authority of the ministers. Nevertheless, his description of the means through which Christ governs the church meshed with the definition of the power of the keys contained in the 1536 Gospels commentary.

Bucer described the ministry of discipline in different ways, depending on his audience. In *De Regno Christi*, he divided it into three components. At its most basic level, what Bucer termed "the discipline of life and manners," it was not restricted to the clergy:

Not only the public ministers of the churches (though these principally), but even individual Christians should exercise a care for their neighbors. By the authority and magisterium of our Lord Jesus Christ, each person should strengthen and advance his neighbors, wherever this is possible, and urge them to progress in the life of God, as his disciples, in his faith and knowledge. And if any fall into error of doctrine or some vice of life or manners, whoever can should with utmost zeal recall such persons from all false doctrine and depraved activity, both for the purity of Christian doctrine and the sedulous conformity of all life to the will of God.[4]

The discipline of penance, on the other hand, was the responsibility of the church's ministers. It was also more limited in scope, applying only to those guilty of grave sin. With regard to these individuals, Bucer wrote,

It is within the office of rectors and elders in the churches to urge not only a true repentance of spirit concerning sins but also the doing of penance and the showing of its fruits, and to bind by the authority of Christ; and they are not to dissolve that bond until these persons have shown good

---

[3] *De Regno Christi*, BOL 15:55; all English translations are taken from *Melanchthon and Bucer*, trans. and ed. Wilhelm Pauck, Library of Christian Classics 19 (Philadelphia: Westminster, 1969), here at 225.

[4] BOL 15:70-71; *Melanchthon and Bucer*, 240.

faith to the Church concerning their true repentance and conversion to
the obedience of Christ through those worthy fruits of repentance.[5]

As in his earlier works, Bucer appealed to both Scripture and the church fathers to
support the need for penitential discipline: Cyprian and the other church fathers
advocated it; Christ in the gospels and the Holy Spirit speaking through St. Paul
required its use.[6]

The third part of the ministry of discipline was the "necessary and common ceremonies of the church," which included "the blessing of places in which the Christian religion is publicly administered, the sanctifying of seasons, in which the people
grow in the Lord and take time for religion; a certain regulation of the ministry of the
word, the sacraments, discipline; sacred offerings, and their distribution to the
poor."[7] In *Von der Kirchen mengel vnnd fähl* the ordering of external ceremonies had
been the fifth component of the church's responsibilities, along with the ministries
of the word, sacraments, absolution, and excommunication;[8] Bucer now combined
the three elements of absolution, excommunication, and ceremonies under the heading of discipline.

In his more detailed lectures on the ministry given to his students at Cambridge,
Bucer defined the ministry of discipline as "the institution and method of living for
God, that is, of doing all things according to the teaching of the gospel, both publicly
and privately." He distinguished between the discipline applied to the clergy and that
which applied "to the whole people of Christ" and was comprised of "certain ceremonies and sacred rites, as well as agreement with the gospel in both morals and actions."[9] The discipline of ceremonies was further subdivided into three categories.
The first consisted of those rites by which individuals were received into the church,
which required "catechization, a confession of faith and a profession of obedience to
Christ." The second category was comprised of those ceremonies which promoted
piety, including both regular public worship and private meetings with the pastor or
other "pious brothers" for admonition. The last category of ceremonies pertained to
the administration of penitential discipline: private and public admonition, abstention from the sacraments, the binding to penance, excommunication, and reconciliation of penitents with the church.[10]

---

[5]BOL 15:74; *Melanchthon and Bucer*, 244.

[6]BOL 15:74-77; *Melanchthon and Bucer*, 244-247.

[7]BOL 15:78-79; *Melanchthon and Bucer*, 248.

[8]BDS 17:163.3-14. The common ceremonies of the church also are listed along with
the other elements of Christian discipline as the third component of the ministry in Bucer's
1543 Catechism; above, p. 171.

[9]*De vi et usu*, SA 570: "Ministerium sequitur Disciplinae, quae est institutio et ratio vivendi Deo, hoc est, faciendi omnia secundum Euangelij doctrinam, publice et private. Haec
vero disciplina duplex est in Ecclesia; alia ordinis Clericalis, alia totius populi Christi. Haec
vero popularis cunctisque Christianis communis disciplina, constat certis caeremonijs, et sa-
cris ritibus, tum consentaneis cum Evangelio, et moribus et actionibus."

[10]Ibid., 570-571: "Caeremoniae vero ac ritus Ecclesiastici, pertinent, alij ad id, ut homines Ecclesiam suscipiantur, alij ad proficiendum pietate in Ecclesia; alij ad abstentionem ab

proposed such a practice for the Strasbourg church in *Von der Kirchen mengel vnnd fähl*, recommending that the pastor and his assistants or elders visit the homes of parish "fellowship" members at least once a year.[20]

Instruction in the essentials of the faith held a key place within the ministry of the church. Both *De Regno Christi* and the lectures on the ministry discussed the practice of catechization, in which "both instructor and catechumen are mutually perfected through question and answer," as well as "holy conferences and the examination of the more difficult questions of our religion" as part of the ministry of doctrine rather than of discipline.[21] However, religious instruction clearly had a disciplinary function as well, especially when it was followed by a profession of faith and obedience. In *De Regno Christi*, Bucer asserted that adults were not to be received into the church through baptism unless they had been instructed in the faith, confessed their sin, renounced Satan and the world, and professed their submission to the gospel. This same confession of sin, renunciation of the world, and submission to obedience was expected of those baptized as children, after they had been catechized. Those who refused catechization, scorned the precepts of Christ, or would not make a profession of faith and obedience were "to be rejected from the company of the saints and the communion of the sacraments." As in his defense of the "Christian fellowships" in Strasbourg, Bucer justified the profession of faith and obedience by the example of the Israelites' renewal of their covenant with God and with a parallel drawn to the oath of citizenship.[22]

Bucer seized the opportunity to establish such a public profession of faith and obedience in the English church. At the end of 1549 he was asked to critique the first edition of the Book of Common Prayer, and in his *Censura* he made several suggestions which would bring the confirmation ceremony prescribed by the prayer book into conformity with his own disciplinary priorities. Bucer accorded a central role to confirmation in the establishment of Christian discipline. As he confidently stated, "in the restoration of this discipline we do not attempt a difficult thing if we approach it earnestly, as faithful ministers of Christ must do, and if we do not overlook the advice which I gave about confirmation and, first of all, about the reception of children and adolescents into the full fellowship of the church."[23] Bucer argued that it was not sufficient for confirmands to be able to repeat their catechism from memory; the children should instead be required to make a solemn and sincere profession of

[20]BDS 17:187.34–188.4.

[21]SA 563: "Verbi vero administratio, cum fiat lectione et recitatione divinarum Scripturarum, earundemque interpretatione et explicatione, indeque desumptis adhortationibus, cum repetitione et Catechismo, qui mutuis perficitur catechizantis et catechumeni interrogationibus atque responsionibus: Item sanctis collationibus, atque difficiliorum religionis nostrae quaestionum excussionibus"; cf. ibid., 567; BOL 15:62–65.

[22]BOL 15:57–59, citation at 59; *Melanchthon and Bucer*, 228–229.

[23]I have used the modern edition of Bucer's original manuscript at Oxford, with an English translation on the facing page, E. C. Whitaker, ed. and trans., *Martin Bucer and the Book of Common Prayer*, Alcuin Club Collections 55 (Great Wakering: Mayhew-McCrimmon, 1974), 137. The *Censura* is also printed in SA, 456–503.

their faith. He described this confession as "of such a kind as might be judged not to originate in the mouth and not be merely a preparation of human teaching: it should be accompanied by signs in the conduct and manner of life in the candidate which the churches might accept as proceeding from a heart which truly believes the gospel and from the teaching of the Holy Spirit."[24] Children could demonstrate their faith by diligent, voluntary attendance at worship, by obedience to their parents, teachers, and all in authority, and by showing an understanding and respect for the divine law and a fear and shame of sin. Those whose lives and conduct did not reflect these signs of faith were to be "left among the catechumens and educated and grounded in divine learning until they display not so much the works of the flesh as the fruits of the Spirit of regeneration." Individuals who were not confirmed, "if indeed they were born of God," would be aroused by the example of those who had been confirmed earlier and spurred on to a more serious effort to learn the catechism and reflect its contents in their lives.[25]

Bucer did not believe that the resulting distinction between "the undoubted people of God and those who in effect declare that they are not yet of his people" would cause any harm to civil society or the state. God himself had commanded that this distinction be made, and the philosophers also recognized that "the honor due to good men is not accorded to the bad."[26] As in his earlier defenses of discipline in general and the "Christian fellowships" in particular, he condemned those who felt the restoration of this type of discipline would be too difficult or impossible to establish in the present church, "as though no Christians were left today, or as though our Lord Jesus Christ, who has received all power in earth and heaven and always has great love for his own people is now either unwilling or unable to give them the power . . . to observe all the things which he has commanded."[27]

Regarding catechization itself, Bucer recommended that it be held more frequently than every sixth week as the prayer book had prescribed. The catechism should be taught every Sunday and feast day, and Bucer praised the practice of some German churches in which the catechism was taught to children on two weekdays in addition to Sundays.[28] Catechism instruction was not to be limited only to those who were not yet confirmed; all children and young people should be required to attend until the pastor excused them.[29]

---

[24]Whitaker, ed., *Martin Bucer*, 103; cf. the provisions of the prayer book in Joseph Ketley, ed., *The Two Liturgies, A.D 1549, and A.D. 1552: With other Documents set forth by Authority in the Reign of King Edward VI*, The Parker Society (Cambridge: Cambridge University Press, 1844), 120–121.

[25]Whitaker, ed., *Martin Bucer*, 103–105.

[26]Ibid., 107–109.

[27]Ibid., 109–111.

[28]In the Strasbourg schools, one afternoon a week was devoted to catechization and a second afternoon to instruction in "Christian conduct"; Ernst and Adam, *Katechetische Geschichte*, 107–115.

[29]Whitaker, ed., *Martin Bucer*, 111–113.

Only those who had been accepted into the "full communion of Christ" through confirmation would be admitted to the Lord's Supper,[30] but admission to the Lord's Supper was not automatically open to all who had been confirmed. Bucer praised the provisions requiring everyone who desired the sacrament to give their names to the pastor and allowing the pastor to bar from the sacrament those who lived in grave sin or open enmity with others and who would not publicly declare their repentance. Any who took offense at such a requirement or who refused to acknowledge their repentance publicly "lacked the Spirit of Christ" and so were not worthy of the sacrament.[31] He was less pleased with the requirement that everyone receive the sacrament at least once a year. He preferred a "weighty exhortation" to pastors to teach their parishioners to receive the sacrament frequently, making use of both public preaching and private admonition. Those who stubbornly refused to attend the communion service and receive the sacrament despite these admonitions were to be excommunicated.[32]

Bucer also argued for the introduction of penitential discipline, asserting that "if it is our desire that the Lord Jesus should truly reign over us, it will be necessary that the whole discipline of penance and of the correction of sinners should be restored in the churches." Fraternal admonition, the public rebuke of those who had openly sinned, the imposition of penance on any whose sins had especially offended the church, and the excommunication of contumacious sinners were all commanded by God, and God's laws were to be obeyed. Only thus could the English church escape "the intolerable wrath of God which today burns so dreadfully in most miserable Germany, for the neglect of this same discipline."[33]

Bucer felt a personal responsibility for the establishment of Christian discipline in England. As in his Gospels commentary and *Von der Kirchen mengel vnnd fähl*, he acknowledged that "this [discipline] cannot be restored unless everyone, or the far greater part of the church, subjects and commits himself to [it] with the greatest consent." Nevertheless, "the blood and damnation of all those who have fallen into sin, when they could have been kept in their duties by this discipline, and of those who persevere in sin, when they could have been brought to repentance by that discipline, will be required from all those who neglected anything which they could have done for the restoration of such discipline."[34] It is not surprising, then, that one of his stu-

---

[30]Ibid., 107, 115.

[31]Ibid., 17–19; cf. Ketley, *Two Liturgies*, 76.

[32]Whitaker, ed., *Martin Bucer*, 29–33; cf. Ketley, *Two Liturgies*, 98.

[33]Whitaker, ed., *Martin Bucer*, 133–137. This plea for penitential discipline followed Bucer's comments on the summons to repentance read on Ash Wednesday.

[34]*Explicatio Martini Buceri in. . . . Ephesios IIII*, SA 534: "Ita, cum eundem Christum, et Spiritum Christi habeamus, si velimus ipsi, quam multos possemus in officio retinere, qui alioqui in gravissima laberentur peccata: quam multos etiam lapsos in peccata, revocare ad poenitentiam salutarem, si hanc ipsam disciplinam haberemus apud nos legitime restitutam, iuxta illa quae commemoravi, praecepta Domini et Spiritus sancti tam gravia. At restituti ea non potest, nisi omnes, aut multo maior portio Ecclesiae se huic disciplinae summa consensione subijciat et addicat. . . . Interim autem omnium eorum sanguis et perditio qui in peccata prolabuntur, cum possent hac disciplina in officio retineri, et in peccatis perseverant, cum revocari possent ista disciplina ad poenitentiam, quae ab illis requiritur, qui quicquam quod suarum partium sit ad restituendam hanc disciplinam intermittunt."

dents wrote to an acquaintance that "Dr. Bucer complains incessantly, both in daily lectures and in his frequent sermons, that we should repent, give up the depraved customs of hypocritical religion, correct the abuses of feast days, attend as well as give sermons more frequently, that we should be bound to maintain discipline of some kind. He impresses on us many things of this kind even *ad nauseum et fastidium*."[35]

Bucer's discussion of discipline in his English works contained little that was new. His broad definition of the ministry of discipline, including elements of church order such as regular public worship and the hallowing of the Sabbath, accords with what he had earlier written both in his 1543 Catechism and in *Von der Kirchen mengel vnnd fähl*. His argument that children should be confirmed only when their profession of faith could be regarded as genuine paralleled the provisions of both the Hessian and the Cologne ordinances that confirmands understand the catechism rather than simply repeat it by rote memory. He repeated his view that through confirmation, children entered into "the full communion of Christ" and came under the disciplinary authority of the pastors. His conviction that pastoral instruction and admonition were to take place publicly, privately, and at home recalls his description of how the "Christian fellowships" were to operate. The ministry of discipline described in Bucer's last writings was the same system which he had advocated for the churches of Germany and especially for his own church in Strasbourg. He saw no need to alter the elements of Christian discipline to fit the circumstances of the English church. On the contrary, because this system of discipline was commanded by God, its establishment was essential for the restoration of Christ's kingdom on earth.[36] This conviction, combined with his feeling of accountability before God, motivated Bucer to preach and teach the necessity of Christian discipline during his last years in England.

[35]Thomas Horton to Franciscus Dryander, TB 20:180 (May 15, 1550): "Dominus Bucerus clamat non cessans nunc in quotidianis lectionibus, nunc in frequentibus concionibus ut penitentiam agamas, ut depravatas consuetudines hypocriticae relligionis abjiciamus, ut abusus festorum corrigamus, ut crebriores in concionibus cum audiendis tum habendis simus, ut disciplinae alicui nos astringamus, hujusmodi multa inculcat nobis etiam ad nauseam et fastidium."

[36]Whitaker, ed., *Martin Bucer*, 135; BOL 15:92–93, 294. Greschat discusses Bucer's conviction that Scripture, and especially the Old Testament, contained laws which were still normative for the church, *Martin Bucer*, 248–249.

10

Conclusion

Bucer's system of Christian discipline evolved along with other elements of his theology. During the 1520s Bucer was particularly vehement in his criticism of the penitential and disciplinary system of the Catholic church. His early works stressed the Christian's freedom from man-made laws, the internal working of the Holy Spirit, and the spiritual nature of the church. Thus he argued that confession could not be compelled and that the power of the keys consisted simply of the word and Spirit working together without regard for any institutional structure. Individual meetings with a priest or pious layman were valuable for counsel and private instruction, especially for those with troubled consciences, but for such meetings to be of any use, the confessor had to be a wise and pious man of proven moral character. In any case, the words of absolution themselves had no intrinsic power to assure sinners of their forgiveness. Although Bucer recognized that some form of church discipline was desirable, he believed that the time was not yet ripe for its establishment. However, he was optimistic that eventually the preaching of the gospel would create a more favorable situation for the exercise of discipline. Such discipline applied only to those within the church, but Bucer defined church membership broadly. Anyone who called himself a Christian was a potential subject for discipline. The most important element of discipline was fraternal admonition, to be repeated as often as there was hope it would bear fruit, but those who contumaciously refused to heed admonition were to be excommunicated.

Many of the features of discipline which Bucer endorsed in the 1520s remained constant throughout his career, but there were also significant developments within the system which had appeared by the mid-1530s. These developments reflect the growing importance which Bucer accorded to the visible, institutional church and its ministers. Working out the implications of his earlier statements, he now explicitly taught that the power of the keys, given to the whole church but exercised by its ministers, regulated admission to the church—originally through baptism, but also through the imposition and lifting of penance and/or excommunication. While he still upheld the voluntary nature of private confession, he was much more forceful in urging its practice, and he defended the mandatory precommunion examination practiced by the Lutherans. On the other hand, his concern for Christian freedom and his sensitivity to charges that it was a means of reintroducing "clerical tyranny" prevented him from instituting such an examination in Strasbourg. Instead, he advocated mandatory attendance at catechism services and supported the pastor's right to exam-ine children before they were admitted to the Lord's Supper for the first time. In ad-dition to this and in order to counter Anabaptist critics, he also suggested a public confirmation ceremony in which those baptized as infants could make their own con-fession of faith. With regard to church discipline proper, he outlined a procedure which involved all Christians but was the particular responsibility of both pastors and lay elders. The disciplinary process began with repeated private admonition and even-tually led to excommunication if the sinner remained contumacious. Excommunica-tion itself resulted in exclusion from all church activities accompanied by some degree of shunning by the faithful, but because the sentence of excommunication was not to be publicly proclaimed, its social consequences were limited. Repentant excommuni-cates, as well as those guilty of grave sin, were to perform some form of penance be-fore they could be readmitted to the full fellowship of the church.

During the second half of the 1530s Bucer continued to refine this disciplinary system, emphasizing two aspects—the use of penitential discipline and the expansion of the public confirmation ceremony to include not only a confession of faith but also a profession of obedience to the church and its ministers. Both acts were given a qua-si-sacramental character through the symbol of the imposition of hands. Chiefly on the basis of passages from the Old Testament, Bucer argued that the public profes-sion of faith and obedience and the imposition of penance for grave sin were required by God. His defense of Christian discipline as something divinely commanded be-came even more strident over the course of the 1540s: what God had willed for his people in the Old Testament, what Christ had commanded in the New Testament, and what the apostles and fathers had established for the early church was to be re-established in the Protestant churches, and the disasters which befell the evangelical estates over the course of the 1540s were due to their neglect of discipline. In his writ-ings on Christian discipline from the later 1540s, he referred constantly to Christ's charge to his disciples, and thus to all his ministers, in Matt. 8:19-20: they were not only to baptize all nations but also to teach the baptized to obey all that Christ had commanded. Bucer's system of Christian discipline was intended to foster such obe-dience to God's commands.

Bucer consciously modeled his system of discipline after the practices of the early church. Although his esteem for the fathers reached back to the 1530s, it was particu-larly as a consequence of his involvement in the religious colloquies and the attempted reformation of Cologne, including the polemical exchange with Johannes Gropper which resulted from the latter, that Bucer became more specific and detailed in incor-porating patristic practices into his own system. His use of the early church model was selective, however, and weighted towards practices from the third and fourth cen-turies. He never entertained the idea that public penance could be performed only once or that it resulted in lifelong debilities. In the Hessian church, which had a more hierarchical structure than did the church of Strasbourg, he reserved the authority to excommunicate to the highest ecclesiastical official, but he always held that individual pastors, acting in the stead of the church, had the right to impose and absolve from public penance. In his last years he argued uncompromisingly for the reintroduction of public penance, but at the same time he recognized, somewhat reluctantly, that not all of the patristic practices could be reestablished in the present-day church. Thus although he wished that those excluded from the sacrament, the "catechumens" as he called them, would leave the church before the beginning of the communion liturgy, he did not insist that pastors expel such individuals.

Bucer's understanding of confirmation and the catechumenate was the most idiosyncratic part of his system of Christian discipline. From very early in his career Bucer distinguished between catechumens and full members of the church, but his ideas on the subject became more sharply defined over time. During the 1530s he repeatedly described those who voluntarily abstained from the Lord's Supper but were not guilty of grave sin or impiety as catechumens. This classification may have been suggested by the fact that catechumens and those undergoing public penance, and thus excluded from the sacrament, had a similar status in the early church. As Bucer further developed his ideas on confirmation, he also regarded those baptized as infants but not yet confirmed as a special category of catechumens. Catechumens in the early church by definition were not yet baptized, and so, given Bucer's defense of infant baptism, there could be no exact re-creation of the catechumenate in the Strasbourg church. However, Bucer's interpretation of the imposition of hands provided the basis for a new definition of catechumen. Although not a sacrament itself, the imposition of hands was a visible sign which indicated the individual's acceptance into the full communion of the church, whether through confirmation or through the reconciliation of penitents.[1] The Anabaptists argued that Christ laid his hands on children and required a profession of faith from adults; Bucer reversed the order, placing baptism, the sacrament of rebirth, first and joining the profession of faith with the imposition of hands in a public confirmation ceremony.

The confirmand's confession of faith and the imposition of hands were integral parts of the confirmation ceremony, but from the practical standpoint of Christian discipline the most important element was the confirmand's profession of obedience to the church and its ministers. Bucer believed that the clergy had no authority beyond the word and the Spirit, but his experience in Strasbourg forced him to acknowledge that if the ministers had no means of coercion, they would be largely ignored by many of their parishioners and therefore unable to carry out their pastoral responsibilities. Bucer's answer to this dilemma was to have the laity voluntarily agree to heed the pastor's coercive authority in a public ceremony. Ideally he would have required that all children in Strasbourg be catechized and then confirmed, but judging from the lack of any explicit mention of confirmation in Strasbourg during the 1540s, he was unable to do more than establish the ceremony on an unofficial and probably irregular basis. The Protestants' rapidly deteriorating political situation during the later

---

[1]Hammann has described the imposition of hands in confirmation as "a sacramental act of the universal priesthood," which parallels its use in ordination as "a sacramental act of specific ministries," *Entre la Secte*, 255, 257–258; cf. his discussion of confirmation, 297–303.

1540s convinced Bucer that something more had to be done to institute Christian discipline and thereby divert God's impending judgment. In this situation he proposed that the formal public profession of obedience made by confirmands be encouraged among Strasbourg's adult inhabitants as well. Once an individual had made the public profession of obedience and been enrolled in a parish "fellowship," he was subject to the coercive authority of the pastor.

Bucer regarded this public profession of obedience as binding and drew parallels between it and the oaths taken by new guild members or by the citizens of a city. Whether made by confirmands or by adults agreeing to enter a parish "fellowship," it was regarded as the point at which an individual became a full member of the church. It should be pointed out, however, that Bucer's distinction between catechumen and full member was not identical with his dualist ecclesiology encompassing both a "multitudinous" church and a professing church, if the latter is equated with the elect. Hammann has stated that Bucer's goal in the exercise of discipline "was not to make of the entire multitude a 'true' community of election . . . but to permit each person to progress towards the holiness of the elect, since the discernment [of the elect] could not be made with certainty."[2] Bucer acknowledged—and implicitly approved of—the fact that children might be confirmed and individuals enrolled in a parish "fellowship" due to social pressure rather than out of genuine willingness to submit to the pastors' disciplinary authority. However, he believed that the church needed some means of encouraging to greater commitment those still unwilling or unready to accept the "full yoke" of Christian discipline. Just as Bucer accepted the magistrate's right to enforce outward conformity in religion,[3] so he also accepted the more indirect compulsion of social pressure as a valid means of leading individuals to submit to Christian discipline.

Bucer was fairly knowledgeable about the complex developments which had resulted in the late medieval penitential and disciplinary system, but he did not see the sharp break between the virtual disappearance of public penance in late antiquity and its gradual replacement by tariff penance. He was extremely critical of tariff penance, which had evolved into the Catholic sacrament, arguing that one could not set fixed penalties for specific sins and rejecting the idea that penance of any kind could satisfy God for sins committed. On the other hand, his appreciation for private confession increased as he saw that it was so highly recommended by many of the church fathers. Bucer's respect for the fathers contrasted with his occasional references to medieval theologians. While he cited patristic writings and practice as authoritative,[4] he used medieval authorities polemically, sometimes citing them out of context or incompletely

---

[2]Ibid., 236–237.

[3]Cf. de Kroon, *Studien*, 8–23, on Bucer's debate with Anton Engelbrecht concerning the role of the magistrate in religion as set forth in the last three of the 16 Articles adopted by the 1533 Synod.

[4]Hammann discusses the ambiguity in Bucer's use of the early church; in some of his writings, the early church functioned only as an example, in others he cited it as normative for Christan belief, *Entre la Secte*, 414–416.

in order to strengthen his own arguments. Bucer clearly rejected the developments in scholastic theology and canon law with regard to the power of the keys, confession, satisfaction and excommunication, and his own system of discipline, defined around the power of the keys, was an effort to recombine the penitential and disciplinary aspects of that power.

Perhaps the most misunderstood part of Bucer's system of discipline is his view of excommunication. Excommunication was to be imposed only after all other means to bring the sinner to repentance had been exhausted. Bucer's division between catechumens and full members of the church meant that excommunication would be necessary only under extreme circumstances. Sinners might drop from the level of full membership to the level of catechumen and be kept from receiving the sacrament, but they would not be fully excluded from the church unless they obstinately refused to heed multiple admonitions. Once the sinner had repented and performed some form of penance, he would be restored to full communion with the church through the minister's absolution and the imposition of hands. In most cases, admonition and the threat of public penance would lead the sinner to repent before excommunication became necessary. Bucer followed Thomas Aquinas and canon law in stating that contumacy was the only grounds for excommunication, and he was cautious in his definition of contumacy: sinners were admonished repeatedly at each stage of the disciplinary process, and as long as there was any hope of reform there was no need to move to the next stage of discipline. Nevertheless, despite his reluctance to see excommunication imposed, Bucer did regard it as essential for the church.

Excommunication was always to be imposed by the proper church authorities. Unlike the penalty of *excommunicatio latae sententiae* in canon law, it could not be automatically incurred. Even when an individual had separated from the church by refusing to attend worship or receive the sacraments, he was not considered excommunicated until or unless he refused to heed admonition to repent. In the face of such contumacy, however, the sinner was to be "handed over to divine judgment" by the leaders of the church and ostracized by the faithful. By the mid-1530s Bucer was quite explicit in arguing that private individuals had no right to "excommunicate" another by avoiding him or her, and he opposed the practice of Anabaptists whose rejection of the official church was interpreted as this type of private imposition of the ban.

Ostracism was an important consequence of excommunication, but it was not to be taken to the extremes required by canon law or practiced by the Anabaptists. Bucer obviously rejected the requirement that those who maintained contact with an excommunicated person were themselves to be excluded from the sacraments. On several different occasions Bucer tried to specify the degree of ostracism to which excommunicates were subject, but it was difficult for him to prescribe exact limits. Moreover, ostracism was to be practiced only by those who had "submitted themselves to Christ," the full members of the church. Because there were many who had not yet made this submission, whether informally through their own devotion or publicly through a confirmation ceremony, the sentence of excommunication was not to be publicly pronounced. As Bucer stated in the Hessian disciplinary ordinance, news of the excommunication would spread quickly enough among the godly; they were the ones responsible for applying the social pressure of ostracism.

Those who were excommunicated had no right to participate in the religious life of the church; in this sense Bucer's understanding of excommunication matched the definition of major excommunication in canon law. Moreover, Bucer believed that civil penalties were to be applied to contumacious excommunicates, but the determination and imposition of these penalties was the responsibility of the magistrate, not of the church. Bucer did not regard the imposition of civil punishment in addition to church discipline as a form of "double jeopardy," punishment twice for the same offense, because the purposes of civil and ecclesiastical discipline differed.[5]

The significance of Bucer's system of Christian discipline can perhaps best be understood when it is compared with similar efforts by later churchmen to indoctrinate and discipline the laity. Wolfgang Reinhard has listed several methods common to Catholics, Lutherans, and Reformed in shaping confessional identity: the formulation of clear theological principles, the establishment and diffusion of new religious norms and the use of education to internalize those norms, the control of the press to produce religious propaganda and limit counterpropaganda, reliance on church discipline to eliminate dissent, and the use of rituals and language to encourage solidarity and a sense of group identification.[6] To a greater or lesser extent many of these elements were present in Bucer's system of Christian discipline. Religious instruction and a carefully defined procedure for church discipline proper were central to the system. The *Tetrapolitan Confession* and the 16 Articles were adopted as Strasbourg's official creed at the 1533 synod; confirmands and those enrolling in a parish "fellowship" were expected to know and understand the basic tenets of their faith as contained in the catechism and the city's official creed. Bucer turned out a steady stream of "propaganda," ranging from his catechisms for children to his lengthy treatise on pastoral care, intended to persuade magistrates and people of the necessity for Christian discipline. He supported the use of ceremonies such as the Saturday evening preparatory service before communion and the precommunion examination which were standard in many Lutheran churches. He attempted to reshape the practice of godparentage to bring it more into line with his understanding of a godparent's function. His most noteworthy use of ritual was the introduction of an evangelical

---

[5]Heinz Schilling emphasizes that both Catholics and Protestants recognized a specifically theological and pastoral aspect of church discipline which resulted in a qualitative difference between ecclesiastical and secular punishment, "Sündenzucht und frühneuzeitliche Sozialdisziplinierung. Die Calvinistische Presbyteriale Kirchenzucht in Emden vom 16. bis 19. Jahrhundert," in *Stände und Gesellschaft im Alten Reich*, ed. Georg Schmidt (Stuttgart: Franz Steiner, 1989), 266; at greater length, "'History of Crime' or 'History of Sin'? Some Reflections on the Social History of Early Modern Church Discipline," in *Politics and Society in Reformation Europe. Essays for Sir Geoffrey Elton on his Sixty-Fifth Birthday*, ed. E.I. Kouri and Tom Scott (London: Macmillan, 1989), 289–310.

[6]Reinhard, "Konfession und Konfessionalisierung in Europe," in idem, ed., *Bekenntnis und Geschichte. Die Confessio Augustana im historischen Zusammenhang* (Munich: Vögel, 1981), 179–188; idem, "Zwang zur Konfessionalisierung? Prolegomena zu einer Theorie des konfessionellen Zeitalters," *Zeitschrift für historische Forschung* 10/3 (1983): 263–268.

confirmation ceremony and the formal enrollment in a parish "fellowship," both of which involved a confession of faith and the promise to submit to the authority of pastors and lay elders. Bucer's system of discipline thus foreshadows many of the methods later used by the confessional churches to shape the religious identity of the laity.

There is an important difference, however, between Bucer and his successors. In a period when the boundaries between confessions were still rather murky and poorly defined, Bucer did not foresee the division of Europe into confessional churches but hoped for a reform of the entire church through the proper use of religious instruction and moral oversight. Doctrinal disagreement and improper conduct would be eliminated by the proper functioning of the entire system of Christian discipline towards all members of the church. While he believed that agreement on certain essential doctrines was necessary, Bucer did not want to define orthodoxy so rigidly that many would be excluded from the church and thus not subject to its discipline and pastoral care.

Reinhard has pointed out that confessionalization occurred together with the formation of the early modern state, and that confessional and political identity went hand in hand.[7] Methods which indoctrinated the laity to accept religious authority were used to teach acceptance of political authority as well. The Strasbourg city council, however, could not make use of Bucer's system of Christian discipline to strengthen its own control over the city because of Bucer's argument that the church and state were two separate and parallel institutions, each with its own sphere of responsibility. Discipline was the responsibility of the church and its ministers, and the magistrate had only a supervisory responsibility over the clergy. Perhaps more realistically than Bucer, the Strasbourg council believed that one must always dominate the other, and it had no desire to give the clergy an opportunity to dictate to the magistrate. The council always regarded Bucer's proposals for pastoral oversight and admonition as attempts by the ministers to usurp secular authority, "to grasp at the sword." Having finally succeeded in winning control of the church after the break with Rome, it was by no means ready to give the Protestant clergy any opportunity to set themselves up as an independent authority. Although it was willing to accept some of Bucer's proposals for discipline, the magistrate refused to loosen its control over the city's church. It did not oppose the pastors' efforts to indoctrinate and discipline the laity as long as the clergy remained clearly subordinate to the magistrate, but it would not tolerate any attempts by the clergy to take the initiative themselves.

For their part, the laity were unwilling to submit to anything which looked to them like a "new papacy." Despite Bucer's arguments that his system of instruction, oversight, and discipline was intended for the betterment of the individual Christian,

---

[7]Reinhard, "Konfession," 188; Heinz Schilling in particular has stressed the political consequences of confessionalization, *Konfessionskonflikt und Staatsbildung. Eine Fallstudie über das Verhältnis von religiösem und sozialem Wandel in der Frühneuzeit am Beispiel der Grafschaft Lippe*, Quellen und Forschungen zur Reformationsgeschichte 48 (Gütersloh: Gerd Mohn, 1981), 365-391.

the laity remained skeptical. They perceived the pastors' efforts only as another attempt to reestablish clerical control. Furthermore, they did not necessarily agree with the pastors' new definitions of right and wrong or of proper and improper conduct.[8] Bucer had little sympathy for the laity's fear that clerical domination might be restored. He saw that fear more as an excuse to lead a "godless, Epicurean life" than as a genuine concern for Christian freedom.

Bucer championed the cause of Christian discipline and pastoral care over the course of his long career as a reformer, first in Strasbourg and then as an exile in England. During that time he never wavered in his criticism of the Catholic church, which he characterized as full of abuses and perversions. He believed that the medieval church had burdened the laity with a penitential and disciplinary system distorted by rules and regulations foreign to the message of the gospel. He wanted to replace the heavy burden of this "papal yoke" with a system of religious instruction and moral supervision which would strengthen the church through pastoral care for each of its members. The ministers of the church had the responsibility before God to see that his people both knew and lived in accordance with the basic tenets of their faith. This was the guiding principle behind Bucer's system of Christian discipline and pastoral care, what he termed "the yoke of Christ." His ultimate inability to see this system fully established was due not to lack of effort on his part, but rather to the failure of both magistrate and laity to see much difference between "the papal yoke" of the Catholics and the "yoke of Christ" as Bucer defined it.

[8]Abray makes this argument for the course of the sixteenth century, *The People's Reformation*, 186–208.

Bibliography

Published Primary Sources

Arbenz, Emil, and Hermann Wartmann, eds. *Vadianische Briefsammlung, 1508–1540.* Mitteilungen zur Vaterländischen Geschichte 24–30a. St. Gallen: Fehr, 1884–1913.

Die Bekenntnisschriften der evangelisch-lutherischen Kirchen. 9th ed. Göttingen: Vandenhoek & Ruprecht, 1982.

[Billick, Eberhard.] *Urteil der Universitet und Clerisie zu Cölne von Martin Bucers Lerung und ruffung gen Bonn, uß Latynischer sprach trewlich verteutsch.* . . . [Cologne: Jaspar von Gennep], 1543.

Bucer, Martin. *Alle Handlungen vnd Schrifften, zu vergleichung der Religion . . . zu Regensburg verhandlet.* . . . [Strasbourg: Wendel Rihel, (1541)]. Stupperich no. 69c.

——. *Die ander verteydigung vnd erklerung der Christlichen Lehr.* . . . Bonn: Laurentius von der Mülen, 1543. Stupperich no. 76.

——. *Bestendige Verantwortung, auß der Heiligen Schrifft.* . . . [Bonn: Laurentius von der Mülen], 1545. Stupperich no. 86.

——. *Ein Christlich ongefährlich bedencken, Wie ein leidlicher anefang Christlicher vergleichung in der Religion zu machen sein möchte.* . . . [Strasbourg: Wendelin Rihel], 1545. Stupperich no. 79.

——. *Common Places of Martin Bucer.* Ed. and trans. D. F. Wright. The Courtenay Library of Reformation Classics 4. Appleford, England: Sutton Courtenay Press, 1972.

——. *Defensio adversus axioma catholicum.* . . . [Strasbourg: Mathias Apiarius, 1534]. Stupperich no. 45.

——. *Enarrationes perpetvae in sacra qvatvor evangelia, recognitae nuper & locis compluribus auctae.* . . . [Strasbourg: Georgivs Vlrichervs Andlanvs, 1530]. Stupperich no. 28.

——. *Enarrationvm in evangelia Mattaei, Marci, & Lucae, libri duo.* . . . 2 vols. Strasbourg: [Johannes Herwagen], 1527. Stupperich no. 14.

——. *Martin Bucer and the Book of Common Prayer.* Ed. and trans. E. C. Whitaker. Alcuin Club Collections 55. Great Wakering: Mayhew-McCrimmon, 1974.

——. *Der newe glaub, von den Doctoren zu Löuen.* . . . [Strasbourg: Wendel Rihel,] 1545. Stupperich no. 82.

——. *Opera Omnia.* Series I. *Deutsche Schriften.* Series II: *Opera Latina.* Series III. *Correspondance de Martin Bucer.* Gütersloh/ Paris/Leiden: Mohn/Presses Universitaires/Brill, 1955–.

——. *Qvid de baptismate infantivm ivxta scripturas Dei sentiendum.* . . . Strasbourg: [Mathias Apiarius], 1533. Stupperich no. 42.

——. *De Regno Christi.* In *Melanchthon and Bucer,* ed. and trans., Wilhelm Pauck, 155–394. Library of Christian Classics 19. Philadelphia: Westminster, 1969.

——. *In sacra qvatvor evangelia, Enarrationes perpetvae, secvndvm recognitae, in qvibus praeterea habes syncerioris Theologiae locos communes.* . . . Basel: Ioannes Hervagivs, 1536. Stupperich no. 28a.

———. *Sacrorvm Psalmorvm libri qvinqve.* . . . [Strasbourg: Georgius Vlricherus Andlanus, 1532]. Stupperich no. 25b.

———. *Scripta Anglicana fere omnia . . . collecta.* . . . Basel: Petrus Perna, 1577. Stupperich no. 115.

———. *Was im namen des Heiligen Euangeli . . . gelehret vnnd geprediget würdt.* . . . Marburg: Herman Bastian, [1543]. Stupperich no. 75.

———. *Wider vffrichtung der Messen, anderer Sacramenten vnd Ceremonien, Vnd des Papstumbs.* Strasbourg: Georg Messerschmidt, 1545. Stupperich no. 87.

———. *Wie leicht vnnd füglich Christliche vergleichung der Religion, vnd des gantzen kirchendiensts Reformation, bey vnß Teutschen zu finden.* . . . [Strasbourg: Crafft Müller], 1545. Stupperich no. 84.

Calvin, Jean. *Iohannis Calvini opera quae supersunt omnia.* Edited by W. Baum, E. Cunitz, and R. Reuss. Corpus Reformatorum 29-87. Braunschweig: Schwetschke, 1863-1900.

Egli, Emil, ed. *Aktensammlung zur Geschichte der Zürcher Reformation in den Jahren 1519-1533.* Zürich: J. Schabelitz, 1879; repr.: Nieuwkoop: B. de Graaf, 1973.

Erasmus, Desiderius. *Opera Omnia.* Ed. Joannes Clericus. Leiden, 1703-1706; repr. London: Gregg, 1962.

Fast, Heinold, ed. *Quellen zur Geschichte der Täufer in der Schweiz.* Vol. 2: *Ostschweiz.* Zürich: Theologischer Verlag, 1973.

Fragments des anciennes chroniques d'Alsace. Mittheilungen der Gesellschaft für Erhaltung der geschichtlichen Denkmäler im Elsass, II. Reihe 13-15, 17-19, 22-23. Strasbourg: R. Schultz, 1888-1911.

Franz, Günther, ed. *Urkundliche Quellen zur Reformationsgeschichte Hessens.* Vol. 4: *Wiedertäuferakten, 1527-1626.* Veröffentlichungen der historischen Kommission für Hessen und Waldeck XI/4. Marburg: N.G. Elwert, 1951.

Friedberg, Emil, ed. *Corpus Iuris Canonici.* 2 vols. 2nd ed. Leipzig: Tauchnitz, 1879-1881.

Gratian. *Decretum divi Gratiani; totius propemodum ivris canonici compendium, summorumque pontificum decreta atque praeiudicia, vna cum variis scribentium glossis et expositionibus; quae omnia pristino suo nitori restituta fuerunt ad fidem veterum codicum.* Lugduni (Lyon): Sennetonios Fratres, 1555.

Gropper, Johannes. *Christliche vnd Catholische gegenberichtung eyns Erwirdigen Dhomkapittels zu Cöllen wider das Buch der gnannter Reformation, so Stenden des Erzstiffts Cöllen vff jungstem Landtag zu Bonn vorgehalten Vnd nun vnder dem Tittel eyns Bedenckens im Trück (doch mit allerley zusätzen vnd veränderungen) vßgangen ist.* Cologne: Grennep, 1544.

Hermann von Wied. *Einfältiges Bedenken. Reformationsentwurf für das Erzstift Köln von 1543.* Trans. and ed. Helmut Gerhards and Wilfried Borth. Schriftenreihe des Vereins für Rheinische Kirchengeschichte 43. Düsseldorf: Presseverband der evangelischen Kirche im Rheinland, 1972.

Herminjard, Aimé-Louis. *Correspondance des réformateurs dans les pays de langue française recueillie et publiée avec d'autres lettres relatives à la Réforme et des notes historiques et biographiques.* 9 vols. Geneva: H. Georg, 1864-1887; repr. Nieuwkoop: B. de Graaf, 1965.

Hubert, Friedrich, ed. *Die Straßburger liturgischen Ordnungen im Zeitalter der Reformation nebst einer Bibliographie der Straßburger Gesangbücher.* Göttingen: Vandenhoeck & Ruprecht, 1900.

Ketley, Joseph, ed. *The Two Liturgies, A.D. 1549, and A.D. 1552; with other Documents set forth by Authority in the Reign of King Edward VI.* The Parker Society. Cambridge: Cambridge University Press, 1844.

Krebs, Manfred, Hans Georg Rott, et al., ed. *Quellen zur Geschichte der Täufer. Elsaß I.-IV. Teil. Stadt Straßburg.* 4 vols. Quellen und Forschungen zur Reformationsgeschichte 26-27, 53-54. Gütersloh: Gerd Mohn, 1959-1988.

Lenz, Max, ed. *Briefwechsel Landgraf Philipp's des Großmüthigen von Hessen mit Bucer.* 3 vols. Publikationen aus den königlichen preussischen Staatsarchiven 5, 28, 47. Leipzig: Hirzel, 1880-1891.

Lombard, Peter. *Sententiae in IV Libris Distinctae.* 3 vols. 3d ed. Spicilegium Bonaventurianum, 4-5. Grottaferrata (Rome): Collegium S. Bonaventurae ad Claras Aquas, 1971-1981.

Luther, Martin. *Werke. Kritische Gesamtausgabe.* Weimar: Böhlau, 1883-1983.

Niccolò de Tudeschi (Panormitanus). *Abbatis Panormitani Commentaria in quartum et quintum Decretalium Libros. Quamplurium Iurisconsultorum, qui probe hucusque aliquid ijs addidisse apparuerunt, et nunc demum Alexandri de Neuo Adnotationibus illustrata. Tomus septimus.* Venice, 1591.

Melanchthon, Philip. *Opera quae supersunt omnia.* Ed. Karl Bretschneider and H. Bindseil. Corpus Reformatorum 1-28. Halle/Braunschweig: Schwetschke, 1834-1860.

Migne, J. P., ed. *Patrologiae Cursus Completus. Series Graeca.* Paris, 1857-1936.

——. *Patrologiae Cursus Completus. Series Latina.* Paris, 1844-1864.

Oecolampadius, Johannes. *Elleboron pro Iacobo Latomo.* Basel: Andreas Cratander, 1525.

——. *Quod non sit onerosa Christianis confessio, paradoxon.* Augsburg: Sigismund Grimm, 1521.

Peter Lombard. See Lombard, Peter.

Pfeilschifter, Georg, ed. *Acta Reformationis catholicae ecclesiam Germaniae concernantia saeculi XVI. Die Reformverhandlungen des deutschen Episkopats von 1520 bis 1570.* 6 vols. Regensburg: Pustet, 1959-1974.

Politische Correspondenz der Stadt Straßburg im Zeitalter der Reformation. 5 vols. in 6. Urkunden und Akten der Stadt Straßburg, Abth. 2. Strasbourg/Heidelberg: Trübner/Carl Winter, 1882-1933.

Reu, Johann Michael, ed. *Quellen zur Geschichte des kirchlichen Unterrichts in der evangelischen Kirche Deutschlands zwischen 1530 und 1600. Teil I: Quellen zur Geschichte des Katechismus-Unterrichts.* Vol. I: *Süddeutsche Katechismen.* Gütersloh: Bertelsmann, 1904; repr.: Hildesheim: Georg Olms, 1976.

Richter, Aemilius Ludwig, ed. *Die evangelische Kirchenordnungen des 16. Jahrhunderts. Urkunden und Regesten zur Geschichte des Rechts und der Verfassung der evangelischen Kirche.* 2 vols. Weimar: Landes-Industriecomtoir, 1846; repr.: Nieuwkoop: B. de Graaf, 1967.

Robinson, Hastings, ed. *Original Letters Relative to the English Reformation written during the Reigns of King Henry VIII., King Edward VI., and Queen Mary: chiefly from the Archives of Zurich.* Second Portion. The Parker Society. Cambridge: Cambridge University Press, 1847.

Röhrich, Timotheus Wilhelm. *Mittheilungen aus der Geschichte der evangelische Kirche des Elsaß.* 3 vols. Strasbourg: Treuttel & Würz, 1855.

Roth, Paul, and Emil Dürr, eds. *Aktensammlung zur Geschichte der Basler Reformation in den Jahren 1519 bis Anfang 1534.* 6 vols. Basel: Historische und Antiquarische Gesellschaft, 1921-1950.

Schieß, Traugott, ed. *Briefwechsel der Brüder Ambrosius und Thomas Blaurer 1509-1548.* 3 vols. Freiburg i.Br.: Fehsenfeld, 1908-1912.

Sehling, Emil, ed. *Die evangelischen Kirchenordnungen des XVI. Jahrhunderts.* Leipzig/Tübingen: Reisland/J.C.B. Mohr, 1902-.

Staehelin, Ernst, ed. *Briefe und Akten zum Leben Oekolampads, zum vierhundertjährigen Jubiläum der Basler Reformation.* 2 vols. Quellen und Forschungen zur Reformationsgeschichte 10, 19. Leipzig: M. Heinsius, 1927-1934.

Stupperich, Robert, ed. *Die Schriften der Münsterischen Täufer und ihrer Gegner. Teil I: Die Schriften Bernhard Rothmanns.* Veröffentlichungen der historischen Kommission Westfalens 32. Münster: Aschendorff, 1970.

Thomas Aquinas. *Summa Theologiae*. Cura et studio Instituti studiorum medievalium Ottaviensis, ad textum S. Pii pp. V iussu confectum recognita. Ottawa: Studium generalis O.P., 1941.

Zwingli, Huldreich. *Huldreich Zwinglis samtliche Werke*. Ed. Emil Egli et al. Corpus Reformatorum 88–. Berlin/Leipzig/Zürich: Schwetschke/Heinsius/Theologischer Verlag, 1905–.

Published Secondary Works

Abray, Lorna Jane. *The People's Reformation: Magistrates, Clergy and Commons in Strasbourg, 1500–1598*. Ithaca, N.Y.: Cornell University Press, 1985.

Adam, Johann. *Evangelische Kirchengeschichte der Stadt Straßburg bis zur Französischen Revolution*. Strasbourg: Heitz, 1922.

Aland, Kurt. "Die Privatbeichte im Luthertum von ihren Anfängen bis zu ihrer Auflösung." In idem, *Kirchengeschichtliche Entwürfe. Alte Kirche, Reformation und Luthertum, Pietismus und Erweckungsbewegung*, 452–522. Gütersloh: Gerd Mohn, 1960.

Anrich, Gustav. "Ein Bedacht Bucers über die Einrichtung von 'christlichen Gemeinschaften'." *Archiv für Reformationsgeschichte Ergänzungsband 5. Festschrift für Hans von Schubert zu seinem 70. Geburtstag* (1929):46–70.

———. "Die Ulmer Kirchenordnung von 1531." *Blätter für württembergische Kirchengeschichte* 35 (1931):95–107.

Augustijn, Cornelis. *De godsdienstgesprekken tussen rooms-katholieken en protestanten van 1538–1541*. Haarlem: F. Bohn, 1967.

———. "Die Religionsgespräche der vierziger Jahre," in *Die Religionsgespräche der Reformationszeit*, ed. Gerhard Müller, 43–54. Schriften des Vereins für Reformationsgeschichte 191. Gütersloh: Gerd Mohn, 1980.

Backus, Irena. "Polemic, Exegetical Tradition and Ontology. Bucer's Interpretation of John 6:52, 53 and 64 Before and After the Wittenberg Concord." In *The Bible in the Sixteenth Century*, ed. David C. Steinmetz, 167–180. Duke Monographs in Medieval and Renaissance Studies 11. Durham, N.C.: Duke University Press, 1990.

Barth, Medard. "Beicht und Kommunionen im mittelalterlichen Elsass; ein Durchblick." *Freiburger Diözesanarchiv* 74 (1954):88–99.

Bellardi, Werner. "Ein Bedacht Hedios zur Kirchenzucht in Straßburg aus dem Jahre 1547." In *Bucer und seine Zeit. Forschungsbeiträge und Bibliographie*, ed. Marijn de Kroon and Friedhelm Krüger, 117–132. Veröffentlichungen des Instituts für europäische Geschichte Mainz 80. Wiesbaden: Steiner, 1976.

———. "Bucer und das Interim." In *Horizons Européens de la Réforme en Alsace. Das Elsaß und die Reformation im Europa des XVI. Jahrhunderts. Aufsätze zum 65. Geburtstag von Jean Rott*, ed. Marijn de Kroon and Marc Lienhard, 267–294. Société Savante d'Alsace et des Régions de l'Est, Collection "Grandes Publications" 17. Strasbourg: Istra, 1980.

———. *Die Geschichte der "christlichen Gemeinschaft" in Straßburg. Der Versuch einer "zweiten Reformation."* Quellen und Forschungen zur Reformationsgeschichte 18. Leipzig: Heinsius, 1934.

———. *Wolfgang Schultheiss. Wege und Wandlungen eines Straßburger Spiritualisten und Zeitgenossen Martin Bucers*. Schriften der Erwin von Steinbach-Stiftung 5. Frankfurt a.M.: Erwin von Steinbach-Stiftung, 1976.

Bériou, Nicole. "Autour de Latran IV (1215): la naissance de la confession moderne et sa diffusion." In *Pratiques de la Confession des Pères du désert à Vatican II. Quinze études d'histoire*, Groupe de la Bussière, 73–92. Paris: Cerf, 1983.

Bizer, Ernst. *Studien zur Geschichte des Abendmahlsstreits im 16. Jahrhundert.* Beiträge zur Förderung christlicher Theologie, 2. Reihe, Sammlung wissenschaftlicher Monographien, 46. Gütersloh: C. Bertelsmann, 1940.

Bornert, René, O.S.B. *La Réforme Protestante du Culte à Strasbourg au XVIe siècle (1523–1598). Approche sociologique et interprétation théologique.* Studies in Medieval and Reformation Thought 28. Leiden: E.J. Brill, 1981.

Bossy, John. "Moral Arithmetic: Seven Sins into Ten Commandments." In *Conscience and Casuistry in Early Modern Europe,* ed. Edmund Leites, 214–234. Ideas in Context. Cambridge: Cambridge University Press, 1988.

Boyle, Leonard E. "The Summa for Confessors as a Genre, and its Religious Intent." In *The Pursuit of Holiness in Late Medieval and Renaissance Religion,* ed. Charles Trinkaus and Heiko A. Oberman, 126–130. Studies in Medieval and Reformation Thought 10. Leiden: E.J. Brill, 1974.

Brady, Thomas A., Jr. *Ruling Class, Regime and Reformation at Strasbourg 1520–1555.* Studies in Medieval and Reformation Thought 22. Leiden: E.J. Brill, 1978.

Browe, Peter. "Der Beichtunterricht im Mittelalter." *Theologie und Glaube* 26 (1934):437–442.

———. "Die Kommunionvorbereitung im Mittelalter." *Zeitschrift für katholische Theologie* 56 (1932):375–415.

———. "Die Pflichtbeichte im Mittelalter." *Zeitschrift für katholische Theologie* 57 (1933):335–383.

Burnett, Amy Nelson. "Church Discipline and Moral Reformation in the Thought of Martin Bucer." *Sixteenth Century Journal* 22 (1991):439–456.

———. "Martin Bucer and the Anabaptist Context of Evangelical Confirmation." *Mennonite Quarterly Review* 68 (1994):95–122.

Cameron, Euan. "The 'Godly Community' in the Theory and Practice of the European Reformation." In *Voluntary Religion,* ed. W. J. Sheils and Diana Wood, 131–153. Studies in Church History 23. Oxford: Basel Blackwell, 1986.

Cardauns, Ludwig. *Zur Geschichte der kirchlichen Unions- und Reformbestrebungen von 1538 bis 1542.* Bibliothek des königlichen preussischen historischen Instituts in Rom 5. Rome: Loescher, 1910.

Chrisman, Miriam Usher. *Strasbourg and the Reform: A Study in the Process of Change.* Yale Historical Publications, Miscellany 87. New Haven: Yale University Press, 1967.

Courvoisier, Jaques. *La Notion d'Église chez Bucer dans son développement historique.* Études d'histoire et de philosophie religieuses publiées par la faculté de théologie protestante de l'université de Strasbourg 28. Paris: Félix Alcan, 1933.

Demura, Akira. "Church Discipline according to Johannes Oecolampadius in the Setting of his Life and Thought." Th.D. diss., Princeton Theological Seminary. Ann Arbor: University Microfilms, 1964.

Deppermann, Klaus. *Melchior Hoffman: Soziale Unruhen und apokalyptische Visionen im Zeitalter der Reformation.* Göttingen: Vandenhoeck & Ruprecht, 1979.

Dictionnaire de théologie catholique. Ed. A. Vacant, E Mangenot, and E. Amman. 15 vols. in 30. Paris: Letouzey et Ané, 1915–1950.

Diehl, Wilhelm. *Zur Geschichte der Konfirmation. Beiträge aus der hessischen Kirchengeschichte.* Giessen: J. Ricker, 1897.

Ditsche, Magnus. "Das 'Richtscheit der Apostolischen Kirche' beim Leipziger Religionsgespräch von 1539." In *Reformata Reformanda, Festgabe für Hubert Jedin zum 17. Juni 1965,* ed. Erwin Iserloh and Konrad Repgen, vol. I, 466–475. Münster: Aschendorff, 1965.

Duggan, Lawrence. "Fear and Confession on the Eve of the Reformation." *Archiv für Reformationsgeschichte* 75 (1984):153–175.

Eells, Hastings. *Martin Bucer.* New Haven: Yale University Press, 1931.

Endriß, Julius. *Das Ulmer Reformationsjahr 1531.* Ulm: K. Höhn, 1931.

Ernst, August, and Johann Adam. *Katechetische Geschichte des Elsasses bis zur Revolution.* Strasbourg: F. Bull, 1897.

Fagerberg, Holsten. *Die Theologie der lutherischen Bekenntnisschriften von 1529 bis 1537.* Göttingen: Vandenhoeck & Ruprecht, 1965.

Fischer, Emil F. *Zur Geschichte der evangelischen Beichte.* 2 vols. Studien zur Geschichte der Theologie und der Kirche, 8/2 and 9/4. Leipzig: Dieterich, 1902-1903; repr.: Aalen: Scientia, 1972.

Fraenkel, Peter (Pierre). "Bucer's Memorandum of 1541 and a 'lettera Nicodemitica' of Capito's." *Bibliothèque d'humanisme et renaissance* 36 (1974):575-587.

——. *Einigungsbestrebungen der Reformationszeit. Zwei Wege–Zwei Motive.* Institut für europäische Geschichte Mainz, Vorträge 41. Wiesbaden: F. Steiner, 1965.

Franzen, August. *Bischof und Reformation. Erzbischof Hermann von Wied in Köln vor der Entscheidung zwischen Reform und Reformation.* Katholisches Leben und Kirchenreform im Zeitalter der Glaubensspaltung 31. Münster: Aschendorff, 1971.

Fuchs, F.J. "Les Catholiques Strasbourgeois de 1529 à 1681." *Archives de l'Eglise en Alsace* 22 (1975):141-169.

Geffcken, Johannes. *Der Bildercatechismus des fünfzehnten Jahrhunderts und die catechetischen Hauptstücke in dieser Zeit bis auf Luther. I: Die zehn Gebote, mit 12 Bildtafeln nach Cod. Heidelb. 438.* Leipzig: Weigel, 1855.

Greschat, Martin. "Die Anfänge der reformatorischen Theologie Martin Bucers." In *Reformation und Humanismus. Robert Stupperich zum 65. Geburtstag,* ed. Martin Greschat and J. F. G. Goeters, 124-140. Witten: Luther Verlag, 1969.

——. "Der Ansatz der Theologie Martin Bucers." *Theologische Literaturzeitung* 103 (1978):82-96.

——. "Martin Bucer als Dominikanermönch." In *Bucer und Seine Zeit: Forschungsbeiträge und Bibliographie,* ed. Marijn de Kroon and Friedhelm Krüger, 30-53. Veröffentlichungen des Instituts für europäische Geschichte Mainz 80. Wiesbaden: F. Steiner, 1976.

——. *Martin Bucer. Ein Reformator und seine Zeit.* Munich: Beck, 1990.

——. "Martin Bucers Bücherverzeichnis von 1518." *Archiv für Kulturgeschichte* 57 (1975):162-185.

Gy, Pierre-Marie. "Le précepte de la confession annuelle et la nécessité de la confession." *Revue des sciences philosophiques et théologiques* 63 (1979):529-547.

Hall, Basil. "Bucer et l'Angleterre." In *Strasbourg au coeur religieux du XVIe siècle. Hommage à Lucien Febvre, Actes du Colloque international de Strasbourg (25-29 mai 1975),* ed. Georges Livet and Francis Rapp, 401-429. Société Savante d'Alsace et des Régions de l'Est, Collection "Grandes Publications" 12. Strasbourg: Istra, 1977.

Hammann, Gottfried. *Entre la Secte et la Cité. Le Projet d'Église du Réformateur Martin Bucer (1491-1551).* Histoire et Société 3. Geneva: Labor et Fides, 1984.

Hareide, Bjarne. *Die Konfirmation in der Reformationszeit. Eine Untersuchung der lutherischen Konfirmation in Deutschland, 1520-1585.* Arbeiten zur Pastoraltheologie 8. Göttingen: Vandenhoeck & Ruprecht, 1971.

Harvey, Andrew Edward. "Martin Bucer in England." Ph.D. diss. Marburg: Bauer, 1906.

Heidrich, Paul. *Karl V. und die deutschen Protestanten am Vorabend des Schmalkaldischen Krieges.* 2 vols. Frankfurter historische Forschungen 5-6. Frankfurt a.M.: Joseph Baer, 1911-1912.

Hinschius, Paul. *System des katholischen Kirchenrechts mit besonderer Rücksicht auf Deutschland.* 6 vols. Berlin: Guldentag, 1869-1897; repr. Graz, 1959.

Hobbs, R. Gerald. "An Introduction to the Psalms Commentary of Martin Bucer." 2 vols. Th.D. diss., Strasbourg, 1971.

Holzmann, H. "Die Katechese des Mittelalters." *Zeitschrift für praktische Theologie* 20 (1898):1-18, 117-130.

Hope (Hopf), Constantin. "Martin Bucer und England. Sein Beitrag zur englischen Reformationsgeschichte." *Zeitschrift für Kirchengeschichte* 71 (1960):82-109.

Hopf (Hope), Constantin. *Martin Bucer and the English Reformation.* Oxford: Blackwell, 1946.

Hulshof, A. *Geschiedenis van de Doopsgezinden te Straatsburg van 1525-1557.* Amsterdam: Clausen, 1905.

Jedin, Hubert. *A History of the Council of Trent.* Vol. I: *The Struggle for the Council.* Trans. Dom Ernest Graf, O.S.B. St. Louis: Herder, 1957.

——. "An welchen Gegensätzen sind die vortridentinischen Religionsgespräche zwischen Katholiken und Protestanten gescheitert?" In idem, *Kirche des Glaubens/ Kirche der Geschichte. Ausgewählte Aufsätze und Vorträge.* Vol. I, 361-366. Freiburg: Herder, 1966.

Jordahn, Bruno. "Katechismus-Gottesdienst im Reformationsjahrhundert." *Luther. Mitteilungen der Luthergesellschaft* 30 (1959):64-77.

Kantzenbach, Friedrich Wilhelm. *Das Ringen um die Einheit der Kirche im Jahrhundert der Reformation. Vertreter, Quellen und Motive des "ökumenischen" Gedankens von Erasmus von Rotterdam bis Georg Calixt.* Stuttgart: Evangelisches Verlagswerk, 1957.

Keim, Carl Theodor. *Die Reformation der Reichstadt Ulm. Ein Beitrag zur schwäbischen und deutschen Reformationsgeschichte.* Stuttgart: Belser, 1851.

Kindler von Knobloch, Julius. *Das goldene Buch von Straßburg.* 2 vols. Vienna: 1885-1886.

Kingdon, Robert M. "The Control of Morals in Calvin's Geneva." In idem., *Church and Society in Reformation Europe,* VIII:3-16. London: Variorum Reprints, 1985.

Klein, Laurentius. *Evangelisch-lutherische Beichte: Lehre und Praxis.* Konfessionskundliche und kontrovers-theologische Studien 5. Paderborn: Bonifacius-Druckerei, 1961.

Knod, Gustav. *Die Stiftsherren von St. Thomas zu Straßburg (1518-1548). Ein Beitrag zur Straßburger Kirchen- und Schulgeschichte.* Beilage zum Programm des Lyceums zu Straßburg. Strasbourg: C.F. Schmidt, 1892.

Koch, Karl. *Studium Pietatis: Martin Bucer als Ethiker.* Beiträge zur Geschichte und Lehre der Reformierten Kirche 14. Neukirchen: Neukirchener Verlag, 1962.

Köhler, Walther. *Zürcher Ehegericht und Genfer Konsistorium.* 2 vols. Quellen und Abhandlungen zur Schweizerischen Reformationsgeschichte 7, 10. Leipzig: Heinsius, 1932-1942.

——. *Zwingli und Luther. Ihr Streit über das Abendmahl nach seinen politischen und religiösen Beziehungen.* 2 vols. Quellen und Forschungen zur Reformationsgeschichte 6-7. Leipzig/ Gütersloh: Bertelsmann, 1924-1953.

Köhn, Mechthild. *Martin Bucers Entwurf einer Reformation des Erzstiftes Köln. Untersuchung der Entstehungsgeschichte und der Theologie des "Einfaltigen Bedenckens" von 1543.* Untersuchungen zur Kirchengeschichte 2. Witten: Luther-Verlag, 1966.

Kohls, Ernst-Wilhelm. "Ein Abschnitt aus Martin Bucers Entwurf für die Ulmer Kirchenordnung vom Jahr 1531." *Blätter für württembergische Kirchengeschichte* 60/61 (1960/1961):177-213.

——. "Holzschnitte von Hans Baldung in Martin Bucers 'kürtzer Catechismus'." *Theologische Zeitschrift* 23 (1967):267-284.

——. "Martin Bucer als Anhänger Luthers." *Theologische Zeitschrift* 33 (1977):210-218.

——. "Martin Bucers Anteil und Anliegen bei der Abfassung der Ulmer Kirchenordnung im Jahre 1531." *Zeitschrift für evangelisches Kirchenrecht* 15 (1970):333-360.

——. "Martin Bucers Katechismus vom Jahre 1534 und seine Stellung innerhalb der Katechismusgeschichte." *Zeitschrift für bayerische Kirchengeschichte* 39 (1970):83-94.

Kretschmar, Georg. "Konfirmation und Katechumenat im neuen Testament und in der alten Kirche." In *Zur Geschichte und Ordnung der Konfirmation in den lutherischen Kirchen,* ed. Kurt Frör, 13-35. Munich: Claudius, 1962.

de Kroon, Marijn. "Bemerkungen Martin Bucers über das Abendmahl in seinem Psalmenkommentar von 1529." In *Bucer und Seine Zeit: Forschungsbeiträge und Bibliographie,* ed. Marijn de Kroon and Friedhelm Krüger, 88-100. Veröffentlichungen des Instituts für europäische Geschichte Mainz 80. Wiesbaden: F. Steiner, 1976.

——. *Martin Bucer und Johannes Calvin, Reformatorische Perspektiven. Einleitung und Texte.* Göttingen: Vandenhoeck & Ruprecht, 1991.

——. *Studien zu Martin Bucers Obrigkeitsverständnis. Evangelisches Ethos und politisches Engagement.* Gütersloh: G. Mohn, 1984.

Krüger, Friedhelm. *Bucer und Erasmus. Eine Untersuchung zum Einfluss des Erasmus auf die Theologie Martin Bucers (bis zum Evangelien-Kommentar von 1530).* Veröffentlichungen des Instituts für europäische Geschichte Mainz 57. Wiesbaden: F. Steiner, 1970.

Lang, August. *Der Evangelienkommentar Martin Butzers und die Grundzüge seiner Theologie.* Studien zur Geschichte der Theologie und der Kirche 2, Heft 2. Leipzig, 1900; repr. Aalen: Scientia, 1972.

Lea, Henry Charles. *A History of Auricular Confession and Indulgences in the Latin Church.* 3 vols. Philadelphia: Lea Brothers, 1896.

Leijssen, Lambert. "Martin Bucer und Thomas von Aquin." *Ephemerides Theologicae Lovanienses* 55 (1979): 266-296.

Ley, Roger. *Kirchenzucht bei Zwingli.* Quellen und Abhandlungen zur Geschichte des Schweizerischen Protestantismus 2. Zürich: Zwingli-Verlag, 1948.

Lienhard, Marc. "Evangelische Alternativen zur Augustana? Tetrapolitana und Fidei Ratio." In *Bekenntnis und Geschichte: die Confessio Augustana im historischen Zusammenhang,* ed. Wolfgang Reinhard, 81-100. Munich: Vogel, 1981.

Lipgens, Walter. *Kardinal Johannes Gropper (1503-59) und die Anfänge der katholischen Reform in Deutschland.* Reformationsgeschichtliche Studien und Texte 75. Münster: Aschendorff, 1951.

Littell, Franklin. "What Butzer Debated with the Anabaptists at Marburg: A Document of 1538." *Mennonite Quarterly Review* 36 (1962): 256-276.

Little, Lester K. "Les techniques de la confession et la confession comme technique." In *Faire Croire. Modalités de la diffusion et de la réception des messages religieux du XIIe au XVe siècle,* 87-99. Collection de l'école française de Rome 51. Rome: Ecole française, 1981.

Locher, Gottfried. *Die Zwinglische Reformation im Rahmen der europäischen Kirchengeschichte.* Göttingen: Vandenhoeck & Ruprecht, 1979.

Mahoney, John. *The Making of Moral Theology: A Study of the Roman Catholic Tradition.* Oxford: Clarendon, 1987.

Martin, Hervé. "Confession et contrôle social à la fin du Moyen Age." In *Pratiques de la Confession des Pères du désert à Vatican II. Quinze études d'histoire,* Groupe de la Bussière, 117-134. Paris: Cerf, 1983.

Massaut, J. P. "La position 'oecuménique' d'Érasme sur la pénitence." In *Réforme et Humanisme. Actes du IVe Colloque, Montpellier, Octobre 1975,* ed. Jean Boisset, 241-281. Centre d'histoire de la Réforme et du Protestantisme. Montpellier: Université Paul Valéry, 1977.

Matheson, Peter. *Cardinal Contarini at Regensburg.* Oxford: Clarendon, 1972.

——. "Martyrdom or Mission? A Protestant Debate." *Archiv für Reformationsgeschichte* 80 (1989): 154-172.

Maurer, Wilhelm. *Gemeindezucht, Gemeindeamt, Konfirmation. Eine hessische Säkularerinnerung.* Schriftenreihe des Pfarrervereins Kurhessen-Waldeck 2. Kassel: Stauda, 1940.

——. "Geschichte von Firmung und Konfirmation bis zum Ausgang der lutherischen Orthodoxie." In *Confirmatio. Forschungen zur Geschichte und Praxis der Konfirmation,* ed. Kurt Frör, 9-38. Munich: Evangelisches Presseverband, 1959.

Michaud-Quantin, Pierre. "A propos des premières *Summae confessorum.* Théologie et droit canonique." *Recherches de théologie ancienne et médievale* 26 (1959): 264-306.

——. *Sommes de casuistique et manuels de confession au moyen âge. XIIe-XVIe siècles.* Analecta Mediaevalia Namurcensia 13. Louvain: E. Nauwelaerts, 1962.

Monter, E. William. "The Consistory of Geneva, 1559-1569." *Bibliothèque d'Humanisme et Renaissance* 38 (1976): 467-484.

Müller, Johannes. *Martin Bucers Hermeneutik.* Quellen und Forschungen zur Reformationsgeschichte 32. Gütersloh: Gerd Mohn, 1965.

Müsing, Hans-Werner. "The Anabaptist Movement in Strasbourg from Early 1526 to July, 1527." *Mennonite Quarterly Review* 51 (1977):91-126.

Neuser, Wilhelm. "Bucers Programm einer 'guten, leidlichen reformation' (1539-1541)." In *Horizons Européens de la Réforme en Alsace. Das Elsaß und die Reformation im Europe des XVI. Jahrhunderts. Aufsätze zum 65. Geburtstag von Jean Rott*, ed. Marijn de Kroon and Marc Lienhard, 227-239. Société Savante d'Alsace et des Régions de l'Est, Collection "Grandes Publications" 17. Strasbourg: Istra, 1980.

Ozment, Steven. *The Reformation in the Cities: The Appeal of Protestantism to Sixteenth-Century Germany and Switzerland.* New Haven: Yale University Press, 1975.

Packull, Werner O. "The Melchiorites and the Ziegenhain Order of Discipline, 1538-39." In *Anabaptism Revisited. Essays on Anabaptist/Mennonite Studies in Honor of C. J. Dyck*, ed. Walter Klaassen, 11-28. Scottdale, Penn.: Herald Press, 1992.

——. "Peter Tasch en de Melchiorieten in Hessen." *Doopsgezinde Bijdragen* 12-13 (1986-1987):107-138.

——. "Peter Tasch: From Melchiorite to Bankrupt Wine Merchant." *Mennonite Quarterly Review* 62 (1988):276-295.

Padberg, Rudolf. *Erasmus als Katechet. Der literarische Beitrag des Erasmus von Rotterdam zur katholischen Katechese des 16. Jahrhunderts. Eine Untersuchung zur Geschichte der Katechese.* Untersuchung zur Theologie der Seelsorge 9. Freiburg: Herder, 1956.

Pauck, Wilhelm. *Das Reich Gottes auf Erden. Utopie und Wirklichkeit. Eine Untersuchung zu Butzers De regno Christi und zur englischen Staatskirche des 16. Jahrhunderts.* Arbeiten zur Kirchengeschichte 10. Berlin: de Gruyter, 1928.

Payne, John B. *Erasmus: His Theology of the Sacraments.* Richmond, Va.: John Knox Press, 1970.

Pollet, Jacques-V., O.P. *Martin Bucer. Études sur la Correspondance avec de nombreux textes inédits.* 2 vols. Paris: Presses Universitaires de France, 1958-1962.

——. *Martin Bucer. Études sur les Relations de Bucer avec les Pays-Bas, l'Électorat de Cologne et l'Allemagne du Nord, avec de nombreux textes inédits.* 2 vols. Studies in Medieval and Reformation Thought 33-34. Leiden: E.J. Brill, 1985.

Poschmann, Bernhard. *Die abendländische Kirchenbusse im Ausgang des christlichen Altertums.* Münchener Studien zur historischen Theologie 7. Munich: Pustet, 1928.

——. *Die abendländische Kirchenbusse im frühen Mittelalter.* Breslauer Studien zur historische Theologie 16. Breslau: Mueller & Seiffert, 1930.

——. *Penance and the Anointing of the Sick.* Trans. and rev. F. Courtney, S.J. Herder History of Dogma. New York: Herder & Herder, 1964.

Rabe, Horst. *Reichsbund und Interim. Die Verfassungs- und Religionspolitik Karls V. und der Reichstag von Augsburg 1547/1548.* Cologne: Böhlau Verlag, 1971.

Reinhard, Wolfgang. "Konfession und Konfessionalisierung in Europe." In *Bekenntnis und Geschichte. Die Confessio Augustana im historischen Zusammenhang*, ed. Wolfgang Reinhard, 165-189. Munich: Vögel, 1981.

——. "Zwang zur Konfessionalisierung? Prolegomena zu einer Theorie des konfessionellen Zeitalters." *Zeitschrift für historische Forschung* 10/3 (1983):257-277.

Roth, Erich. *Die Privatbeichte und die Schlüsselgewalt in der Theologie der Reformatoren.* Gütersloh: C. Bertelsmann, 1952.

Rotscheidt, W. "Martin Butzers Rechtfertigung seiner Wirksamkeit in Bonn 1543." *Monatshefte für rheinische Kirchengeschichte* 37 (1943):10-23.

Rudolf, Friedrich. "Oswald Myconius, der Nachfolger Oekolampads." *Basler Jahrbuch* (1945):14-30.

Rummel, Erika. *Erasmus' "Annotations on the New Testament": From Philologist to Theologian.* Erasmus Studies 8. Toronto: University of Toronto, 1986.

Rusconi, Roberto. "De la prédication à la confession: transmission et contrôle de modèles de comportement au XIIIe siècle." In *Faire Croire. Modalités de la diffusion et de la réception des messages religieux du XIIe au XVe siècle*, 67–85. Collection de l'école française de Rome 51. Rome: École française, 1981.

Russo, François, S.J. "Pénitence et Excommunication. Etude historique sur les rapports entre la théologie et le droit canon dans le domaine pénitentiel du IXe au XIII siècle." *Recherches de science religieuse* 33 (1946): 257–279, 431–461.

Schilling, Heinz. "'History of Crime' or 'History of Sin'? Some Reflections on the Social History of Early Modern Church Discipline." In *Politics and Society in Reformation Europe. Essays for Sir Geoffrey Elton on his Sixty-Fifth Birthday*, ed. E. I. Kouri and Tom Scott, 289–310. London: Macmillan, 1987.

——. *Konfessionskonflikt und Staatsbildung. Eine Fallstudie über das Verhältnis von religiösem und sozialem Wandel in der Frühneuzeit am Beispiel der Grafschaft Lippe*. Quellen und Forschungen zur Reformationsgeschichte 48. Gütersloh: Gerd Mohn, 1981.

——. "Sündenzucht und frühneuzeitliche Sozialdisziplinierung. Die Calvinistische Presbyteriale Kirchenzucht in Emden vom 16. bis 19. Jahrhundert." In *Stände und Gesellschaft im Alten Reich*, ed. Georg Schmidt, 265–302. Stuttgart: Franz Steiner, 1989.

Seidel, Karl Josef. *Frankreich und die deutschen Protestanten. Die Bemühungen um eine religiöse Konkordie und die französische Bündnispolitik in den Jahren 1534/35*. Reformationsgeschichtliche Studien und Texte 102. Münster: Aschendorff, 1970.

Sohm, Walter. *Territorium und Reformation in der hessischen Geschichte 1526–1555*, ed. G. Franz. 2nd ed. Veröffentlichungen der historischen Kommission für Hessen und Waldeck XI/1. Marburg: Elwert, 1957.

Spijker, Willem van 't. *De Ambten bij Martin Bucer*. 2d ed. Kampen: Kok, 1987.

Staehelin, Ernst. *Das theologische Lebenswerk Johannes Oekolampads*. Quellen und Forschungen zur Reformationsgeschichte 21. Leipzig: M. Heinsius, 1939.

Stalnaker, John C. "Anabaptism, Martin Bucer, and the Shaping of the Hessian Protestant Church." *Journal of Modern History* 48 (1976): 601–643.

Stenzel, Karl. "Die geistlichen Gerichte zu Straßburg im 15. Jahrhundert." *Zeitschrift für die Geschichte des Oberrheins* 68 (N.F. 29) (1914): 365–446; 69 (N.F. 30) (1915): 52–95, 201–253, 343–383.

Stollberg, Dietrich. "Osiander und der Nürnberger Absolutionsstreit." *Lutherische Blätter* 17 (1965): 153–168.

Strauss, Gerald. *Luther's House of Learning. Indoctrination of the Young in the German Reformation*. Baltimore: Johns Hopkins University Press, 1978.

Stupperich, Robert. *Der Humanismus und die Wiedervereinigung der Konfessionen*. Schriften des Vereins für Reformationsgeschichte 53/2 (160). Leipzig: M. Heinsius, 1936.

——. "Der Ursprung des 'Regensburger Buches' von 1541 und seine Rechtfertigungslehre." *Archiv für Reformationsgeschichte* 36 (1939): 88–116.

Tentler, Thomas N. *Sin and Confession on the Eve of the Reformation*. Princeton, NJ: Princeton University Press, 1977.

——. "The Summa for Confessors as an Instrument of Social Control." In *The Pursuit of Holiness in Late Medieval and Renaissance Religion*, ed. Charles Trinkaus and Heiko Oberman, 103–126. Studies in Medieval and Reformation Thought 10. Leiden: E.J. Brill, 1974.

Theologische Realenzyklopädie. Ed. Gerhard Krause and Gerhard Müller. Berlin/New York: de Gruyter, 1977–.

Trusen, Winfried. *Um die Reform und Einheit der Kirche. Zum Leben und Werk Georg Witzels*. Katholisches Leben und Kämpfen im Zeitalter der Glaubensspaltung 14. Münster: Aschendorff, 1957.

Varrentrapp, Conrad. *Hermann von Wied und sein Reformationsversuch in Köln. Ein Beitrag zur deutschen Reformationsgeschichte*. Leipzig: von Duncker & Humblot, 1878.

Vercruysse, Jos E. "Schlüsselgewalt und Beichte bei Luther." In *Leben und Werk Martin Luthers von 1526 bis 1546. Festgabe zu seinem 500. Geburtstag*, ed. Helmar Junghans, 1:153–169; 2:775–781. 2 vols. Göttingen: Vandenhoeck & Ruprecht, 1983.

Vodola, Elisabeth. *Excommunication in the Middle Ages*. Berkeley: University of California Press, 1986.

Vogt, Herbert. "Martin Bucer und die Kirche von England." Ph.D. diss., Westfälische-Wilhelms-Universität, Münster, 1966.

Vorgrimler, Herbert. *Busse und Krankensalbung*. Handbuch der Dogmengeschichte IV/3. Freiburg i.Br.: Herder, 1978.

Wartenberg, Günther. "Die Leipziger Religionsgespräche von 1534 und 1539. Ihre Bedeutung für die sächsisch-albertinische Innenpolitik und für das Wirken Georgs von Karlowitz." In *Die Religionsgespräche der Reformationszeit*, ed. Gerhard Müller, 35–41. Schriften des Vereins für Reformationsgeschichte 191. Gütersloh: Gerd Mohn, 1980.

Wendel, François. *L'Église de Strasbourg, sa constitution et son organisation (1532–1535)*. Études d'histoire et de philosophie religieuses 38. Paris: Presses universitaires de France, 1942.

Williams, George Huntston. *The Radical Reformation*. 3d ed. Sixteenth Century Essays and Studies 15. Kirksville, Mo.: Sixteenth Century Journal Publishers, 1992.

Index